Quebec

Montreal

St. Lawrence River

Ft. Chambly
Ft. St. Jean

CANADA

Part of
Massachusetts

Ontario

Ft. Ticonderoga

Lake
Champlain

Kennebec River

Saint
John

Oswego

Rome

Ft. Stanwix
(later Ft. Schuyler)

Mohawk River

NEW YORK

Albany

Hudson River

West
Point

New York
City

iladelphia

NEW
JERSEY

Delaware Bay

DELAWARE

MARYLAND

sapeake
Bay

NEW
HAMPSHIRE

Ft. Western

MASS.

Hartford

Norwich

CONN.

R.I.

Boston

New Haven

New London

Newport

Bay of Fundy

NOVA
SCOTIA

Delaware River

The
Thirteen
Colonies

© Claudia Carlson, 1993

The Man in the Mirror

BENEDICT ARNOLD

Engraving by I. Fielding, 1783
from a drawing by Pierre Eugène du Simitière, c. 1777.

THE MAN
in the
MIRROR

A Life of Benedict Arnold

CLARE BRANDT

To Amenia Free Library
Happy reading —
Clare Brandt

13919

5/19/94

RANDOM HOUSE   NEW YORK

Library of Congress Cataloging-in-Publication Data
Brandt, Clare.
The man in the mirror: a life of Benedict Arnold/Clare Brandt.
—1st ed.
p. cm.
Includes bibliographical references and index.
ISBN 0-679-40106-7
1. Arnold, Benedict, 1741–1801.   2. United States—History—
Revolution, 1775–1783.   3. American loyalists—Biography.
4. Generals—United States—Biography.   5. United States.
Continental Army—Biography.   I. Title.
E278.A7B73   1993
973.3′092—dc20
[B]   92-45118

Manufactured in the United States of America on acid-free paper
24689753

Cartography copyright © 1994 Claudia Carlson
Book design by Lilly Langotsky

TO C., C., C. AND D.

Contents

Chronology

1741	Arnold born, January 14		
1752	Goes to Rev. Cogswell's school in Canterbury		
1755	Returns to Norwich as Lathrops' apprentice	1756–63	French and Indian War
1762	Moves to New Haven		
		1765	Stamp and Quartering Acts, Stamp Act Congress, riots in the colonies
		1766	Stamp Act repealed
1767	Marries Margaret Mansfield	1767	Townshend Acts
1768	Benedict, Jr., born		
1769	Richard born	1770	"Boston Massacre"
1772	Henry born	1773	Tea Act, Boston Tea Party
1774	New Haven militia troop organized	1774	First Continental Congress; British close port of Boston
1775	APR. Marches to Boston with militia troop	APR. Revolutionary War begins
	MAY Captures Ticonderoga with Ethan Allen	MAY Second Continental Congress convenes in Philadelphia
	JUNE Wife dies	JULY George Washington takes command of Continental Army

AUG.   Joins Continental
   Army at Cambridge
SEPT.–NOV.   March up
   the Kennebec River
DEC. 31   Wounded at
   Quebec

1776

JAN.   Paine's *Common Sense*
   published
MAR.   British withdraw from
   Boston

MAY–JUNE   Retreat from
   Canada
JULY   Supervises fleet at
   Skenesboro, Hazen
   court-martial

JULY   Declaration of
   Independence promulgated

SEPT.   British take New York
   City

OCT.   Battle of Valcour
   Island

NOV.   Continental Army in full
   retreat across New Jersey
   and into Pennsylvania

DEC.   Brown and Hazen
   file charges against
   Arnold at Albany;
   Arnold goes to Rhode
   Island

DEC.   Continental victories at
   Trenton and Princeton; army
   goes into winter quarters in
   New Jersey

1777   FEB.   Passed over for
   promotion
MAR.   Meets Betsy
   Deblois
APR.   British raid on
   Danbury
MAY   promoted to
   major general; goes to
   Philadelphia
JULY   joins General
   Schuyler in Northern
   Department

JULY   Ticonderoga falls to
   British; British army in
   New York sails for
   Chesapeake

SEPT.–OCT.   Battles of
   Saratoga, to hospital
   in Albany

SEPT.   British take Philadelphia
AUTUMN   "Conway Cabal"
   attempts to replace
   Washington with Gates

1778 FEB. Departs Albany for New Haven	FEB. U.S.-French alliance signed; Continental Army in winter quarters at Valley Forge
APR. Writes again to Betsy Deblois	
MAY Goes to Valley Forge	
JUNE Enters Philadelphia	JUNE British withdraw from Philadelphia to New York
SUMMER Meets Peggy Shippen	
1779 JAN. (prob.) Becomes engaged to Peggy Shippen	Stalemate in the war
FEB. Reed publishes eight charges against Arnold	
MAR. Congressional committee recommends court-martial on two charges	
MAR. 22 Purchases Mount Pleasant	
APR. 3 Congress orders court-martial on four charges	
APR. 8 Marries Peggy Shippen	
EARLY MAY Offers services to British	MAY 31 British capture Stony Point; Americans retake it six weeks later
JUNE 1 Court-Martial convenes and adjourns	
AUG. Correspondence with Major André lapses	
OCT. Threatened by mob, reopens correspondence with André	

DEC. Court-martial
reconvenes

DEC. British launch southern
strategy, Clinton and army
sail for the Carolinas

1780 JAN. 19 Court-martial
verdict
MAR. Edward Shippen
Arnold born
APR. Begins campaign
to get command of
West Point

MAY British take Charleston,
South Carolina

JUNE Trip to
headquarters, West
Point and Connecticut
AUG. 3 Receives
command of West
Point; arrives there
Aug. 5

AUG. Cornwallis defeats Gates
at Camden, South Carolina

SEPT. 11 Aborted
meeting with André at
Dobbs Ferry
SEPT. 14 Peggy and
baby arrive
SEPT. 17 Meets General
Washington at King's
Ferry
SEPT. 22 (early A.M.)
Meets André; returns
to Robinson house
SEPT. 23 Receives
Joshua Smith's report;
argument with Varick;
Major André captured
SEPT. 25 Escapes after
receiving Jamison's
letter
SEPT. 26 Arrives in
New York

OCT. 2 André hanged

NOV. Peggy reaches
New York

OCT. American militia defeats
British force at King's
Mountain, North Carolina

DEC. Sails for
    Chesapeake

1781   JAN. Morgan defeats
                                       Cornwallis at Hannah's
                                       Cowpens
                             MAR. Cornwallis badly
                                       bloodied at Guilford
                                       Courthouse

JUNE Returns to New
    York

AUG. James born

SEPT. Leads raid on
    New London   OCT. 17 Cornwallis surrenders
                                         at Yorktown

DEC. Sails for England

1782   MAR. Parliament votes not to
                                       pursue war in America; new
                                       prime minster orders peace
                                       negotiations

1783   SEPT. 3 U.S.-British peace
                                       treaty signed

1784 Files for compensation
     as a Loyalist

1785 Sophia Matilda born;
     sails for New
     Brunswick

1786 John Sage born

AUG. Sails for Jamaica,
    then London

1787 JULY Returns to New
     Brunswick with family

SEPT. George born

1788 SUMMER Trading voyage
     to London

1789   MAY French Estates-General
                                       meet for the first time in
                                       more than a century
                             JULY 14 Storming of the
                                       Bastille

AUTUMN Peggy goes to
    Philadelphia

1790 SPRING Peggy returns to
Saint John

1791

JULY Louis XVI attempts to
leave France, but is arrested
and returned to Paris

DEC. Arnolds sail for
England

1792

APR. France declares war on
Austria

JULY 1 Duel with Lord
Lauderdale

AUGUST Mob storms Tuileries;
French royal family is
imprisoned

"SEPTEMBER MASSACRES" in
France; Year One of the
French Republic is
proclaimed

DEC. Louis XVI goes on trial
for treason

1793 George III awards
pensions to Arnold
children

JAN. Louix XVI guillotined

FEB. France declares war on
Great Britain

SUMMER The Terror
commences in France

1794 SPRING Sails to West
Indies; captured by
French, then escapes

In England, habeus corpus
suspended in response to
pro-French radical threat

JULY 28 Robespierre guillotined;
end of Terror; the Directory
assumes control in France

1795 July Returns to
England

High inflation in England, food
shortages, civil unrest;
assassination attempt on
George III.

OCT. Benedict, Jr., dies

1796

French and British begin to talk
peace

DEC. Offers plan "to
liberate Chile, Peru [*et
al.*]"

1797	SEPT. Coup d'état in France; peace negotiations with England broken off
	OCT. France makes peace with Austrians
1798 JAN. Offers to command fire ships	JAN.–FEB. Napoleon threatens to invade England
JUNE William born	AUG. 1 Battle of the Nile; Lord Nelson annihilates French fleet
1799	MAR. Second Coalition formed: Russia, Austria join war against France
	NOV. Coup in France; Napoleon becomes first consul
	DEC. George Washington dies
1800 JUNE Edward leaves for India	
1801 JUNE 14 Arnold dies	

Introduction

During the chilly predawn hours of September 22, 1780, in the sixth year of the Revolutionary War, the most celebrated American hero of that war held a secret meeting with a British spymaster on the shore of the Hudson River near his headquarters. Major General Benedict Arnold had been spying for the British for more than a year. In August, he had requested and obtained command of the crucial American fortress at West Point, with the express purpose of turning it over to the enemy. His fee was to be twelve thousand pounds sterling.

The coup would be both dramatic and cataclysmic, which perfectly suited Arnold's style. He was well aware that the American war effort was virtually moribund. The Continental army was undermanned, underfed and underarmed; Congress had no money to pay the men or to purchase supplies; and for many months the individual thirteen states had failed to meet their obligations for manpower and provisions. Commander in Chief George Washington was beginning to run out of improvisations, and morale among the civilian population plummeted deeper with every passing day.

All that stood between the fledgling United States of America and ruin was the royal government of France, whose infusions of money, ships and men had kept the Continentals going for the past three years. But French support, too, was beginning to flag. King Louis XVI, unwilling to waste his resources on a lost cause, seemed to be looking for an excuse to extricate himself from America. The loss of West Point to the British would provide that excuse.

In short, had Arnold's plot succeeded—which it very nearly did—the American war effort would have been dealt a lethal psychological and strategic blow, and it is very likely that today's schoolchildren throughout the fifty colonies would stand beside their desks each morning pledging allegiance not to the flag of the United States of America but to Her Majesty Elizabeth II. Little wonder that, during recess, those schoolchildren still revile their enemies with the epithet "Benedict Arnold."

Arnold's motives in turning traitor have heretofore been difficult to pin down. He himself claimed to have offered his services to the British "from a principle of love to my country," i.e., for political and ideological reasons; but this is patently untrue. Arnold had no politics and no ideology. He also contended, quite mendaciously, that money played no part in his decision. Money was extremely important to Arnold; but by itself it does not account for his treason, nor does it explain the many other dramatic, inconsistent and even bizarre actions that punctuated his career.

Arnold was undoubtedly disgruntled by the shoddy treatment he had received at the hands of Congress; but nearly every other Continental officer had been treated badly and was equally angry. Like Arnold, the entire officer corps was deeply resentful at the attrition of civilian support for a war in which they had all made personal sacrifices of fortune and health. But only one of these officers turned his coat: the best battlefield general on either side of the conflict, the hero of Saratoga and of Valcour Island, the man who had led his army into the hell of the Kennebec wilderness and brought them safely to Quebec in 1775, the gallant, the enterprising, the audacious "Genius of War."

The historian's challenge is to reconcile the two Arnolds—the Patriot-Hero and the Traitor—and thereby to explain why this able, courageous, intelligent, articulate American patriot suddenly reversed himself and offered his services to his sworn enemy. None of the obvious reasons—money, anger, ambition—fully explains his turnabout, nor did he experience a psychic break in his life in 1779. Quite the contrary, his treason was perfectly consistent with every-

thing that went before. Arnold the Patriot-Hero and Arnold the Traitor were one man whose every action, from the most admirable to the
most reprehensible, flowed from a single source deep inside his heart.

He was, to be sure, a mass of outward contradictions: Arnold had
astonishing physical valor but no moral courage, a rigid code of
"honor" without a shred of inner integrity, and superior intelligence
with no understanding. To fill in the gaps, to become the ideal hero
he wished to be, Arnold became a master of self-delusion. We all
delude ourselves in small ways from time to time to ease our way
through life; Arnold did so in gigantic ways with every breath he took,
and his delusions occupied the center of his being. Even after his
treason came to light in 1780, for example, he refused to acknowledge any culpability and maintained the fiction of the Patriot-Hero
until the day of his death, a very long twenty years later. His strength
and fortitude in this, as in all things, were of heroic proportions. He
never gave in, and he never gave up.

Arnold's character was firmly rooted in the soil of eighteenth-
century New England, which meant that he suffered (as his countrymen have always suffered) from the great American virus: social
insecurity. America's rejection of the traditional European determi-
nants of social class—birth and family—has proved to be both its
greatest strength and its greatest weakness. (In Arnold's day, the loss
of these guideposts was much more recent and therefore more keenly
felt.) In the long run, it is extremely beneficial to society to reward
accomplishment and riches rather than pedigree; but in the short run
it can be extremely tough on the individual, for if a person may rise
as far as his talents will take him (theoretically, at least), his fall
becomes entirely his own fault. Where there is great opportunity
there is also great fear; and we Americans feel that we have to keep
up the effort, every day, in order to prove our worth.

Benedict Arnold rode the roller coaster of success and failure all
his life, starting with a disastrous and traumatic plunge in early
adolescence. That he survived that first blow is testimony to his
intelligence and tenacity. But he did not survive internally. The early
wounds remained beneath the surface, festering, growing and eventually erupting under the pressures of war and public celebrity. Finally, they brought him down.

Throughout his life, Benedict Arnold fought like a lion against
his enemies, both British and American, and against his own demons.
He was always on the attack. His contemporaries, from the lowliest
soldier to the greatest figures in the land, could neither ignore him
nor remain neutral: Arnold—then and now—was either loathed inor-

dinately or admired extravagently. (Yes, there are modern Americans who champion his cause.) He had staunch allies and implacable enemies, but no friends, until, at the age of thirty-seven, he wooed and won a remarkable woman who precipitated the greatest crisis of his life and with him faced its consequences.

This book tells the story of two wars: the war of America against Great Britain and the war of Benedict Arnold against the world. Each was a battle for survival. Arnold waged his war with far less gentility than his counterparts in the other struggle; he fought all out, no holds barred and no prisoners taken. Whatever else may be said of him, he was a giant of a man.

The Man in the Mirror

Chapter 1

"A VERY UNCERTAIN STAY"

1741-1762

His given name means "blessed," from the Latin *benedictus.*

The surname Arnold derives from an ancient German word meaning "the eagle's power."

Benedict Arnold, a singularly American specimen of eagle, was hatched in an aerie on the steep, rocky cliff that overhangs the convergence of the Yantic and Shetucket rivers in eastern Connecticut. The landscape of the town of Norwich is precipitous and adamantine, much like the interior landscape of its most infamous son. In this inhospitable setting, the eagle's quest for daily sustenance requires stamina, audacity and a talent for improvisation, the same attributes that propelled Benedict Arnold's quest for a more elusive prize: sustenance for the heart.

Arnold's father was a Rhode Islander of distinguished family (his great-grandfather had been one of the colony's original proprietors), who migrated to Norwich in the 1730s, took the measure of the bustling river community and abandoned his vocation of barrel-making to become a trader. Trade was the lifeblood of New England's economy, and in Norwich, one of the region's largest and most prosperous towns, nearly every member of the community depended directly or indirectly on the commercial traffic with Canada, the West Indies and Europe. Within a few years the former barrel-maker had garnered sufficient social and financial credit to win the hand of the young widow Hannah Waterman King, daughter of an old and respectable Norwich family and herself a pillar of rectitude.

The Arnolds' firstborn son, named Benedict for his father, died at the age of eight months, presumably of the same affliction that took his half-sister Hannah on the same day. According to custom, the dead children's names were given to the next born of the same gender. Benedict Arnold, the future traitor, was born on January 14, 1741, followed a year later by a sister Hannah and eventually by two more sisters and a baby brother. The senior Arnold established his family in a handsome house in the genteel environs of Chelsea Parade, where he and his wife assumed a prominent role in Norwich society.

The children learned their lessons at the local elementary school and their theology at the First Church of Norwich, where the Arnold family sat in a private pew in the most fashionable section. Winter afternoons found young Benedict and his friends skating on the cranberry bog across the road from the Arnold house, or sledding headlong down the steep hills toward the river bank. In summer the boys fished for striped bass, mackerel and eels in the Thames River (which is formed by the convergence of the Shetucket and the Yantic) or, in a daredevil mood, tested their courage with a swim at the brink of Yantic Falls a mile above the town. They wandered along the wharves at Chelsea Landing, the commercial center of Norwich, where coastal packet boats and oceangoing brigantines disgorged goods and passengers. There the sons of prosperous shipowners, like young Benedict Arnold, might embark for the twelve-mile sail downriver to New London, where the broad harbor flowed out into open water and the world beyond.

Benedict was an exceptionally alert and energetic child, a natural leader of his group. His budding self-confidence was constantly undermined, however, by his mother's stern piety. "Nobody," she admonished her son, "can be anything . . . but what God makes or permits them to be. Fix your dependence on Him alone, who is all in all." Mrs. Arnold did not hold with hubris; and while she was willing to pay eighteen pounds for her children to sit in the fashionable part of the church, she squelched in them any signs of self-aggrandizement. Hers was an exacting God who made demands but gave no promises, who inspired fear without hope and shame without absolution.*

Just before Benedict's tenth birthday, his three-year-old brother, Absalom, died and was buried in the family plot in the Norwich Burying Ground, his tiny headstone lined up in a row with his deceased older siblings. As the only surviving son, young Benedict was now groomed for advancement. His parents enrolled him in a private academy in Canterbury, fourteen miles upriver, to embark on a classical curriculum under the direction of the Reverend Dr. James Cogswell, a recent graduate of Yale College. Classical scholars were a rarity in the colonies, as were graduates of the colleges they were being prepared to enter (Yale, no doubt, in the case of Dr. Cogswell's students). Attendance at the school automatically elevated the ten-year-old into the rarefied atmosphere of the colonial elite.

"It is with a great deal of satisfaction that I commit my uncultivated child to your care under God," Hannah Arnold wrote to Dr. Cogswell. "Pray don't spare ye rod and spoil ye child. . . . If you should find him backward and unteachable, pray don't be soon discouraged but use all possible means, again and again." Young Benedict himself received the following maternal instructions: "Be dutiful to superiors, obliging to equals, and affable to inferiors, if any such there be. Always choose that your companions be your betters, that by their good examples you may learn." Above all, she stipulated, "keep a steady watch over your thoughts, words and actions." Thus armed, the lad took his place among some half dozen schoolmates, who recited their declensions and ate their meals in the small keeping room of Dr. Cogswell's house and slept in the crowded loft above.

During Benedict's second summer in Canterbury a yellow fever epidemic swept through Norwich. "Deaths are multiplied all round us," Mrs. Arnold wrote her twelve-year-old, "and more daily expected . . . your uncle Zion Arnold is dead . . . Captain Bill has lost all his sons, John Post has lost his wife, John Lathrop and his son Barnabus are both dead. . . . How soon our time will come we know not," she reminded him; "Pray, my dear, whatever you neglect, don't neglect your precious soul which, once lost, can never be regained."

Within the month Benedict's eight-year-old sister, Mary, was

*Mrs. Arnold's rhetorical style strongly suggests adherence to the teachings of the "Great Awakening" or "New Light," a Devil-ridden revivalist movement that flourished in New England in the 1740s. The schoolmaster she eventually chose for her son, the Reverend James Cogswell, was nevertheless a doctrinally conservative "Old Light."

dead. "My dear," his mother wrote, "I should send for you to ye funeral, but ye contagion is such I am afraid. But I must exort you to prepare for death yourself. Beg of God to sanctify this death to your awakening; how soon sickness and death may meet you, you nor I don't know. Prepare to meet your God before your feet stumble on ye dark mountains." Before the epidemic had spent itself, Elizabeth, the baby of the family, was also taken, leaving Benedict and his sister Hannah—namesakes of the dead—the only surviving children.

Understandably, Mrs. Arnold's preoccupation with death began to verge on the obsessive. Again and again she sounded the alarm: "We have a very uncertain stay in this world, and it stands us all in hand to see that we have an interest in Christ, without which we must be eternally miserable." Her son apparently did not need reminding: among the few mementos of his childhood that he found worth preserving were his mother's letters, including one written a year after his sisters' deaths informing him that his father was in a "poor state of health."

Mr. Arnold's affliction did not kill outright. Alcoholism, unlike yellow fever, is a leisurely scourge. In the course of his inexorable decline Benedict's father lost control of his business affairs, so that when the boy was fourteen—a stocky lad, about five feet nine and full of restless energy—his world turned upside down. Gone was the money for his education; gone, too, was his father's business, which he might have expected to inherit. He was removed forthwith from Dr. Cogswell's school and brought back to Norwich as an apprentice in the apothecary shop of his mother's kinsmen, the brothers Daniel and Joshua Lathrop.

Given the circumstances, young Benedict was extremely lucky: the Lathrops, both graduates of Yale, were prominent members of Norwich society. Like most of their neighbors, they traded on the side, and the shop attracted a large clientele in search of European and West Indian goods as well as elixirs and mustard plasters. Even more attractive perhaps to young Arnold, he boarded with his fellow apprentices in Daniel's elegant, comfortable house across the road from the shop, under the benign care of Mrs. Lathrop, whose three sons had all died young.

Nevertheless, the lad's private turmoil can be imagined. Having confidently set forth from Norwich, the eldest son of a respectable family, to travel a path that he and everyone else fully expected to take him to the pinnacle of American society, he had been forced to return and face his friends and neighbors, the apprenticed son of a bankrupt and a drunk. His humiliation was severe; but like many adolescent agonies it remained buried, working its destruction secretly, silently and slowly, deep beneath the skin.

To all appearances, Arnold's seven-year apprenticeship with the Lathrops was an unqualified success. An avid learner, he mastered the apothecary's trade with ease. In the process, his quick wits, cool head and meticulous attention to detail so impressed the Lathrops that before he left his teens Arnold had already sailed for them on several trading voyages as supercargo (the officer in charge of purchasing and selling cargo). The sea attracted him; it was open, clean and unpredictable. He crossed the chill Atlantic to the great city of London, and sailed among the warm green islands of the Caribbean, where frigate birds soared above the turquoise sea, impossibly high. He learned to traffic with men of all ranks, colors and nationalities; he saw what money could buy; he sampled exotic tastes and acquired cosmopolitan appetites; and presumably, because he was young and lusty and not unattractive, he enjoyed the company of women.

By the time he reached twenty, the young man had seemingly mastered his early disappointment and become his own man. His diligence, self-discipline and competence had earned the world's respect. He was a solid success, well on the way to autonomy and prosperity.

But Arnold's outward assuredness teetered on the brink of an inner abyss that had been gouged in his soul by the earthquake that had struck when he was fourteen. The humiliation, helplessness and anger of that cataclysm had been working inside him ever since, deepening and widening the chasm until it could no longer be sounded or bridged. The space where self-assurance and self-respect should have developed was empty. For all his accomplishments, Benedict Arnold was a hollow young man, driven by a craving for reassurance and confirmation that could never be satisfied, even by his own well-earned triumphs. Whatever he had was never enough; the more he gained, the more he needed. His was a hunger of heroic proportions—one that would inevitably consume him.

Arnold's mother died when he was eighteen, precipitating his father's final, swift collapse. The elder Arnold was arrested for public drunkenness, being "disabled in . . . his understanding and reason, appearing in his speech, gesture and behavior, which is against the peace of our lord ye King and laws of this colony." He died in 1761, leaving twenty-year-old Benedict and his sister Hannah the owners of a fine house and very little else.

Within the year Arnold had made a clean break from the town where his name, he felt sure, could never be separated from his father's disgraceful history. He would make his own name, his own history. Borrowing money from the Lathrops, he rented a shop in New Haven, near the harbor and the smell of the sea, where he hung out a sign proclaiming himself

B. Arnold Druggist
Book-Seller, &c
From London
Sibi Totique

"Sibi Totique"—"For himself and for all."

Chapter 2

"SIBI TOTIQUE"
1762-APRIL 1775

New Haven was considered to be "the most beautiful [town] in New England, if not in all America." Its houses, each with a private garden behind, were arranged around three hundred small squares or parks, with a large, elm-shaded central square bounded by the "grand buildings with steeples and bells" of Yale College. To the north of town stood "a lofty mountain," to the south lay the broad, busy harbor opening into Long Island Sound.

More to the point, as far as Arnold was concerned, it was the fastest growing town in Connecticut, teeming with new business opportunities, new ideas and new people. The latter, mostly merchants, shopkeepers and traders like himself, were dubbed "the interlopers" by the old guard. Occasionally, as he stood behind the counter of his shop waiting on his contemporaries, the youthful scholars of Yale, Arnold may well have reflected on his own aborted education. By now, however, he studied a different text, whose primary lesson was: never be brought up short. Bankruptcy had destroyed his childhood world and his confidence in the future; therefore, money would become his shield.

To Arnold, money meant far more than financial security; it was also a crucial ingredient of self-respect. For a young man who had overcome so many obstacles, his inner reservoir of self-esteem was astonishingly empty. (Psychologists tell us that the development of self-esteem depends on unconditional love received in childhood.) This left him utterly dependent on the outside world for confirmation of his own worth. He was well aware of his talents and accomplishments, to be sure; but pride is not the same as self-assurance—indeed, it often signals the opposite. Arnold needed money as a tangible expression of the world's regard, and he craved it not so much for its own sake (although he certainly enjoyed the things it could buy) as for its ability to confirm his substantiality to the world and to himself.

The young entrepreneur lived two lives, one in his Chapel Street shop, the other on the high seas. During the winter he minded the store, peddling necklaces and earrings, buttons and buckles, books, tea, maps, Francis's Female Elixir and "a very large and fresh assortment of drugs and chemical preparations . . . and many other articles, very cheap, for cash or short credit." Thanks to his industry and business acumen the shop soon expanded into larger quarters in Leather Lane, and Arnold was able to pay back his loan from the Lathrops and move his sister Hannah to New Haven to keep house and manage the business during his long absences at sea.

Each year, from early spring until late autumn, he sailed the Atlantic and the Caribbean. Always quick to learn and eager to be his own master, he acquired enough proficiency to command the ships he sailed in. In Quebec he traded linen and homespun for furs, timber and cheese; and in the West Indies, cattle for slaves and molasses. Books for his shop were purchased in London: Dr. Johnson's dictionary, *Paradise Lost, Woman of Pleasure,* the essays of Pope, *Low Life above Stairs, Practical Farrier* and *Harwood on Death-Bed Repentance.* His advertisements appeared regularly in the *Connecticut Gazette:* "Benedict Arnold wants to buy a number of large genteel fat horses, pork, oats and hay, and has to sell choice cotton and salt, by quantity or retail, and other goods as usual."

But Arnold was extremely unlucky in his timing. No sooner had his business started to thrive than the British government began to interdict the West Indian and Canadian trade upon which it depended. From London's point of view, the new policy was both logical and just: the recent British victory over the French and their Canadian Indian allies had brought peace and prosperity to the thirteen lower colonies while burdening the London government with an enormous war debt and vast new territories to administer (primarily Canada itself). It was time for New England and the other American colonies to accept their share of the burden. Laws prohibiting direct trade between New England and the French West Indies had been on the books for years; now they would be enforced.

The New England colonists naturally cried foul. With the full connivance of British officialdom, direct trade with the West Indies and Quebec had become their lifeblood. Now the rules had been changed without warning, transforming them overnight from traders into smugglers. British warships appeared off the coast from the Caribbean to the St. Lawrence, seizing colonial vessels and condemning their cargoes of molasses, lumber and cotton. Trader after trader faced financial ruin, and the entire economy of New England began a dramatic downward slide. Meetings were held in every town; new political organizations, reflecting every shade on the political spectrum, began to churn out pamphlets; and a series of formal protests was delivered—and ignored—in London.

Smoldering colonial resentment burst into flame in 1765 with the announcement of a new tax on newspapers, legal documents and other forms of printed matter (called the Stamp Act, after the official stamp that indicated the tax had been paid; a similar tax had been collected in England for nearly a century). Mobs took to the streets, their raucous behavior and radical slogans frightening conservative Americans as much as they did the British. Cooler heads in nine of the thirteen colonies appointed delegates to a Stamp Act Congress, which met in New York in October to try to gain control of the situation. Their address to King George III, framed in highly conciliatory and conservative language, fell on deaf ears in London. But throughout America its message, as well as the marvel of its conception, reverberated loud and clear. For the first time, delegates from the various colonies had met face to face on their own initiative, without the sanction or the participation of the British government, had overcome their long-standing mutual distrust and hammered out a set of common principles and goals.

Their principles were conservative and their goals modest. What they sought was the restoration of their traditional rights as British citizens, principally life, liberty and property, the three "natural rights of man" expounded a century before by the English philosopher John Locke and widely accepted as the basis of British constitutional law. Locke contended that the primary function of government was to protect these natural rights, and that it could impinge upon them—by taxing property, for example—only with the sanction of the people's elected representatives. Accordingly, Americans could not be taxed by Parliament, where they had no representation, but only by their own colonial assemblies.

Most thinking American colonists adhered to these broad principles, forming a conservative Whig majority at the center of the political spectrum. Far to the right, a minority of ultraconservative Tories upheld the dictates of king and Parliament without demur, while on the left a handful of radicals, following John Locke's argument to its logical conclusion, argued that it was the duty of every loyal American to overthrow a government that had so consistently demonstrated its unwillingness to protect their rights.

For the majority, however, independence from the mother country was unthinkable in 1765, and they maintained their loyalty to the crown while vigorously protesting every new parliamentary assault on their livelihoods and Lockian sensibilities.

In April 1765 Benedict Arnold, who had just turned twenty-four, joined one of the most influential Whig organizations on the continent, the secret fraternity of Free and Accepted Masons. An import from France, Freemasonry's vigorous antiautocratic, anti-Catholic credo had gained wide acceptance in America. The Masons wielded vast influence through individual members' ownership of most of the major newspapers in the colonies. As champions of representative government, Freemasons were almost by definition Whigs; as members of a transcontinental fraternity, they were accustomed to thinking in intercolonial terms; and finally, as initiates in an often persecuted order, they knew how to keep secrets.

It is doubtful, however, that Benedict Arnold was attracted by the politics or philosophy of Freemasonry. He liked its style. Freemasons tended to be prosperous, well educated and articulate, and membership gave Arnold, "the interloper," automatic entree to the highest levels of business and society in Connecticut and throughout the thirteen colonies (membership in the right club being more important in fluid societies such as America's than it is in societies which, like Great Britain's, are traditionally stratified by birth). The gentlemen Arnold met at Hiram Lodge No. 1 were everything the young entrepreneur longed to be: prosperous and socially secure.*

Because Arnold still lacked the financial base for his social as-

---

*Latter-day Masons have frequently tried to deny that Arnold was ever a member of their order, and in the visitors' book at a New York City lodge where Arnold signed in as a "Visiting Brother" in 1774, someone later drew a line through his name.

cent, his response to the new British trade interdictions was predictably strong. Whig politics appealed to his deepest personal inclinations as well as to his pocketbook, so he absorbed his Masonic brethren's newspapers and mastered their rhetoric. His commitment was genuine, but shallow. Arnold's politics were a reaction to a personal threat, and he adhered not to the natural rights of man but to his own rights. In this he was not alone—what was remarkable was his talent for camouflaging the fact. Arnold was a quick study. He talked like a Whig so convincingly, and eventually fought like a Whig so energetically, that he persuaded everyone (including himself, to some degree) that his dedication to the cause ran deep. At bottom, however, Benedict Arnold's only cause was Benedict Arnold.

One morning in January 1766, shortly after his return to New Haven from a trading voyage, Arnold learned that one of his sailors, a man named Peter Boles, had secretly approached a royal customs officer to inquire about the reward for informing on Arnold for smuggling. Arnold's reaction was typically impulsive and forthright: he sought out Boles, "gave him a little chastisement" (in the parlance of the time) and ordered him out of town. But Boles lingered in a local tavern, his fear of further chastisement apparently outweighed by his resentment against Arnold. One cannot help but wonder what Arnold had done to provoke such a dogged vengeance. In the afternoon, he caught up to Boles again and forced him to sign a prepared written statement confessing "malicious, wicked and cruel intentions . . . instigated by the Devil," a nice New England touch, and swearing "never hereafter to make information . . . against any person or persons whatever for importing contraband or other goods."

But later that same night a shout from the street informed Arnold that Boles was still in town and that a group of his former shipmates (whose livelihoods were also dependent on free trade) had gathered to administer a little chastisement of their own. With Arnold in the lead, the party dragged Boles from the tavern, tied him to the town whipping post and administered "forty lashes with a small cord." Next they conducted him to the edge of town and charged him never to return "lest he should be saluted with a second part of the same tune, with new additions in a higher strain."

Virtually all of New Haven, from the loftiest shipowner to the humblest sailor, applauded Arnold's conduct, with the notable exception of a conservative majority on the city council who indignantly ordered his arrest, together with nine others, for "unlawfully and riotously [assembling] with intent . . . to assault, batter, wound and evilly entreat the person of Peter Boles." The outcome of their trial was never in doubt, since numerous witnesses verified the charges. The judges, however, all good Whigs, had the final say: after declaring Arnold and the others guilty as charged, they awarded Boles token damages of fifty shillings.

An irate conservative, protesting the award in a public letter to the editor of the *Connecticut Gazette,* specifically impugned the motives of Benedict Arnold, whose impassioned response condemned in turn the motives of Americans who would "vindicate, protect and caress an informer, a character, particularly at this alarming time, so justly odious to the public. . . . Every such information tends to suppress our trade," Arnold wrote, "so advantageous to the colony, and to almost every individual, both here and in Great Britain, and which is nearly ruined by the late detestable Stamp and other oppressive acts—acts which we have so severely felt, so loudly complained of, and so earnestly remonstrated against, that one would imagine every sensible man would strive to encourage trade and discountenance such useless, such infamous informers."

Arnold's rhetoric, as well as his conduct, earned high marks from his Masonic brethren, who highly approved of civil disobedience in defense of trade and natural rights. No doubt he also appeared a champion to the sailors of New Haven, who recognized a tough infighter when they saw one. Equally gratifying was the approbation he received from Miss Margaret Mansfield, to whom he became engaged about the time of the Boles adventure. Margaret was the daughter of Samuel Mansfield, a prosperous trader who also served as High Sheriff of New Haven County, which meant that the marriage promised to accelerate Arnold's rise in society at the same time that it satisfied his domestic desires.

Arnold was a passionate man and an ardent lover, and he sailed to the West Indies in March 1766 dreading the long separation from his fiancée. Miss Mansfield was less forthcoming. "Dear girl, it seems a whole age since I left you," he lamented from the island of St. Croix in May. "Were you sensible what pleasure it would give me to have only one line from you you'd embrace every opportunity of writing me." Despite her epistolary indifference, the couple was married shortly after his return to New Haven, and on St. Valentine's Day the following year, 1768, their first son, Benedict, was born.

Arnold's little family was soon facing bankruptcy. Like most traders, he had always operated on credit, and several successive years of economic depression landed him in debt to the tune of £1,400. The hopes of every colonial Whig had surged when the Stamp Act was repealed in 1766, only to be dashed the following year (shortly after Arnold's marriage) by a new set of stringent customs regulations called the Townshend Acts. In the ensuing months, British customs officers were assaulted in every port city in the colonies, and informers like Peter Boles were routinely tarred and feathered by mobs comprised of the communities' most illustrious members.

At sea, Arnold could escape from politics and lawsuits, creditors and debtors. There the challenges were concrete and the storms finite. But he was always extremely lonely for his wife and "the little pledge of our mutual love. . . . My dear girl," he yearned, "you only can imagine how long the time seems since we parted . . . I shall think every day an age until I see you." On every ship from New Haven he eagerly sought a letter from her, but he was usually disappointed.

The Arnolds' second son, Richard, was born in August 1769, only a few weeks after his father and the rest of New Haven's trading establishment had agreed to join Boston, New York and Philadelphia in suspending all trade with Great Britain until the Townshend duties were repealed. It was a desperate measure taken by desperate men. Parliament's response was to dispatch two British army regiments to Boston, America's busiest port and the cradle of the resistance. The following spring a small detachment of redcoats, under extreme provocation, fired into a mob at the customhouse, killing five and wounding six unarmed civilians. The so-called "Boston Massacre" heightened both tensions and discourse throughout the colonies. "Good God," Benedict Arnold fulminated from St. George's Key in the Caribbean, "are the Americans all asleep and tamely giving up their glorious liberties, or are they all turned philosophers that they don't take immediate vengeance on such miscreants? I am afraid of the latter, and that we shall all soon see ourselves as poor and as oppressed as ever heathen philosopher was."

In December 1770 Arnold returned from the tropics to a frigid welcome at home: a Jamaica trader named Forbes had been spreading rumors in New Haven that Arnold was habitually drunk in the islands, that he "kept a whore or two [and had contracted] the venereal disease." (Again, one has to wonder what Arnold had done to provoke such a peculiarly nasty form of retribution.) The tale was soon embellished with a number of lively circumstantial details concerning a duel over a whore that Arnold had "cow'd out [of]."

It is difficult to know which imputation he minded most, whoring or cowardice. It is not difficult, however, to imagine his wife's reaction to the threat of venereal disease, and Arnold's correspondence strongly suggests that he slept alone that winter. He begged friends in Jamaica for sworn depositions as to "my character in the bay, my manner [of] living . . . and the comp[any] I kept," as well as "my being in perfect health all the time," emphasizing that the "peace [and] reputation of an injured and innocent family is at stake." His protestations of innocence may have been genuine; his indignation certainly was. Eventually he prevailed, and the Arnolds' third son, Henry, was conceived exactly a year after his father's return from Jamaica.

The couple celebrated their reunion by borrowing to the hilt to build a fine new house on Water Street, a fashionable thoroughfare facing the harbor where the town's most prominent merchants and shipowners lived. The move would confirm Arnold's elevation in status from shopkeeper to merchant—a real ascension but a subtle one, in a society in which a few prominent families still lived above the store and social rank had more to do with wealth than occupation. The house would be a showplace, with pediments and porticos, lofty ceilings, a curving staircase, English wallpaper in the parlor and a carriage house behind. Like all houses it would be part dwelling, part mirror and part statement, a fitting symbol of Benedict Arnold's substantiality.

Unfortunately, the project also came to represent the lurching progress toward cataclysm of American-British relations. Arnold obtained a loan for the house thanks to an easing of credit after repeal of the Townshend duties, but before his grandiose plans could be carried out, a new set of commercial and political measures (the Tea and "Intolerable" Acts) brought trade to a virtual halt. He was unable to keep up with his payments and construction came to a halt, leaving the house only half finished.

As tensions mounted day by day between the colonies and Great Britain, so did Arnold's personal anxieties. He sailed on a series of increasingly fruitless voyages, haunted by the specter of his wife's helplessness before their creditors and of his children's threatened futures. "My Dearest Life," he wrote to Margaret in the summer of 1773 from Quebec, "You cannot imagine how much trouble and fatigue I have gone through [here] . . . two of my people have informed against me, which had near cost me my vessel . . . had not my friends interposed which, with the addition of ten or fifteen pounds to the villains, settled the matter." Having saved his ship from confiscation, he planned to sell her and return home overland via Lake Champlain. But there was no market for brigantines in Quebec, so, desperate for cash, he loaded her with a cargo of horses and sailed instead to Barbados. As usual, he had received no letter from home and lived from day to day "under the greatest anxiety and suspense, not knowing whether I write to the dead or the living."

When Margaret finally wrote it was to plead for help: her father was on the verge of bankruptcy. "I know of no way he can extricate himself," her husband responded, "but by giving up his effects and taking benefit of the Insolvent Act. . . . If he should think proper to do this I will assist him all that is in my power, but all that I am worth at present, saving my house, will not half pay his debts . . . and it is no better than throwing the money away to attempt it." Arnold ordered his wife to sell the goods he was shipping home to pay their debts, expressly forbidding her to use any of the money to bail her father out.

When she reported the deaths of two close friends, the ghosts of Arnold's childhood returned to haunt him. "May their loud and affecting calls awaken us to prepare for our own exit, whenever it shall happen," he wrote to her. Above all he feared for his children: "Pray, my dear," he urged Peggy, "keep our little ones at school and spare no pains to give them a good education . . . it is of infinite concern."

While Arnold was in Barbados in March 1774, the British, in retaliation for the Boston Tea Party, closed the port of Boston and eradicated many of the traditional powers of the Massachusetts Assembly. Once again the colonies drew together to frame a response. Local Committees of Correspondence had already been created to articulate grievances and regulate intercolonial communications. Now these extralegal bodies took a more active role, coordinating food shipments to Boston and organizing a meeting of representatives from all the colonies to be held in Philadelphia in September.

The First Continental Congress both affirmed its allegiance to the British crown and insisted on an immediate return to the trade regulations of the early 1760s. If Parliament failed to comply within sixty days, all thirteen colonies pledged to adopt nonimportation regulations and to convene a second congress the following spring. The measures were promptly ratified by the Connecticut General Assembly, and committees were established in every town to enforce compliance. Two months later, in the absence of a response from London, the nonimportation rules went into effect.

Now citizens of every colony, "anxious for the safety of their country and desirous of contributing all in their power to the support of their just rights and liberties," began to organize local troops of militia. Benedict Arnold and sixty-four other New Haven men hired one Edward Burke at three pounds a month to instruct them in military drills and maneuvers. For Arnold it was a welcome release, a chance to act on his deep frustration and intensely personal anger against the British for jeopardizing the new life he had fought so hard to create. If Parliament meant to steal the fruits of his labor and destroy his dreams, it would have to be taught that Benedict Arnold would not take it lying down.

The company received its official charter as the Governor's Second Company of Foot Guards, and each member outfitted himself at considerable expense in a splendid scarlet coat with silver buttons, a ruffled shirt, linen vest and black breeches and stockings. Arnold thrived on all of it: the dashing uniform, the close-order drill, the pressure of impending emergency and, most of all, his own election as company captain. The vote not only confirmed his standing in the community, it also bolstered his interior sense of worth. Arnold was given rank because he was able, intelligent and authoritative; he cherished it for its explicitness. The insignia on his uniform automatically conferred on Captain Arnold the status and respectability that citizen Arnold so earnestly desired. Mundane matters could be swept aside when he was marching at the head of his company, and the beat of the drum drowned out the cries of creditors and cleared his mind of ghosts.

Scarcely a month after his election, New Haven was electrified by news of the bloody confrontation at Lexington and Concord: it was war at last, and Captain Arnold leaped to greet it. Summoning his men that same afternoon, he announced his intention of marching to Boston to reinforce the Massachusetts militia. The majority agreed to join him, and the following morning, April 22, 1775, resplendent in scarlet and ruffles, he paraded his troop, some fifty strong, on New Haven Green, with half the town on the sidelines—including, no doubt, his wife, his children and some of his most persistent creditors.

The drama threatened to turn to farce when it was announced that the Board of Selectmen, under orders from a conservative town council, refused to furnish its militia troop with gunpowder. Arnold, who would rather have died than appear ridiculous, promptly marched his men to the tavern where the board met and sent an orderly inside to demand the keys to the powderhouse. After a pause, there stepped through the door of the tavern the venerable David Wooster, sixty-four years old, founder and Worshipful Master of the New Haven Masonic Lodge and a veteran of the French and Indian War. Wooster, speaking for the council, declared that Arnold and his men should not take up arms against the king without first seeking proper authority.

Proper authority indeed, Arnold expostulated; wherein did it lie? Certainly not in the royal governor of Connecticut, who could hardly be expected to sign a chit for gunpowder to be used against British troops. Certainly not in the Second Continental Congress, which would not convene for another month. Arnold presented the select-men with a choice: either to turn over the keys to the powderhouse or to stand by while he and his men gained entrance by other means. He must have been extremely persuasive. The keys were handed over forthwith, and after a final parade and a solemn address by the Reverend Jonathan Edwards, Benedict Arnold and his Foot Guards marched away to war.*

*Powderhouse Day is still celebrated in New Haven, with marching on the Green and a reenactment of the Arnold-Wooster confrontation.

Chapter 3

"I AM DETERMINED
TO INSIST ON MY RIGHT"

APRIL-JULY 1775

During their second day on the march, April 24, 1775, Arnold led his troop in signing a formal covenant in which all disavowed "from the heart . . . every thought of rebellion to His Majesty as supreme head of the British Empire." Like most of the New England militia converging on Boston that week, Arnold and his men considered themselves loyal subjects who had been, "in the course of Divine Providence, called to the honorable service of hazarding our lives in defence [of] . . . the liberties and unalienable rights of mankind."

Of the thousands of Americans who endorsed these noble sentiments, few had deeply pondered the political principles on which they rested. Like militia Captain Benedict Arnold, they were more devoted to their personal rights than to the natural rights of mankind, and the exalted rhetoric of the covenant that Arnold distributed among his men was doubtless standard Masonic issue flowing through his pen.

He did, however, subscribe wholeheartedly to the passage in which his men pledged to pay "that regard to the advice, admonition and reproof of our officers which their station justly entitles them to

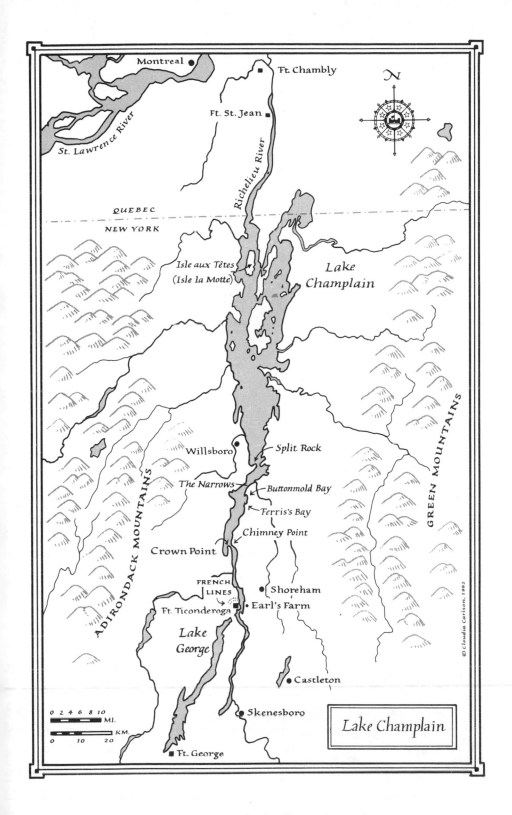

Montreal

Ft. Chambly

Ft. St. Jean

St. Lawrence River

Richelieu River

QUEBEC

NEW YORK

Isle aux Têtes
(Isle la Motte)

Lake
Champlain

Willsboro

Split Rock

The Narrows

Buttonmold Bay

Ferris's Bay

Chimney Point

Crown Point

FRENCH
LINES

Shoreham

Ft. Ticonderoga

Earl's Farm

Lake
George

ADIRONDACK MOUNTAINS

GREEN MOUNTAINS

Castleton

Skenesboro

Ft. George

0 2 4 6 8 10
MI.

0   10   20
KM.

© Claudia Carlson, 1993

Lake Champlain

expect." Unfortunately, however, the use of the plural—offi-cers—served to subvert the chain of command. Militia recruits in 1775 typically swore to obey orders arrived at by a council of *all* their officers, in which each man had an equal vote and the majority ruled, a misguided form of military democracy that persisted, with disastrous consequences, to the end of the war.

Somewhere north of Hartford, the Foot Guards' path crossed that of militia Colonel Samuel H. Parsons, a Harvard-educated lawyer and Connecticut assemblyman who was returning from a visit to the American lines outside Boston. Arnold had a knack of establishing rapport with men of superior station, and he and Parsons enjoyed a friendly exchange of information before going their separate ways. The redcoats, Parsons said, were confined inside Boston by a motley collection of colonial militia units thinly stretched throughout the suburbs. The enemy could not be starved out as long as their ships controlled the harbor, nor could they be dislodged without artillery— and practically all the artillery in the thirteen colonies was in British hands.

Arnold eagerly informed Parsons of some eighty pieces of heavy artillery that were virtually there for the taking: at the old fortress of Ticonderoga, which he had visited the previous year on an overland trip from Canada. Ticonderoga, situated at the southern end of Lake Champlain (see map, page 21), had originally been constructed by the French to defend against a British invasion of Canada from the lower colonies. Time after time during the French and Indian War, the British had tried and failed to take the fort, and the gallons of blood spilled on both sides during these heroic episodes had raised Ticonderoga to the status of a legend.

At the end of the war in 1759, however, with England in con-trol of both Canada and the lower colonies, Ticonderoga's useful-ness came to an end, and the British permitted the old fort to deteriorate. By the time Arnold visited there in 1774, the ramparts and walls were crumbling, and a garrison of only fifty men mounted guard over the artillery, the storehouses and the seventy-ton British sloop that was anchored off the dock. As the only ship of any size on Lake Champlain, the sloop by itself virtually guaranteed control of the waterway.

Taking his leave of Parsons, Arnold continued north toward Boston, his brain resounding with the name *Ticonderoga*. The epic deeds of the fort's conquerors and defenders—men such as General Jeffrey Amherst, whose successful assault in 1759 had precipitated the end of the war—were inscribed in the lists of immortals. Captain

Benedict Arnold now determined that his name would be added to the roster.

On reaching Cambridge several days later, Arnold sought out Dr. Joseph Warren, Worshipful Master of St. Andrew's Masonic Lodge (whose members had perpetrated the Boston Tea Party sixteen months before) and chairman of the Massachusetts Committee of Safety, a recent addition to the growing list of ad hoc Whig organizations whose overlapping memberships and activities frequently resulted in competition rather than cooperation. Warren promptly pushed a resolution through his committee appointing Benedict Arnold a colonel of the Massachusetts militia with orders to enlist up to four hundred men in the western part of the colony, to capture Fort Ticonderoga and to dispatch its cannon to Boston.

Arnold's overnight promotion from Connecticut captain to Massachusetts colonel—which was typical of the uncoordinated improvisations resorted to by the committees and militias of the thirteen several colonies during the early stages of the war—was heady stuff for a thirty-four-year-old military neophyte with a boundless craving for recognition. Arnold was not bothered at all by the catch-as-catch-can nature of the expedition. He loved to improvise and hustle on his own, with no one looking over his shoulder; his talents shone brightest when he was in charge. So he plunged headlong into the enterprise, disregarding the primary drawback of independent command—singular responsibility in case of failure—in favor of the vision of the solitary victor reaping all the laurels.

But across this vision fell the shadow of a potential rival. A letter had been circulating in Cambridge for several weeks urging that Ticonderoga be taken as soon as hostilities commenced. Its author was John Brown, a Yale-educated lawyer from Pittsfield, Massachusetts (and, ironically, cousin-in-law to Benedict Arnold, having married the sister of Rhode Island attorney Oliver Arnold). Brown had just returned from a reconnoitering expedition into Canada via Lake Champlain at the behest of the Massachusetts Committee of Correspondence (as opposed to Dr. Warren's Committee of Safety). Not only had Brown been first with the idea of capturing Ticonderoga, he had the means readily at hand, having already engaged the services of Ethan Allen and his Green Mountain Boys to mount the assault at the Correspondence Committee's orders.

The Green Mountain Boys, a.k.a. the Onion River Company, were a group of freewheeling land speculators who had organized into a guerrilla band in the early 1770s to defend their vast holdings in the New Hampshire Grants (now Vermont) against the territorial incursions of the Province of New York. Though rough and undisciplined, under Ethan Allen's leadership they had created havoc to the point where Allen and his principal lieutenants were now posted as outlaws by New York. As a fighting troop the Boys were intimately acquainted with the territory surrounding Fort Ticonderoga; as local landowners they had a personal stake in defending it. But their greatest threat to Arnold was their readiness: with Allen and the Boys beside him, John Brown could march on Ticonderoga at once, while all Benedict Arnold had were ambitious plans and a piece of paper from the Massachusetts Committee of Safety.

Arnold hastily ordered his trusted aide Eleazer Oswald, of the Connecticut Foot Guards, to enlist troops and follow as quickly as possible while he rode ahead with a single orderly.* Galloping across the entire breadth of Massachusetts in three days, he reached Williamstown on the evening of May 8, where, dining at the tavern of Nehemiah Smedley, he learned the worst: John Brown and several militia officers from Massachusetts and Connecticut had passed through a few days before on their way to join the Green Mountain Boys.

The following morning at first light, Arnold and his servant were in the saddle heading north. All day they rode through the high valleys of the Green Mountains and across the border into the New Hampshire Grants. Finally, toward dusk, they reached the village of Castleton, where Arnold discovered John Brown and the others in the local tavern conducting a council of war.

Arnold boldly introduced himself. Ethan Allen, it turned out, was not present, having already departed for Shoreham to organize the crossing of Lake Champlain. The others identified themselves: John Brown, several of Allen's lieutenants, and the chairman of the council, Connecticut militia Captain Edward Mott, whose presence was indirectly Arnold's doing. As an officer in Samuel Parsons's militia regiment, Mott had been ordered by Parsons (on behalf of, but without consulting, the Connecticut Assembly) to capture Ticonderoga; and Parsons himself, of course, had gotten the idea from Benedict Arnold.

Brown and Mott, gratified to learn that the Massachusetts Committee of Safety concurred in their project, freely confided their plan of attack to Arnold. The following morning at dawn, two small de-

---

*Oswald and about twenty of the Foot Guards volunteered for the Ticonderoga expedition. The rest served on the lines in Cambridge for a month or two and then returned home.

tachments would make their separate ways to Crown Point and Skenesboro (headquarters of the vast estates of Philip Skene, a wealthy Tory whom Arnold had encountered on his trip up the lake the previous year) to capture boats and bring them secretly to Shoreham. The main body would embark after dark, cross the lake and attack the fort at first light. Scouts had informed them that the British garrison was still unaware of the outbreak of hostilities, so the surprise should be complete.

The 140 recruits had all insisted on being commanded by their own officers, and the chain of command had been determined by the number of men each officer had brought with him. Accordingly, Ethan Allen would lead the assault, with James Easton, a Pittsfield innkeeper and militia captain, as second-in-command and Seth Warner of the Green Mountain Boys third, "to rank according to the number of men that each one raised."

It was a commendable plan—but there was no room in it for Benedict Arnold. Another man might have bowed to superior organization and experience and offered his services in a spirit of cooperation, but Arnold's spirit did not encompass cooperation. As the highest ranking officer present, he felt his way was clear, and, producing his document from the Massachusetts Committee of Safety, he coolly demanded to be placed in command of the whole enterprise.

"Shockingly surprised," Mott, Brown and the others naturally refused, patiently explaining again the logic of their command structure. Arnold, however, admitted no logic other than rank. The more they expostulated, the more adamant he became. He had tremendous staying power and (as we have already seen) a talent for personal provocation, with the result that by the time the meeting broke up, Edward Mott, John Brown, James Easton and the others would sooner have murdered Benedict Arnold than take orders from him.

Early the following morning, Arnold rode the twenty miles to Shoreham to confront Ethan Allen, whom he found near the lakeshore directing preparations for the crossing. Resplendent in a makeshift uniform of yellow breeches and green coat with gold epaulets, Allen exuded self-assurance. His manners, like his uniform, were rough; and if his lip curled at the ruffled shirt and drawing-room diction of Colonel Arnold, the colonel no doubt returned the compliment.

As the two were taking each other's measure, a contingent of Green Mountain Boys unexpectedly strode into view: the detachment that should have been on its way to Skenesboro to collect boats for the crossing. Rumors of the previous evening's dustup had spread among Allen's men, whose jealousy for their own independence far exceeded their sense of mission. Refusing to follow Edward Mott to Skenesborough, they had marched instead to Shoreham to inform Allen in person that if he did not lead them they would "club . . . their fire-locks and march . . . home."

Ethan Allen and Benedict Arnold, faced with a threat to the mission itself, grudgingly agreed to a joint command. For both of them, the act of accommodation was as repugnant as it was unfamiliar. The very qualities they held in common—courage, brazenness and a hunger for personal glory—were the qualities that would doom their collaboration.

Meanwhile, the first order of business was transport. Since the Skenesboro mission had been aborted, small foraging parties were dispatched to scour the neighborhood for rowing boats of any description. Allen's plan was to embark the men at midnight in a small cove, screened by woods, near the farmhouse of his friend James Earl.

Earl's farm lay on the east bank of Lake Champlain's narrow southern "finger". Directly across that water lay a flat, cleared point of land that had been occupied in Ticonderoga's glory days by an extensive system of redoubts and trenches known as the French lines. Immediately south of the lines, on a high, rocky cliff that loomed magnificently above the surrounding woods, hills and water, stood Ticonderoga itself, with the gaping breaches in its gray stone ramparts and parapets clearly visible from the edge of James Earl's woods, only three quarters of a mile away.

By midnight a motley collection of rowing craft was beached in the little cove, and the embarkation commenced. The first crossing was made silently and without incident. Arnold and Allen, riding in the lead boat, landed north of the fort and conducted a hasty head count. Only eighty men were present, about one third of their force. However, dawn was approaching, and there was no time to wait for the others. Guided by a local youth named Nathan Beeman, whose intimate knowledge of the ground came from playing games about the fort with the children of the British garrison, the party crept stealthily in the faint predawn light along the lakeshore and up the cliff under the fort's eastern curtain wall. Skirting the corner bastion, they made their way toward the main gate along the narrow path between the fortress wall and Lake Champlain, which lay at the bottom of a sheer hundred-foot drop on their left. Scrambling through a breach in the wall, they darted across the open space under the guns of the sleeping fort toward the massive outer gate. It was locked, but the wicket was not. With Arnold and Allen neck and neck in the lead, the men poured into the low tunnel that passed under the earthworks to the interior of the fort. A single sentry burst out of the guardhouse door and aimed his gun; his flint flashed in the pan. Shouting the alarm, he turned tail and ran before them through the tunnel.

On his heels, Arnold and Allen erupted onto the broad central parade ground, bordered by barracks whose peaked roofs and gables were just being touched by the first rays of the rising sun. The men surged behind them onto the parade, emitting piercing Indian war whoops as they swarmed into the barracks to rouse the sleeping British soldiers. The two rival commanders, moving as one—sticking together like burrs, in fact; neither would let the other out of his sight—wheeled to the left and ran up the narrow wooden stairway that led to the second-floor quarters of the garrison commander, Captain William Delaplace.

A British officer, incompletely clad but totally self-possessed, emerged from Delaplace's door. Allen brandished his sword above the man's head and screamed against the din that if "a single gun [was] fired in the fort, neither man, woman or child should be left alive." Arnold echoed his call for surrender "in a genteel manner," and gallantly attempted to legitimize the mayhem occurring on the parade below by producing his commission from the Massachusetts Committee of Safety. When the Britisher hesitated and offered to palaver, an infuriated Allen lunged toward him with fire in his eye, at which juncture another officer appeared in the doorway: Captain Delaplace himself, fully clothed thanks to the time bought by his stand-in, the cool-headed Lieutenant Jocelyn Feltham. Delaplace took only a moment to assess the situation and formally surrender the fort. Benedict Arnold's baptism of fire was over, after ten minutes and without a single fatality.

"The sun seemed to rise on that morning with a superior lustre; and Ticonderoga and its dependencies smiled on its conquerors, who tossed about the flowing bowl, and wished success to Congress, and the liberty and freedom of America." So wrote Ethan Allen, who joined in the tipsy celebration and looked benignly on as the Boys plundered the fort, which duty, one British officer reported, "was most rigidly performed as to liquors, provisions, etc." By ten o'clock in the morning the rest of the men had been ferried across the lake, Ticonderoga's supply of rum was considerably diminished and the party was in full swing.

Benedict Arnold was appalled. All day he stalked about the fort attempting to organize parties to repair fortifications, inventory cannon and distribute ammunition. A counterattack could be expected from St. Jean within days; Crown Point must be captured and secured, the British sloop located and seized and, most important, the cannon sent on its way to Boston. But the men turned their backs on his orders. When he exhorted, they smirked; when he threatened, they yawned. By the end of the day he had made such a nuisance of himself that Edward Mott and James Easton, styling themselves the "Committee of War for the Expedition against Ticonderoga and Crown Point," dashed off a letter to the Massachusetts Congress (which theoretically had jurisdiction over both the Massachusetts Committee of Correspondence and the Massachusetts Committee of Safety) complaining that Arnold's refusal to relinquish command, despite "not having enlisted one man . . . causes much difficulty" and suggesting that his "further procedure in this matter [is] highly inexpedient, both in regard to expense and defence."

Arnold was justifiably furious at the feckless behavior of Allen and his men. Although vastly less experienced than they, he sensed instinctively the shape and urgency of the strategic situation and was enormously frustrated at his inability to act on his insight. But he was also frightened at his own helplessness. Alarm bells went off in Arnold's head, as they always did when he felt himself at the mercy of other men's actions. (With drunkenness as a factor, the alarms perhaps rang louder than usual.) He went instantly on the defensive, insisting more rigidly than ever on his rights and, at the same time, denying responsibility for any lapse in judgment or behavior.

"[Ethan] Allen," he complained to Joseph Warren, "is a proper man to head his own wild people, but entirely unacquainted with military service; and as I am the only person who has been legally authorized to take possession of this place, I am determined to insist on my right, and I think it my duty to remain here against all opposition, until I have further orders." Although his rigid insistence on command was, in a narrow sense, justified by the behavior of Allen's men, his tactlessness served only to alienate the people on whom the success of the mission depended.

In the ensuing days, Arnold carried on virtually alone. He toured Ticonderoga's fortifications with engineer Bernard Romans and wrote detailed estimates of the men and material required to restore them. He made inventories and prepared lists of the manpower and provisions necessary to hold the fort against a counterattack. Many of the cannon intended for Boston were "buried in the ruins," he reported to Joseph Warren, "[and] a large number of iron and some brass and mortars, etc., [are] lying on the edge of the lake . . . covered with water." Nevertheless, he remained confident of recovering and dispatching them to Massachusetts—if he received sufficient manpower and equipment.

But even as he was executing his military orders with such energy and dedication, Arnold was devoting massive inner resources to the pursuit of his private demons. The alarm bells continued to sound; the specters of failure and humiliation howled at the gates, personified in this case by Ethan Allen, Edward Mott, John Brown and James Easton, whose behavior not only jeopardized the mission but whose very existence jeopardized Benedict Arnold's vision of himself as the conquering hero of Fort Ticonderoga.

He became particularly obsessed with Brown and Easton after they were dispatched as couriers to the Continental and Massachusetts congresses, respectively. Arnold convinced himself that the two were deliberately slandering him before the politicians in Watertown and Philadelphia. It wasn't true: although Brown and Easton did indeed take pains to characterize Arnold as a troublemaker and to minimize his participation in the capture of Ticonderoga, they did not have to lie in order to make their point. Furthermore, their enthusiasm in pursuing the matter may be directly attributed to Arnold's own arrogance and want of tact.

But Arnold's fixation on Brown and Easton became the cornerstone for a house of mirrors that he constructed in the ensuing weeks, a house in which his own image remained inviolable, while his rivals were reflected as a pair of scoundrels whose sole mission was to destroy the reputation of the only competent and civilized American officer on Lake Champlain, himself. In this house, Arnold's conduct as a brave soldier and patriot appeared invariably correct and his motives invariably pure. Anyone who said different was a liar. This simple but potent argument permitted Arnold to forego introspection (the poison of the insecure) and blame all his troubles on the jealousy and malice of others.

The house of mirrors became a private refuge in which Arnold could shape and misshape events to correspond to his delusions. From within, he clearly perceived that every failure was the fault of someone else. From the outside, however, it was quite apparent that Benedict Arnold's perceptions were badly skewed.

Meanwhile, Allen and the others made their plans without him. The Green Mountain Boys, nursing hangovers, murmured insults and threats and even took a shot or two in his direction "with their fusees" (as Arnold noted in his regimental memorandum book, which he faithfully kept despite the lack of a regiment). After Allen's lieutenant, Seth Warner, successfully stormed the crumbling old fortress at Crown Point and seized its entire garrison (one sergeant and ten men), Allen, in high good humor, dashed off a note to the Committee of Safety at Albany—capital of a colony in which he was currently posted as an outlaw—demanding "immediate assistance from you both in men and provisions" and signing himself "Your friend, Ethan Allen, Commander of Ticonderoga."

Arnold, isolated and virtually impotent, requested Joseph Warren to withdraw his commission, "that a proper person might be appointed in my room." The desire to step down was genuine: in the absence of control, Arnold's instincts often urged him to flee. (The call to duty always rang clearest when it harmonized with his own self-interest.) But, at the same time, had he possessed the faculty of introspection he would have known that being superseded would be intolerable to him. He made the request in the total absence of self-knowledge. It is not surprising, therefore, that when it was eventually granted, he would literally, if briefly, lose his wits.

By now Arnold and his rivals were reporting to (and attempting to undermine one another with) at least six separate political bodies: the Massachusetts Committee of Safety, the Massachusetts Provincial Congress, the Connecticut General Assembly, the Connecticut Committee of Correspondence, the Albany Committee of Correspondence (which frequently deferred to the New York Committee of Safety) and the Second Continental Congress, all extralegal ad hoc organizations that had sprung up in response to financial and political pressure from Britain. There were no clear lines of responsibility among them, although theoretically the Second Continental Congress, which was just getting under way in Philadelphia, had the ability to override the others and wield power in the best interests of all the colonies. But Congress's power was severely limited by long-standing jealousies among the various colonies; and the delegates in Philadelphia, inexperienced in governance and deeply divided, particularly on the crucial question of "independency," spent much of their time and energy pussyfooting around the political sensibilities of their several constituencies while they wavered between conciliation and defiance of Great Britain. As a result, militia officers like Benedict Arnold found themselves fighting a deadly enemy in the field with no reliable political support behind them—a situation that did not improve, even after Congress committed itself to independence the following year.

Throughout the early days at Ticonderoga, Arnold's inner tur-moil was masked by his superb performance as a military officer. Seventy-two hours after the capture of the fort, scouts reported that the British sloop was docked at St. Jean at the far northern outlet of Lake Champlain, loaded with supplies and ready to sail in support of a British counterattack on Ticonderoga. By now the Green Mountain Boys, loaded with booty, had begun to depart for home, leaving the fort's garrison dangerously undermanned. It was clear to Arnold that the best way to save the fort was to seize the sloop and thereby prevent the enemy from coming up the lake.* That very afternoon he was presented with the means to do it: the arrival of Eleazer Oswald with fifty recruits aboard a small schooner they had captured at Skenesboro. By sunset Arnold had armed the ship (rechristened *Liberty*), provisioned her and set sail for St. Jean, without telling Ethan Allen or any of the others.

He anchored the first night off Crown Point, the site of an im-mense British fort that had been consumed by a spectacular fire and explosion two years before. The narrow strait between Crown and Chimney points marks the end of Lake Champlain's southern finger. Beyond it, the lake abruptly widens into a 120 mile long hourglass-shaped inland sea, bounded on either side by chains of high moun-tains. The winds that swirl inside this vast elongated bowl make sailing on the lake notoriously treacherous and frustrating. *Liberty's* voyage north was no exception. All the first day she beat against a strong headwind, past isolated homesteads nestling in the little coves that scallop Champlain's shoreline, past huge flocks of migratory Canada geese rocking in the water and stilt-legged herons standing in the shallows or rising silently to fish. By evening the ship had nego-tiated the narrows at the center of the hourglass and anchored off Split Rock. The following day a fair wind carried Arnold all the way down the main lake to within thirty miles of St. Jean, and there it died, leaving him becalmed.

Arnold transferred half the men to bateaux and rowed all night. Just before dawn they slipped into a tiny mosquito-infested creek about a mile from St. Jean, whence he sent scouts ahead to recon-noiter. They returned with good news: the sloop was at the dock, lightly guarded by a small British garrison that seemed oblivious to their presence. Arnold led his men stealthily forward to the edge of the clearing around the fort. It was his first solo combat command.

---

*Up the lake means south, down the lake means north, since Champlain flows from south to north.

He "briskly march[ed] up in the faces" of the British sergeant and nineteen men, who, taken completely by surprise, surrendered without firing a single shot.

From his prisoners Arnold learned that the captain of the garrison was expected back from Montreal at any moment with "a large detachment for Ticonderoga [and] a number of guns and carriages for the sloop, which was just fixed for sailing." He quickly ordered his men to load all the stores and provisions aboard the sloop and to destroy the rest of the boats, with the exception of five bateaux that he took in tow. By nine o'clock in the morning he had set sail for Ticonderoga with *Liberty* close behind.

At midday, sailing before a brisk breeze, Arnold's little fleet came upon an arresting sight: Ethan Allen, with a "party of 100 mad fellows" in four boats, rowing hell-for-leather for St. Jean. Allen had gotten wind of Arnold's expedition and, determined not to be outshone, had impulsively rounded up some men and chased his rival down the lake. But not being the planner Arnold was, he had forgotten to bring provisions, and by the time Arnold swooped down on them, Allen and his men were "in a starving condition."

This time it was Arnold who had the upper hand and Allen who was reduced to frustrated expostulation. Displaying his prize, Arnold announced his intention to arm the sloop and the schooner and thus establish American control of Lake Champlain. Allen retorted that the best way to forestall a British attack on Ticonderoga was to take and hold St. Jean itself, implying that if Arnold had any guts he would have remained there. Holding St. Jean itself was of no consequence, Arnold correctly rejoined, as long as American ships controlled the lake. Allen, brushing aside warnings of British reinforcements, vowed to persevere. Denouncing the scheme as "wild [and] impractical," Arnold nevertheless magnanimously provided Allen's men with provisions, and the two parted. Toward sunset the following day, *Liberty* and *Enterprise* (as Arnold had rechristened the sloop) approached Ticonderoga "and, having saluted the fort, came to anchor."

He quickly set about arming the two ships with whatever guns he could lay his hands on, mostly small swivels mounted on the gunwales—inadequate, but better than nothing. He personally scoured the countryside for provisions, reinforcements and timber for wheel carriages to transport the cannon to Boston. His sense of mission was crystal clear, his efficiency and initiative remarkable—and his insecurity overwhelming. The slanders that he was convinced John Brown and James Easton had spread in Philadelphia and Watertown preoccupied him constantly. Would they be believed? Would his coup at St. Jean be sufficient to expunge them from the record? "I have had intimations given me," he brooded to Joseph Warren, "that some persons had determined . . . to injure me in your esteem by misrepresenting matters of fact . . . [but] I have the satisfaction of imagining I am employed by gentlemen of so much candor that my conduct will not be condemned until I have the opportunity of being heard."

Two days after Arnold's return to Ticonderoga, Ethan Allen suddenly reappeared, his troop having been ignominiously surprised and chased away from St. Jean by a detachment of two hundred British regulars, the very reinforcements Arnold had warned him about. Allen blustered in his report to the Continental Congress, "[if] I had but five hundred men with me at St. Jean, when we [*sic*] took the King's sloop, I would have advanced to Montreal." But in fact he was considerably, if temporarily, chastened, and the Green Mountain Boys decamped in droves.

After hearing Allen's story, Arnold sailed the sloop and the schooner up to Crown Point, where he proposed to "make a stand," assuring his masters in Massachusetts that "these places will not be given up unless we are overpowered by numbers or deserted by Providence, which has hitherto supported us." From his headquarters on board the schooner he sent out urgent requests for gunpowder—"out of twenty-six barrels found here there is not one pound good"—and reinforcements: "every man within fifty miles . . . who can be of service . . . and bring all the powder that can be found, and as many spades, pick-axes, and hoes, as they have," also "seamen, gunners, carpenters, etc." to fit out and man the two vessels, on which "our safety . . . in a great measure depends."

A few days later, Arnold's scouts informed him that the St. Jean garrison, deprived of transport for an attack up the lake, had withdrawn to Chambly. The threat against Ticonderoga had vanished, thanks to Arnold's foresight and courage. But this personal victory was offset by a serious setback on another front: the arrival of an official three-man fact-finding commission from the colony of Connecticut, which presented itself at Crown Point to question him concerning the "critical situation" at the forts stemming from his differences with Ethan Allen.

Allen himself arrived hot on the commissioners' heels. The question that burned in Arnold's brain was, whose version of events would they believe? Fortunately, he was able to bolster his narrative with concrete evidence of vigilance and efficiency: his careful inventories of arms and supplies, and his plans for fortifying Ticonderoga and transporting the cannon to Cambridge. As for his courage and industry, the sight of *Enterprise* anchored off Crown Point provided ample demonstration. The commissioners concluded that "Colonel Arnold has been greatly abused and misrepresented by designing persons, some of which were from Connecticut. Had it not been for him everything here would have been in the utmost confusion and disorder; people would have been plundered of their private property, and no man's person would be safe that was not of the Green Mountain party."

Temporarily bested, Ethan Allen agreed to step aside until matters could be "regulated and an officer appointed to take the command." Meanwhile, he informed the commissioners, he proposed to lead his Green Mountain Boys on a military expedition into Canada, and he wrote to the Canadian Indian tribes reminding them that he had "hunted with them many times, and know how to shoot and ambush like Indians, and am a great hunter" and promising "money, blankets, tomahawks, knives, paint and anything that there is in the army" if they would join him. The commissioners frostily declined to support such a hare-brained scheme, leaving Allen in limbo.

As for Benedict Arnold, his short-lived triumph turned to fretful apprehension on receipt of the news that Massachusetts had resigned its responsibility for the Ticonderoga expedition to the colony of Connecticut, thus depriving him of the official protection and support of Joseph Warren. Worse still, in thanking him formally for his "exertions in the cause," the Massachusetts Congress omitted any specific personal praise of his accomplishments. Arnold's imagination fed on such omissions, and he concluded that the congress, taken in by the lies of James Easton, no longer trusted him.

Within hours, however, this bad news was eclipsed by total disaster: the Continental Congress, despite "indubitable evidence that a design is formed by the British ministry of making a cruel invasion from the province of Quebec upon these colonies," ordered both Arnold and Ethan Allen to strip Ticonderoga and Crown Point of all arms and provisions and retreat to the southern end of Lake George, where "an exact inventory [can] be taken of all . . . cannon and stores, in order that they may be safely returned when the restoration of the former harmony between Great Britain and colonies, so ardently wished for by the latter, shall render it prudent."

"Ticonderoga," Arnold protested in a prompt reply to Congress, "is the key of this extensive country." To abandon it would be to invite a British invasion. At the very least, the whole Champlain Valley would become subject to "continual alarms" from Canada, which, he cogently suggested, "will [in the long run] probably cost more than the expense of repairing and garrisoning" the fort. Furthermore, he argued, if Ticonderoga were evacuated, the settlers in the Champlain Valley, "about five hundred families . . . to whom a remove would be entire ruin, as they have large families and no dependence but a promising crop on the ground . . . will be left at the mercy of the king's troops and Indians."

The argument, with its nice balance of humaneness, tactical acuity and thrift, represents Arnold at his best. Unfortunately, it occupied only a small part of his letter to Congress, the bulk of which was devoted to a list of his personal services at Ticonderoga and a litany of complaints against Ethan Allen. This inept attempt to play at politics backfired badly, with the result that for every member of Congress who discovered in Arnold an officer of intelligence, resourcefulness and enterprise, another saw a braggart, a complainer, a troublemaker. Both responses were accurate; and from this moment on, Congress's attitude toward Arnold remained deeply divided, even after he had proven himself to be one of their most effective officers.

While awaiting a response to his letter, Arnold chose to ignore the withdrawal order. On June 4, he paraded the garrison at Crown Point, embarked his men aboard the sloop, the schooner and several bateaux, and weighed anchor for a reconnoitering expedition down the lake. For ten days he sailed the length and breadth of the waterway, sending out scouts and holding powwows with the local Indians. The intelligence he received was encouraging: not only had the Canadian Indian tribes pledged to remain neutral in the war but the merchants of Montreal had categorically refused to cooperate with British Governor Sir Guy Carleton in organizing and financing the defense of their city against an American invasion, despite Sir Guy's threat to burn the town if they refused. Carleton did not have enough troops to fortify both Montreal and Quebec, and he desperately needed help from both civilians and Indians, help that the chiefs assured Arnold would not be forthcoming.

It was obvious to Arnold that Canada should be invaded before reinforcements could arrive from England. To take and hold Quebec, he argued in a cogent letter to the Continental Congress, would be less expensive in the long run than trying to stop the British at Ticonderoga. Asserting that the citizenry of Canada was "determined to join us whenever we appear in the country with any force to support them," he presented Congress with a detailed operational plan for the invasion and offered, "if no person appears who will undertake to carry the plan into execution," to command it himself.

That he was unqualified from inexperience to lead a major mili-

tary operation never occurred to him. Arnold felt he could do anything, given the chance, and his argument in favor of invasion was
well conceived. However, at the time he wrote it he was undergoing
an acute crisis of confidence. The Massachusetts Congress, having
written him a letter of fulsome praise for his "fidelity, knowledge,
courage and good conduct" at Ticonderoga, had at the same time,
and without informing him, acquiesced in the appointment of a new
commander for the forts, a Connecticut colonel named Hinman.

Despite his repeated requests to be relieved of command, Arnold
could not accept the actual event. In his mind, a perfectly routine
order became an attack on his character and reputation. He could
not bear the implied criticism, the public humiliation of it. The Massachusetts Congress had unwittingly tapped into his deepest fears,
and he lashed out at the man he held responsible for his reputation
with that body, James Easton. Arnold challenged Easton to a duel.
When Easton refused to draw his sword on the spot, Arnold "kicked
him very heartily [before witnesses] and ordered him from [Crown]
Point immediately."*

This exploit did not postpone the day of reckoning, of course,
and Colonel Hinman's arrival at Crown Point put Arnold under enormous pressure. To turn over the command, he felt, would be ac-
quiescing in his own disgrace, which was unthinkable. He was
cornered, and like an animal he lunged to defend himself, losing all
sense of the occasion and of his own long-term best interests.

Citing a technical flaw in Hinman's written orders, Arnold refused to surrender command of Crown Point. The puzzled colonel
prudently retired to Ticonderoga to await events. Five days later, an
inspection committee from the Massachusetts Congress arrived. Arnold would not parley with them. The committee chairman, Walter
Spooner, insisted that he at least peruse their written instructions. He
did so in their presence, and was devastated: not only was the committee empowered to issue him orders and reenlist his men under
Colonel Hinman, they were also directed, if they found him wanting,
to discharge him and order his return to Cambridge to render an
accounting of his expenditures.

Arnold turned to stone. Blurting out his resignation, he stalked
from the room. All the following day he remained in his quarters

---

*In one sense, Easton deserved it, having claimed in public that he person-
ally had led the assault on Ticonderoga and taken Captain Delaplace's surrender,
a claim that Delaplace himself refuted in a letter to the newspaper *Oracle of
Liberty.*

aboard the schooner *Liberty,* unable to face the committee or his men. At the end of the day he received Spooner's written orders to deliver up the command to Colonel Hinman and then to repair promptly to Congress to settle his accounts.

"It appears to me very extraordinary," Arnold responded, "that the [Massachusetts] Congress should first appoint an officer and afterwards, when he had executed his commission, to appoint a committee to examine if he was fit for his post. I think the examination should have been prior to the commission." As for his expenses, he claimed that, having received no money from the Massachusetts Congress, he had been forced to dig into his own purse to the tune of £100 to feed his men (a complaint that would be echoed by every officer in the Continental Army throughout the next eight years). Finally, his being superseded by an officer of the same rank but younger in seniority clearly indicated that "the Congress are dubious of my rectitude or abilities" and constituted a "disgraceful reflection on [me] and the body of troops [I] command." For all these reasons, he announced, summoning every shred of dignity at his command, "[I] decline holding my commission longer."

Later that same day, Edward Mott and several other men were taken captive aboard *Liberty* by Arnold's men and held for several hours at bayonet point before being released. The circumstances surrounding this curious event are murky. According to Mott, Arnold had planted a rumor among his men that they would be "defrauded out of their pay," and then, playing on their anger, persuaded them to sail with him for St. Jean to turn themselves and the schooner over to the British. Arnold's version of events naturally diverged: he himself, he claimed, had been held hostage by the men in order to induce the committee to pay them their back wages.

The truth lies buried somewhere between the two versions. Although Arnold was perfectly capable of manipulating his men to defend what he construed as his honor, it is extremely difficult to imagine him contemplating treason at this juncture. He was certainly desperate, but not yet desperate enough to take such a risk. There was too much to lose: reputation, of course, first and foremost; but also home, family and a budding career in an army in which he felt he could shine.

The point, perhaps, is not whether Mott's astonishing accusation was true or untrue, or even whether he himself believed it. (If he, and the others who took it up later, did not believe it, the infernal nature of the lie clearly indicates the depths of their hatred of Arnold.) The point is that Benedict Arnold was by now so controversial that his enemies knew that they could say extravagant, even explosive, things about him and someone would believe them.

Wild accusations aside, authentic reports of Arnold's behavior toward Colonel Hinman and the Massachusetts committee soon reached the ears of the Continental Congress, where they did much to undercut the credit he had received for saving Ticonderoga from a British counterattack. His champions in Congress, who recognized his military aptitude and valued his enterprising spirit, were confounded, and the anti-Arnold faction found new adherents.

Meanwhile, at Crown Point, Arnold's humiliation was made complete. A few days after the crisis on board *Liberty,* the "polite, generous and manly" Colonel Hinman appointed James Easton commander of Crown Point, and when Arnold's men were mustered, many of them volunteered to reenlist under Easton's command.

Arnold departed Crown Point on July 5. He had several days before reaching his first stopover, Albany, to ponder his next move. Should he resign his commission and thus forego the war?—an unattractive prospect, but no less attractive than swallowing his pride in order to remain in military service. His conflict was resolved in an abrupt and shocking manner when, in Albany, he received a letter from New Haven informing him that his wife was dead.

Chapter 4

"AN IDLE LIFE . . .
A LINGERING DEATH"

JULY-AUGUST 1775

Marriage had given ballast to Arnold's life; now he was cast adrift. "[My existence], but for the consideration of the public and my dear, innocent [children], is not worth reserving," he lamented in a letter to Connecticut Congressman Silas Deane, adding that "an idle life under my present circumstances would be but a lingering death." Philosophy was beyond him; the war would be his anchor. In the cause of his country he could, with perfect impunity, seek the action he craved.

The means were directly at hand in the person of forty-two-year-old Major General Philip Schuyler, newly appointed commander of the Northern Department (as the Hudson-Champlain theater would henceforth be known) of the newly created Continental Army, whose commander in chief, General George Washington, was currently en route to join the main army outside Boston.

What Washington would find was not an army at all, but a motley collection of local militias, each with its own officers and rules. In order to transform them into a unified, viable fighting force, he would have to rely heavily on the few American officers who had gained military experience fighting for the British in the French and Indian War, men such as the quintessential New York aristocrat Philip Schuyler.

Congress's choice of Schuyler for the Northern Department was a shrewd one: not only had he fought over much of its ground during the late war, he also owned a goodly piece of it. The vast Schuyler estates that stretched for miles north of Albany had been in the family for more than a century. The landed gentry of the Province of New York came as close as any colonial upper class to replicating the manners and attitudes of the British landed aristocracy, with the possible exception of the Virginia squirearchy into which George Washington had been born. Both Washington and Schuyler bore themselves with the sublime self-assurance that is bred into the children of a privileged, stable class, and their fellow men, over whom they towered so effortlessly, regarded them as genuinely superior beings. Cultivation and elegance came naturally to them, as did the easy affability that the best American aristocrats have always assumed in order to subsist in a supposedly egalitarian society.

Established landowning aristocracies are traditionally suspicious of persons in trade, and the Schuylers of New York were no exception. Philip Schuyler's people did not make money, they *had* money. The fact that an ancestor had stooped to make it sometime in the not-so-distant past did not signify. Secure in their income and estates, they regarded the making of money as crass at best and corrupt at worst—an attitude that placed them at odds with their New England neighbors, whose social ladder rested on solidly commercial footings.

Philip Schuyler, standing tall and erect, every inch the patrician, was distrusted and disliked by the New England troops over whom he was to exert control. A notable exception was the New Haven shopkeeper Benedict Arnold, who was strongly attracted by the New Yorker's demeanor and by the patrician world of grace and urbanity that he discovered in the parlor of the general's elegant Albany mansion, where he soon ingratiated himself with Mrs. Schuyler and her daughters.

Colonel Arnold was also gratified by General Schuyler's good opinion of Colonel Arnold, gleaned from favorable reports of his conduct at Ticonderoga. Schuyler had already requested Congressman Silas Deane to obtain Arnold's appointment as deputy adjutant general in the Northern Department. "I dare not mention it [directly] to Congress," he warned Deane, well aware of the fierce rivalries within that body and of Arnold's equivocal reputation, nor "would [I] have it known that I had ever hinted it, as it might create jealousy."

Although Congress had never answered Arnold's letters regarding Canada (which he naturally took as a personal affront), it appeared they had heeded his arguments: Schuyler's orders were to fortify Ticonderoga and, if he deemed it practicable, to mount an invasion of Canada down the lake. The decision to invade or not to invade was left entirely up to Schuyler. Thanks to the slowness and uncertainty of communications—it took about a week for the average courier to travel from Philadelphia to Albany, if he got there at all—Congress was forced to grant its commanders in the field genuine autonomy in military matters. Unfortunately, however, they insisted on retaining tight control over such life-and-death decisions as the appointment of adjutants, commissaries and mustermen.

For General Schuyler, as well as for the future of the colonies, the decision was a crucial one. If he invaded Canada, captured Montreal and Quebec and persuaded the Canadians to join the rebellion, the British would doubtless be forced to sue for peace. If he failed, he would bear the sole responsibility. In the absence of disciplined troops and experienced officers, Schuyler naturally hesitated to order an invasion immediately, despite the urgings of his new friend Arnold, who argued cogently that the invasion must be undertaken before the British could reinforce Quebec and Montreal.

Arnold was desperate for action and a chance to prove himself. He was also anxious to ingratiate himself further with Philip Schuyler. In one of their early conferences, he reported to the general that at Ticonderoga, under the command of his successor, all was "anarchy and confusion . . . everything to do and nothing done. . . . The officers complain they have no orders to act; it is well they have not, for the men obey none." This assessment was confirmed when Schuyler made a personal inspection trip to the fort a few days later. Approaching the dock after dark, his party landed and slipped past the first guard post unchallenged, after which, he reported to General Washington, "with a pen-knife only I could have cut off both guards [at the second post, one of whom was sound asleep] and then have set fire to the block-house, destroyed the stores and starved the people."

The experience only confirmed Schuyler's reluctance to invade Canada with the troops at hand. Arnold, whose appointment as adjutant had not been approved by Congress, became restless. With the summons of the Massachusetts Congress hanging over him, he departed Albany in mid-July to settle his accounts, introduce himself to the new commander in chief, and scan his prospects in the Continental Army.

During a brief stopover in New Haven to visit his children, now in the charge of his sister, Hannah, the strains of the previous months caught up with him, and he suffered his first attack of gout, that excruciatingly painful disease of the joints that was to plague him for the rest of his life. Frequently triggered by stress, gout attacks appear without warning and last for a period of two to ten days, during which even the slightest touch or movement is torment to the victim.

While Arnold waited out the attack (two painkillers were in wide use at the time, alcohol and laudanum; there is no evidence regarding his use of either), he prepared his Ticonderoga accounts for the Massachusetts Congress and caught up on his business affairs. The recent military exertions of Colonel Benedict Arnold had done nothing to suppress the commercial appetites of Benedict Arnold, merchant of New Haven. Like many of his countrymen, Arnold believed that business should be kept strictly separate from politics. So when Captain John Gordon of *Peggy,* one of Arnold's brigantines, suggested a trading voyage to British Quebec, the owner gave his blessing and wrote to a Canadian friend requesting his help in supplying the ship.

After barely a fortnight at home, fit and eager for action, Arnold set off for Cambridge, where, toward the end of July, he presented himself at the headquarters of General George Washington of Virginia. It was barely a month since the commander in chief had joined his army, but already his presence had had an effect. Washington was on the lines every day, personally supervising all aspects of life in the far-flung, makeshift camp, from the guarding of ammunition depots to the digging of latrines. His insistence on the strict subordination of men to officers had raised an outcry among the zealously egalitarian New Englanders, which deterred him not a bit. While waiting for the real war to begin—he could not attack Boston without the cannon from Ticonderoga, which would take another eight months to arrive—he concentrated on transforming his ragtag militia troops into an army.

Even more impressive than General Washington's policies and accomplishments, however, was his private character. The men around him were consistently awed by his natural authority, graceful style and apparently endless forbearance, all stemming from a vast reservoir of personal assurance. Washington was bedrock. Lose his temper he might; become discouraged he might; but he never wavered. His self-confidence, virtually free of conceit, was deeply rooted in his soul.

He was also profoundly ethical, and his behavior was dictated by principle and conviction. Arnold, with no ethics, no principle and no convictions other than those he had picked up as a matter of expediency, could not comprehend what drove a person like Washington. He might envy the commander in chief his self-confidence, and even admire his demeanor, but he could never understand him. The war threw Arnold and Washington into the same boat, but it did not put them in the same class.

Naturally, none of this was apparent on first meeting. Washington welcomed Arnold as a soldier (a problematical one to be sure; the general was well aware of the colonel's reputation for contentiousness) and as a brother in Freemasonry. Soon Arnold was coming and going freely at headquarters, rubbing elbows with the commander in chief's inner circle and striking up a particular friendship with his adjutant general, Horatio Gates.

At forty-seven, Gates was the old man of the headquarters staff, older by four years than his commander in chief, with whom he had served in Virginia two decades before. At the end of the French and Indian War, Gates had returned to England to pursue a career in the British Army and quickly run up against that institution's literal interpretation of the phrase "an officer and a gentleman." Gates was the illegitimate son of the housekeeper to the Duke of Leeds, a fact that effectively blocked his line of promotion. Resigning from the army, he recrossed the ocean and settled in Virginia at the behest of George Washington. Horatio Gates was a competent and experienced officer with a gigantic chip on his shoulder. Like his new friend Arnold, he harbored a vast ambition with a deep underlying reservoir of insecurity.

Congenial as the atmosphere at headquarters might be, Arnold craved action. Within days of his arrival he learned that the commander in chief was contemplating an overland expedition to Quebec via the Kennebec River, in support of General Schuyler's projected invasion via Lake Champlain. The object was to force Canada's royal governor, Major General Guy Carleton, to make a difficult choice. Most of Carleton's troops had been sent to Boston earlier in the year. In the face of a two-pronged attack, he would either have to divide his depleted garrison between Quebec and Montreal (see map, page 46), in which case he might lose both, or concentrate his forces at one and concede the other. Montreal controlled the invasion route via Lake Champlain. If the Continentals took it, they would have a stable base of operations in Canada with reliable supply lines, and the British would no longer present a threat to the Hudson Valley. If they took Quebec, on the other hand, the British would lose access to the sea and be starved out of the country entirely.

Benedict Arnold conceived a desperate longing for command of the Kennebec expedition. Its difficulties did not daunt him—the long and arduous trek through an uncharted wilderness, with an assault on the bastion of Quebec at the end of it—and he set about trying to convince General Washington that, inexperience notwithstanding, he was the man for the job. He submitted a specific plan for the expedition, wrote letters on the commander in chief's behalf to potential suppliers and sought intelligence about the route, taking pains all the while to impress Washington with his intimate knowledge of Quebec and its people and assuring the general that the town would "fall into our hands an easy prey."

Throughout August Arnold lived in suspense, shuttling between Cambridge, where plans for the expedition went ahead despite the absence of a decision from General Schuyler, and Watertown, where the Massachusetts Congress picked over his account books and finally, grudgingly, granted him about three quarters of what he said he was owed. (After appealing the ruling to Silas Deane, he received the balance from Congress six months later.) Even after General Schuyler announced that the invasion was on, no commander was named for the Kennebec, and an impatient Arnold declared his intention of departing for home. He was stopped by a note from Horatio Gates: General Washington, having considered "your plan . . . [wished to] converse with you upon it when you next meet."

Washington's hesitation is understandable. Although Arnold had much to recommend him—familiarity with Quebec, an enterprising spirit, a clear sense of mission and an obvious devotion to the cause of his country—his inexperience and his reputation for disharmony spoke against him. The leader of the Kennebec division would have to exert control over a dozen or more independent companies whose battle-hardened commanders were not used to taking orders from novices. It took the commander in chief another two weeks to make up his mind while Arnold lingered at headquarters, making himself useful. Then, all at once, it was his.

Chapter 5

"OUR GALLANT COLONEL"

SEPTEMBER-NOVEMBER 1775

On the morning of September 6, 1775, the newly appointed commander of the Continental Army's Kennebec expedition, Colonel Benedict Arnold, reviewed his troops on Cambridge Common accompanied by his friend, Adjutant General Horatio Gates.

Parading before them were ten companies of New England volunteers, all purportedly "active woodsmen, and well acquainted with bateaux," plus three rifle companies garbed Indian-style in "deep ash-colored hunting-shirts, leggins, and moccasins" and armed with rifles, tomahawks and scalping knives.

Arnold's junior officers consisted of two lieutenant colonels, two majors and ten captains, most of whom had considerably more knowledge of war and life than their thirty-four-year-old commander. These men faced a formidable task: to conduct more than a thousand troops, with provisions and equipment, nearly four hundred miles through the wilderness, up one major river and down another, over portages and chains of mountains where the route was virtually unknown—and, ideally, to accomplish this so expeditiously that Governor Carleton would be taken unawares and Quebec would fall without a fight.

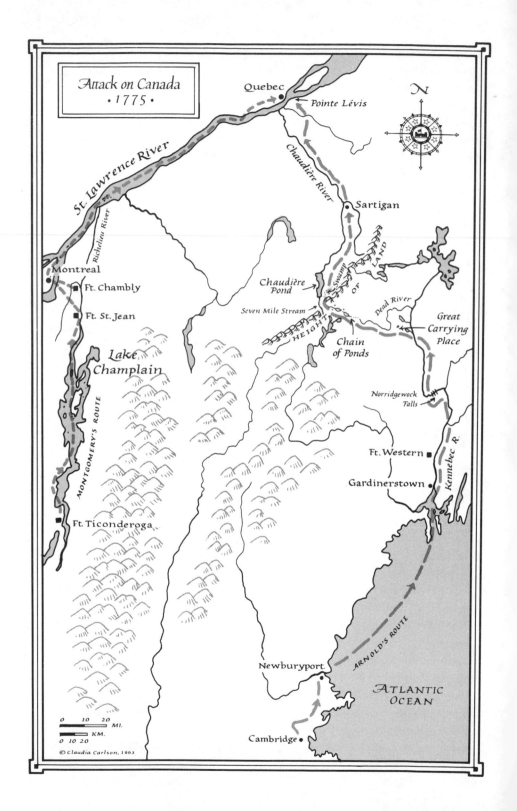

Attack on Canada
· 1775 ·

The company captains ranged in age from thirty-eight-year-old Simeon Thayer, a veteran of Rogers's Rangers and a wig-maker in civilian life, to nineteen-year-old Samuel Ward, son of the governor of Rhode Island. The expedition's surveyor was Sergeant John Pierce and its doctor twenty-two-year-old Isaac Senter, who had interrupted his medical studies to volunteer for the army. Eleazer Oswald, Arnold's faithful comrade from the New Haven Foot Guard, served as secretary. The senior officer in the group was forty-six-year-old Lieutenant Colonel Roger Enos of Connecticut, who had fought under General Jeffrey Amherst and on whose experience and steadiness Arnold particularly relied.

By far the most interesting officer in the detachment was the formidable Daniel Morgan, captain of the Virginia rifle company. During his service against the French and Indians, Morgan once struck a superior officer in a fit of rage and survived the punishment: five hundred lashes. Now, at forty, his six-foot frame constructed entirely of muscle, heart and guts, he took no nonsense from anyone, and his men took no orders from anyone but him. Morgan's prowess as both woodsman and warrior would be crucial to the success of the expedition, and Arnold knew it.

"The drums beat and away they go," an enthusiast reported on the day the first division marched, "as far as Newburyport by land, from there they go in sloops to Kennebec River, up it in bateaux . . . scale the walls [of Quebec] and spend the winter in joy and festivity among the sweet nuns." Surveyor Pierce enjoyed the trip to Newburyport, particularly the "taverns very plenty" where he drank "toddy on the Province['s] cost [and] 1000 pretty girls." Young Dr. Senter was more preoccupied with "the fleas and other Tory insects [which made] not a little free with our property," but he noted philosophically that everyone being "in the same predicament, afforded a seeming alleviation."

Arnold himself, after seeing the last detachment off, rode the forty miles from Cambridge to Newburyport in a single day, September 15. He had much to ponder as he passed through the columns of marching men, whose lives during the perilous weeks ahead would depend on his judgment. Lacking introspection, immune to self-doubt, he did not question his ability to bring them through safely, nor did he doubt their ultimate success. His appointment as commander was, in itself, a confirmation of his powers. He had taken a risk, overstretched himself—and caught the brass ring. Now, with a fresh start and a clear mandate, he never doubted that he would prove himself once and for all.

General Washington's final written orders were troubling, however. The commander in chief addressed himself at length to the logistical and tactical difficulties of Arnold's command, and also to its political intricacies, warning him particularly of the dangers of alienating Canada's civilian population. No matter what the circumstances, the commander in chief instructed, the men were to be kept under tight control and to pay full value for supplies and lodging. "Should any American soldier be so base and infamous as to injure any Canadian or Indian in his person or property, I do most earnestly enjoin you to bring him to such severe and exemplary punishment as the enormity of the crime may require. Should it extend to death itself it will not be disproportional to its guilt at such a time and in such a cause. . . . Upon your conduct and courage and that of the officers and soldiers on this expedition," the commander in chief emphasized, ". . . the safety and welfare of the whole continent may depend."

Arnold did not need reminding; the significance and complexity of the task were what had drawn him to it in the first place. Much more troubling was a passage in which General Washington seemed to go out of his way to remind Arnold of his status. Once the detachment was united with General Schuyler's army, the commander in chief instructed, "you are by no means to consider yourself as upon a separate and independent command. . . . Upon this occasion and all others, I recommend most earnestly to avoid all contention about rank. In such a cause, every post is honorable in which a man can serve his country."

Why should Washington feel it thus necessary to belabor the obvious? For Arnold, there could be only one explanation: the general's mind must have been fouled by the calumnies of his enemies. This was partly correct. Washington had indeed heard reports of Arnold's behavior at Ticonderoga and, having carefully weighed them, concluded that Arnold was extremely defensive in matters of rank and control. Accurate as the assessment was, Arnold could neither comprehend nor appreciate it. In his eyes he had behaved impeccably at Ticonderoga, and anyone who said otherwise was a villain and a liar.

At Newburyport, Arnold's men embarked and sailed north in ships belonging to a wealthy local trader. Rough seas during the night "occasioned most of the troops to disgorge themselves of their luxuries so plentifully laid in ere we embarked," and at dawn the ships were obliged to make their way in rain and heavy wind between the low, rocky offshore islands at the mouth of the Kennebec River. As they regrouped inside the harbor, the weather cleared, and flocks of cormorants and seagulls wheeled and screeched in the overhead sun while their delicate cousins, the long-legged cranes, breakfasted among the gently lapping waves at water's edge.

Less inviting was the view inland of the broad, blue Kennebec River flowing out of a dark and seemingly impenetrable forest wilderness. Arnold's fleet set sail, his flagship in the van. Guided by a local pilot, the ships threaded their way among the shoals at the river's mouth and sailed upriver between stands of shadowy pines and maples brushed with early autumn color, past marshes choked with yellowing ferns, past meadows of goldenrod and purple aster, and past the settlements of the lower valley with their sawmills, cornfields and farms. The men were in high spirits, although a contrary wind kept them at the oars most of the day. Bets were placed as to who could shoot the greatest number of seals, cranes and hawks; and in the evening the troops dined sumptuously ashore on salmon, lobster and roast beef, courtesy of the local inhabitants. The ever-resourceful Surveyor Pierce and his party even managed to discover and consume "seven or eight bowls of egg rum."

Arnold's ship pushed ahead of the others and anchored after dark at the settlement of Gardinerstown. There, over supper in the comfortable home of shipbuilder Reuben Colburn, Arnold learned two pieces of sinister news: hostile Mohawks were reported to be gathering on the Chaudière River, and the two hundred bateaux in Colburn's shipyard were largely unfinished. (Little wonder: Colburn had been given only two weeks to build them.) Arnold refused to be intimidated by rumors of Indians (which eventually proved false), but the shortage of bateaux was much more serious. As if to remind him of the need for haste, the weather turned sharply colder the following morning as the men transferred their supplies and equipment to the available bateaux and commenced the long pull up to Fort Western, where the whole division would rendezvous.

The bateaux used by Arnold's expedition were an uneasy compromise between the traditional Maine logging bateaux and lighter craft designed for speed and portability. The boats had to be heavy enough to bear the hundreds of barrels of flour, pork, dried peas and gunpowder on which the expedition depended, yet light enough to be carried around portages. About twenty feet long, the bateaux constructed by Reuben Colburn had bottoms solid enough to withstand the sharp glacial material of the Kennebec bottom and flared sides to carry them over the waves in white water. Heavy and light, solid but portable: these contradictory demands were impossible to fulfill, as

Arnold's men would soon discover. That first afternoon, however, they engaged in lighthearted, impromptu races; and Private Samuel Barney boasted that his bateau "beat anyone that there was," although he had to confess, "I blistered my hands very bad."

Arnold himself arrived at the old trading post of Fort Western by evening and promptly called a council of officers to announce the order of march. Two advance parties would set off the following morning to scout the route and gather intelligence, with the main body departing in separate divisions on four succeeding days, in order to avoid bottlenecks at the portages. The whole detachment would rendezvous at Chaudière Pond, on the far side of the Height of Land, which formed the border with Canada.

Next morning, in a cold, driving rain, Arnold watched as Surveyor Pierce with eight men pushed off upriver in canoes, followed closely by a small scouting party under the command of Lieutenant Archibald Steele, "a man of an active, courageous, sprightly and hardy disposition." The rest of the day he was engrossed by two disparate but equally disturbing incidents: a trial for murder and a squabble over command.

During a raucous party the previous night, a young soldier named McCormick had fired his pistol into a crowded room, killing one of his fellow revelers. Found guilty by court-martial, he confessed at the foot of the gallows to shooting the man—by mistake, having intended the bullet for his commanding officer, Captain Simeon Thayer, who had tried to break up the party. Arnold issued a reprieve and sent McCormick to Cambridge in custody, recommending to General Washington that he be "found a proper object of mercy." The martinet, it appeared, had a soft side.

Much more threatening was the challenge to his authority issued by Daniel Morgan and his men. Arnold had assigned the rifle companies to the first division, where their skills as woodsmen would be put to use marking trails and clearing roads. Morgan's men, however, objected to serving under the division commander Arnold had appointed, Lieutenant Colonel Christopher Greene, and Morgan himself, claiming that General Washington had given him an independent command, categorically refused to take orders from anybody but Arnold. This put Arnold in a terrible bind: if he gave in to Morgan, his authority, and perhaps his reputation at headquarters, would suffer; but if he did not give in, he realized, from looking into Daniel Morgan's eyes, that the Virginians would not march under Greene. Arnold had no choice but to transfer Greene to the second division and send the first forward under Morgan's command. (General Washington, on receiving Arnold's report of the incident, confirmed Arnold's authority to dictate the chain of command, but by the time his letters reached them, both Morgan and Arnold had more pressing matters on their minds.)

Greene's division left Fort Western the day after Morgan's, September 26, and the third division pushed off one day later under the command of Major Return Jonathan Meigs (whose mother, during her courtship, had mended a quarrel by bidding Meigs's future father to "Return, Jonathan," which pleasing event he duly commemorated in naming his firstborn son). Arnold himself set off the same day by canoe, fully confident, he wrote to General Washington, of reaching Quebec by the middle of October, three weeks hence. He left behind most of the supplies and heavy equipment in the charge of Roger Enos, the commander of the fourth division, whose task it was to secure the line of retreat and to resupply the forward divisions, which were traveling light.

Arnold's ebullience was considerably diminished by the time he reached Daniel Morgan in the van, forty-eight hours later. Passing through the forward divisions, he had seen the entire army "up to their waists in water," pushing and hauling the heavy bateaux against the icy current. Promises to the contrary notwithstanding, the men were far from experienced boatmen, but the boats were also at fault. Hastily constructed of green pine, they had already begun to leak and break apart, soaking the men's clothing, provisions and ammunition. In order to save his medical supplies, Dr. Senter, on the fourth day out of Fort Western, paid four dollars out of his own pocket for a new bateau, "well built . . . seasoned, etc., fit for the business." Private Samuel Barney, who had cheerfully blistered his hands in a race the week before, now grumbled about his "dam'd bad bote," and Captain Simeon Thayer "heartily wish[ed] the infamous constructors" of the bateaux would someday "be obliged to trust to the mercy of others more treacherous than themselves, that they might . . . undergo the just reward of their villainy."

Arnold lingered the entire second week at Norridgewock Falls as each detachment in turn struggled over the brutal portage. Teams of oxen were hired to haul the heavier items—barrels of flour and dried peas, boxes of gunpowder—over a steep road whose very existence testified to the perseverance and ingenuity of Daniel Morgan and his men. Everything else was carried by hand: clothing, cook pots, rifles, strings of salt pork and fish on long poles and, finally, the bateaux themselves upended and hoisted on hand spikes. "Now we are learning to be soldiers," a private in Captain Ward's company noted laconically in his diary at the end of his first day on the portage.

Above Norridgewock the army, now spread out over ten or

twelve miles, climbed laboriously out of the lowlands. Soon high snow-capped mountains loomed on all sides, a "dismal" sight in the eyes of Simeon Thayer. During a three-day soaking rain the men's clothing froze at night "a pane of glass thick, which," Thayer commented, "proved very disagreeable, being obliged to lie in them." On the seventeenth day out of Fort Western, October 11, Arnold reached the Great Carrying Place, a twelve-mile portage, divided by three large ponds, that led from the Kennebec to the Dead River. There he ordered construction of a small shelter for the sick, which Dr. Senter promptly christened "Arnold's Hospital, and no sooner finished than filled." The young physician did his best to treat a wide variety of ailments including dysentery; but many of the men concocted their own herbal teas, and a local guide taught one company how to extract liquid from the "Balm of Gilead fir . . . [which] was heating and cordial to the stomach."

Perilously behind schedule, the detachment now faced a severe food shortage. The waters of the Kennebec, seeping and washing through the bateaux day after day, had ruined virtually every barrel of flour and leached the salt from the army's supply of pork and fish. Arnold put the men on short rations—three quarters of a pound each of pork and flour per man per day—and dispatched an urgent message back to Roger Enos to forward supplies immediately. He marveled at the men's "spirit and industry," which, despite their hunger and fatigue, seemed "to overcome every obstacle." They supplemented their meager diet with some "fine salmon trout" caught in one of the ponds at the Great Carrying Place, and hunted moose in the surrounding woods. Others, however, including the rowing champion Samuel Barney, began to steal food from their companions.

Spirits rose when the two advance scouting parties returned from the Dead, which they described as a "fine, deep river" with "short carrying places . . . and plenty of moose." Arnold immediately ordered Archibald Steele back up the trail to penetrate the Chaudière valley in search of information and supplies, and dispatched an Indian courier to gather intelligence from a trusted friend in Quebec, the merchant John Dyer Mercier. Confident that the worst was over, Arnold vowed in separate dispatches to General Schuyler and General Washington that he would reach the city with his army inside a fortnight.

The Dead River, however, did not live up to its name, and the effort of pulling the boats against its swift current began to sap the men's remaining strength. Arnold called a two-day halt and sent Major Bigelow to the rear with twelve bateaux and nearly a hundred men to bring up emergency supplies, ordering Roger Enos to come up as quickly as possible with the rest. Meanwhile, he and the forward detachments launched their boats again in a driving rain that fell unremittingly for the next forty-eight hours. The river rose eight feet during the second night and washed through the campsites of the sleeping army. Arnold and his party managed to drag their drenched belongings up a small slope behind their camp, where they "passed the remainder of the night in no very agreeable situation." Others, less fortunate, lost everything they owned and spent the predawn hours in the water.

First light revealed a dismal landscape of swirling water and bare trees, in which the crooked course of the river could not be discerned. Nevertheless, with the example and encouragement of Arnold and his fellow officers, the men embarked and began to pull at their oars. All day they strained against the merciless current, while Simeon Thayer attempted to cheer his men with the observation that the portages were so "entirely overflowed that our bateaux went through the woods without the trouble of carrying them." During the day "several boats return[ed from upriver] loaded with invalids, and lamentable stories of the inaccessibleness of the river and the impracticality of any further progress into the country." At this juncture, Major Bigelow and his hundred men returned from the rear carrying two barrels of flour and a message from Roger Enos that he could spare no more.

The unexpectedness of the blow made it all the more devastating. With his army on the verge of disintegration, Arnold summoned all his powers of mind, spirit and instinct in order to preserve the one thing that was keeping his men going: their courage. In the process, he demonstrated for all time that he was a leader of men. He summoned an emergency officers' council on the evening of October 23 (the twenty-ninth day out of Fort Western) and got approval of two resolutions. First, Colonel Enos was ordered to send all but his most able-bodied men back to Norridgewock and to bring the rest forward with the remaining provisions as quickly as possible. Second, Arnold himself would set off immediately with a small detachment on a forced march to the French settlements along the Chaudière River to obtain provisions and send them back.

The effect was immediate. A rifleman named Morison, who had blanched in the face of impending famine ("We had not contemplated warring with such a dreadful enemy," he wrote in his diary), now cheerfully applauded the decisiveness and wisdom of "our gallant colonel"; and Dr. Senter, who the day before had described the

Dead River valley as "a direful howling wilderness," now reported that the army was "fired with more than Hannibalian enthusiasm, American Alps nor Pyrenees were obstacles."

For two days Arnold and his small detachment, with Connecticut Captain Oliver Hanchet as second-in-command, rowed and portaged in a driving snowstorm across the chain of ponds at the head of the Dead River. Icy winds ripped the last leaves from the trees and whipped up dangerous whitecaps on the open water. Near dark on the second day the little party disembarked and commenced to cross the "terrible carrying place," the Height of Land that forms the border between Canada and the lower colonies. For hours they stumbled upward in the dark with their canoes and baggage and finally camped near midnight at the top of the pass.

At dawn, in the valley far below their campsite, Chaudière Pond was revealed—not a pond at all but an enormous lake in the midst of a vast plateau. Arnold led a small detachment with canoes to row down Seven Mile Stream while Oliver Hanchet scouted the best overland route to the lake. After Hanchet and his men floundered all day in a vast swamp with water up to their waists, Arnold dispatched warnings and specific directions back to the main army. He also passed along a report from the Chaudière that Archibald Steele had delivered that afternoon in person: the French settlers appeared extremely friendly and were eagerly preparing to supply the army. (Some forty miles to the rear, "the whole valley was made to ring with our exultations," a Connecticut private reported on hearing the news.)

Even more significant in the long run, Steele reported that the American invasion strategy was working: Governor Carleton was known to be at Montreal with the bulk of his force preparing to face the oncoming army of Philip Schuyler—leaving Quebec with only a handful of troops and one small frigate to patrol the St. Lawrence crossing.

Galvanized by the news, Arnold vowed to cross the St. Lawrence and attack the city as soon as a sufficient number of his men came up—provided, of course, that the British did not become aware of his presence in time to prevent it. Surprise was crucial, and Arnold was vexed by the failure of John Dyer Mercier to respond to his letters.

For most of its hundred-mile length, the Chaudière River lives up to its name—it means "cauldron" in French. Three of Arnold's boats capsized in white water the first afternoon. During the enforced pause to pull the men out of the water, Arnold sent a scout forward, who reported a major falls just ahead. If they had gone over, the whole party would "inevitably have been dashed to pieces and all lost." Reaching the first French settlement the following day, Arnold immediately dispatched a number of live cattle and five hundred pounds of flour back to the men, with instructions for "those who have provisions . . . [to] let this pass on for the rear, and those who want will take as sparingly as possible, that the whole may meet with relief."

Two days later, the first contingents of Arnold's army appeared out of a blinding snowstorm. Barely able to walk, gaunt and wasted, they brought disastrous news: Roger Enos had turned back with his entire detachment—nearly one third of the army—taking with him most of the ammunition and food.

When the men in the forward detachments had learned about Enos's defection, anger had served to buttress their courage. They cursed and reviled the defectors, and Captain Henry Dearborn's company "made a general prayer that Colonel Enos and all his men might die by the way, or meet with some disaster, equal to the cowardly, dastardly and unfriendly spirit they discovered in returning back." Meanwhile, having no other choice, they marched, most of them barefoot by now, across the Height of Land (Arnold had ordered them to abandon their bateaux) and down into Canada.

Having missed their colonel's warning, or been too weak to take it in, most of the men landed in Oliver Hanchet's swamp, where they floundered "up to [their] arm pits in water and ice" for three days and nights. Those who survived stumbled down the steep, rocky, frozen terrain of the Chaudière valley, helping one another along, until their captains issued orders for every man to save himself and leave the stragglers to die.

Dr. Senter's meager supply of flour was mixed with water "in imitation of shoemaker's paste, which was christened Lillipu." When the flour ran out, the doctor reported, "cooking being very much out of fashion, we had little else to do than march." Some of the men chopped up pieces of rawhide "singeing first the hair, afterwards boiling them and living on the juice or liquid that they soak'd from it for a considerable time." Others boiled shaving soap, candles, lip salve, cartridge boxes, and finally their moccasins, "under the vague but consolatory hope that a mucilage would take place." They ate roots, tearing them from the soil with their nails and eating "them raw, even without washing." Eventually they slaughtered and ate their pet dogs, skin, feet and all.

On November 2, Dr. Senter, marching in the van, saw "a vision of horned cattle, four footed beasts . . . drove by animals resembling

Plato's two-footed featherless ones. Upon a nigher approach our vision proved real! Exclamations of joy—Echoes of gladness resounded from front to rear! with a te deum." As the cattle were slaughtered, many of the men wept, others simply sat and stared. Some tore at the animals' flesh and ate it raw; many gorged themselves and became ill.

These were the men—their health and numbers decimated, but their spirit apparently intact—with whom Benedict Arnold was to capture Quebec.

Speed was crucial: the British would soon learn of the army's appearance at the Chaudière settlements. Arnold must get his remaining able-bodied men—fewer than seven hundred—across the St. Lawrence before the enemy could prepare. Leaving the army camped near the village of Sartigan to rest and recover and follow as soon as it could, Arnold pushed ahead with a small detachment to Pointe Lévis to organize the river crossing. En route he learned that General Schuyler's army, led by Brigadier General Richard Montgomery (who had taken command of the invasion when Schuyler fell sick), had captured St. Jean and Chambly and was advancing on Montreal. But another messenger brought ill tidings: Arnold's Indian courier, either by accident or design, had been captured at Quebec and all his letters seized. John Dyer Mercier was in prison, and the British lieutenant governor had sent to Montreal for reinforcements. Two frigates with gunboats now patroled the St. Lawrence between the city and Pointe Lévis, and all the canoes and bateaux on Arnold's side of the river had been confiscated.

The view from Pointe Lévis was forbidding. Directly across the swift, gray waters of the St. Lawrence, atop a massive rock, stood the city of Quebec, its stone walls washed with dim light from the winter sun which traced a low arc far to the south, from whence, across a flat, frozen landscape, Arnold's men were struggling toward him. How was he to carry them the last mile to the gates of the city?

The men began to straggle in, looking "very ghostly and meager" after a march of several days in a blinding snowstorm over a "terrible road, mud and mire to the horses' bellies." Arnold quickly dispatched Simeon Thayer back to Sartigan to bring the invalids down in boats and ordered Major Meigs out into the countryside to scour for canoes. (Surveyor Pierce celebrated his arrival at Pointe Lévis by holing up in his quarters with four bottles of Madeira.) But no sooner had Meigs collected a number of boats than the wind shifted to the north and began to blow a gale, turning the St. Lawrence into a roiling, churning torrent, impossible to cross. The men, chilled to the bone, were kept busy constructing scaling ladders for the assault.

Arnold's impatience was intense. He knew that 150 British reinforcements had reached Quebec during the previous week, and on the morning of November 12 he saw with his own eyes a sizable British vessel sail downriver and anchor off the city. By evening he learned that she had landed two hundred seasoned British regulars under the command of Colonel Allan Maclean. Arnold immediately called a council of officers, which convened to the strains of dance music—the local inhabitants were entertaining the American soldiers at a "fine ball [down the street, with] music of diverse sorts such as bagpipes, fiddle, fife, [and] German flute"—to consider the following question: assuming they could cross the river within the next few days, should they persevere in their plan to attack the city immediately, or wait for General Montgomery's army to arrive?

Arnold himself argued strenuously in favor of attack, citing intelligence sources inside Quebec who assured him that the city's defenses remained weak and disorganized despite the British reinforcements. It was an argument he longed to believe: either the attack would take place now under his command, or General Montgomery would lead it later. To his "mortification," however, his officers—Daniel Morgan, Simeon Thayer, Oliver Hanchet, Archibald Steele, Return Jonathan Meigs, Christopher Greene and the others—overruled him.

If only he had arrived a few days sooner, there would have been no question of delay. He had done everything in his considerable power to bring his army to the goal. If only the Dead River had not flooded, if only Roger Enos had possessed a backbone, if only his courier had not been captured . . . but it was fruitless to speculate. He had done the best he could against impossible odds, and now he would be denied the fruits of his labors.

Ironically, in hindsight, his officers appear to have made the correct decision. The arrival of the two hundred British regulars had indeed tipped the balance, thanks in part to their numbers and training and also to the talents of their commander, the energetic and able Colonel Maclean, who took charge of the weak and divided city and converted it into a determined armed camp in a matter of days. But if any of Arnold's intelligence sources sounded the alarm, he paid no attention. His courage was up; and his good judgment fell victim to his craving for personal triumph.

On the afternoon following the officers' council, the wind died, and Arnold began to embark his men after dark in the forty-odd canoes and barges that had been secreted in a cove several miles upriver. It would take at least four crossings to bring the whole army over, but it must be risked. About nine P.M., Arnold gave final orders to Oliver Hanchet, whom he left in command of the small guard remaining at Pointe Lévis, and stepped into the lead canoe with Daniel Morgan, Dr. Senter and a local pilot. Morgan's riflemen pushed off into a fast-moving ebb tide and began to paddle silently across the St. Lawrence.

Chapter 6

"THE NURSERY OF HEROES"
NOVEMBER-DECEMBER 1775

The three-mile crossing seemed to take forever. Reaching the middle of the river, the pilot steered straight for the riding lights of two British frigates, then silently, in slow motion, Arnold's canoe slipped undetected between the ships. There was a sudden lurch and a splash of icy water; everyone froze, gripping the sides, as the craft rocked in the wake of a guard boat that passed much too close for comfort.

Drawing in under the steep palisades that line the river's northern shore, the canoe cautiously entered Wolfe's Cove, named in honor of British General James Wolfe, who had landed an army there in 1759 and defeated the French General Montcalm in battle the following day. (Richard Montgomery had served under Wolfe in that campaign, as had the British general who now opposed him at Montreal, Governor Sir Guy Carleton.) The cove was the only landing site near the city where a gap in the towering cliff gave access to the plateau one hundred feet above. Fortunately, the overconfident British had failed to station sentries there, and Arnold and his men were able to disembark unchallenged. As the canoes pulled silently back into the river to fetch the second division, Arnold dispatched sentries in both directions along the shore and up the steep path to the open flats west of the city walls known as the Plains of Abraham.

An hour passed. No musket fire or cry of alarm broke the black silence of the river. Some of the men, chilled to the bone, built a small fire in a deserted hut. Finally, toward midnight, a canoe emerged from the gloom, then another and another. The second wave disembarked and the boats returned to the river. Hours passed. At four A.M. the third wave began to appear. One man, half drowned, nearly insensible and "seemingly chilled to the heart," was dragged ashore and carried to the fire: Archibald Steele, whose canoe had broken apart in the swift river current. After seeing his men safely aboard other craft, Steele had reached a canoe that was already overloaded; so he threw his arms over the stern, instructed the steersman to sit on them and was towed the rest of the way through the icy water. Happily, the lieutenant was not "a man . . . to be dispirited by slight matters, [and] friction soon restored him to his usual animation."

Suddenly a sharp challenge rang out from the darkness: a British patrol boat had pulled into the cove to investigate the fire. Arnold returned the hail as a friend, but the boat continued to approach and reluctantly he ordered his men to fire. "Screaming and dismal lamentations" resounded over the water, and the craft withdrew. They had been discovered; there would be no more crossings.

Five hundred men quickly followed Arnold up the steep defile to the Plains of Abraham. From the top of the cliff they could hear the regular cries of the night watch on the ramparts of the sleeping city. Every instinct urged him to lead an immediate surprise attack, in defiance of his officers' counsel—but the scaling ladders were still at Pointe Lévis, waiting for the fourth river crossing, one that would never take place. The fire that had brought Archibald Steele back to life was also the ruination of Benedict Arnold's glorious coup.

In the dark, the men fanned out over the Plains of Abraham, appropriating empty houses whose owners had sought protection inside the city walls. Arnold established his headquarters in the suburb of Sainte-Foy, about a mile from the ramparts, at the abandoned farmhouse of the commander of the Quebec city militia, Major Henry Caldwell, a staunch Tory. There, shortly after dawn on a "fair, serene and pleasant morning," a courier rushed in to inform him that Colonel Maclean was mobilizing the garrison for a sortie. Arnold was elated: a head-to-head battle on the Plains of Abraham offered his only remaining hope for a personal triumph, on the model of the immortal Wolfe.

For hours he waited, anxiously scanning the walls for signs of an impending attack. By noon he could stand the suspense no longer. Citing the capture of an American sentry as a pretext, he marched his men in two columns toward the walls. At a distance of eight hundred feet they stopped, gave three lusty cheers and paraded in a circle. If Allan Maclean would not come out to fight, Arnold would provoke him. But Maclean refused to take the bait. He ordered his gunners to lob a few cannon shots at the parade and then permitted the Americans to withdraw in good order.

Arnold was keenly disappointed. Unfortunately, he was also seduced into believing what he had always wanted to believe: that Maclean's garrison was too weak to risk a fight and that the civilian population of Quebec city refused to support him. He was badly mistaken. The Quebec garrison was somewhat undermanned, to be sure, but it was extremely well deployed and armed, and the civilian population—including the commercial establishment, whom Arnold had counted on to force Governor Carleton to capitulate to the Americans—stood firmly behind it. Maclean's failure to attack was a sign of prudence, not weakness: why should he risk a battle before learning whether or not the Americans had taken Montreal?

Arnold, however, continued to cling to the image of a weak and divided Quebec, in part because his lust for a personal victory warped his usually sound judgment, and in part because his nature could not comprehend the sea change that had taken place among the city's merchants and traders. The men of commerce in Montreal and Quebec—men whom Arnold had known for years—had heretofore largely opposed Governor Carleton's efforts to defend the two cities, partly because some of them were secretly in sympathy with the political and economic objectives of the American revolution, and partly because they wished to avoid a war that would inevitably wreak destruction on their property and livelihoods. But when Montgomery's army crossed the border, they had been forced to look inside their hearts, and there they discovered that loyalty to king and country overrode all other considerations.*

Benedict Arnold, who recognized no god higher than his own self-interest, could not conceive that other people did. An overriding allegiance to country or sovereign or deity was out of his ken.

---

*Even the merchants of French descent, whose resentment of their British overlords might well have led them to support the Americans, were restrained from doing so by threat of excommunication—another motive that Benedict Arnold could never understand. (The French Catholic bishop of Canada was strongly allied with the British, for complicated political reasons that are not relevant to this story.)

Wharves and warehouses he understood, fidelity he did not; so he persisted in his fatal conviction that the commercial interests of Canada remained firmly pro-American. His failure to see the truth fell well within the normal range for the species—people often believe what they want to believe—but in Quebec in 1775, Arnold's self-delusion would prove fatal to his men, his cause and his commanding general.

The first few days in camp were clear but extremely cold, and the men shivered in their ragged summer uniforms. Food and drink were plentiful, but General Washington's injunction to "pay the full value for all provisions or other accommodations which the Canadians may provide" was widely disregarded. The larders and cellars of the empty houses invited plunder; Surveyor Pierce, for instance, who had no money to make purchases, nevertheless dined on "fryed stakes" washed down with generous drafts of wine, brandy and rum. It was futile to try to stop it. The men were hungry, and Arnold did not have enough money to pay them all. Nor would the Canadians take their money: Continental currency was only as good as the Continental Army's prospects for winning the war, which at the moment were extremely uncertain. Arnold and his officers tempered justice accordingly. On the fourth day in camp, a soldier court-martialed for stealing received a pardon while another convicted of sleeping on guard received twenty lashes.

A messenger arrived with the welcome news that General Montgomery had taken Montreal and would reach Quebec with his army in about a fortnight. Arnold's satisfaction was short-lived: a spy inside the city informed him that a British attack was imminent, Colonel Maclean's abrupt change of strategy having been prompted by intelligence regarding American ammunition supplies. Arnold ordered an immediate inventory and discovered that Maclean knew more about his situation than he did. More than a hundred of his muskets were unserviceable, and his supply of cartridges totaled less than five rounds per man. The position before Quebec being clearly untenable, Arnold assembled his detachment before dawn on the morning of November 19 (their fifth day on the Plains of Abraham) and ordered a withdrawal to the settlement of Pointe-aux-Trembles some twenty-five miles to the west, where they could await Montgomery and his army in relative safety.

"The ground [being] frozen and very uneven," a private in Oliver Hanchet's company reported, "we might have been tracked all the way by the blood from our shattered hoofs." The shattered pride of their colonel was less visible; his bleeding was internal. The ignominy of retreat was only part of the story. Arnold was also aware that some of his junior officers had known about the ammunition shortage for days but had chosen not to tell him.

The officers' motives are as murky to us as they were to Arnold. Fear of the enemy was surely not a major factor; soldiers who are afraid to fight do not withhold information leading to a withdrawal from battle. More likely, they were afraid of their colonel, whose courage and optimism in the face of disaster seemed bound to lead them into jeopardy. Men who lack resolution are often frightened and offended by the resolution of their superiors. It is even possible that one or two of Arnold's officers, more intuitive than the rest, had begun to sense his vast capacity for self-delusion. Or perhaps these independent-minded New England farmers and artisans simply resented his style of military discipline. Whatever the reason, the incident served notice that several of the junior officers harbored serious misgivings about the campaign and about their colonel. Inevitably their grumbling filtered down into the ranks, and by the time the army reached Pointe-aux-Trembles, certain New England companies had become infected with the germ of despair.

To lose the confidence of underlings—even of a few among many—can be devastating to an insecure man like Arnold, although his pride might not permit him to show it. During the army's two-week stay at Pointe-aux-Trembles, he commanded with his usual efficiency and attention to detail, giving orders for everything, from the manufacture of moccasins for the entire army to the placement of a guard at a ferry landing several miles to the rear to cover the crossing of Oliver Hanchet and his men from Pointe Lévis. The latter was dangerous duty, and Surveyor John Pierce, a good friend of Hanchet's but also a charter member of the doom-and-gloom faction, pleaded sick and was excused from marching with a relief column to the ferry, although that same afternoon found him riding out into the countryside on a pleasure expedition, where he consumed a "bottle of very good wine."

The weather turned colder still, forming a thick crust of ice in the river every night. The first blizzard of the season dropped more than twelve inches of snow in a few hours, and the local people stuck small spruce and cedar trees in the drifts to mark the main road. Several New England volunteers who had reached the end of their terms of enlistment packed up and headed for home. It was a sinister portent: most of the men's enlistments would expire on December 31, less than six weeks away.

Oliver Hanchet was one of the officers whom Arnold trusted to stay the course; so it was all the more shocking when Hanchet, on returning to camp from Pointe Lévis, refused Arnold's orders to establish a forward post at the riverfront settlement of Sillery, three miles west of Quebec's Lower Town, in anticipation of the army's return to the Plains of Abraham. The mission was not only suicidal, Hanchet explained, but pointless, because the entire campaign was defunct. In fact, the Connecticut captain continued, his entire company was making preparations to march for home when their enlistments expired on December 1, only four days hence.

Concealing his shock and dismay, Arnold declined to respond directly, instead summoning the two Rhode Island captains, Simeon Thayer and John Topham, to whom, in Hanchet's presence, he presented the mission. In one eager breath the two friends volunteered to lead it, finally flipping a coin to determine who would gain the honor. Thayer won the toss, and the three captains departed, the victor to prepare for his mission, Topham to nurse his disappointment, and Hanchet perhaps to brood on the tactical arts of high command.

Thayer and his men, after rowing all night in a "prodigious snowstorm," established themselves "in a most disagreable situation" at Sillery. Daniel Morgan and his rifle company also returned to Quebec at this time to establish sniper posts in the suburbs, many of whose inhabitants—including Arnold's recent landlord Henry Caldwell—had emerged from the city to burn down their own houses rather than permit them to shelter the returning American army.

On December 2, Arnold's independent command came to an end with the arrival of Brigadier General Richard Montgomery. The two were of an age—both in their mid-thirties—but Montgomery was as different from his colonel as a man could be. Where Arnold was stocky, Montgomery stood tall and slender; where Arnold was prickly, Montgomery exuded a serene confidence; where Arnold was confrontational, Montgomery displayed an unflagging amiability that quickly earned him "the voluntary love, esteem and confidence of the whole army," including Benedict Arnold, who, for the only time in his career, did not seem to resent being superseded.

The reason is not difficult to determine: Montgomery admired Arnold and took pains to tell him so. "I find Colonel Arnold's corps an exceedingly fine one," he reported to Philip Schuyler after reviewing the Kennebec detachment. "There is a style of discipline among them much superior to what I have been used to see this campaign, [and Arnold] himself is active, intelligent and enterprising"—high praise from a British officer and gentleman who had fought side by side with the immortal Wolfe.

It was therefore all the more mortifying when, a few hours after Montgomery's arrival, the general and the colonel both stood witness as Oliver Hanchet publicly paraded his company and announced its imminent departure for home. Arnold threatened and cajoled to no avail, and only the personal intervention of "the virtuous General [Montgomery]" persuaded Hanchet and his men to delay their departure for the time being.

To Montgomery it was a familiar story; many of his own troops had departed for home after the fall of Montreal. To induce them to stay he had promised each man a bounty of one dollar, a suit of clothes and a share of any captured British stores. Congress had expressly forbidden the latter, for obvious reasons, but Montgomery felt he had no choice, and he urged General Schuyler to persuade the government to honor his commitments. Schuyler, who himself had been forced "to coax, to wheedle and even to lie" to retain his troops, wrote to George Washington—who coaxed and wheedled every day—that longer terms of enlistment were crucial to the survival of the Continental Army. Most of the army's volunteers, however, were small farmers whose presence at home was vital to their families' survival and who therefore, if asked to sign up for more than a few months at a time, would not join at all. Furthermore, in an army that was underpaid and underfed, the reenlistment rate was extremely low.

Montgomery's force was now reduced to three hundred regular troops and one artillery company under the command of Captain John Lamb, a first-rate officer with great courage and an uncontrollable temper. At Montreal, Lamb had announced his company's imminent departure, citing the indisputable fact that supporting his men and equipment on a captain's pay had pushed him to the edge of personal bankruptcy. Without artillery, of course, there was no point in going to Quebec, so Montgomery persuaded Lamb to remain by giving him "a little money on account," probably out of his own pocket.

Among the officers who went home from Montreal was Arnold's nemesis James Easton. John Brown, however—now Major John Brown of the Continental Army—came to Pointe-aux-Trembles with Montgomery's army, and his appearance was troublesome to Arnold, particularly after it became apparent that General Montgomery thought well of Brown and had promised him a promotion. Brown's prowess as a soldier cut no ice with Arnold, however. Brown—the man responsible for damaging his reputation with Congress and the commander in chief—was the enemy; and Benedict Arnold never forgot an enemy.

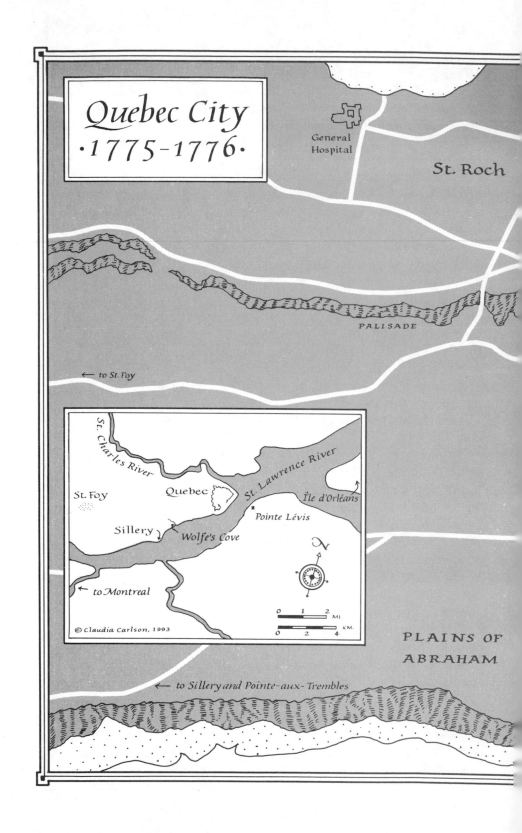

Quebec City
·1775-1776·

General Hospital

St. Roch

PALISADE

← to St. Foy

St. Charles River

St. Lawrence River

St. Foy

Quebec

Île d'Orléans

Pointe Lévis

Sillery

Wolfe's Cove

N

← to Montreal

© Claudia Carlson, 1993

0   1   2 MI.

0   2   4 KM.

PLAINS OF
ABRAHAM

← to Sillery and Pointe-aux-Trembles

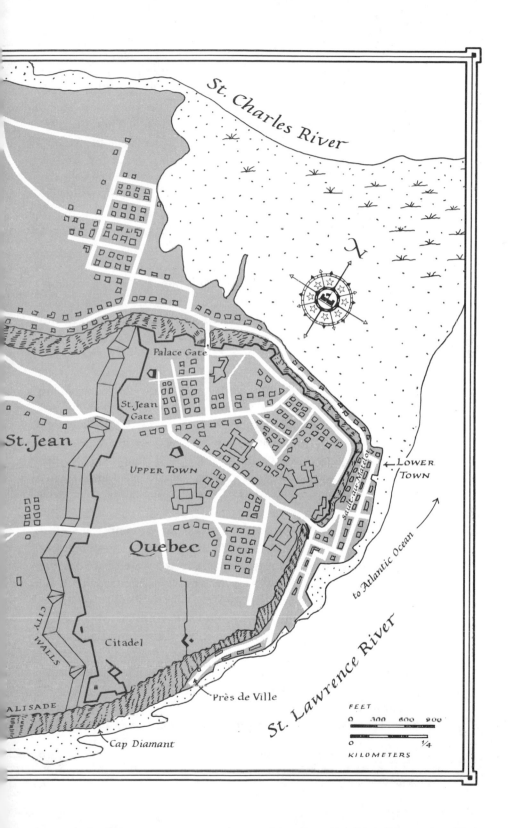

St. Charles River

N

Palace Gate

St. Jean
Gate

St. Jean

UPPER TOWN

LOWER
TOWN

Sault-au-Matelot

Quebec

to Atlantic Ocean

CITY WALLS

Citadel

Près de Ville

St. Lawrence River

PALISADE

Cap Diamant

FEET

0   300   600   900

0   ¼

KILOMETERS

While Arnold's men celebrated the arrival of fresh provisions—Surveyor Pierce gleefully noted "rum, pork and flour"—and strutted around camp in captured uniforms from the 7th and 20th British regiments,* Arnold himself sat down with the general to consider a strategy for the reduction of the bastion of Quebec. Theoretically, they had two choices, assault or siege. Neither was very promising. They lacked the manpower and equipment for an assault as well as the supplies and clothing necessary to maintain a winter siege on the Plains of Abraham. Their decision, however, was dictated not by tactics but by the calendar. Most of the men could be expected to decamp on December 31 when their enlistments expired, making a protracted siege impossible. An assault it would have to be, and before the end of the month.

Unfortunately, Governor Carleton had managed to escape capture at Montreal and make his way to Quebec. (Arnold, en route to Pointe-aux-Trembles, had seen Carleton's ship sailing downriver and heard the guns of Quebec salute his arrival.) A popular governor and a valiant general, Carleton's presence in Quebec was bound to stiffen the city's resolve. Nevertheless, Arnold remained convinced that Quebec would fall to an assault. He spoke contemptuously of its "wretched, motley garrison of disaffected seamen, marines and inhabitants" and assured Montgomery that a majority of the population was in favor of capitulation. He was so persuasive that by the time the army returned to the Plains of Abraham on December 4, Montgomery was also sneering at "Maclean's banditti, the sailors from the frigates . . . [and] the citizens obliged to take up arms."

But in partaking of Arnold's certitude, Montgomery added a grain of salt. He appreciated, as Arnold did not, that the vast majority of Canada's citizens would never openly throw in their lot with the Americans until Quebec was firmly in American hands. Only if he could take the city, and afterward man and fortify it against a counterattack that would inevitably come in spring when the ice left the river and reinforcements arrived from England, only then would Canada's citizens dare to offer their services openly. Benedict Arnold said, Support me and I will take Quebec, to which the Canadians by and large replied, Take Quebec and we will support you.

"Fortune often baffles the sanguine expectations of poor mortals," General Montgomery wrote in announcing the assault plan to

---

*Which means that one of Arnold's men was walking around in a spare uniform belonging to Captain John André, a member of the 7th Regiment. André, who will appear later in the story, had been taken prisoner at St. Jean.

General Schuyler. "I am not intoxicated with the favors I have received at her hands, but I do think there is a fair prospect of success." They would attack at night during the first heavy snowstorm, he informed Schuyler, in order to create maximum confusion inside the city. Montgomery himself would lead the main assault by escalade against the bastion at Cap Diamant, while a feint on the Lower Town drew off defenders. Once the guns of Cap Diamant had been captured and turned on the town, the Lower Town would be attacked in force and the Upper Town would be forced to capitulate (see map, pages 66–67).

While waiting for the weather to cooperate, Montgomery would employ his artillery in such a way as to persuade Governor Carleton that he was settling in for a siege. He ordered Oliver Hanchet to construct an artillery battery close to the city walls; when Hanchet refused, Simeon Thayer volunteered to undertake the mission. During six successive bitterly cold nights, Thayer and his men men crept forward to the chosen site, placed fascines, packed snow between them and poured water to form a wall of ice. The battery opened up on the seventh morning and was promptly penetrated by a British cannonball, killing two and wounding three. Five more were dead by the end of the day. Nevertheless, Thayer and his men remained at their exposed post for nearly a fortnight.

If their guns did little damage to the enemy, their courage and ingenuity lifted morale among their fellows. "Who but Yankoos would have thought of such a contrivance?" one soldier wrote home, "or who but enthusiasts for liberty would carry on a siege at such a season of the year?" To Montgomery, who "never expected any other advantage from our artillery than to amuse the enemy and blind them as to my real intention [an assault]," the sacrifice of Thayer's men was a painful necessity. To other elements of the army it was a matter of little concern. During the first night, while Thayer and his men crept forward under the enemy's guns, several of his fellow officers—friends of Oliver Hanchet—stole into the Lower Town and strolled through the streets, on a lark.

Benedict Arnold, it must be reported, had also discovered a diversion from the exigencies of war: lining his pocketbook. The brigantine *Peggy*, which he had dispatched from New Haven on a trading voyage the previous summer, had been trapped at Quebec in September after the American invasion prompted a British commercial embargo. Her captain, John Gordon, had managed to save the vessel from confiscation by transferring ownership to a Canadian friend and then quietly taking her into winter harbor at the Île d'Orléans to await events.

When Arnold reached the Plains of Abraham with his army in November, he ordered Gordon to load the ship with horses, salt and hay and, at the first opportunity, to slip her past the British guard boats and out to sea. Although this constituted trading with the enemy, it did not violate any written law. The spirit of commerce flourished unabated in wartime America, and delegate after delegate had risen before Congress to denounce any attempt to regulate the commercial activity of their constituents, war or no war. (Accordingly, Arnold's petition to Congress the following year for restitution for the loss of *Peggy,* which by then had been turned into a fire ship at Quebec, was treated as business as usual.)

In other words, in exploiting the war for personal gain, Arnold behaved no better and no worse than a large proportion of his fellow Americans. What he never understood was that men who *did* behave better might disapprove. In the absence of a personal ethical code, Arnold relied solely on external justifications for any questionable action. "Everybody's doing it" had always been his motto (and the motto of every red-blooded prewar New England trader). Now he expanded his credo to include, "It isn't technically illegal." He never realized that to men of true principle these arguments are irrelevant; he never realized that men of conscience might judge him by a different standard. But if Arnold's lack of conscience spared him any uneasiness over *Peggy,* her captain was punished for his craftiness forthwith: contracting smallpox during a visit to the American camp, Captain Gordon died in early December, leaving *Peggy* anchored at the Île d'Orléans, loaded and ready for sea.

On returning to the Plains of Abraham, Arnold had moved into second-best quarters at Menut's Tavern in St. Roch while General Montgomery established his headquarters at Holland House, an elegant stone dwelling in the suburb of Sainte-Foy. There the two commanders made final preparations for the assault and waited, day after crystalline day, for a blizzard to mask it. A week went by, and then another. Sometimes the mutual cannonading made it seem "as if the heavens and the earth were coming together." Arnold was forced to move his quarters farther from the ramparts after his house received a direct hit, and the proprietress of a nearby French brothel died when a ball passed through her house just as she was "administering a spiritous potion to one of our lads."* Dr. Senter, who had set up

---

*If she was the same woman who, a few nights earlier, had persuaded four drunken young Americans to desert, the cannonball could be viewed as evidence that God was on the American side.

shop in the General Hospital just half a mile outside the walls, reported that during one evening in mid-December, "agreeable to prescription, fifty-five more of the fire pills were given to the Carletonians. . . . Operated with manifest perturbation, as they were (as usual) alarmed. Bells beating, dogs barking, etc. Their cannonade still continued on the battery. . . . Forty-five more pills as cathartic [the next] night."

But in fact, the cannonading made more noise than it did harm. It was Daniel Morgan's silent "skulking riflemen," plying their trade from concealed positions close to the walls in the suburb of St. Roch, who struck real fear into the hearts of the Quebecois. "To fire on those who appear on the ramparts . . . this is the American way of making war," sneered a British officer; "they are worse than Savages."

Meanwhile, out on the windswept Plains of Abraham, the American army waited. The weather grew so cold that "no man after having been exposed to the air but ten minutes could handle his [gun] to do execution." The meager huts, infested with "lice, itch, jaundice, crabs, bedbugs and an unknown sight of fleas," gave little comfort. The pallid winter sun touched the Plains only briefly in the middle of the day, its sallow rays highlighting a moonscape of swirls, lumps and ridges formed by the drifting snow. Beneath the icy crust the snow was deeper than a man was tall, and Arnold's soldiers slid along awkwardly in their moccasins, trying not to fall through. Soon Dr. Senter was treating as many cases of pleurisy and pneumonia as he was gunshot wounds. Worse still, smallpox broke out in camp, and as the infection spread, the young doctor, defying orders from headquarters, secretly ordered one of his assistants to inject him with a primitive form of inoculum.*

By mid-December the army was reduced by sickness and injury to about eight hundred able-bodied soldiers. The men were kept busy making cartridges, distributing scaling ladders and collecting hemlock boughs to wear in their hats during the assault, in order to avoid shooting one another in the dark. But most of their energy was devoted to withstanding the cold and inuring themselves to the stark, windswept landscape where everything had turned a steely winter gray: sky, earth, river and the walls of the city they had come to conquer.

Day after arctic day passed, with no storm in sight. The suspense

---

*So little was known about the disease that opinions were sharply divided on the efficacy of inoculation.

took its toll, and by December 23 the cabal of restless, disaffected men that had gathered around Oliver Hanchet seemed on the verge of mutiny. Arnold attempted to seize the initiative by calling an officers' council at his headquarters, but promptly lost his temper when Hanchet took the floor to denounce him openly. As the shouting match grew louder, Richard Montgomery suddenly entered the room. In the hush that followed, the general began to speak, and within minutes he had persuaded the two antagonists to agree to an uneasy reconciliation.

Three days later, however, Hanchet and two other company captains from the Kennebec division, William Goodrich and Jonas Hubbard, informed Montgomery that they would not participate in the assault unless transferred out of Arnold's command. Concealing his "great mortification," Montgomery declared that he would not transfer them, nor would he "compel them, that he wanted no persons with him who went with reluctance." When the meeting ended inconclusively, his heart sank: the loss of three companies could easily spell ruin. At the very least, he explained to General Schuyler, "I shall . . . be obliged to change my plan of attack, being too weak to put that in execution I had formerly determined on."

The plan of attack was doomed in any case, as Montgomery and Arnold learned after an aborted assault during a short-lived storm on the night of December 27. General Carleton, it appeared, had learned their plan and concentrated his forces on Cap Diamant. An alternate scheme was quickly adopted, in which a feint would be made against Diamant while a two-pronged attack in force was launched against the Lower Town: from the south by Montgomery with three hundred Continentals, and from the north by Arnold at the head of the artillery company and his five hundred "famine-proof veterans" of the Kennebec. Once the Lower Town was secured, if Governor Carleton refused to capitulate, the combined armies would attack the Upper Town. It was an inferior plan, leaving Cap Diamant's guns in control of the defenders, but it would have to do.

Meanwhile, Montgomery had to employ every ounce of his considerable powers to mitigate the men's growing sense of anxiety and suspense. His Christmas Day address "enraptured" the army, one soldier reported, and another described "the fire of patriotism kindled in our breasts, and we resolved to follow wherever he should lead." Simeon Thayer's company took another tack: hunting down four malingerers who had failed to turn out on the night of the aborted assault, they placed halters around their necks and paraded them through the camp. Morale surged. Surveyor Pierce, appalled by the army's reawakened ardor, got "very drunk [and] . . . spewed unaccountable." Dr. Isaac Senter, on the other hand, requested Arnold's permission to command those men of Oliver Hanchet's company who had "signif[ied] their earnest desire of going [on the assault] with the rest of their fellows who went through the woods." Arnold declined with thanks, explaining that Senter would "be wanted in the way of your profession."

December 30 dawned gray and milder. By evening the wind blew hard and it began to snow. At midnight, in a full-blown blizzard, the men began to assemble for the assault. As Arnold's detachment gathered at the guardhouse in St. Roch, he noted the presence of Oliver Hanchet, William Goodrich and Jonas Hubbard with their companies. At five A.M., according to plan, the forward column set off with Arnold in the lead. At his side marched the faithful Eleazer Oswald, with Daniel Morgan and John Lamb and their companies close behind. Their object was to surprise and overrun the first barricade in Sault au Matelot, while the main body—Thayer, Meigs, Steele, Hanchet and the rest—came up. The whole detachment would then attack and capture the second barricade and enter the Lower Town to rendezvous with Montgomery.

"The storm was outrageous," one of Arnold's men reported. Head down, shoulders hunched, Arnold ran virtually blind along the narrow street under the high city wall. Every landmark was all but obliterated by the driving snow. Behind him, Morgan and the others followed literally in his footsteps so as not to lose the way.

As Arnold passed under Palace Gate, the unexpected sound of pealing bells penetrated the howling of the wind: the alarm had been given inside the city, much too soon. Soon he could hear the sharp crack of musket fire, and by the time he made the turn into Sault au Matelot, his "whole right flank was exposed to an incessant fire of musketry from the stone walls and from the pickets of the garrison." His men could neither return fire nor protect themselves in the narrow street; all they could do was run. Approaching the first barricade, Arnold shouted to Lamb to bring up his six-pounder; but the gun was stuck in a snowdrift back at the corner, far out of range.

Arnold, Morgan, Oswald and a score of men rushed forward, thrust their muskets into the portholes of the barricade and began to fire. Ladders were brought up and put in position. At this juncture, a musket ball entered Arnold's calf "about midway and, in an oblique course, passed between the tibia and fibula [and] lodged in the gastroennemea muscle at the rise of the tendon achilles." He fell bleeding in the snow. There was no refuge from the incessant musket fire that rained down from the walls, but Arnold refused to withdraw. Finally, growing faint from loss of blood, he consented to be carried to the hospital. It was his first battle, and he had lasted less than an hour.

With a man supporting him on either side, Arnold made his way back up Sault au Matelot and along the St. Charles River shore "under the continual fire of the enemy from the walls, at no greater distance than fifty yards." He shouted exhortations to the men of the rear detachments who were making their way to the front in the pale predawn light. All around him soldiers fell dead or wounded, including one of the men who was helping him; but another took his place as Arnold made his halting, painful way to the rear.

It was daybreak when Arnold was placed on Dr. Senter's operating table in a hospital already overflowing with wounded men. Senter probed Arnold's heel, found the bullet and extracted it. New patients arrived faster than the doctor could treat them, and couriers raced in and out bearing muddled, contradictory reports of the progress of the battle. Rumors raced through the hospital, to the unceasing background accompaniment of cannon fire and the screams of the wounded.

At nine o'clock the most devastating of the rumors was confirmed: Richard Montgomery had been killed at Près de Ville, and his detachment had withdrawn to the Plains of Abraham. A deep gloom settled over the hospital—virtually everyone genuinely mourned Montgomery, including Benedict Arnold. But there was no time to indulge grief. A large detachment of enemy troops had reportedly sallied out Palace Gate and was moving freely through St. Roch. If this was true, Arnold's detachment was trapped and the hospital itself was in danger of attack. Dr. Senter urged Arnold "to be carried back into the country where they would not readily find him . . . [but he] would neither be removed, nor suffer a man from the hospital to retreat." He ordered a small detachment of walking wounded to mount two field pieces in the street before the hospital gates, then placed his sword and two loaded pistols on the cot at his side and announced "that he was determined to kill as many as possible if they came into the room. We were now all soldiers," Senter reported, "even to the wounded in their beds."

The makeshift gun crew returned in triumph, having gotten off several shots at an advancing enemy column before being forced to retire, whereupon the British had also withdrawn, dragging the American guns behind them. Arnold dispatched runners to headquarters and out into the countryside in search of information and reinforcements. Particulars of Montgomery's death were reported: he and two aides had been struck by grapeshot after breaching the second picket barrier at Près de Ville. On seeing his general fall, second-in-command Colonel Donald Campbell had panicked and turned tail with the whole detachment, leaving Arnold's men entirely on their own to "either carry the Lower Town, be made prisoners, or [be] cut to pieces."

Arnold had to wait nearly forty-eight hours to learn the fate of his detachment. On the morning of January 2, Major Return Jonathan Meigs, now a British prisoner on parole, appeared beside his bed. (Meigs had been sent out to collect the officers' baggage; he returned to prison three days later.) The major was a laconic storyteller, and his tale was brief. After overrunning the first barricade, Daniel Morgan had led the way down the narrow street under a devastating crossfire from houses on both sides and from the walls of the city high above. He had paused before the second barricade for the main body and Lamb's artillery to come up, but only the companies of Thayer and Meigs appeared, the rest being lost in the storm in the maze of streets and alleys to the north. Dawn improved the enemy's marksmanship, and the men became sitting ducks.

At the end of half an hour Morgan could wait no longer. He threw his men against the second barricade. The ladders were in position and Morgan was on the point of going over when it was discovered that all the guns were too wet to fire. Helpless, he ordered a withdrawal, but by then it was too late: the street behind was blocked by the British column that had come out Palace Gate—the same detachment that had already taken prisoner a large proportion of the men in the rear, whom they came across floundering in the snow in search of their companies.

Trapped in the open in the narrow street before the barricade, under incessant cannon and musket fire from a concealed enemy that outnumbered them three to one, Arnold's men held out for three hours with the "awful voice of Morgan" cursing the foe and urging them to hold fast. "Here," as Major Meigs put it, "we found some brave officers and men." Finally even the formidable Virginian had to admit defeat, and he surrendered rather than sacrifice the entire detachment.

Taken prisoner were Morgan, Eleazer Oswald, Oliver Hanchet, Archibald Steele (with two fingers shot away), Simeon Thayer and his friend Topham, Christopher Greene, Return Jonathan Meigs, John Lamb (wounded in the temple near his left eye) and four hundred other officers and men. Colonel Henry Caldwell, who watched them file through the barricade, later remarked to a friend, "You can have no conception what kind of men composed their officers . . . one major was a blacksmith, another a hatter. Of their captains, there was a butcher . . . a tanner, a shoemaker, a tavern-keeper, etc. Yet they all pretended to be gentlemen."

So ended what Surveyor Pierce (who was too ill with toothache to participate in the attack) called "the most terrible night and day I ever saw."

In reporting the occasion, a Philadelphia newspaper hailed America as "the nursery of heroes," adding that as long as the country was "struggling in so glorious a cause as that of liberty and virtue, she will not want generals to lead forth her armies and direct them to victory and triumph." One of those generals,* lying in a bed in the General Hospital outside the walls of Quebec, agreed. "I have no thoughts of leaving this proud town until I first enter it in triumph," he wrote to his sister. "That Providence which has carried me through so many dangers is still my protection. I am in the way of my duty and know no fear."

*Arnold was promoted to brigadier general on January 10, 1776.

Chapter 7

"SHINING IN HISTORY"

JANUARY-MAY 1776

On his thirty-fifth birthday, January 14, 1776, Arnold received a letter written by General Washington nearly six weeks before, congratulating him on the Kennebec detachment's arrival at Pointe Lévis and expressing the hope that "before this . . . [you will] have met with the laurels which are due to your toils, in the possession of Quebec." In recognition of Arnold's accomplishment, the commander in chief appointed him to command a regiment in the newly reorganized Continental Army, with places for all the officers of his detachment "in the rank they now bear." He also informed Arnold that Roger Enos had been court-martialed and "acquitted on the score of provision."*

Arnold was not insensitive to irony, and in thanking the commander in chief for "the notice you have been pleased to take of me

---

*Washington had been forced to hold the trial without waiting for Arnold's evidence, since Enos's enlistment was about to expire and by law he could not be court-martialed after leaving the service—a rule that Congress changed within the year.

and my officers," he commented mordantly that most of those gentlemen were currently "provided for in an unexpected manner not very pleasing to me." He made no comment whatsoever about Enos.

Washington's praise, gratifying though it was, was irrelevant to Arnold's present situation. Five days after the battle, he was forced to remove himself from the hospital to Holland House in order to reassume command of the army, the surviving field officers having refused to serve under Montgomery's second-in-command, Colonel Donald Campbell, whose ignoble flight from Près de Ville was the talk of the camp. The defeat had "struck an amazing panic into both officers and men," and Arnold's first task was to persuade his dazed and frightened troops to make a stand against a British garrison that now outnumbered them two to one. From his bed at headquarters, totally incapacitated and in constant pain, he managed to emanate such confidence and energy that the men lifted their heads and began to function again as an army.

Arnold placed every able-bodied man on twenty-four-hour alert and deployed them as convincingly as possible. When the British had not attacked by the end of the first day, he began to hope they would not come out at all. "I pray God they may not," he wrote to the American commander at Montreal, General David Wooster (the same David Wooster who had denied him the keys to the New Haven powderhouse the previous April), "for we are in [a] miserable condition to receive them." He urged Wooster to send guns, reinforcements, "three or four hundred pair of snowshoes, a few barrels of sugar for the hospital, and fifty light shovels." Most of all, he urged his old companion in Freemasonry to come himself, and quickly: "The burden lies very heavy on me, considering my present circumstances. I find myself unequal to the task."

An attack of gout intensified his suffering; nevertheless, while awaiting Wooster's arrival, he issued reports, prepared inventories and requisitioned ammunition and provisions. The men were ordered "to lay on their arms constantly and to mount guard every other night. Their duty is exceedingly hard," Arnold reported to the Continental Congress, "however [they] appear alert and cheerful." At his orders, a small detachment of men crossed the frozen river to construct a battery on Pointe Lévis, which, one American soldier rhapsodized, "plays sweetly upon the Lower Town and has drove them into the Upper Town." A disdainful Quebecois, however, tallied the battery's total score during its first three weeks as follows: "killed a boy, wounded a sailor, and broke the leg of a turkey."

General Wooster, Arnold soon learned to his dismay, had no intention of coming to Quebec at all, a council of his officers having agreed "to a man" that he ought to remain at Montreal. Instead, he sent along a colonel to assist with day-to-day operations until Arnold's wound would permit him to resume active command.

By the middle of January, more than a hundred of Arnold's soldiers had packed up their belongings and left for home (Surveyor John Pierce among them). Among the pitiful troops left were only fourteen of the original Kennebec detachment, those gallant troops who had so admired him. Ordered to take up guard duty near the ramparts, the fourteen refused, changing their minds only when threatened with a punishment of thirty-nine stripes. Then, toward the end of the month, Arnold learned that nearly a quarter of the men imprisoned in Quebec had enlisted in Colonel Allan Maclean's British corps of Royal Emigrants.

Little wonder that his spirits began to flag, despite the brave front he presented to the outside world. He had vowed to Congress "to put the best face on matters and betray no marks of fear," and succeeded so well that the British did not dare to attack. Thanks to his leadership and ingenuity, his army had survived against the odds. Nevertheless, in responding to a heartfelt tribute from Philip Schuyler, Arnold protested becomingly that he was "much more anxious of being a good citizen than shining in history, which I really should not have thought of had not you been pleased to compliment me on that head."

Schuyler was only reflecting sentiment in the colonies at large: the march up the Kennebec had made Benedict Arnold a public hero. In the short run, the fulsome praise of the world at large was extremely satisfying to him; in the long run, however, it destroyed him, because it became a necessity rather than a luxury. Outward approval was Arnold's only source of self-esteem, and he could never get enough of it. Becoming famous served only to raise the stakes: a popular hero has much more to lose than an anonymous local merchant. The birth of a new public persona—Benedict Arnold, Patriot-Hero—put more pressure on Arnold's fragile sense of inner worth than it could bear. How could he ever live up to it?

Like all popular images, Arnold's was a mixture of fact and fancy. The title of "Hero" was well deserved; the attribution of "Patriot" was a myth. But, standing alone in the spotlight, it was all he had to cling to, and so Arnold the Hero wedded himself to the myth for life. The fears still possessed him, of course, more strongly than ever—fear of losing face, of being pitied, of being poor, of being ashamed. The myth became his armor, and he would do anything to preserve it.

Arnold was deeply troubled by the fact that Congress, although granting him a promotion to brigadier general, had failed to respond to his reports. An army of "at least five thousand men, with an experienced general," should be dispatched to Canada at once, he wrote from his sickbed at Holland House, to capture and garrison Quebec before the arrival of British reinforcements. Congress neither sent an army nor deigned to answer his letters. Instead, it asked him for an immediate, detailed accounting of all his expenditures in Canada to date. Arnold naturally protested: "The multiplicity of accounts which daily arise here . . . renders it impossible for a commanding officer to pay that attention to them which they deserve and, at the same time, do his duty as a soldier." Continental money was virtually useless, he added, and there was no hard currency with which to purchase supplies and pay the men. The only remedy was to take and hold Quebec: "If the capital is taken," he informed Congress, "I believe paper money will soon have a currency." Meanwhile, "our credit extends no farther than our arms."

It was a cogent argument, but the man who wrote it was seething inside. An insecure nature will often turn careless inadvertencies into deliberate snubs. In Arnold's view, Congress was ignoring him. If he deserved promotion, surely he also deserved serious consideration of his proposals. They had not even acknowledged his letter; instead they had asked him to account for the money he had spent. Why did they not trust him?

An explanation—or what may have passed for an explanation, in Arnold's imagination—presented itself toward the end of January in the person of John Brown, the man solely responsible, in Arnold's eyes, for Congress's lack of trust in their new brigadier. Brown had traduced Arnold to Congress in the aftermath of Ticonderoga, had he not? Now Arnold refused Brown's request for the promotion that had been promised him by General Montgomery.

Brown, who was just as tenacious and unforgiving as Arnold, naturally lodged a protest—directly to Congress. The new-fledged Patriot-Hero could not support such a threat to his persona. All his fears and insecurities came rushing to the fore, and, as at Ticonderoga, he lashed out impulsively to defend himself, losing all sense of fitness and proportion.

He dashed off a letter to John Hancock, the president of Congress, accusing Brown and James Easton of plundering baggage belonging to British officers captured at Montreal. This outrage, he reported, "is the public topic of conversation at Montreal and among the officers of the army in general"; he argued, "and, as such conduct is unbecoming the character of gentlemen or soldiers, I believe it would give great disgust to the army in general if those gentlemen were promoted before those matters were cleared up."

Brown denied the charge vehemently and challenged Arnold to

present his evidence at a public court of inquiry. Arnold refused to call the court. Instead, he chose to do some traducing of his own. On learning that a Canadian volunteer named Duggan was about to depart for Congress, Arnold summoned the man and tried to persuade him to "impeach to Congress one certain dam'd rascal and villain who . . . was guilty of the worst of crimes." Refusing at first to give the "villain's" name (an uncharacteristic hedge; perhaps some dilatory instinct was trying to pull him back from the brink of disaster), he finally succumbed to Duggan's insistence and gave it. Duggan protested that he "knew of no such charges against Major Brown and would carry no such message to Congress unless he [Arnold] would put [it] in a letter." This Arnold would not do, insisting instead that "the best way" was for Duggan to "impeach him, and I will enforce it." The man remained firm, however, and Arnold dismissed him, venting his frustration thereafter by repeating the accusation privately to anyone who would listen.

This behavior went far beyond the habitual Arnold pugnacity and tactlessness. Only a man with a tenuous hold on reality overplays his hand so recklessly. Arnold's failure to call the court, and his bizarre and evasive suggestions to Duggan, strongly suggest that he had no evidence to substantiate his charge against Brown. (Luggage belonging to enemy officers captured by Brown's command had indeed disappeared, although the perpetrators were never identified.) There is only one explanation: he had retreated into his house of mirrors, where his image remained spotless, where everything that went wrong was someone else's fault and anyone who said different was a liar.

From this bastion of self-delusion Arnold emerged to do battle with his traducer. But many of the stones he cast so blindly ricocheted and hit him instead. Brown's and Easton's friends—and they had many friends—rallied their forces to fight back. Cracks appeared in the immaculate image Arnold was trying so hard to protect, and shards of rumor penetrated as far as Philadelphia, where Duggan was able to recite a strange tale of General Arnold's fixation.

Miraculously, Arnold's delusions survived without a scratch. The mirrors of his inner citadel proved shatter-proof. Retreating there in the aftermath of the battle, totally oblivious to the self-destruction he had wrought, he continued to gaze on an image of himself that remained unscathed.*

---

*Brown never received satisfaction, being denied a court of inquiry into Arnold's charges by Congress, then by General Wooster and finally by General Schuyler.

•   •   •

In Quebec, it was the coldest winter in living memory—"cold enough," the French said, "to split a stone." The snow blew and drifted until householders inside the city entered and left their dwellings through second-story windows. Outside the walls, on the icy, windswept wasteland of the Plains of Abraham, the American army froze and sickened and endured. To discourage the spread of smallpox, Arnold confined the men to quarters when not on duty. A Green Mountain Boy named Josiah Sabin [sic] managed to obtain a supply of illegal inoculum from the hospital and established a brisk trade among the frightened men. Despite precautions—all his clients "were sent into his room blindfolded, were inoculated, and sent out in the same condition"—Sabin was eventually caught and brought before Arnold; but "after a considerable controversy and many sharp words between [Sabin's commanding officer] Colonel [Seth] Warner and General Arnold, he was set at liberty without punishment."

By the end of February Arnold was "able to hobble about [his] room," and all his old energy and optimism returned. Several thousand reinforcements had been promised by the end of the month, and he harbored the hope of mounting a surprise assault on the city. Meanwhile, he confided to General Washington, the situation was "so very perplexing that I have often been at a loss how to conduct matters . . . the service requir[ing] a person of greater abilities and experience than I can pretend to." Confident of being in the commander in chief's good graces, Arnold for the first time employed the informal salutation "Dear General," rather than the more distant "May It Please Your Excellency."

The weather turned unexpectedly mild and "very clear, the northern lights were equal to a moon"—a reminder that spring was coming, and with it a fleet from England. Several days of arctic wind ensued, however, followed by a week of alternating snow and rain that culminated on March 11 in an overnight snowfall of more than a foot. By this time Arnold was up and about, traveling the length and breadth of his camp and disliking what he saw. (Like many convalescents, he overdid it, riding fourteen miles the first day, "which fatigued me so much I have hardly been able to walk since.") Fewer than a thousand reforcements had arrived, far below his expectations, and nearly half of them were already sick enough to be hospitalized. Most of the new men were militia, engaged only until April 15, the beginning of the planting season in New England. Short of manpower, of ammunition, of supplies and of credit, Arnold and his army labored, as he put it, "under almost as many difficulties as the Israelites did of old, obliged to make brick without straw."

On April Fool's Day, Brigadier General David Wooster finally arrived on the Plains of Abraham to take command of the army. At sixty-four, Wooster was one of the oldest officers in the Continental Army and one of the least competent. Renowned for his courage under fire, he was also known to take more eggnog than was good for him. Quarrelsome and unpredictable, Wooster was insubordinate to superiors, inconsistent toward subordinates and unfailingly tactless in dealing with civilians.

General Washington, well aware of Wooster's shortcomings, had denied the old war-horse his militia rank of major general in the Continental Army. Demoted to brigadier—the only Continental officer thus downgraded—Wooster had then been bypassed by General Schuyler for command of the invasion into Canada in favor of Richard Montgomery, a junior brigadier. Still smarting from that indignity, Wooster arrived at Quebec determined to demonstrate who was boss.

Toward the end of the first afternoon, as he and Arnold rode together near the walls, Arnold's horse shied on an alarm and fell on his bad leg, temporarily confining him to bed. There he fumed in frustration while Wooster threw his weight around the camp. Within the week, unable to tolerate Wooster's arrogant incompetence, Arnold announced his intention of withdrawing to Montreal to assume command of its garrison. Thus David Wooster, through sheer brazen idiocy, managed to accomplish in a few days what the British had failed to do during four months: to drive Benedict Arnold away from the city he had come to capture.

Traveling west in easy stages, his mind released from the daily chores and obligations of a baffling command, Arnold took a careful look around him and realized for the first time that the civilian population of Canada was not, as he had believed only two weeks before, "generally in our favor." Quite the contrary, he now saw clearly that "they are only waiting for an opportunity to join our enemies"—and that it was America's fault.

The principal problem was money: Continental currency was worthless, and Canadians in all walks of life now regarded "Congress and the United Colonies as bankrupt." The army could neither supply nor pay its soldiers; and men with guns in their hands will not go hungry. "Flagrant abuses" against the citizenry occurred every day. "Women and children have been terrified and forced [to furnish supplies] . . . a priest's house has been entered with great violence," and one farmer who asked to be paid was run "through the neck with a bayonet." The result was that a vast majority of the population had become staunch "Tories, who would wish to see our throats cut and perhaps would readily assist in doing it. . . . [In short], we have brought about ourselves, by mismanagement, what Governor Carleton himself could never effect."

By the time he reached Montreal, Arnold knew that the army would have to withdraw from Quebec as soon as British reinforcements arrived, which could be expected in about six weeks. It was a bitter pill, which he resolutely swallowed, and he promptly began to make preparations for an orderly, staged retreat upriver.

He found an able assistant and kindred spirit in the interim commander of the Montreal garrison, Colonel Moses Hazen, a prosperous local farmer eight years his senior who had joined the American army at the time of the invasion and been appointed colonel of his own regiment. Hazen, who had been born in Massachusetts and served in the French and Indian War, heartily endorsed Arnold's gloomy assessment of the situation in Canada, and Arnold responded by entrusting him with command of the important posts of St. Jean and Chambly, which guarded the army's supply lines as well as its line of retreat, should that become necessary.

Soon after Arnold's arrival, a new commander for the army in Canada passed through Montreal on his way to relieve General Wooster: Major General John Thomas, an experienced officer but "an utter stranger in the country and much terrified with the smallpox." Thomas's demeanor may not have encouraged Arnold, who knew that only a miracle could sustain the army on the Plains of Abraham, but his presence at least indicated that Congress was paying attention.

This was confirmed by the arrival on April 27 of a distinguished three-man congressional commission headed by the venerable Benjamin Franklin. (Nearing seventy, Franklin had just returned from a sojourn in England with all his curiosity, intelligence and charm intact.) Arnold, displaying his flair for grand occasions, greeted the commissioners at the ferry landing with full military honors and rode beside their carriage to headquarters at the elegant Château de Ramezay, where they were introduced to the leading lights of Montreal society, including "a large assemblage of ladies, most of them French. After drinking tea and sitting some time," a commission aide reported, "we went to an elegant supper, which was followed with the singing of the ladies, which proved very agreeable and would have been more so, if we had not been so much fatigued with our journey."

But as Arnold already knew and the commissioners quickly learned, the elegance and politesse were window dressing. During the ensuing days in the grand parlors of the château, the singing of ladies gave way to the strident pleas of a multitude of Congress's creditors—desperate men, many of them personally known to Arnold from his trading days, who had gone heavily into debt to supply the American army and now found themselves unable to borrow enough to feed their own families. What they demanded, and deserved, was immediate payment in hard currency and firm assurances that the Continental Army was in Canada to stay. The commissioners could furnish neither.

In these circumstances, Congress's specific charge to Franklin and the others—to draw Canada into a federal union with the thirteen lower colonies—was clearly irrelevant. American debts in Canada now totaled nearly £35,000, according to estimates furnished by Arnold. In addition, the commission bluntly informed John Hancock a few days after its arrival, "the violences of our military in exacting provisions and services . . . without pay [has turned the Canadians'] good disposition toward us into enmity, makes them wish our departure, and accordingly we have daily intimations of plots hatching and insurrections intended for expelling us, on the first news of the arrival of a British army." They presented Congress with two alternatives: send £20,000 in hard currency immediately (an impossibility, as everyone knew), or order the army to withdraw from Canada.

Provisions for a disciplined, orderly withdrawal as far as Montreal would have to be executed within the month, when the first British fleet of the season could be expected to land troops at Quebec. Otherwise, Arnold warned the commissioners, the retreat would become a rout in which the enfeebled and demoralized army might disintegrate entirely, leaving the way open for a British attack on Montreal. He had already suggested to generals Washington and Schuyler two sites on the upper St. Lawrence River where the retreating Americans could make a stand, the first being Deschambault, at a bend in the river about twenty-five miles west of Quebec (see map, page 87). Now the commissioners ratified his judgment by giving him cash out of their own expenses to fortify the site and build gunboats.

It was already too late: shortly after dawn on the morning of May 10, the clattering of horses' hooves was heard in the courtyard of Château de Ramezay, and Colonel Donald Campbell burst through the door to announce that a British fleet had landed at Quebec and the American army was in headlong retreat upriver.

Chapter 8

"NICE AND DELICATE HONOR"

MAY-AUGUST 1776

Pausing only to order mobilization of the garrison, Arnold rode swiftly eastward, intent on finding General Thomas and convincing him to make a stand at Deschambault. He was too late. At Sorel, less than forty miles east of Montreal, Arnold met the first panic-stricken elements of Thomas's runaway army and learned the worst (probably from Dr. Isaac Senter, one of the few members of that pitiful company capable of telling a coherent story).

Having been informed within hours of his arrival at Quebec that a British fleet was rendezvousing at the mouth of the St. Lawrence, General Thomas had chosen to disbelieve the report. (The fleet had indeed arrived several weeks earlier than anyone expected, after a harrowing trip across the ice-ridden north Atlantic.) He refused to send scouts or to order any preparations whatsoever for a withdrawal. Four days later, at dawn, the aptly named enemy frigate *Surprise* appeared off the Lower Town with two other vessels. All morning they disembarked troops, and still Thomas did nothing. At noon, General Carleton led a sortie in force onto the Plains of Abraham, sending the scattered, unmobilized American army flying

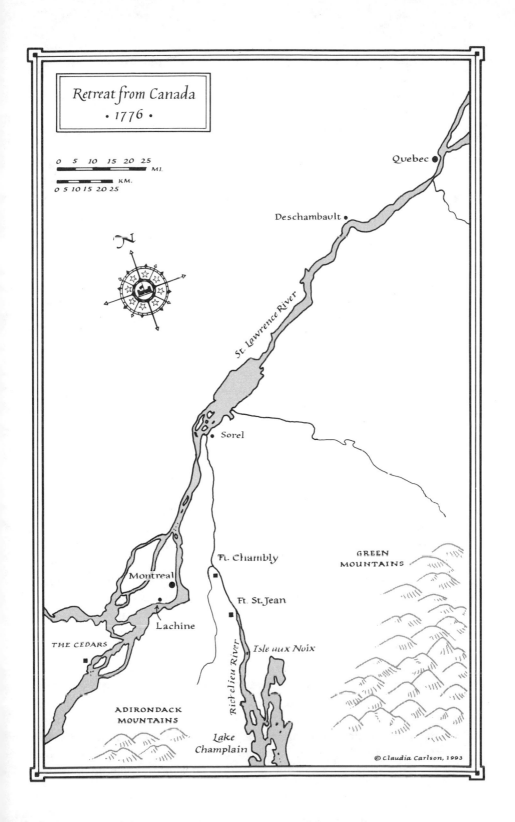

Retreat from Canada
· 1776 ·

0   5   10 15 20 25
                    MI.
0 5 10 15 20 25
            KM.

N

Quebec

Deschambault

St. Lawrence River

Sorel

Ft. Chambly

GREEN
MOUNTAINS

Montreal

Ft. St. Jean

Lachine

Isle aux Noix

THE CEDARS

Richelieu River

ADIRONDACK
MOUNTAINS

Lake
Champlain

© Claudia Carlson, 1993

before him "in the most irregular, *helter skelter* manner. . . . All the
camp equipage, ammunition . . . and most of our sick fell into their
hands," Dr. Senter lamented, "with all hospital stores." The road
west was "strewed with arms, cartridges, clothes, bread, pork, etc.
. . . orderly books and papers which . . . should not have been left.
Look whatsoever way one would, he saw men flying and loaded carts
driving full speed." All the artillery at Sillery was abandoned, and at
Holland House, Colonel Allan Maclean's men found General
Thomas's dinner sitting on the table, still warm.

Arnold had no time to indulge in anger. There was urgent news
from Montreal: a large force of British troops and Indians was advancing on the Cedars, a strategic American outpost in the wilderness
west of the city. Montreal was now threatened on two sides. Arnold
rode immediately back to headquarters at the Château de Ramezay.
By the time he got there, the Cedars had fallen and its entire garrison
had been taken prisoner.

He issued an urgent call for reinforcements and marched west
with a small detachment. Two days later at Lachine, his force now
numbering five hundred, Arnold dispatched a flag of truce to the
enemy encampment across the river, demanding the surrender of all
the American captives lest he "sacrifice every Indian who fell into my
hands and . . . follow them to their towns and destroy them by fire
and sword." An answer came back from his British counterpart the
following morning: if he dared to attack, all the prisoners would be
killed.

"Words cannot express my feelings at the delivery of this message," Arnold reported to Benjamin Franklin and his fellow commissioners. "Torn by the conflicting passions of revenge and humanity,
a sufficient force to take ample revenge, raging for action, urged me
on the one hand; and humanity for five hundred unhappy wretches,
who were on the point of being sacrificed if our vengeance was not
delayed, plead[ed] equally strong on the other." As usual, Arnold
chose action. His reasoning was cogent: the restless, unpredictable
Indians might kill the captives even if he failed to attack, and the
British would not be able to stop them. He proposed to a council of
officers to ferry the detachment across the river at night and mount
a surprise attack at dawn on the enemy's flank.

The council voted in favor of the plan, but only after a strenuous
and emotional debate in which Arnold suffered a deep wound at the
hands of his friend, Moses Hazen, who had arrived on the scene
posthaste from Chambly as soon as he received his general's summons. Arnold demanded a great deal from those he called friend,

primarily unwavering loyalty and unquestioning support. His fragile ego could tolerate no less. When Hazen argued in council against the attack, Arnold considered it an act of personal betrayal. (Several other officers had also disapproved of the plan, but Hazen was the only one Arnold cared about.) Deeply affected by his friend's apostasy, he struck back hard, and by the time the council disbanded, words had been uttered that no man could forgive.

In the event, the debate was irrelevant. After midnight, as the men were preparing to embark in their bateaux, a message arrived from the enemy offering to exchange the American captives for an equal number of British troops held in military prisons. Arnold agreed (after wringing additional concessions from the British officer in charge, who was obviously desperate to avoid a massacre), the captives were released and Montreal reprieved, at least for the moment.

But the incident had taken a heavy emotional toll, and riding back to the city, bone weary, Arnold finally faced a brutal fact that he had been avoiding for weeks: the American army would have to withdraw from Canada. Even if Congress suddenly were to conjure up the inclination and wherewithal to reinforce and finance the campaign, it would be too late. The army was moribund. Witness the Cedars: the garrison there could have easily held out until the arrival of reinforcements, Arnold had learned from the prisoners; instead, its commander, who lived in abject fear of Indians, had surrendered without a fight. Witness also the disease-ridden, demoralized troops he had seen at Sorel, who would never be able to defend Montreal against General John Burgoyne and an army of six thousand fresh British regulars and Hessian mercenaries, who were expected to land at Quebec within days.

"My whole thoughts are now bent on making a safe retreat out of this country," Arnold wrote to his friend Adjutant General Horatio Gates; "however, I hope we shall not be obliged to leave it until we have had one bout more for the honor of America. . . . The commissioners," he added, "this day leave us, as our good fortune has long since; but as Miss, like most other Misses, is fickle and often changes, I still hope for her favors again and that we shall have the pleasure of dying or living happy together." Whatever the outcome, he assured Gates, "I shall ever be happy in your friendship and society, and hope, with you, that our next winter quarters will be more agreeable." Ironically, shortly after dispatching this letter, Arnold learned that Gates himself had been appointed to lead the army in Canada with an independent command.

In the interim, a new commander swaggered through the revolving door of leadership: General John Sullivan, who unexpectedly succeeded to the command when General Thomas died of smallpox. Sullivan passed through Montreal on June 2 on his way to Sorel. A man of lukewarm ability and burning ambition, he boasted to General Washington a few days later that he had already accomplished more "than has been [done] in Canada since the surrender of St. Jean [the previous autumn]." He condemned his predecessors for deliberately lying to Congress about the sorry state of the army, and then, oblivious to the contradiction, vowed to lead that same army in an assault against Quebec. Arnold, of course, knew better, and he labored in Montreal to keep his garrison in line and to organize an orderly withdrawal.

He had been empowered by the commissioners to seize supplies, by force if necessary, from the local merchants. "Nothing but the most urgent necessity can justify such harsh measures," the commissioners explained to Congress; "we have been constrained [to permit it only] . . . to prevent a general plunder which might end in the massacre of your troops and of many of the inhabitants." In carrying out the order, Arnold requested each merchant to label his parcels in order to obtain eventual reimbursement by Congress. (The gesture was naïve at best and cynical at worst, but it had to be made.)

The first baggage train of requisitioned goods departed Montreal for Chambly on June 6, under the command of a Major Scott, Arnold having first persuaded General Sullivan with considerable difficulty that the supplies should be used to support a retreat rather than a return to Quebec. Two days later, Sullivan suffered a devastating— and entirely avoidable—defeat along the St. Lawrence, at the hands of General Burgoyne's newly arrived army. "I now think only of a glorious death or a victory obtained against superior numbers," he blustered to General Schuyler, who promptly reminded him that his death, glorious or otherwise, was quite irrelevant to his primary mission: the survival of his army as a fighting force. Arnold also tried to temper Sullivan's braggadocio, assuring his commander that "there will be more honor in making a safe retreat than hazarding a battle against such superiority. . . . The junction of the Canadians and the colonies, an object which brought us into this country, is now at an end. Let us quit them and secure our own country before it is too late." These arguments, he added, were "not urged by fear for my personal safety. I am content to be the last man who quits this country, and fall so that my country may rise. But let us not fall all together."

Meanwhile, Arnold had received a dispatch from Major Scott informing him that the supplies in the baggage train had been denied storage room by the commander of the Chambly garrison, Moses Hazen. In a fury, Arnold rode to Chambly to see to Hazen himself. There, sprawled on the river bank, unguarded, he found hundreds of packages, bales and boxes of provisions and clothes "broken open, plundered and huddled together in the greatest confusion . . . [making it] impossible to distinguish each man's goods or ever settle with the proprietors."

In Arnold's eyes, the sight justified his new image of Hazen as the enemy, and also offered a means of proving to the world that the man who had turned on him was a treacherous and unreliable officer. His revenge would have to be postponed, however; saving the Montreal garrison came first. Back at headquarters, he waited anxiously for news from the front. Finally, on June 15, he dispatched his aide-de-camp, James Wilkinson, downriver in search of news. Wilkinson returned within hours, having literally run into the vanguard of the British army. The Americans were in full retreat—and Sullivan had failed to alert Montreal.

Now Arnold's careful preparations paid off. He ferried the entire garrison across the river overnight, scuttled his bateaux and marched south, destroying all the bridges in his wake. At St. Jean he met the remnants of Sullivan's army, exhausted from their retreat up the Richelieu River in bateaux in a heavy rain. "The fatigue [of the journey]," Sullivan reported to Congress, "was beyond anything that ever I went through, and what was never done by an army in our situation before"—a claim, one hopes, he did not attempt to make within earshot of Benedict Arnold.

At an officers' council, Arnold and the others finally persuaded Sullivan to order a full retreat. The preservation of the army must be their first priority now: General Burgoyne had brought with him from England the frames for fourteen gunboats, shipwrights to construct them and a large supply of naval stores. Fort Ticonderoga would be at risk by the end of summer. If it fell, the way would be open for a British advance on Albany and the Hudson Valley.

At Isle aux Noix, in a sea of mud, the army paused to regroup. Malaria and dysentery spread through the camp, together with swarms of blackflies and mosquitoes. "The raging of the smallpox deprives us of whole regiments in the course of a few days," General Sullivan reported to the commander in chief. In the hospital (a converted barn), Dr. Lewis Beebe labored among patients who "could not see, speak or walk—one, nay two, had large maggots, an inch long, crawl out of their ears, were on every part of the body. No mortal will ever believe," he wrote, "what these suffered unless they were eye witnesses. . . . Death is now become a daily visitant in the camps, but as little regarded as the singing of birds."

Arnold was ordered ahead to report to General Schuyler. Covering two hundred miles in record time, he rode into Albany at midnight on June 24 and straight into a personal, political and military quagmire.

Philip Schuyler's patrician nose was painfully out of joint, thanks to Congress's appointment of Horatio Gates to an independent command in his department. The antipathy between Gates and Schuyler had rich and complicated origins. Beneath his cool, aristocratic manner, General Schuyler harbored an obsessive solicitude for his public reputation (a clue, perhaps, to his mutual affinity with Arnold), and he therefore regarded the appointment not only as an intrusion on his authority but as a criticism of his conduct.

The fact that the appointee was Horatio Gates made things even worse. Since becoming an American, the illegitimate son of the duke's housekeeper had taken great pains to cultivate his image as a man of the people, a role that Schuyler disdained. Gates was extremely popular with the egalitarian New England troops, whose dislike of the New York aristocrat was nourished by the ancient and often bloody rivalry between their provinces. No sooner had Gates's appointment been announced in the northern army than "the officers, as well as men, of one colony [began] insulting and quarreling with those of another"—determined, apparently, to follow their generals' example in everything.

Benedict Arnold liked and admired both men: Gates because he was a kindred spirit, brusque and aspiring; Schuyler because he was a model of the secure and self-assured gentleman Arnold wished to be. Once Gates arrived in Albany, however, it was nearly impossible to stay in their respective good graces. At their first meeting, Schuyler expressed the opinion that since the army had left Canada, Gates no longer had an independent command. Gates objected strenuously—he had fought too long and hard for the appointment to subordinate himself now to Schuyler. In one particularly icy exchange, Schuyler remarked that "if he were superseded, it would give him great pleasure to be superseded by a gentleman of General Gates's character and reputation," but that Congress had no right to "put him under the command of a younger officer [i.e., a major general with less seniority], nor [to] oblige him to be a suicide and stab his own honor." After days of wrangling, the two reluctantly agreed to "cooperate, that no evil might result to the service." But Schuyler still insisted that until Congress made its wishes known, he would continue to "stand upon punctilios with General Gates that I would otherwise with pleasure waive."

Arnold accompanied the two generals to Crown Point to view the shattered remains of the army, now reduced to little more than "a mob . . . ruined by sickness, fatigue and desertions and void of every idea of discipline or subordination." "Everything about this army is infected with the [smallpox]," Gates informed General Washington, "the clothes, the blankets, the air, and the ground they walk upon." He immediately established a quarantine hospital at Fort George, which was jammed within the month with nearly three thousand patients.

On July 7, Schuyler outlined the prospects to a council of officers. Generals Carleton and Burgoyne could be expected to sail up the lake with their army as soon as the new fleet was ready, in order to capture Ticonderoga and march on to Albany before the onset of winter. From a secure base at Albany, they would then be poised to march down the Hudson River in the spring, in coordination with a British thrust up the Hudson from New York City. General Howe, having abandoned Boston in March (shortly after the arrival of the Ticonderoga cannon), was currently positioning his army to attack New York. Gaining control of the city and its harbor was the prelude to an attack on his primary strategic object: the Hudson River Valley.

As Howe—and Washington, Schuyler and Arnold—well knew, the event would probably decide the fate of the American Revolution. The Hudson crossings were crucial to the Continental war effort, permitting provisions, supplies and reinforcements to flow between the middle colonies and the New England states. If General Washington lost control of the river, his army would wither and die and the war would be over.

The northern army's mission was clear: to stop the British on Lake Champlain and thus frustrate Howe's grand design. The odds against defeating the enemy in battle were enormous, but there was another way to achieve the same effect. Carleton and Burgoyne would have to attack Ticonderoga early enough in the season to make the long and arduous march to Albany before winter came or—in case they failed to take the fort—to sail back to Canada before the lake froze over. In other words, time was on the side of the Americans; delay would be just as effective as victory.

The council of officers voted to abandon Crown Point and concentrate their meager ground forces at Ticonderoga. The old fort's defensive situation was far from ideal, with high hills overlooking it from the rear and its east-bank supply lines vulnerable to attack. To protect the flow of supplies, the council voted to build a fortified camp across the lake from the fort and connected to it by a floating bridge. The new camp was promptly christened Mount Independence, in honor of the Declaration of Independence that had recently been promulgated in Philadelphia.

More to the point, as far as Arnold was concerned, the council ordered construction of "a naval armament of gondolas [heavy, flat-bottomed gunboats with forty-man crews, entirely dissimilar to the Venetian craft of the same name], row galleys [and] armed bateaux . . . [in order to] secure our superiority on Lake Champlain." Arnold desperately wanted command of the fleet—a risky and solitary command, made to order for the hero of the Kennebec. His maritime experience recommended him for the job, as did his proven ability to infuse men with his own courage under fire. But no commander was named by the council; instead, General Gates requested Arnold to oversee construction of the fleet in the Continental shipyard at Skenesboro.

Before leaving Crown Point to take up his new duties, Arnold took advantage of an interlude as senior officer at the fort (Schuyler had returned to Albany, Gates to Ticonderoga) to take care of some old business: he ordered the arrest and court-martial of Moses Hazen for dereliction of duty in failing to guard the requisitioned goods at Chambly. Rumblings immediately reverberated throughout the army, where Moses Hazen had many friends. "General Arnold is very busy in making experiments upon the field officers," one of them commented; "I heartily wish some person would try an experiment upon him, viz. to make the sun shine through his head with an ounce ball and then see whether rays come in a direct or oblique direction." Oblivious to the controversy and confident in his right, Arnold spent the week before the trial on an inspection tour at Skenesboro.

He had last visited the site before the war, as a guest in Philip Skene's commodious manor house during an overland trip from Canada. Located at the southernmost tip of Lake Champlain, the headquarters of Skene's 34,000-acre patent encompassed houses and offices, a blockhouse, sawmill, iron forge, flour mill, barns, stables, tenant houses and slave quarters. Now the family was gone, and all activity centered in the shipyard, which General Schuyler had established the previous spring.

Six gondolas were on the stocks when Arnold arrived. Flat-bottomed, heavy, unwieldy and slow, the gondolas nevertheless possessed one cardinal virtue: they were easy and quick to build. Given the urgent necessity to launch the greatest number of guns onto Lake Champlain in the shortest possible time, Arnold was forced to accept the gondola as the backbone of his fleet. But as a sailor he preferred the larger and more maneuverable row galley, and soon after his arrival at Skenesboro, construction on several two-masted Spanish-style galleys commenced. He expected to finish nine gondolas and two galleys within the month. Once they were rigged at Ticonderoga and outfitted at Crown Point, he wrote General Gates, "I think we shall have a very formidable fleet."

A "formidable fleet" perhaps—but utterly lacking experienced seamen to sail its ships and point its guns. "As there is no prospect of reprisals" on the lake (taking enemy prizes in which all the men would share, a common practice in eighteenth-century naval warfare), Arnold suggested offering generous bonuses in order to attract experienced volunteers. But General Schuyler's coffers were virtually empty; he did not even have cash to purchase naval stores and gunpowder for the fleet. Arnold refused to be daunted. Confident in his nautical expertise, to which both Schuyler and Gates deferred, he returned to Ticonderoga, called on Gates and bluntly asked for command of the fleet. Gates complied with "infinite satisfaction," assuring Congress that Arnold was "perfectly skilled in maritime affairs" and expressing the conviction that "he will thereby add to that brilliant reputation he has so deservedly acquired."

Buoyed by Gates's endorsement, Arnold hoisted sail and ran full speed ahead into the court-martial of Moses Hazen, entirely confident that his initial broadside—the testimony of Major Scott—would blast his opponent out of the water. Too self-involved to appreciate the depths of resentment he had provoked in Hazen, he underestimated his adversary's capacity for revenge.

On the first morning of the trial, Hazen raised an objection to Scott's appearance on the grounds that his testimony was tainted: Scott himself had been so careless with the goods in transit, Hazen averred, that most of the damage had occurred before the baggage train reached Chambly. Before Arnold could protest, Hazen produced eyewitnesses who swore that his assertion was true.

Arnold was utterly confounded. Unarmed with facts to refute the charge, he defended himself instead with rhetoric, declaring *on his honor* that Scott had delivered the goods at Chambly intact. The court, however, was more interested in evidence than in Benedict Arnold's honor, and citing Scott's "overstrained zeal" to testify as an indication of bias, refused to let him appear.

Arnold then sat furious and helpless while Hazen administered the coup de grâce: most of the goods at Chambly had disappeared, he explained to the court, because Benedict Arnold had stolen them.

This bombshell shattered whatever was left of Arnold's composure. He rose to his feet, denounced the proceedings, reviled the officers of the court in particularly pointed and insulting language, and stalked from the room.

By accident or design, Arnold's outburst served a very useful purpose: it deflected attention away from Hazen's accusation. The integrity of the members of the court had been publicly impeached, and as officers and gentlemen they had to respond. The question was, how far could they go in demanding satisfaction of a man who was their superior officer, a renowned hero, the newly appointed commander of the fleet on Lake Champlain and the confidant and protégé of Major General Horatio Gates.

Colonel Enoch Poor, the president of the court, wrote Arnold a careful letter expressing the court's "just resentment" and requesting "an open acknowledgement of your error." Unwittingly, he had asked Arnold to perform the only act of personal courage of which he was incapable: admitting that he was wrong. Arnold responded the only way he knew how, by attacking. "I am not very conversant with courts-martial," his answer read, "but this I may venture to say, they are composed of men not infallible . . . [and] as soon as this disagreeable service is at an end (which God grant may soon be the case), I will by no means withhold from any gentleman of the court the satisfaction his . . . very nice and delicate honor . . . may require."

The court promptly acquitted Moses Hazen and issued a warrant for Arnold's arrest on charges of "contemptuous, disorderly" behavior and the use of "profane oaths and execrations and . . . menacing words . . . in the presence of said court." Before the warrant could be carried out, however, Horatio Gates overturned it by dissolving the court, explaining to Congress that he was "obliged to act dictatorially . . . the instant they demanded General Arnold to be put in arrest. The United States must not be deprived of that excellent officer's service at this important moment."

Arnold fled to his domain at Skenesboro, complaining to anyone who would listen of the "grossest abuse offered me by Colonel Hazen, who claimed the protection of the court and was by them countenanced." Although his protest was justified—Hazen had indeed been permitted to utter an unsupported allegation openly in a courtroom where he himself, rather than Arnold, was on trial—it did not address the allegation itself.

Arnold never directly denied stealing the goods—which may be read either as a dignified response to outrageous calumny or as a confounded silence in the face of the truth. His contemporaries accepted whichever assessment conformed to their existing biases. Arnold's own rigid friend-or-foe mentality had made it nearly impossible for his army acquaintances not to take sides, for or against him. He all but challenged the world to choose between him and his enemies; and the world chose, not deliberately but passionately. Almost nobody in his immediate circle or in Congress was lukewarm about Benedict Arnold, even before his outburst in the Hazen courtroom. Many men perceived that outburst as a poignant howl of outraged innocence; others simply heard the squeal of a bank manager caught with his hand in the till.

More than two hundred years later, the question still remains: did Arnold steal the goods on which the lives of his men depended? It is difficult to imagine that he did. He cherished his men's respect almost as much as he cherished his shiny new image as America's Patriot-Hero. The fact that he later proved capable of larceny does not mean that he was guilty of it in 1776. There was, to be sure, an army rumor about bundles of linens marked "B.A. and sent to Connecticut." General John Sullivan heard it, believed it, and repeated it to a congressional committee in Philadelphia at virtually the same moment that Moses Hazen was accusing Arnold in open court at Ticonderoga. But where Arnold was concerned there were always rumors, because there were always men angry enough to go to any lengths to avenge the wrongs he had done them. But rumors are not hard evidence, and in the absence of the latter one must consider the larger picture—which strongly indicates that he did not commit larceny in 1776, because he had too much to lose.

His later career is not entirely irrelevant, however. Moses Hazen's bombshell may well have set off reverberations deep in the cellar of Arnold's gleaming house of mirrors, where dwelt the unacknowledged, darker Arnold, a self-absorbed, grasping creature whose mercenary appetites would one day spawn the most sordid crimes. Arnold's craving for money was deeply rooted in his personality: money helped to stave off his childhood fears; it meant respectability and unassailable security. He needed money as he needed air to breathe. Without it, he knew no inner peace.

In other words, Arnold's binary image in the world was the sign of a binary being—the bright and shining Patriot-Hero with the strange, distorted shadow. To the end of his days, Arnold never acknowledged the greedy, self-destructive, corruptible creature that lurked behind the cellar door of his pristine mirrored house. But others caught a glimpse of him from time to time, and they never again trusted his upstairs self. To these men, Arnold's military exploits and patriotic rhetoric did not ring true. They sensed the hollowness at the core; and their instincts were perfectly correct. (Ironically, they never questioned his loyalty, only his probity. In the event, of course, both probity and loyalty would be cast aside the moment they ceased to serve Arnold's inner needs.)

In Congress, therefore, although General Gates's dissolution of the court-martial was pronounced "prudent," Arnold himself continued to be looked at askance. "Many reports injurious to your character about the goods seized at Montreal" had made the rounds in Philadelphia, Congressman Samuel Chase warned him, adding gravely, "Your best friends are not your countrymen."

Chapter 9

"THE COUNTENANCE OF THE ENEMY"

AUGUST - OCTOBER 1776

At Crown Point on August 17, Arnold was again confronted by a junior officer's brazen insubordination; but where Moses Hazen's defiance had led to high drama, that of Jacobus Wynkoop quickly turned to farce.

Wynkoop was a New York army captain who had been appointed by General Schuyler the previous spring to take command of the four existing American vessels on Lake Champlain (all captured from the British the previous year) and to organize the shipyard at Skenesboro. Shunted from Skenesboro to Crown Point when Arnold arrived, the feisty "Commodore," as he styled himself, ruled his domain and nursed his resentment from his headquarters aboard the captured schooner *Royal Savage*.

His indignation boiled over shortly after Arnold arrived at Crown Point to supervise the outfitting of the first four completed gondolas. When firing was heard down the lake early on the morning of August 17, Arnold immediately dispatched a hundred men in bateaux to bring back an oar-making detachment posted seven miles below, and then ordered the two small schooners to sail immediately to cover their retreat up the lake. To his amazement, Wynkoop's flagship fired a shot across the schooners' bows, bringing them to a stop. "Sir," trumpeted the commodore in a note delivered within minutes to Arnold's headquarters, "I know no orders but what shall be given out by me. . . . If an enemy is approaching, I am to be acquainted with it and know how to act in my station."

"You surely must be out of your senses," Arnold fired back; "if you do not suffer my orders to be immediately complied with . . . I shall be under the disagreeable necessity of convincing you of your error by immediately arresting you." Receiving no reply, he boarded *Royal Savage,* and within minutes the schooners were on their way down the lake. (They returned by evening; it was a false alarm.)

"A strange infatuation seems to prevail in people," General Schuyler responded on receiving a report of the incident. "How Wynkoop should imagine that he was not to obey General Arnold's orders . . . I cannot imagine." But Arnold, who was intimately acquainted with the potency of "strange infatuations," pleaded for clemency. "I believe the Commodore was really of opinion that neither of us had authority to command him," he wrote to General Gates after carrying out orders to arrest Wynkoop and send him to Ticonderoga. "He now seems convinced to the contrary, and sorry for his disobedience of orders. If it can be done with propriety, I wish he may be permitted to return home without being cashiered."

Gates, however, eagerly seized on the Wynkoop incident as a means of embarrassing the man who had appointed him commodore in the first place, Philip Schuyler—whose authority over Gates himself had just been confirmed by Congress. In passing Wynkoop along to Albany, Gates solemnly noted that "many officers of rank in [the Northern] Department say he is totally unfit to command a single vessel at this important hour of business. . . . The times will not admit of trifling," he enjoined his superior; "decision alone must govern on these occasions." Schuyler responded pointedly that Wynkoop's fate would be decided by Congress, "by whom (and not by me) he was appointed," and he took the occasion to remind his rival that "the want of subordination and discipline in an army cannot be too much lamented. It is the source whence all disorder and misfortune arise."*

---

*The Wynkoop affair was referred to the Marine Committee of the Continental Congress, where it died a lingering death. Wynkoop never received a ruling, but three years later he did get paid for his time of service on the lake at the rate of $60 a month.

On August 24, Arnold set sail from Crown Point with six new gondolas and the four captured British vessels: *Royal Savage,* mounting twelve guns; the eight-gun schooner *Revenge;* the *Liberty* schooner, in which he had sailed to St. Jean the year before; and *Enterprise,* the twelve-gun British sloop he had captured there. Two additional gondolas and four row galleys were to join the fleet as soon as they were completed. Meanwhile, his principal mission was to gather intelligence. Hearsay reports had been received of "several large [British] vessels" on the stocks at St. Jean, but their dimensions and armaments remained a mystery, as no American scout had been able to penetrate the enemy shipyard.

Arnold was confident that whatever ships the British were building, they would not be ready to sail until the end of September, some six weeks hence. Meanwhile, his strategy was dictated by a very specific set of orders from General Gates: he was to station his fleet at either Split Rock or Isle aux Têtes (see map, page 104; Isle aux Têtes is an antiquated name for Isle La Motte) and "maintain possession of those passes" if possible. If, however, the British "fleet should have so increased as to force an entrance into the upper part of the lake," he was to withdraw his ships to Ticonderoga immediately. Under no circumstances was he to venture beyond Isle aux Têtes, and under no circumstances was he to provoke a fight. The preservation of the fleet was paramount, Gates stipulated. "It is a defensive war we are carrying on; therefore, no wanton risk or unnecessary display of the power of the fleet is at any time to influence your conduct."

With these injunctions in mind, but keeping his own thoughts to himself, Arnold boarded *Royal Savage* and headed north into the broad expanse of Lake Champlain. He vastly preferred the enemy before him to the enemies behind. The British were clearly visible and forthright in their dealings—unlike his treacherous accusers, the politicians who did not trust him and the feuding generals whose backbiting threatened the very cause in which they served. Arnold was poor at politics because he refused to recognize it as a game. (Persons who are incapable of laughing at themselves are seldom good at games.) But he was very good at war, and on the open water he had some latitude in which to maneuver as he chose.

He pushed his little fleet hard and anchored the second night at Willsboro, where "a violent storm at northeast" obliged him to drop back to the shelter of Buttonmold Bay. When the storm abated, the flotilla sailed again, anchoring on September 3 in the narrow defile just south of Isle La Motte, where it was spied by a troop of British soldiers who raced back to St. Jean with a wild tale of *"four hundred bateaux filled with Rebels* [emphasis added].''

Unfortunately, Arnold's intelligence about the British was no more accurate, although fresh reports did indicate that both General Carleton and General Burgoyne would sail with the fleet, accompanied by more than seven thousand seasoned British and Hessian troops. The debilitated American garrison at Ticonderoga would be no match for such a force. Arnold would have to stop them on the water, or at least delay them long enough to make an attack on Ticonderoga unfeasible. With the fate of the northern army, and possibly the entire Hudson Valley, resting on his flotilla, Arnold took small comfort in the appearance during the first week of September of the small six-gun galley *Lee* and the gondola *Jersey*. He had expected all the galleys by now, confident that they would prove "vastly superior to any naval strength I can conceive it possible for the enemy to bring on the lake this fall." The delay was occasioned primarily by the dysentery, jaundice and "putrid, intermitting and bilious fevers" that raged at Skenesboro and Ticonderoga during the waning days of summer. Many of Arnold's crewmen had fallen ill as well, and he requested General Gates to dispatch "a watch coat or blanket and one shirt" for each man, to protect them against the cold autumn winds. "Rum," he added, "is another necessary article."

He moored his fleet in a line off Isle La Motte and dispatched scouts to penetrate the secrets of the British shipyard at St. Jean. On September 6, a small detachment sent ashore to cut fascines* was "attacked by a party of savages, who pursued them into the water . . . [and] before they could row off, three were killed and six wounded." Accompanying the Indians was a British officer, who left behind "a laced beaver hat, the button marked 47th Regiment." After midnight that night, Arnold was awakened by reports of lights and the sound of axes on either shore: the British were erecting batteries. He set sail at first light and dropped back to a less vulnerable anchorage, where he remained for ten days, scanning the southern horizon for his galleys and the northern shoreline for his scouts, training his "wretched motley crew[s]" in the handling of boats and conducting gun drills with no ammunition.

By mid-September only one additional gondola had appeared. Even more welcome was the arrival of Colonel Edward Wigglesworth,

---

*Fascines were bundles of sticks fixed "on the bows and sides of the gondolas to prevent the enemy's boarding and to keep off small shot"—probably an Arnold improvisation.

"a good seaman," Gates assured Arnold, "[who] appears to be much of a gentleman and has, as far as I can learn, an unimpeached good character." The fleet's second-in-command, Brigadier General David Waterbury, was to sail north in about ten days with three large galleys and a final gondola. Waterbury was "an able seaman and a brave officer [with whom Arnold was on] the best terms," giving General Gates confidence that "no dispute about command or want of confidence in each other will retard the public service."

Intelligence received from a British deserter was only somewhat reassuring: most of the British ships at St. Jean—four or five sloops, a number of gondolas and several large floating batteries—were still on the stocks, but one of the batteries would apparently mount more than twenty eighteen-pounders in addition to mortars. The report was unreliable (like Arnold's scouts, the man had not actually seen the shipyard), but its premonition of British firepower was disconcerting, and Arnold was glad to learn from Gates that the three galleys were being outfitted "with utmost diligence." (Gates enclosed in this letter a copy of the Declaration of Independence and ordered Arnold to forward it to the British with his next flag.)

Three days later, September 17, Arnold finally received an incontrovertible piece of intelligence that changed everything: in addition to the schooners, sloops, gondolas and batteries he already knew about, the British had on the stocks at St. Jean a three-masted ship of war "designed to mount twenty guns, nine- and twelve-pounders . . . [which] will be completed in a fortnight." Her name was *Inflexible,* she measured eighty feet from stem to stern, and "with a working breeze [she] alone could sweep the lake clear of all that floated on it."

Arnold had no defense against such a vessel. His only hope resided in the calendar: given the lateness of the season, General Carleton might well decide he could not wait for *Inflexible* to be completed. If he sailed without her, and if Arnold's remaining ships arrived in time—two very large *if's*—the Continental fleet might yet save Ticonderoga.

He decided to withdraw to the sheltered anchorage at Valcour Island, where, he assured Gates, "there is a good harbor, and if the enemy venture up the lake, it will be impossible for them to take advantage of our situation." Sailing south along the western shore line, now ablaze with autumn color against the backdrop of Adirondack peaks, Arnold, looking ahead, may have seen the rocky cliff of Valcour Island hovering in the air above the level of the lake like a disembodied spirit—the result of a recurrent low-lying mist that

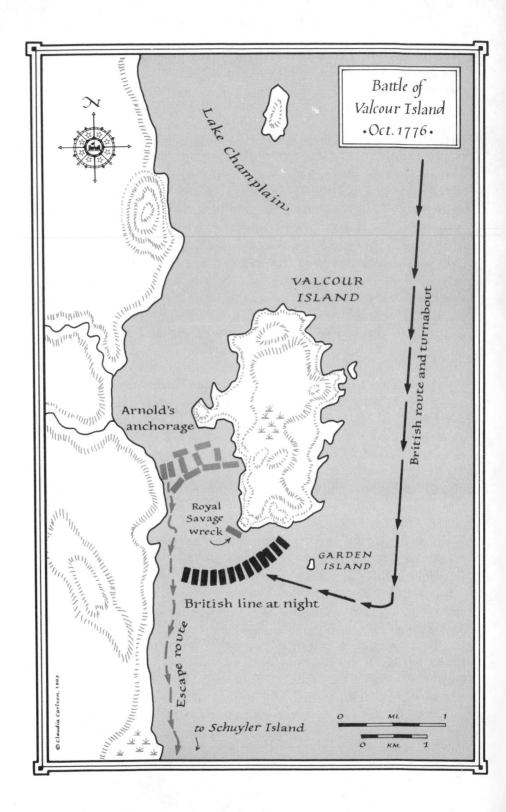

N

Battle of
Valcour Island
·Oct. 1776·

Lake Champlain

British route and turnabout

VALCOUR
ISLAND

Arnold's
anchorage

Royal
Savage
wreck

GARDEN
ISLAND

British line at night

Escape route

© Claudia Carlson, 1993

to Schuyler Island

0   MI.   1

0   KM.   1

frequents Lake Champlain in autumn. He reached Valcour on September 23 and anchored his ships facing south in a line across the channel between the island and the mainland (see map, page 104).

The weather grew "very severe." On September 30 a sail was seen to the south: the new galley *Trumbull*—"not half finished or rigged, her cannon much too small," carrying no gunpowder, no warm clothing and manned by landlubbers. "I hope to be excused," Arnold wrote to Gates, "(after the requisitions so often made) if with five hundred men, half naked, I should not be able to beat the enemy with seven thousand men, well clothed, and a naval force, by the best accounts, near equal to ours. . . . I am surprised at their strange economy or infatuation below. Saving and negligence, I am afraid, will ruin us at last." In desperation he sent *Liberty* down to Ticonderoga for supplies, although he could ill afford to have her absent from the fleet.

After a second long week of waiting, with no sign of the enemy, General Waterbury arrived with the galleys *Washington* and *Congress*, a hundred troops, no seamen and a vastly inadequate supply of naval stores, for which Gates apologized: "Where [supplies are] not to be had, you and princes of the earth must go unfurnished." But at least there were now as many of the maneuverable galleys as there were senior officers, and with Waterbury and Wigglesworth already aboard *Washington* and *Trumbull* respectively, Arnold transferred his flag to *Congress*.

Waterbury brought devastating news of General Washington's defeat on Long Island. "It appears to me our troops or officers are panic struck," Arnold fulminated, "or why do a hundred thousand men fly before one quarter of their numbers? Is it possible my countrymen can be callous to their wrongs or hesitate one moment between slavery or death?" With the British now poised to take New York, the danger to the Hudson Valley was all the more immediate, and Arnold assured both Schuyler and Gates on October 7 that he and his men were eager "for an opportunity of meeting the enemy who, I believe, will hardly be in a condition to see us this fall."

Shortly after dawn on the cold, clear morning of October 11, as the peaks of the Adirondacks were catching the first rays of the sun, Arnold heard signal guns on the north shore of Valcour Island and promptly alerted the fleet: the British were coming, in strength as yet unknown. An incredulous General Waterbury appeared aboard *Congress* to inquire if Arnold actually intended to give battle in the channel. Surely, Waterbury protested, they should sail immediately and fight the enemy "on a retreat in Main Lake." Arnold disagreed:

with a strong north wind at their backs, the heavier British ships would easily overtake and annihilate the fleet before it could make its escape. After Waterbury departed, Arnold was free to train his spyglass on the open water beyond the point of Valcour Island, where, within the hour, the British fleet appeared, running south under full sail, a beautiful and fearsome sight. *Inflexible* was in the lead, followed by the schooners *Maria* and *Carleton*, twenty oared gunboats, four longboats, a fleet of war canoes packed with Indians and, bringing up the rear, a mammoth three-hundred-man fourteen-gun floating battery called *Thunderer*.

The British were well beyond Valcour before they came about and began to beat upwind toward Arnold's position.* The appearance of *Inflexible* had destroyed any illusions Arnold might have harbored of a glorious victory. Outgunned and outmanned two to one, all he could hope for was a glorious defeat. As he watched, the enemy's oared gunboats began to pull ahead of *Inflexible*, *Maria* and the others. In order to engage them before the rest could come up, he ordered the galleys and *Royal Savage* forward. Unfortunately, *Royal Savage* fell to leeward almost immediately and became a sitting duck for the approaching gunboats, which drew within range at about eleven A.M. She took their concerted fire for an hour and then, hung up on the rocks at the point of Valcour Island, her guns fell silent as her captain and crew made their escape.

The engagement between the galleys and gunboats then became "general and very warm." At midday the enemy schooner *Carleton* drew near and fired off several deadly broadsides. But she was well ahead of the other heavy British ships, and Arnold was able to concentrate his guns on her to such good effect that after an hour she had to be towed out of range by longboats.

For another five hours, while *Inflexible* still struggled upwind, the gunboats and Arnold's little fleet rained on each other "a very hot fire with round and grapeshot" at a range of about seven hundred yards, while "a large number of Indians on the island and each shore . . . [kept up] an incessant fire" on the American ships. General Waterbury's galley, *Washington*, "was hulled a number of times [and] her mainmast shot through," while Arnold's own galley, *Congress*, "received seven shot between wind and water, was hulled a dozen times, had her mainmast wounded in two places and her yard in one."

---

*The British commodore later claimed not to have known the American fleet was there, but his junior officers said that he was lying, and an unseemly public squabble ensued.

Arnold himself, galvanized by his first experience of naval combat, seemed oblivious to the interminable roar and thud of cannon fire, the blinding, choking black smoke, the smell of burning wood and canvas, the screams of the wounded and the slippery footing on *Congress*'s bloody deck. Impatient with his gunners' ineptitude, he aimed the guns himself, "which," he later reported, "I believe did good execution." The British agreed: assessing the damage to their gunboats afterward, one officer commented admiringly that "the cannon of the rebels were well served"—so well that an enemy boarding party of "upwards of one thousand men in bateaux" lingered out of range the entire afternoon, unable to perform its appointed task.

Toward evening, *Inflexible* finally came into position and fired five broadsides, to devastating effect. The American line fell silent. Only the approach of night brought a temporary reprieve. In the gathering dark, the enemy ships began to drop out of range and to anchor in a line across the entrance to the channel. In the morning, at their leisure, they would bring *Inflexible, Maria* and *Thunderer* into position, blast Arnold's ships out of the water and be on their way to Ticonderoga.

Arnold's fleet had expended more than three quarters of its ammunition, and most of his ships were severely damaged. The gondola *Philadelphia,* having taken a twenty-four-pound shot in her starboard bow, sank an hour after the battle was over.* Only the galley *Trumbull,* one small schooner, a sloop and a single gondola were relatively seaworthy, and even they could not escape. Both the strong contrary wind and the distance around the island precluded an exit through the channel to the north. He was trapped.

As darkness fell, Arnold conceived a desperate plan. The British flagship *Maria,* having remained well out of range during the battle, now came to anchor all the way out at Garden Island, at the far end of the British line—which pulled the entire line much farther out into the lake than necessary and left a gap of more than a mile between the mainland shore and the closest enemy ship. This, plus a boon from nature in the form of a dense fog, was all Arnold needed. After dark, with *Trumbull* in the lead and *Congress* in the rear, the wounded Continental fleet rowed in single file with muffled oars down the mainland shore. Each ship was guided by a blinkered lantern on

---

*Raised from the bottom of Valcour Bay in 1935, *Philadelphia* is now on display at the National Museum of American History of the Smithsonian Institution in Washington, D.C., where she is hailed as "the oldest American man-of-war in existence."

the stern of the vessel in front, barely discernible in the fog. One by one, they slipped through the gauntlet and out into the open lake, where all set sail for Crown Point.

At dawn, with *Trumbull* and the three undamaged ships far ahead of the others, nature withdrew her blessing: the wind shifted to the south, leaving Arnold's *Congress*, General Waterbury's *Washington* and seven severely damaged gondolas still in sight of Valcour Island. Fortunately, the contrary wind delayed the enemy as well, giving Arnold time to lead his little brood of wounded vessels into the lee of Schuyler Island for emergency repairs. In early afternoon, with the British still mired in confusion and chagrin back at Valcour, they got under way again. At daybreak the following day, the wind shifted again to the north, and by mid-morning Arnold could see the British squadron bearing down on him en masse.

Washington was leaking so badly that General Waterbury urgently requested permission to scuttle her, but Arnold ordered him instead "to push forward to Split Rock, where he would draw the fleet in a line and engage them again." By the time the two galleys reached Split Rock, the gondolas were well in front, and Arnold ordered Waterbury to turn with him and make a stand to cover their escape. *Washington*, however, could do no more. Caught in the treacherous crosswinds of the palisades, she took several British broadsides, struck her colors and surrendered.

Now *Inflexible*, *Maria* and *Carleton* turned all their attention to the galley *Congress*—three Goliaths bearing down on a single David. Arnold fought them off for more than two hours in a running battle through the Narrows. *Congress*'s "sails, rigging and hull . . . were shattered and torn in pieces," and more than a third of her crew was felled by an "incessant fire . . . [of] round and grapeshot." Emerging into the upper lake, with the gondolas limping along in front, Arnold hugged the eastern shore and focused his entire energy on outwitting his pursuers: at all costs, he must keep his ships and men from falling into enemy hands.

Just south of Buttonmold Bay lay a small cove belonging to the homestead of one Peter Ferris, a patriot known to Arnold. Arnold gave the signal and suddenly *Congress* and the gondolas swerved to the left, passed through the rocky inlet at the entrance to the cove and ran aground on the beach just below Ferris's house. The British ships' superior size and weight was instantly converted from an asset to a liability. Taken unawares, *Inflexible*, *Maria* and the others had to jibe around and beat back into range, which gave Arnold the time he needed to dump all his cannon overboard and set his vessels afire.

At the end, he saw to it that *Congress*'s colors were left flying; this was no surrender.*

Amid the crackling of flames and explosions of ammunition, Arnold gathered the two hundred survivors and set off along the woodland trail to Crown Point, nine miles to the south, accompanied by Peter Ferris and his family (who returned to their homestead a few weeks later to discover that the British had burned all the buildings and fences, cut down the apple trees and slaughtered the livestock). Reaching the fort at four A.M., Arnold roused the garrison commander, who ordered an immediate withdrawal to Ticonderoga. "Exceedingly fatigued and unwell, having been without sleep or refreshment for near three days," Arnold himself finally reached Ticonderoga that evening and reported to General Gates.

New York City, Gates informed him, had fallen to the British more than three weeks before. General Washington and the Continental Army were on the run in Westchester County, leaving General Howe in a position to push up the Hudson River the moment Carleton's army broke through to Albany.

The outcome of the campaign would depend on Fort Ticonderoga after all. During the two months Arnold had been absent, the French lines north of the fort had been repaired and fortified, and a "beautiful strong breastwork or lines, mounting twenty-five pieces of cannon from six- to thirty-two-pounders," had been constructed across the lake on Mount Independence. Unfortunately, a great deal of it was show. Gates lacked both tools and manpower to finish the fortifications, and the cannon he had been promised had never arrived. An urgent call for reinforcements had been dispatched to all the neighboring states, but whether they would arrive in time to save Ticonderoga from a seven-thousand-man enemy assault force depended entirely on how quickly the British moved. Most of the northern army's ammunition allotment had gone to Arnold's fleet. Ten of the navy's sixteen ships had been lost in the battle of Valcour, leaving only six small Continental vessels to defend Ticonderoga from the guns of *Inflexible*. (They were the *Liberty* schooner, one brand new galley and the four sail that had escaped with Colonel Wigglesworth after the battle.)

Morale was understandably low. On the evening after Arnold's arrival, General Waterbury and the crew of *Washington*, released by the British on parole, arrived at the Ticonderoga landing, where, in

*The galley *Congress* is still embedded in the stiff mud at the bottom of Ferris Bay.

the words of Gates's aide, they made such a "dangerous impression" on the guard with their "warm . . . acknowledgement of the kindness with which they had been treated" by their British captors that the aide immediately "placed the boats containing the prisoners under the guns of a battery, and gave orders that no one should be permitted to land, and no intercourse take place with the troops on shore." Gates, apprehending a real "danger [in] permitting these men to have any intercourse with our troops, accordingly . . . ordered [them] to proceed . . . and they went forward that night without being permitted to land."

But Gates was not inexperienced in matters of morale. He placed Arnold in command of the French lines, and in his general orders issued a clarion call: "The fleet has acted a noble part. Let it not be said that the cause of all America [was lost] by the supineness of the Northern Army." Within twenty-four hours, the Battle of Valcour Island was on its way into American mythology. "No man ever maneuvered with more dexterity, fought with more bravery, or retreated with more firmness" than Arnold at Valcour, army doctor James Thacher rhapsodized. "[When finally overcome by superior strength, he] set fire to his vessel and would not quit her till she was so completely in flames that it was impossible for the enemy to strike her colors on their arrival, and they were left flying among the flames to the last. This . . . was supporting a point of honor in a manner almost romantic," the doctor allowed, "yet so it was . . . [and at Ticonderoga] we now feel more confidence in our strength." A colonel on the French lines observed new "life and spirits . . . [in the men, and] a determined resolution to defend the place to the last extremity."

The British disembarked their army at Crown Point, and General Carleton boasted that "he would be in possession of Ticonderoga [within the week] and on his way to Albany, where he was to have his winter quarters." A week passed, and still he did not come. During those seven days, the eastern shore of the lake remained inexplicably free of British scouts, and reinforcements and supplies arrived every hour at Mount Independence, "free and unmolested." Two released American prisoners brought a message from General Carleton: he had postponed his attack only to give Ticonderoga an opportunity to surrender. "Simple man," scoffed one Continental patriot, "to think that such gasconade would have any effect to intimidate the minds of the brave Americans."

Shortly after dawn on October 28—more than a fortnight after Arnold's arrival at Ticonderoga—signal guns announced the approach of the enemy by land and water. "The whole camp presented a terrific blaze of fire arms issuing from every quarter to prepare for battle," an eager young captain from Pennsylvania reported. "Column after column presented their fronts along the lines, with fixed bayonet, whose glistening fire arms reflecting the bright rise of the sun presented a luster . . . more radiant than the sun itself. What mind could resist a flash like this! The sounds of the drums to arms, the reports of the alarm cannon, and the cry of the sergeants to the men in hurrying them from their tents of 'Turn out! Turn out!' would make even a coward brave. These were, however, the times that tried men's souls, and here only the sunshine and summer soldier shrank from the expected conflict."*

Enemy troops and Indians could be seen disembarking on both sides of the lake north of the French lines. When two armed boats approached, Arnold's troops fired, and they withdrew. A prolonged hush followed. Every American eye was trained on the enemy positions, but there was no sign of movement. Finally, at dusk, the British began to reembark in their bateaux. By sunset, they were gone.

During the next few days, General Carleton embarked his seven thousand troops into their proud ships and sailed back to Canada. Three weeks later the Narrows were frozen solid. Overcoming the determined American garrisons at Ticonderoga and Mount Independence would have taken more time than Carleton had, and Albany was a long, arduous march away. If he had sailed from St. Jean a month earlier, the outcome would no doubt have been different. Four weeks had made the difference—exactly the amount of time Carleton had waited for *Inflexible,* a ship he thought necessary to sweep the Continental fleet from the lake.

Dodsley's (London) *Register* later ascribed General Carleton's retreat to "the countenance of the enemy." The specific countenance to which the *Register* referred—the countenance that had forced Carleton's withdrawal and thereby preserved the Hudson Valley and the Continental Army for another critical season—was the countenance of Benedict Arnold.

---

*Thomas Paine, *The American Crisis,* 1776: "These are the times that try men's souls. The summer soldier and the sunshine patriot will, in this crisis, shrink from the service of his country; but he that stands it *now,* deserves the love and thanks of man and woman."

Chapter 10

"OUR EVIL GENIUS"

NOVEMBER 1776 -JULY 1777

Many of Arnold's countrymen saw it differently.

"You must have heard that a few days ago we had a fine fleet, but General Arnold, our evil genius to the north, has, with a good deal of industry, got us clear of [it]," wrote General William Maxwell, whose relish in slandering Arnold stemmed from his service as a judge at the court-martial of Moses Hazen. Maxwell's malevolence was matched only by his power of invention: "Our fleet, by all impartial accounts, was much the strongest," he recounted, "but [Arnold] suffered himself to be surrounded between an island and the mainland . . . still our people repelled them with ease the first afternoon. In the night, he gave orders to every vessel to make the best of their way, by which they became an easy prey, beat by one, twos and threes. . . . This was a pretty piece of admiralship, after going to their doors almost, and bantering them for two months or more, contrary to the opinion of all the army."

Even more believable, though just as false, were the allegations of Brigadier General David Waterbury, commander of the galley *Washington*. Faced with the unenviable task of explaining to Congress why his was the only ship in three days of fighting to strike her colors and surrender to the British, Waterbury intimated that Arnold had deliberately left him behind to surrender to the enemy in order to buy time to make his own escape. This self-serving concoction not only distorted the facts, it accused Arnold of physical cowardice, the one human frailty to which he never yielded. Nevertheless, it was widely circulated and believed, especially among Arnold's enemies in Congress and the army.

The counterclaims of Arnold's champions were equally extravagant. In a rush to defend their hero against Waterbury and his ilk, they transmogrified him into a clairvoyant who had known all along that the fleet must be sacrificed in order to delay the British and effect their ultimate withdrawal to Canada. Giving battle in the Valcour channel, however, was not part of a secret master plan formulated ahead of time by Arnold in direct defiance of General Gates's orders. It was simply a masterful improvisation in the face of a terrible situation. Arnold's instincts were brilliant, his leadership inspired and his courage unexcelled. But the fact that his scrambling had saved his country did not become clear until after the war was won.

For Arnold, the second battle of Valcour Island—the battle in hindsight over his conduct—was more vexatious and grueling than the first. It seemed that the greater a military hero he became, the worse his enemies spoke of him. Devoid of equanimity and inner confidence, buffeted by every passing rumor, lie and innuendo, as the weeks passed he clung more desperately than ever to the image of his better self, the genuine, but unstable, Patriot-Hero. He came to deny any aspect of his being that did not conform to the image, reinforcing the cellar door lest the ordinary, human, vulnerable, hungry, imperfect Benedict Arnold emerge to blur the outline in the upstairs mirrors. Eventually, his habitual avoidance of introspection became pathological. He would admit no failing, take no responsibility for any of his problems. The potency of his image was thereby preserved—but his grip on reality slipped and weakened with every passing day.

With Ticonderoga and the Hudson Valley safe until spring, Arnold and Horatio Gates were ordered to march south with the bulk of the northern army to reinforce General Washington, who was currently attempting to gain control of his army's panic-stricken retreat through New Jersey. The soldiers of the main army, demoralized by the pasting they had received in the battles for Long Island, Manhattan and Westchester, were deserting in droves. In mid-August, before Long Island, Washington had commanded nearly twenty-eight thousand men; in early November, he crossed the Hudson River into New Jersey with about five thousand.

The commander in chief's desperate calls for militia had gone virtually unanswered. When he reached the Delaware River and crossed into Pennsylvania, Congress ignominiously fled its capital, Philadelphia, for the relative safety of Baltimore. The British halted on the New Jersey side of the river and waited: they knew as well as Washington did that the majority of his troops planned to decamp when their enlistments expired at the end of December. Barring the unexpected, by the end of the year it would all be over.

Passing through Albany with General Gates at the end of November, Arnold ran into a snare prepared for him by his two nemeses, Moses Hazen and John Brown. Both men had come to town in order to file formal charges against him, Hazen for defamation of character, and Brown for thirteen alleged misdemeanors in Canada ranging from the outlandish—that Arnold was personally responsible for the spread of smallpox in the Canadian army—to the breathtaking—that in 1775 at Ticonderoga he had made "a treasonable attempt to make his escape . . . to the enemy."

Brown's charges were couched in the form of a petition to General Gates, which Gates at first refused to act on, reluctantly promising to forward it to Congress only after Brown called personally at headquarters to press the matter. Arnold was grateful to Gates for keeping the charges private; still he had to wonder if his enemies in Congress might not exploit the petition to block the promotion to major general which his performance at Valcour had surely earned him. Most of the charges were nonsense; but one at least was bound to ring alarm bells in the halls of Congress: that "to the eternal disgrace of Continental arms," Arnold had stolen goods requisitioned from the merchants of Montreal.

Moses Hazen's charge—that, in a note written the previous July to the Canadian commissioners, Arnold had accused Hazen by implication of stealing a wagonload of rum at Chambly—was less easily deflected. At a court of inquiry, held on General Gates's orders, eyewitnesses for both parties managed so thoroughly to obscure the five-month-old history of the rum in question that the judges were unable to ascertain Hazen's guilt or innocence, leading them to rule that Arnold's note constituted "an aspersion of Colonel Hazen's character, [and that] therefore [Hazen's] complaint [was] just." Although the verdict carried no punishment—and Horatio Gates refused to impose any—Arnold was left with the humiliation of having been publicly bested yet again by Moses Hazen and the uncomfortable thought that his persecutors would never let him forget it. (The charges have a pleasant symmetry: Hazen, who had defamed Arnold in a courtroom at Ticonderoga, now accused Arnold of defamation; and Brown, whom Arnold had charged with stealing, now returned the favor.)

A week before Christmas, Arnold and Gates passed through Nazareth, Pennsylvania, and lodged at the Sun Tavern in Bethlehem with a group of their fellow officers. There Arnold received urgent orders from General Washington to proceed to Rhode Island and "take such measures as in your opinion will be most likely to give opposition to, and frustrate the intents of" a large British fleet that had been sighted off the coast. Washington could not spare a single man from the main army (in fact, he was in the process of stripping New England of all its Continental troops to reinforce it), and he counted heavily on Arnold's ability to attract local militia volunteers.

Discouraging though the prospects were, Arnold was heartened by the commander in chief's confidence. Washington had even scratched out the conventional closing his secretary had written at the end of the letter ("your most obedient servant") and substituted in his own hand the more personal "I am, dear sir, with great esteem and regard," a mark of singular friendship. Arnold quickly rode the few short miles to headquarters to receive the commander in chief's final orders, and headed east toward Rhode Island.

On Christmas night, only three days after Arnold's departure, General Washington recrossed the Delaware River in secret and routed a large contingent of holiday-besotted Hessians at Trenton, taking more than a thousand prisoners. It was a desperate gamble—made possible by the reinforcements from the northern army—that paid off at once in a startling upsurge of enlistments and reenlistments. On January 1, Washington struck again, surprising and soundly defeating a camp of British regulars at Princeton. General Howe, utterly confounded, withdrew his army from southern New Jersey, permitting the Continentals, with the pressure off their capital city, to withdraw into winter quarters near Morristown.

While Washington was reaping laurels in New Jersey, Benedict Arnold was slogging in a backwater of the war. The British had landed six thousand men at Newport, on the southern tip of an island at the mouth of Narragansett Bay, to establish a foraging base. Week after week, as they dug in and hardened their fortifications, Arnold issued desperate calls for militia that went virtually unanswered. "We have it yet in our power to be free and happy, if we will exert ourselves," he wrote to Samuel Chase on hearing of General Washington's triumphs in New Jersey; but the able-bodied men of New England seemed disinclined to any exertion whatsoever. The only bright spot was the presence of Eleazer Oswald, who had been released on parole from prison in Quebec, along with Daniel Morgan, John Lamb and the rest of the Kennebec detachment. (As long as Oswald was on parole, he could serve Arnold only in an unofficial capacity. He and most of the others were formally exchanged several weeks later, and Lamb and Morgan promptly set about raising new regiments for the Continental service.)

On a trip to Boston in February, Arnold was introduced to the "beautiful . . . straight, tall, elegant" Elizabeth Deblois and fell headlong into love. He wrote her ardent love letters, full of foolish fondness; but "the heavenly Miss Deblois" refused to answer. Lavish presents, dispatched via his emissary, Mrs. Henry Knox (wife of the Continental Army's chief of artillery), were likewise spurned. Betsy's indifference to Arnold probably had little to do with the fact that her father was an avowed Tory. More likely it stemmed from the difference in their ages: Arnold was thirty-six, and she had just turned fifteen.

Crushed, but refusing to admit defeat, Arnold returned to Providence and his stagnant command. There he was informed that Congress had promoted five new major generals. His name was not among them.

Adding insult to injury, all five men on the list had been brigadiers a shorter time than he. "Congress have doubtless a right of promoting those [whom] . . . they esteem most deserving," he wrote to General Washington; but "their promoting junior officers . . . I view as a very civil way of requesting my resignation as unqualified for the office I hold. My commission," he continued, "[I] received with pleasure only as a means of serving my country; with equal pleasure I resign it when I can no longer serve my country with *honor*."

Arnold's words were bound to strike a chord in the heart of a man whose sense of honor ran deep—much deeper, in fact, than his own. Arnold's vaunted honor was concerned solely with appearances, i.e., pride and public dignity; Washington's was rooted in substance—internal probity and private integrity. (Nearly every aspect of their characters followed the same pattern; for example, Washington's devotion to his country's cause was deep and durable, while Arnold's was shallow and mutable.)

In addition to sympathizing with Arnold personally, the com-

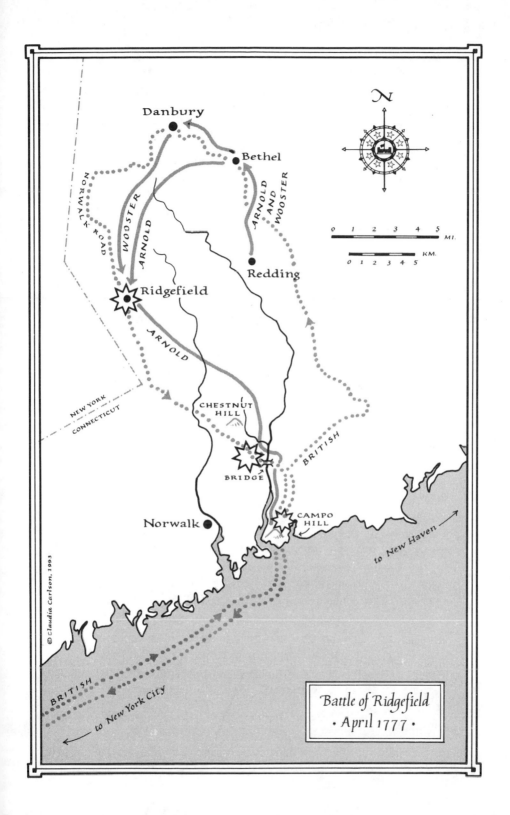

Danbury

Bethel

NORWALK ROAD

WOOSTER

ARNOLD

ARNOLD AND WOOSTER

Redding

Ridgefield

ARNOLD

NEW YORK
CONNECTICUT

CHESTNUT
HILL

BRIDGE

BRITISH

Norwalk

CAMPO
HILL

to New Haven

N

0 1 2 3 4 5
MI.

0 1 2 3 4 5
KM.

BRITISH

to New York City

© Claudia Carlson, 1993

Battle of Ridgefield
· April 1777 ·

mander in chief was anxious not to lose his invaluable services, and he desperately tried to persuade Congress to right the wrong. "Surely a more active, a more spirited and sensible officer fills no department in your army," he pleaded with his friend Congressman Richard Henry Lee. "It is not to be presumed, being the oldest brigadier, that he will continue in the service under such a slight," and he warned Lee that Congress's predilection for basing promotions on political, rather than military, criteria would lose them "two or three other very good officers" as well.*

Washington requested Arnold to postpone making a decision until Congress had time to reconsider, which, in effect, gave Arnold an honorable way to do what he wanted to do: remain in the army. War brought out the best in him. At the same time, it earned him the regard of patricians like George Washington and Philip Schuyler, men whose exalted sphere he would otherwise never have penetrated. The vast majority of Arnold's fellow soldiers might wish to end the conflict and go home; but civilian life no longer beckoned him, and the fruits of victory—freedom and independence from the British yoke—meant little to him. The war itself had more meaning to General Benedict Arnold than the goals for which it was fought.

"Every personal injury shall be buried in my zeal for the safety and happiness of my country, in whose cause I have repeatedly fought and bled and am ready at all times to risk my life," he magnanimously assured the commander in chief. But underneath the rhetoric, he was seething with fantastical delusions of persecution. "I cannot . . . help thinking it extremely cruel to be judged and condemned without an opportunity of being heard or even knowing my crime or accusers," Arnold wrote to his friend Horatio Gates. "I know some villain has been busy with my fame and easily slandered me." But no matter how severely wronged, Arnold assured his friend—coining the phrase that would become his leitmotiv—"[I remain] conscious of the rectitude of my intentions."

At this juncture, word came from Boston that Betsy Deblois had explicitly and forevermore rejected his suit. At the same time, plans for an attack on Newport were officially abandoned, and in despair, Arnold departed Rhode Island, determined to visit General Washington and, if necessary, Congress in order to confront his future head-on.

*Just before making the promotions, Congress had adopted a new state quota system whereby Connecticut already had more than its share of major generals.

Stopping over briefly in New Haven to visit his family, he was awakened in the predawn hours of April 26 by the arrival of a courier from the senior military commander in the district, his old companion in arms General David Wooster. Two thousand enemy troops had been landed from a British fleet the evening before at Cedar Point, some thirty miles west of New Haven, and were now on the march toward the Continental supply depot at Danbury (see map, page 117).*

Arnold rode west all morning, rallying militia along the way, and in the afternoon rendezvoused with Wooster and a local militia troop at Redding. Six hundred strong, they marched north all afternoon in a driving rain, pausing at Bethel at eleven P.M. to give the exhausted men a rest. During the night, a Continental colonel with fifty men from the Danbury garrison arrived with a report that the enemy had entered the town during the afternoon, packed up all the military stores they could carry, destroyed the rest, set the town on fire and were now poised to march at dawn back to their transports at Cedar Point.

Too late to save the depot, Arnold and Wooster determined to prevent the enemy from regaining their ships. The British were undoubtedly aware of their presence at Bethel and might well decide to take an alternate route. Obliged to divide their meager force, the two generals set off at daybreak, Wooster marching north with two hundred troops and Arnold leading the main body, some four hundred men, westward to cut the Norwalk road. All morning Arnold and his detachment bushwacked through the woods in the pouring rain. He soon learned that the enemy was indeed retreating down the Norwalk road (specifically in order to "avoid Mr. Arnold," their general later acknowledged), so he quickened the pace and reached the village of Ridgefield at eleven A.M., just as the rain stopped and the sky began to clear.

Firing could be heard to the north: General Wooster was attacking the British rear. Arnold swiftly ordered a barricade thrown across the road at the northern edge of town. Abutting the site on one side was a farm clearing with a sheer drop-off behind; to the left was a high rock ledge that overlooked the barricade. It was far from ideal,

*British supply lines across the Atlantic had become dangerously attenuated, and they needed the military stores at Danbury almost as much as the Continentals did. The depot had became vulnerable during the January emergency, when General Washington transferred virtually every soldier out of western Connecticut to reinforce the main army.

but he had no time to be choosy. The enemy soon "appeared in one grand column that filled the road full for more than half a mile in length."

Sighting the barricade, the British halted, brought their artillery forward and, under its cover, began slowly, inexorably, to advance. Arnold's militia, outnumbered four to one and armed only with muskets, held in good order for more than an hour. Two enemy flanking parties, each larger than the entire American contingent, broke off from the main body and began to move in on the barricade from both sides. Only when they overran the rocky ledge and began to fire down on the men at point-blank range did Arnold order a retreat.

Remaining at the barricade with the rear guard, Arnold was thrown to the ground beneath his wounded horse with his foot caught in the stirrup. An alert enemy soldier leaped down from the rocky ledge and ran at him, bayonet at the ready. Arnold extricated his pistol in the nick of time, shot the man dead, disengaged himself from the stirrup and followed his men down the main street of Ridgefield "through a shower of small and grape shot."

Gaining the outskirts of the village, Arnold spread the word among his officers to collect their troops and rendezvous in the morning at the bridge across the Saugatuck River, ten miles below, where he planned to make a stand. He rode through the spring evening down the steep rocky ledges and wooded plateaus of eastern Connecticut, as the land takes one giant step after another in its plunge toward Long Island Sound. Bivouacked at night, Arnold learned that General Wooster had been gravely wounded in the action north of Ridgefield and was not expected to live. The feisty general's courage and resourcefulness in the battle had earned Arnold time to erect the barricade at Ridgefield, a fact that he fully acknowledged a few days later, after Wooster had died.

At nine A.M. Arnold reached the bridge to find Eleazer Oswald with a small troop of reinforcements and, best of all, three field pieces belonging to John Lamb's artillery company. Lamb himself, Oswald announced, was on the way. Arnold placed his cannon about two miles north of the bridge. At mid-morning, when the advance British column appeared in the road, he fired the six-pounder, felling several redcoats and bringing the whole detachment to a halt. After a pause, the main body of the enemy came up and began to advance straight at Arnold's position, as though to attack him head-on. Then, on a signal, the entire column abruptly wheeled left into the woods and began to cross a ford about a mile above Arnold's position. Caught off guard, he ordered his men back to the bridge to attack the enemy's flank; but the British, "running full speed" in remarkable order, got there first, and while two regiments of regulars fended off Arnold's men, the rest passed safely by.

He chased them all the way to Cedar Point, four miles below. By the time he reached the broad beach, the enemy's landing craft were taking on troops under the cover of artillery fire from the top of Campo Hill and from three armed escort vessels that had drawn in close to shore. John Lamb arrived and promptly led a charge up the hill. Blind in one eye from the wound he had received at Sault au Matelot, Lamb was just as pugnacious and spirited as ever. He was hit by grapeshot and fell to the ground behind a stone wall. Several minutes passed, and everyone assumed he was dead—but up he rose, bleeding from his left side, and gathered his men for a more or less orderly retreat under overwhelming enemy fire.

Arnold fared no better against the enemy's positions on Campo Hill. He led by example, as always; but his raw militia troops, exhausted and intimidated by their forty-eight-hour struggle against a disciplined and experienced enemy, finally crumbled in the face of a bayonet attack mounted with great precision by four regiments of redcoats. "Expos[ing] himself almost to a fault," Arnold rode to the front of the line and "conjured [his men] by the love of themselves, posterity, and all that is sacred not to desert him; but it was all to no purpose, their nerves were unstrung . . . they became panic struck, and there was no stopping them."

As darkness fell, the last British troops embarked safely, and the fleet weighed anchor and set sail for New York—a sight that seems to have dealt a deathblow to Benedict Arnold's vaunted fellow feeling for the soldiers under his command. Furious and frustrated, he sneered in a report written that same night, "The militia . . . I wish never to see another of them in action."

Arnold's conduct at Ridgefield and Cedar Point earned him promotion to major general, but without official restoration of his seniority over the men who had been promoted in February. Restless and frustrated, he decided to go to Philadelphia to appeal the decision in person. His military reputation was mightier than ever: perhaps the time was ripe to claim his due from Congress.

On May 20, only a few days after Arnold's arrival in the capital city, John Brown's thirteen charges against him were given a formal reading in Congress. "Conscious of the rectitude of my intentions," he protested to John Hancock, "I must request the favor of Congress to point out some mode by which my conduct and that of my accusers, particularly Lt. Col. John Brown, may be inquired into." With

Arnold's congressional critics temporarily silenced, Hancock complied with uncharacteristic dispatch. At a hearing before the Board of War, Arnold, who had taken great pains to prepare himself, presented "a variety of original letters, orders, and other papers" pertaining to his command at Montreal, and called Charles Carroll, late commissioner to Canada, to testify to his "character and conduct" there. John Brown, who was at home in Pittsfield, Massachusetts, had not been notified of the hearing and did not appear—with the inevitable result that the board officially absolved Arnold of the charges so "cruelly and groundlessly [promulgated in Brown's] publication."*

Arnold's rejoicing over his public vindication turned to anger and frustration during the ensuing weeks, as it became clear that Congress had no intention of addressing the two urgent matters that had brought him to Philadelphia in the first place: the restoration of his seniority and the settlement of his public accounts. He submitted detailed accounts of his personal expenditures for the army, dating from the Kennebec campaign to the present, to which Congress could not have responded even if it wanted to: on the eve of its first birthday, the fledgling United States of America was broke. (Lacking the power to tax its citizens, Congress's only way of paying its bills was to issue paper currency. The original 1775 issue was two million dollars, which had swelled by 1779 to two hundred million dollars, with predictable inflationary consequences.) As for his seniority, they never officially discussed it, granting him instead the gift of a fine horse, "properly caparisoned," to replace the animal killed under him at Ridgefield.

Arnold's disenchantment was mirrored by that of Philip Schuyler, who was also in Philadelphia to answer a set of extremely serious, but unsubstantiated, charges before Congress. The two men met frequently, their mutual outrage drawing them closer together than ever before. Much of Schuyler's wrath was directed at Horatio Gates, whose partisans had been spreading rumors in the capital that their chief would soon replace Schuyler as head of the Northern Department. After Schuyler was exonerated of the charges against him, and his command was officially confirmed, Gates himself came to Philadelphia to demand a transfer to a different department.

---

*A week after the Board of War's verdict, Arnold was appalled to learn that they intended to publish John Brown's charges as part of their public report. "The liberty of the press I hold sacred," he declared, but "if the printer . . . takes an unbecoming liberty with my character, I shall take an opportunity of calling [him] to account."

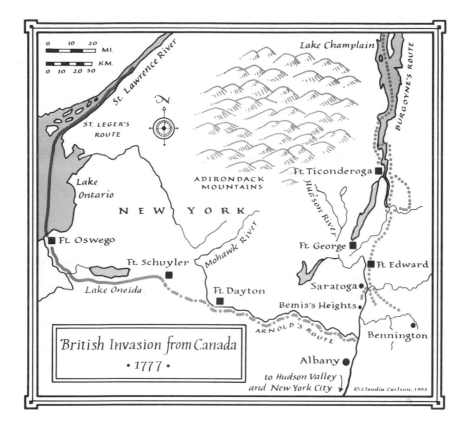

With the feud between his two mentors growing more virulent by the hour, Arnold could no longer remain friends with both. Faced with the choice between Gates, whose steadfast protection and support had surely merited his undying gratitude, and Schuyler, the courtly patrician who had befriended him, Arnold instinctively chose form over substance, style over fidelity. His inexorable slide toward Schuyler may also have been influenced by the prospects for the coming campaign: with General Burgoyne known to be massing an army in Canada for an attack up Lake Champlain, momentous operations were promised in the Northern Department.

General Schuyler departed Philadelphia in early June. A month later, the capital was galvanized by the news that Ticonderoga had fallen to the British without a fight and that General John Burgoyne was on the march toward Albany. The enemy's strategic goal was the same as the previous summer: to capture the Hudson Valley and its vital river crossings and thereby bring the war to an early close. Burgoyne would attack the valley from the north while the British army in New York moved up the Hudson to meet him. This time, there was a new and sinister addition. Far to the west, a powerful flanking detachment of British and Indians led by General Barry St. Leger had already come within striking distance of Fort Schuyler, which commanded a strategic portage a hundred miles up the Mohawk River. If they captured the fort, there was little to stop them from linking up with Burgoyne and ensuring the subjugation of the valley before the summer was out (see map, page 123).

All that stood between General Burgoyne and Albany was Philip Schuyler's vastly outmanned and outgunned northern army. With no possibility of reinforcements from the main army—General Washington needed every man to counter British operations in New Jersey—Schuyler would need a large infusion of northern militia. "If General Arnold has settled his affairs and can be spared from Philadelphia," the commander in chief wrote to John Hancock, "I would recommend him for this business and that he should immediately set out for the Northern Department. He is active, judicious and brave, and an officer in whom the militia will repose great confidence. Besides this, he is well acquainted with that country and with the routes and more important passes and defiles in it. . . . I could wish him to be engaged in a more agreeable service—to be with better troops," he continued, "but circumstances call for his exertions in this way, and I have no doubt of his adding much to the honors he has already acquired." Congress complied, dispatching orders for Arnold to proceed immediately to Washington's headquarters and thence to the northern army.

Arnold had no intention of refusing the order, but he was not above using it as leverage to obtain the object of his desire. He faced a delicate situation: Arthur St. Clair, one of the generals who had been promoted over him, was currently serving in the northern army, and Arnold did not wish to establish a precedent by acknowledging St. Clair's seniority, even indirectly. On the other hand, he was longing to shake the dust of Philadelphia from his heels and take to the field.

"The duty every honest man owes his country," he wrote to John Hancock on the very day his orders were signed—but before they were delivered—

> obliges me to address myself to the honorable Congress on a subject which I am sorry to have occasion to mention: my being sometime since superseded by a number of junior officers, which is generally, but by the army in particular, viewed

as an implied impeachment of my character and declaration of Congress that they thought me unqualified for the post that fell to me in the common line of promotions. I therefore hope Congress will do me the favor to accept my resignation, which upon my honor I do not ask from a spirit of resentment (though my feelings are deeply wounded), but from a real conviction that it is not in my power to serve my country in the present rank I hold. . . . Honor is a sacrifice no man ought to make; as I received, so I wish to transmit to posterity.

There was no risk that Congress would accept his resignation under the present circumstances. Nevertheless, the following morning, having received no reply (Congress wisely tabled his letter), he wrote awkwardly and nervously again, offering to accept his orders until such time as Congress approved his withdrawal from the army. Before they could change their minds he left town. Pausing briefly at headquarters, where he promised General Washington to "waiv[e] all dispute about rank . . . [and] act in concert" with Major General St. Clair, he proceeded to Fort Edward, where he arrived on July 21 to Philip Schuyler's "high satisfaction."

Chapter II

"THE FURY OF A DEMON"

AUGUST-OCTOBER 1777

The northern army had been retreating for two weeks before a heavily armed and supplied British force of some nine thousand men. Too weak to stand and fight, Schuyler's only recourse was to slow the enemy down by destroying bridges and blocking roads in his wake, a strategy that had so far kept Burgoyne's progress to barely a mile a day.

"We are daily insulted by the Indians," Arnold reported to General Washington. The "infernal savages . . . joined by a number of more savage and infernal Tories, painted like furies, are continually harassing and scalping our people and the miserable defenceless inhabitants. Whole families of the latter have been inhumanly butchered without distinction of age or sex, and some (I am credibly informed) have been roasted alive in presence of the *polite and humane British Army,* and no doubt contributed greatly to their pleasure & satisfaction." General Schuyler, an old hand with the Indians, complained that these incidents had produced an "unaccountable panic" in his army. "A few shot from a small party of Indians has more than once thrown them into the greatest confusion.

The day before yesterday, three hundred of our men who were advanced about a mile and a half came running in, being drove by a few Indians, certainly not more than fifty."

In the long run, however, the atrocities redounded on the British: American militia from the surrounding settlements flocked to reinforce General Schuyler in record numbers, and Benedict Arnold was inspired to ask the commander in chief to transfer Daniel Morgan and his regiment of sharpshooters to the Northern Department. Their presence, he correctly surmised, would put the army "in a condition to see General Burgoyne with all his Infernals on any ground they might choose."

Ironically, while Schuyler and Arnold were conducting a masterful retreat through the woods of northern New York before a vastly superior enemy force, a small body of pale-faced "infernals" along the Delaware River had outmaneuvered them both. Arnold's Philadelphia sources advised him that congressional sentiment was running strongly in favor of accepting his resignation, and that Philip Schuyler, having been designated official scapegoat for the loss of Ticonderoga, was about to lose his command to General Gates. Profoundly threatened by both eventualities, Arnold sat down on August 5 to write his first letter in many months to his old friend Horatio Gates.

The bulk of the letter was devoted to the northern army's current situation; but toward the end, almost in passing, he remarked that "a few days since I was informed that Congress had accepted my resignation" (which was not true, but it provided a preamble to his peroration). "No public or private injury or insult," he vowed, "shall prevail on me to forsake the cause of my injured and oppressed country until I see peace and liberty restored to her or nobly die in the attempt." Signing the letter "Your affectionate friend," he dispatched it to Philadelphia, where Gates received it a few days after receiving official notification of his appointment to command the Northern Department.

That same week, however, after a lengthy and rancorous debate, Congress voted to deny Arnold his seniority and to accept his resignation from the army. One of his triumphant enemies declared that Arnold had "conducted almost without blemish in resigning, if a man may be said to do so, who leaves a patriotic exertion because self love was injured in a fanciful right incompatible with the general interest of the Union." But Congressman Henry Laurens complained bitterly that Congress's "reasoning upon this occasion was disgusting. [Arnold] was refused not because he was deficient in merit or that his demand was not well founded, but because he asked for it, and that granting at such instance would be derogatory to the honor of Congress." The lawmakers' profound ambivalence about their "good old servant, General Arnold," was reflected in such unseemly squabbling and also in a basic administrative oversight: whether by accident or design, Arnold was not officially notified that his resignation had been accepted.

Camped with the northern army at the junction of the Hudson and Mohawk rivers, only eight miles above Albany, generals Schuyler and Arnold received a welcome piece of intelligence: the British fleet had set sail from New York—not up the Hudson, as they had feared, but down the coast toward Delaware Bay. (Philadelphia fell to the enemy a month later.) One prong of the three-prong attack on the Hudson Valley thus receded, but the second suddenly jumped into the foreground. On August 7, two exhausted Continental officers arrived at headquarters with news that the enemy's flanking operation to the west had achieved its first goal: Fort Schuyler was under siege.

Arnold promptly volunteered to lead a relief detachment. At Fort Dayton a few days later, his men surprised and captured a small troop of enemy scouts and soldiers, among whom was a young civilian named Han-Yost Schuyler, the scion of a prominent local Loyalist family (and a distant cousin to Arnold's friend the general). Han-Yost was apparently afflicted with some mild mental disorder whereby he had come to be revered by the Indians of the Mohawk Valley as a visionary, so when his relatives appeared to plead for his release, Arnold proposed a bargain: Han-Yost's freedom for his participation in a daring ruse.

Scouts had informed Arnold that the enemy's Indian allies at Fort Schuyler, disgruntled by the paucity of spoils on the expedition, were on the verge of deserting. On his instructions, therefore, Han-Yost Schuyler returned to the British camp outside the fort, gathered the Indians about him and announced that Arnold was on the march toward them with an overwhelming force. When asked by the British commander to be more specific, the young man simply rolled his eyes in his head and stared fixedly at the treetops, thereby convincing the Indians that Arnold's host was as multitudinous as the leaves on the trees and persuading them to decamp. In the process, one enemy officer reported, the Indians "grew furious and abandoned, seized upon the officers' liquor and clothes, and became more formidable than the enemy we had to expect." Unable to maintain the siege alone, the redcoats broke camp and retreated back into Canada, leaving Han-Yost to approach the gate of Fort Schuyler alone and announce to the astonished American garrison that the siege had been lifted.

Leaving two regiments of militia to guard Fort Schuyler, Arnold returned to the northern army within the week. His coup, which had eliminated a powerful enemy threat and dramatically decreased their chances of capturing the Hudson Valley, received the applause it justly deserved; but it was overshadowed by another victory won the same week at Bennington, Vermont, in which local militia units routed a large enemy foraging detachment, inflicting more than nine hundred casualties, half of whom were British regulars.

It was thus a severely weakened General Burgoyne who was now obliged to make his way to Albany alone, with no diversions in the offing and no reinforcements to protect his increasingly attenuated supply lines. Suddenly American prospects along the Hudson looked rosier, and militia by the hundreds began to report to the Continental camp. By the first week in September the army boasted six thousand troops, with another four thousand posted across the Hudson. Burgoyne's inexorable march to Albany was stalled; and Thaddeus Kosciusko, the brilliant Polish military engineer who had recently come to America as a Continental volunteer, was ordered to choose a likely site to erect fortifications and make a stand. "Our people are in high spirits and wish for action," Arnold wrote to John Lamb; "a few days, in all probability, will determine the fate of General Burgoyne's army or that of ours."

Unfortunately, the northern army was by this time locked in an internecine battle that drained its energy and threatened to destroy its effectiveness. During Arnold's absence, Horatio Gates had arrived to assume command, General Schuyler had retired to his home in Albany, and the hostility between the two rivals' partisans had rent the army from top to bottom. Schuyler continued to exert considerable influence, primarily through daily correspondence with his protégé and former secretary, Richard Varick, who had remained with the army as muster-master general. Varick found fault with General Gates's every word and gesture, and his posture of open ridicule was replicated by his mentor's admirers, whose gossiping and sneering in turn aroused deep resentment among the adherents of General Gates.

Arnold's taste was for real war, clean war, against an agreed-upon enemy; nevertheless, in the current atmosphere, it was impossible not to take sides between his two superiors. At first, Gates seemed to go out of his way to oblige, giving Arnold command of a division that included Daniel Morgan's riflemen, Henry Dearborn's regiment of light infantry (which had been specially trained to fight in conjunction with Morgan's sharpshooters, woodsman-style) and two regular infantry brigades commanded by Ebenezer Learned, a doughty veteran who had been part of the Fort Schuyler relief detachment, and Enoch Poor—the erstwhile president of the controversial Hazen court-martial at Ticonderoga who had tried to have Arnold arrested for contempt of court.

The honor of commanding such an elite division (as well as the pleasure of giving orders to Enoch Poor) failed to win Arnold over. He had already made his choice between Philip Schuyler's patrician universe and the plebian terra firma of Horatio Gates. Once having made it, any gratitude he felt toward Gates for favors past and present was expunged from his emotional record book. He took his division and promptly turned on his one-time friend and protector with no apparent qualm. At first, Arnold was perhaps unaware of the signals he was sending—he was a colossally insensitive man; but they were clearly read by General Gates.

Arnold's first offense (in Gates's eyes) was to cultivate the friendship of the Schuyler faction's chief agent provocateur, Richard Varick. Varick's efficiency and ingenuity recommended him to Arnold (he had been largely responsible for supplying the fleet on Lake Champlain the previous autumn), as did his affection for General Schuyler and his family. Horatio Gates, on the other hand, regarded Varick quite correctly as a Schuyler spy and viewed Arnold's cultivation of the young man with deep suspicion.

Gates's doubts became near-certainties when Arnold appointed nineteen-year-old Matthew Clarkson as his aide-de-camp: Clarkson was not only Richard Varick's good friend but also a cousin of General Schuyler's aristocratic aide, Henry Brockholst Livingston. But Gates's jealousy and resentment did not become cast in stone until the day that young Livingston himself appeared in camp and dined in Arnold's tent, whereupon Gates issued general orders publicly countermanding Arnold's assignments for two newly arrived militia units, assignments that he himself had specifically ordered Arnold to issue.

"Placed . . . in the ridiculous light of presuming to give orders I had no right to do," Arnold promptly called at headquarters to request clarification. Not surprisingly, a quarrel ensued (which Varick gleefully described to Schuyler as "a little spirit"). In the end, Gates acknowledged the error and promised to rectify it; but he failed to do so. By the time the army moved north to fortify the ground chosen by General Kosciusko, Arnold was fuming, the rumor mill was relentlessly grinding, and Varick and Livingston were regaling their general in Albany with every delicious detail. For his part, Schuyler did nothing to moderate the young men's mischief-making or to remind them of their mission. Quite the contrary, he egged them on.

The new camp was situated on Bemis's Heights, a high bluff (named after a local tavern keeper) that overlooked the Hudson River. By the time Arnold's division arrived, General Kosciusko was already erecting artillery emplacements along the edge of the escarpment to prevent Burgoyne's army from passing along the river road one hundred feet below. Denied the use of the road, the British would be forced to mount the heights and attempt to advance inland, which Kosciusko proposed to thwart by constructing an extensive U-shaped breastwork extending west from the cliff across the rough, wooded terrain of the heights (see map, page 134). If Kosciusko's assumptions proved correct—and if the fortifications were completed in time—General Burgoyne would either have to give battle or turn back.

Arnold's division was stationed on the American left. He posted Daniel Morgan and Henry Dearborn about a quarter of a mile in front of his main body and beyond them his advance pickets, whose bivouac lay near the farm buildings of John Freeman, a Loyalist who was traveling with Burgoyne. The clearing at Freeman's farm, and at two smaller farms near the American headquarters, were hemmed in on all sides by woods and thick underbrush—tiny islands of openness in a dense forest wilderness.

Within hours of arriving in camp, Arnold was ordered out on a reconnaissance mission. He led his detachment north through thick scrub and nettles, plunging down banks of steep ravines and scrambling noisily up the other side. The woods glowed with early autumn colors—rusty oak, golden birch, burgundy sumac, and lush dark evergreens. Arnold discovered Burgoyne's army pitching its tents in a cleared field just east of the Freeman farm buildings, and after taking "a view of the enemy's encampment" and capturing eight prisoners, he returned to camp "without loss."

Then, for a full week, the two armies kept their distances. Given the terrain, enemy movements were nearly impossible to ascertain or predict, and persistent early morning fogs, "so dense you could in very truth grasp [them] with your outstretched hands," increased the army's sense of isolation and vulnerability. Expecting an attack at any moment, Arnold's men labored on the breastworks by day and slept on their arms at night, jumping at every alarm. Finally, shortly after dawn on September 17, Arnold was ordered forward to meet a British attack. Groping his way through the fog at the head of his division, he was advancing through the forest, virtually blind, when the fog lifted suddenly and he saw before him not the massed British right, as expected, but a couple of dozen enemy soldiers digging potatoes in a field. A single report from Morgan's rifle felled one of the hapless redcoats, and the rest took to their heels.

Two days later, September 19, after the fog lifted in mid-morning, scouts across the Hudson reported that the entire British army was on the move in three columns, one (the left) marching down the river road, the center and right ascending the heights. Arnold raised the alarm and his division prepared to meet them. They stood at the ready for an hour, with no orders forthcoming from General Gates. Finally Arnold dispatched a courier to headquarters to request permission for Morgan and Dearborn to advance and reconnoiter. Gates refused. The northern army, it appeared, would take the attack inside its fortifications.

Arnold was appalled. His raw militia could not be expected to withstand a frontal assault by British regulars, even with the protection of a breastwork. He was convinced they should advance and fight American-style, in the woods, where Morgan's and Dearborn's special troops could operate to best advantage. Another hour passed, and Arnold began to fear that the enemy was outflanking him to the west; but again Gates refused to permit a single scout to advance.*

Finally, toward noon, when a British cannonball landed at the edge of Arnold's camp, Gates gave permission for Morgan and Dearborn to advance. Within minutes Arnold could hear brisk firing to the north and the sound of Morgan's turkey call rallying his men in the forest. A courier brought news that Dearborn had been beaten back by the enemy's advance guard. Clearly, Arnold's troops were being attacked in force, giving him license to send his division into battle with or without Horatio Gates's permission.

Dispatching Enoch Poor's brigade forward in support of Dearborn, Arnold himself rode to an advance picket on high ground about half a mile behind the action, where he received a steady stream of couriers and ordered up reinforcements. The sound of cannon and musket fire grew heavier, black smoke rose above the treetops, and in the lulls Arnold could hear the screams of the wounded.

---

*I do not mean to imply that Gates was either cowardly or inept. He was an experienced officer, and his overall strategy of waiting Burgoyne out, within his fortifications, is regarded as judicious by a number of military historians.

Morgan and Dearborn were engaged in a deadly seesaw battle with the massed British right in a cleared field near the Freeman farm. At first Morgan's sharpshooters, firing from the woods, broke the enemy line, whereupon Dearborn's men burst from the trees "heroically, like veterans indeed," and pursued them to the far end of the clearing. There, under cover of their cannon, the British re-formed and charged with bayonets, driving Dearborn's infantry back into the forest. Having regained their initial positions, the two armies then repeated the deadly sequence—Morgan's rifles broke the British line, Dearborn drove them back and was driven back in turn—time and again, back and forth across the blood-soaked field, for four inconceivable, death-dealing hours.

Arnold, "infuriated by the conflict and maddened by Gates's refusal to send reinforcements, which he repeatedly called for, and knowing [his men] were meeting the brunt of the battle . . . seemed inspired with the fury of a demon." Surprisingly, he remained at his post, an uncharacteristic act of restraint that was entirely correct under the circumstances. Leadership on the field was not lacking with officers such as Morgan, Dearborn, Poor and Learned in command. What was needed was an overview of the battle and intelligence regarding the enemy, which Arnold was well positioned to provide. He was much more valuable to his men where he was, and he knew it.

Toward the end of the afternoon, Arnold perceived from the reports that several battalions from the enemy's center column were shifting toward the west to reinforce their beleagured right. Riding pell-mell to headquarters, he burst into Gates's presence and demanded troops to attack the weakened British center. At first Gates refused; and by the time he realized that Arnold was correct and ordered up the reinforcements, it was too late: Burgoyne's center had already been reinforced by Hessian troops from the river road. (One British military historian has asserted that if Arnold had gotten the troops when he asked for them, and succeeded in breaking the British center, Burgoyne would have been defeated then and there. He also states unequivocally that Benedict Arnold was the British Army's "most formidable opponent" in the war.)

Now Arnold's brave men, "who had something more at stake than fighting for sixpence per day," struggled on for two more hours against the hardened British right and center. Only at nightfall did both sides retire, leaving "the field . . . covered with dead almost for several acres." Thus ended what Major Dearborn correctly called "one of the greatest battles that ever was fought in America, and I

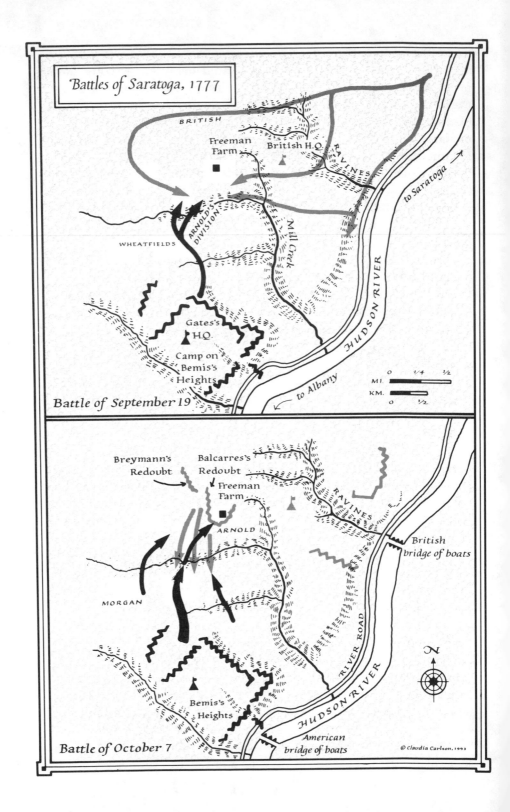

Battles of Saratoga, 1777

BRITISH

Freeman Farm

British H.O.

RAVINES

to Saratoga

ARNOLD'S DIVISION

Mill Creek

WHEATFIELDS

HUDSON RIVER

Gates's H.O.

Camp on Bemis's Heights

MI.   0   1/4   1/2

KM.   0   1/2

to Albany

Battle of September 19

Breymann's Redoubt

Balcarres's Redoubt

Freeman Farm

RAVINES

ARNOLD

British bridge of boats

MORGAN

RIVER ROAD

HUDSON RIVER

N

Bemis's Heights

American bridge of boats

© Claudia Carlson, 1993

Battle of October 7

trust we have convinced the British butchers that the cowardly Yankees can and, when there is a call for it, will fight.''

Arnold returned to his quarters exhausted but elated at his men's courage and conduct, and was there greeted by Richard Varick bearing yet another tale of the "Face of Clay," Horatio Gates. Dining in Gates's tent during the battle, Varick had managed to provoke an argument with his commander and resigned on the spot as muster-master general. His pique played right into Arnold's frustration over Gates's conduct of the battle, and impulsively Arnold invited the young man to join his staff as "supernumerary aide."

The American army rested that night to the sound of wolves howling among the bodies on the battlefield. Arnold arose before daybreak and prepared to renew the attack. The British had been badly bloodied; surely this was the moment to strike and finish the job. But "the day dawned thick and misty; fog obscured everything at a distance of twenty yards"; and General Gates stood pat. Neither did the British renew the attack, although scouts reported that they were building fortifications in the clearing at the Freeman farm.

For five days Arnold fumed, as his men resumed work on the fortifications and jumped for their guns at every small alarm. Good news arrived from the north: a small American militia detachment had surprised a British troop near Ticonderoga, freed a large body of prisoners and then made its way into the French lines before retiring. This stylish coup, which clearly demonstrated the vulnerability of Burgoyne's line of retreat, earned high acclaim for its bold leader, none other than John Brown. The whole camp on Bemis's Heights erupted in "a general Whooray," and Arnold's own division fired "thirteen cannon . . . for the thirteen United States," followed by "three cheers . . . which rang in the ears of the enemy"—and also, no doubt, in the ears of Benedict Arnold.

During the celebration, an Indian scout came into camp with a Tory prisoner, and General Gates "gave him to them for a while. They took him and buried him up to his neck and had their powwow around him, after that they had him up and laid him aside of a great fire and turned his head and feet awhile to the fire, hooting and hollowing [*sic*] around him, then he was handcuffed and sent to Albany gaol." A few days later the Indians "brought in twenty-seven regulars and Hessians, also Tories, who were given up to them to buffet"; but the following day, when the Indians presented Gates with two captured British regulars and one scalp, he paid them "twenty dollars for each prisoner but would give nothing for the scalp."

On September 25, five days after the battle, an astonished Arnold read in general orders that "Colonel Morgan's corps, not being in any brigade or division in this army, are to make returns and reports only to headquarters, from whence alone they are to receive their orders." Adding insult to injury, Gates's official report to Congress, which circulated in camp on the same day, noted "the general good behavior of the troops" during the battle but made no special mention of Arnold's brave division.

Arnold stormed into Gates's headquarters "in great warmth." His division alone had been engaged on the nineteenth, he protested; surely their "spirit and firmness in action" deserved special recognition. As for Morgan and Dearborn, their companies were, and always had been, an integral part of the division, and Gates had no right to remove them.

Gates must have been expecting a scene. Perhaps he had even rehearsed, as his performance seemed carefully calculated to drive his old friend over the edge. At first Gates professed not to know what the fuss was all about, blandly remarking that everybody knew that Arnold had resigned his commission in the Continental Army and was no longer on regular service, and that therefore his so-called command was merely a temporary detachment of special troops which Gates could dispose of as he wished.

Arnold, dumbfounded and embarrassed to learn in this manner (and in the presence of Gates's smirking staff) that his resignation had been accepted, could only sputter that Gates himself had given him command of the left, an argument which the general and the onlookers dismissed with contempt. Hostility Arnold could tolerate; ridicule he could not. Driven to the wall, he blurted out the words that Gates had been waiting to hear: he would leave camp forthwith, he announced, and appeal his case directly to Congress. Gates immediately acquiesced, remarking airily that his presence would soon become irrelevant anyway, since command of the left was to devolve on Benjamin Lincoln, a major general senior to Arnold who was on the verge of joining the northern army. It was the last straw: Lincoln was one of the officers who had been promoted over Arnold the previous February. "High words and gross language ensued, and Arnold retired in a rage."

He was trapped. With a decisive battle looming and victory perhaps within their grasp, Arnold desperately wished to remain with the army; but he knew that Gates would never back down. Deliverance came from an unexpected quarter. Enoch Poor and Benjamin Lincoln—the two men most likely to rejoice at Arnold's departure

(Poor because of their mutual history, Lincoln because of the awkwardness over seniority)—spearheaded a drive to persuade him to remain. All the officers of Poor's brigade signed and circulated a public address thanking Arnold "for his past service and particularly for his conduct during the late action and requesting his stay," while Lincoln personally offered to try "to bring about a reconciliation." Bowing to the will of his fellow officers, Arnold graciously consented to remain in camp.

At this juncture, one of Gates's aides dropped a hint that Arnold would be restored to command if he dismissed young Brockholst Livingston from his staff. (Gates was meanwhile plying Livingston's cousin, Henry Beekman Livingston, with dinner invitations and offers of "an advanced post on the left," which Henry B.—an admirer of Benedict Arnold—declined.) Arnold was furious at the suggestion, but he reluctantly accepted the young man's offer to resign when it became apparent it might actually do some good. Within hours of Livingston's departure (which was delayed by one day at Arnold's request, "lest it should appear like a concession"), Gates expressed in general orders "his grateful thanks to the officers and soldiers of General Poor's brigade and General Learned's brigade and [Morgan's] regiment of riflemen [and Dearborn's] corps of Light Infantry . . . for their gallant behavior in the action of the 19th instant, which will forever establish the fame and confirm the reputation of the arms of the United States." This was as far as he was prepared to go. Arnold informed Gates in writing of his decision "to sacrifice my feelings . . . and continue in the army at this critical juncture when my country needs every support," but there was no response, and command of the left remained with General Lincoln.

Surprisingly, General Gates's secretaries continued in daily orders to refer to the left as "Arnold's division," and Arnold himself on one occasion challenged General Lincoln's right to give orders to his men. Officially, however, he was a general in command of nothing, and his presence in the camp was superfluous. Richard Varick attributed Gates's conduct to jealousy, but nineteen-year-old Brockholst Livingston was probably closer to the truth: "The reason of the present disagreement between two old cronies is simply this," he reported to General Schuyler: *"Arnold is your friend."*

By the beginning of October, General Gates was well aware of his opponent's increasingly desperate situation. Burgoyne had suffered nearly twice as many casualties on September 19 as the Americans had (600 and 320 respectively), and enemy soldiers had been deserting in droves ever since while the American ranks swelled with new enlistments. Vastly outnumbered, Burgoyne would have to decide within days either to give battle or to turn back while there was still time to reach Canada before the onset of winter. "Perhaps," Gates speculated, "his despair may dictate to him to risk all upon one throw; he is an old gamester, and in his time has seen all chances." Burgoyne was a thorough professional, as were the troops he commanded, and if he chose to give battle the outcome was far from certain. American morale was extremely high, however, and Henry Dearborn boasted that "if Mr. Burgoyne and his army are not subdued this month, it will [not] be for want of spirit in us."

October 7 dawned clear and pleasant for once. Shortly after first light, Daniel Morgan's corps appeared from the woods, soaked to the skin and disgruntled after a night in the open. (The fact that these experienced woodsmen had become "bewildered in the woods" during a reconnoitering expedition behind enemy lines illustrates the extraordinary difficulty of the terrain.) Before they could finish breakfast, an aide from headquarters galloped into camp with orders to advance: the British were coming through the woods in approximately the same manner as on September 19, but in greater force.

Dearborn, Poor and Learned marched forward to meet them, while Morgan—who had learned a hard lesson on the nineteenth—circled into the deep woods to outflank them to the west. Soon Arnold could hear the first smacks of musket fire, and a courier rushed by with news of a major engagement in a wheatfield southwest of the Freeman farm. Arnold fumed and paced in helpless rage. This was *his* division, *his* battle, *his* war. Did anyone—Horatio Gates or the president of Congress—have a right to keep him from it? The answer, after an hour of suspense, was no. Arnold jumped on his horse and rode hell for leather toward the sounds of battle.

Bursting from the woods into the wheatfield, he beheld "a scene of complicated horror and exultation." The field was covered with dead and dying men, most of them British. Morgan's sharpshooters, firing from the cover of trees on the British flank, had taken a terrible toll. (General Burgoyne himself had received two shots, which passed harmlessly through his hat and waistcoat.) Now the enemy was in full retreat, and Arnold galloped to the head of Learned's brigade and shouted at the men to follow him in pursuit.

Plunging into the woods at the far end of the field, Arnold crashed through the underbrush after the fleeing redcoats and erupted into the clearing at the headquarters of the Freeman farm, which was now dominated by two mammoth, newly constructed British redoubts. Flourishing his sword above his head, Arnold raced toward the fortification on his right (called Balcarres's Redoubt, after its commander, Lord Balcarres), screaming at Learned's men to follow. He seemed transformed by battle. Giving himself up utterly to it, he began to operate outside himself, beyond conscious thought, becoming, as one of the men put it, "the very genius of war."

Raked by enemy musket and cannon fire, he and the men hurled themselves across the open space and attacked the redoubt head-on. Forced to fall back, Arnold reformed his men and charged again. Nearly the whole division was engaged by now, but the enemy inside their barricade stood firm as the Continentals attacked again and again, led by Arnold's inspired example.

From the corner of his eye, Arnold spied Henry Dearborn's corps forming on the far side of the battlefield for an assault on the second enemy redoubt (commanded by Hessian Colonel Heinrich von Breymann). He quickly wheeled his horse and galloped straight for them through the crossfire, reaching Dearborn unscathed but in a state of such heightened excitement that he inadvertently hit one of the men on the head with the flat of his sword. (The man survived, and Arnold could not remember the incident afterward. One historian has likened Arnold's ride to the charge of the Light Brigade at Balaklava: "Magnificent, but it is not war.")

Dearborn and Morgan attacked Breymann's redoubt from the front while Arnold led a small detachment around its left flank. As he entered the barricade from the side, his horse fell and pinned him to the ground. Dearborn's men had just come over the top. They rushed to his aid and extricated his leg—the same leg he had wounded at Quebec. It was crushed and bleeding copiously from a bullet wound. A litter appeared, and the genius of war was lifted onto it and carried back to the hospital on Bemis's Heights as the sounds of battle grew fainter and fainter with distance and the coming on of dark.

Chapter 12

"THE DICTATES OF MY HEART"

OCTOBER 1777 - MAY 1778

───────────────────────────────────────

The field hospital was all noise, pain and confusion. Arnold's leg was torn by musket fire and broken in several places, but he adamantly refused permission to amputate. Dawn brought news of victory: General Burgoyne had abandoned his fortifications at the Freeman farm and withdrawn across a deep ravine. The day turned warm. Through his shock and pain Arnold could hear intermittent firing, and during the afternoon General Lincoln was brought in, his leg wounded in a skirmish. That night, as a heavy rain beat on the hospital tents, Burgoyne's army began to slog north toward Ticonderoga, and the following day General Gates led his army in pursuit.

Benedict Arnold spent October 11, the first anniversary of the battle at Valcour Island, in transit to the Albany hospital. Chief surgeon James Thacher assessed his wounds, heeded his agony and sat up with him the first night. Soon the hospital was filled to overflowing with American and British casualties, keeping Dr. Thacher and his staff of "thirty surgeons and mates . . . constantly employed."

Richard Varick became a frequent visitor at Arnold's bedside. By the end of the week he was able to report that the British had been surrounded near Saratoga and forced to surrender their entire army. (Later, the two battles on Bemis's Heights came to be known as the "Battles of Saratoga," the name by which they are known today.) "Gentleman Johnny" Burgoyne himself arrived in Albany on October 21, during the season's first snowfall, and took up lodgings with Philip Schuyler. The American general, together with "his lady and daughters, [gave] their unfortunate guest a friendly and polite reception, characteristic of this noble spirited family," despite the fact that only a few days before Burgoyne's troops had burned to the ground their mansion at Saratoga. Burgoyne was due to sail soon for England, while his troops proceeded to a prison camp near Boston.

To Richard Varick, the American victory was marred by the fact that it would redound to the credit of the insufferable Gates. He was able to report, however, that on at least one social occasion in Albany, General Gates had been forced to listen politely while his opposite number, John Burgoyne, regaled the company with praise for Benedict Arnold's "bravery and military abilities, particularly in the action of the 19th [of September]."

Gates's triumph came on the heels of General Washington's crushing defeat at Brandywine Creek outside Philadelphia, which led to the ignominious evacuation of that city by an angry and embarrassed Congress. A small group of Gates's partisans—known as the "Conway Cabal," after its guiding spirit, Brigadier General Thomas Conway—was thereby emboldened to instigate an effort in Congress to have Gates replace Washington as commander in chief. Whether or not General Gates directly encouraged the cabal, its very existence puffed him up to the point where he deliberately affronted his old comrade in arms by failing to report to him officially on the outcome of the northern campaign.

Washington, well aware of the machinations of the cabal, refused to rise to the bait. He confined himself to a mild reprimand; but he let Gates know precisely how he felt by singling out his rivals, Arnold and Lincoln, for rewards of a very personal nature: each received from the commander in chief an elegant set of French epaulets and sword knots sent him by "a gentleman in France . . . to be disposed of to any friends I should choose"; and on the day the surrender at Saratoga was announced to the main army, the passwords in camp were "Lincoln" and "Arnold."

To receive such particular approbation from General Washington was a high honor. Even more soothing to Arnold's wounded sensibilities, perhaps, was the restoration of his seniority by the Congress of the United States. But his victory had been purchased at an awful price: his wounded leg refused to heal. Week after week, as the other beds in the Albany hospital slowly emptied, he lay in agony, staring at the walls and wondering if he would ever fight, or sit a horse, or even walk, again. One day he appeared to be on the mend, the next he relapsed into weakness and excruciating pain. A gout attack in November stalled his recovery completely. In January he sat up for the first time, but the wounds reopened and he was back to where he had started three months before. For a man who loathed inactivity and shunned introspection, it was a living hell.

Meanwhile, the revolution itself seemed on the verge of foundering. General Washington's army, decimated by desertion and battle, ravaged by sickness, ill clad, ill fed and apparently friendless in its own country, withdrew into winter quarters at Valley Forge as though to its deathbed. Congress spent the winter in exile in York, Pennsylvania, where it distinguished itself in Arnold's eyes by voting against the establishment of peacetime pensions for Continental officers. Horatio Gates, who had refused to serve under the commander in chief, accepted instead a congressional appointment as chairman of the Board of War. One of his first acts was to order a midwinter invasion of Canada under the leadership of a twenty-year-old French volunteer, Continental Major General Marie Joseph Paul Yves Roch Gilbert du Motier, Marquis de Lafayette. The young man reached Albany in February expecting to set off at once with 2500 troops. He quickly learned from generals Arnold, Schuyler and Lincoln that the troops did not exist, nor did the provisions, forage and arms that Gates had promised him. Lafayette reluctantly recommended that the invasion be called off, which embarrassed Gates and caused one of his aides to try to shift blame for the cancellation to Arnold's machinations. "The malice of this man is so bitter," the aide wrote, "[that he] reminds one of a taper, sinking in its socket, which emits a feeble gleam just before it expires."

Arnold was not above influencing the young Frenchman against Gates—whom he called *"the greatest poltroon in the world,* and many other genteel qualifications"—but the politicizing of the army, dramatically demonstrated by the machinations of the Conway Cabal, was repugnant to him, and he regarded Congress's mistreatment of its officer corps as scandalous. Most Continental officers had abandoned prosperous businesses, farms and professions in order to serve their country; now it appeared their sacrifices would be neither compensated nor recognized. As another of Arnold's hospital visitors (Washington's young aide-de-camp Alexander Hamilton) reported, the entire officer corps, already frustrated by congressional inconsistency in matters of promotion, seniority and reimbursement for expenses, now appeared on the verge of resigning en masse.

As for the rank and file, they had received no pay since August, and there was not "one whole shirt to a brigade. For God's sake," one officer pleaded, "if you can't give us anything else, give us linen that we many be enabled to rescue the poor worthy fellows from the vermin which are now devouring them." Two men were killed during a mutiny that took place in Enoch Poor's brigade—the brave men Arnold had led against the redoubt at Freeman's farm on October 7.

For Arnold, whose inner reservoir of strength had already been drained by weeks of intense physical pain and frustration, such events perhaps loomed larger than they might have otherwise. No longer could he brush them aside and lose himself in action. Hemmed in by the four walls of his hospital room, entirely at the mercy of his own thoughts, he became prey to a painful question that inevitably rose up from the depths: were the Continental Army and the Congress of the United States worthy of his sacrifices and exertions?

Arnold was neither the first nor the last Continental officer to ask himself this question—even the great Washington had his dark moments. But he *was* the only Continental officer to contemplate the dire condition of the troops and the pettiness and ineptitude of the Congress and answer it by turning his coat. He did not take that giant step for two more years, but the mental preparation for it surely began in the dark early days of 1778.

The explanation is simple: most of Arnold's fellow officers were sustained by a deep commitment to the crusade for independence, which permitted them to sweep all obstacles aside. Arnold had no such commitment. Most of the others operated from a deep personal sense of honor, which Arnold entirely lacked. What Benedict Arnold wanted was a hero's reward: a secure place at the top of the heap in a peacetime world. Nothing less would do, and if the war was lost he would be left with nothing. The inner satisfaction of having fought honorably and well in a just cause would never compensate this man for a term in a British military prison. His personal crusade was far more important to him than that of his country. So far they had been successfully fused. Now, perhaps, it began to occur to him that the two might not be identical after all.

Three months of churning speculation, physical agony and deep uncertainty reduced Arnold to a lonely, fragile and vulnerable man. He found his thoughts returning to Betsy Deblois, the Boston girl who had captured his heart the previous spring. Betsy had since become engaged to another man, but her mother had forbidden the marriage.

Perhaps, he felt, there was hope. For weeks the thirty-six-year-old hero lay in his bed trying to drum up the courage to write a love letter to a sixteen-year-old girl. He dispatched it on April 8:

> Twenty times have I taken up my pen to write to you, and as often has my trembling hand refused to obey the dictates of my heart, a heart which has often been calm and serene amidst the clashing of arms . . . [but which] trembles with diffidence and the fear of giving offence when it attempts to address you. . . . Neither time, absence, misfortunes nor your cruel indifference have been able to efface the deep impressions your charms have made. Will you doom a heart so true, so faithful, to languish in despair? . . . Dear Betsy, suffer that heavenly bosom (which surely cannot know itself the cause of misfortune without a sympathetic pang) to expand with friendship at least, and let me know my fate. If a happy one, no man will strive more to deserve it. If, on the contrary, I am doomed to despair, my latest breath will be to implore the blessing of Heaven on the idol and only wish of my soul.

For once Betsy replied promptly; her answer was no.

"You entreat me to solicit no further for your affections," Arnold responded:

> Consider, dear madam, when you urge impossibilities I cannot obey, as well might you wish me to exist without breathing as cease to love you. . . . Consult your own happiness and, if incompatible with mine, forget there is so unhappy a wretch, for let me perish if I would give you one moment's pain. . . . I hope a line in answer will not be deemed the least infringement on the decorum due to your sex, which I wish you strictly to observe.

She never answered the letter;* but all of Arnold's hopes for the future seemed to have become fixated on her, and he refused to give up his suit. His blind obsession with Betsy is mute evidence that he was teetering on the brink of an emotional abyss; her persistent silence seemed bound to push him over the edge.

Arnold's correspondence with Betsy was conducted from Middletown, Connecticut, where he sojourned for two months after his release from the hospital, visiting his children at school and under-

---

*Betsy had many subsequent suitors but never married. She lived into her eighties.

going further surgery to remove "some loose splinters of bone remaining in the leg, which will not be serviceable until they are extracted. This will be a work of time," he informed General Washington, "perhaps two and possibly five or six months. The callus is strongly formed in my leg. I never enjoyed a better state of health, and it is with the utmost regret I find myself at present unable to repair to headquarters and take the command your Excellency has been so good as to reserve for me."

He continued on to New Haven on May 4, where he received a hero's welcome. "Several Continental and militia officers, the cadet company, and a number of respectable inhabitants from this place" escorted him from the outskirts of town to a ceremony on the Green and a thirteen-gun salute. When the cheering died, however, there was only his sister Hannah and the family account books, neither of which proved soothing to his troubled soul. He lingered less than a week, arriving by coach at the Continental camp at Valley Forge on May 20.

General Washington's apparently moribund army—more than one quarter of whom had perished during the winter from illness, malnutrition and exposure—had been resuscitated at the eleventh hour by His Majesty Louis XVI, King of France. Louis had been a child of five in 1759 when his father's army was driven out of America by Great Britain. Eager since the outset of the revolution to support the thirteen colonies—and, in the process, to humiliate his country's ancient rival and regain his colonies in Canada and the Caribbean—Louis and his ministers had prudently waited to commit themselves until the fledgling United States of America demonstrated its military and political viability. The victory at Saratoga provided that proof, and twenty-four hours after learning of Burgoyne's surrender, the government of France extended formal diplomatic recognition to the new country and prepared to enter the war at its side.

France's entry into the war promised not only large infusions of troops and money but also a significant reduction of pressure, since the British would have to divert troops and ships from the thirteen colonies to protect their valuable holdings in the West Indies. Sir Henry Clinton, the new British commander in chief, was known to be on the verge of withdrawing from Philadelphia in order to concentrate his strength in New York City, and a British peace commission was on its way to America with offers to fulfill all the colonies' demands short of independence. (Because of the latter stipulation, Congress refused to meet with the commissioners, who returned home empty-handed.)

The arrival of spring, therefore, brought a sharp rise in morale in the threadbare army that sprawled over the hilly woods above the Schuylkill River, eighteen miles northwest of Philadelphia. Daily drills and bayonet practices conducted by General Friedrich von Steuben, a Prussian volunteer, instilled a new sense of confidence in the rank and file, and the officers' spirits were lifted by congressional approval of seven-year pensions (which fell far short of the lifetime half-pay that General Washington had requested, but it was better than nothing). By the time Arnold arrived, the camp was shaking off its doldrums and bustling with plans for the spring campaign.

Many of the men at Valley Forge had fought with Arnold on Bemis's Heights, and he received the boisterous, heartfelt hero's welcome that was his due. General Washington greeted him warmly and ushered him into his inner circle, which included the Marquis de Lafayette, aide-de-camp Alexander Hamilton, Major General Nathanael Greene (who had served at Washington's side throughout the war and become one of his most trusted advisers) and Brigadier General Henry Knox, the army's chief of artillery. (It was Knox who had brought the cannon from Ticonderoga to Boston, across the Berkshire Mountains, during the winter of 1776; and it was Knox's wife who had introduced Arnold to Elizabeth Deblois.)

But Arnold received the troops' salute from a seat in a carriage, and when he alighted to enter the commander in chief's headquarters, he did so on crutches. There was no place for a crippled general in the coming campaign, no matter how great his talents. While Greene, Knox, Henry Dearborn and Arnold's other comrades looked forward to commanding wings, brigades and companies, he was assigned to remain behind in Philadelphia as military commandant after the British withdrawal.

It was Philadelphia's dubious distinction to harbor the largest population of Tory Loyalists of any city in the country. In the aftermath of the British occupation, it would be the task of the American military and civil authorities (including the Pennsylvania Council and the Congress of the United States, which were supposed to share power in the capital city) to cooperate in healing the financial, political and social wounds of the city's deeply divided citizenry. The post of military commandant, therefore, would demand political acuity, sound judgment, tact and absolute probity.

Under these circumstances, it is little wonder that Arnold's appointment set alarm bells ringing among his enemies in Congress and the army. Their warnings proved more apt than anyone could have predicted: for somewhere along the road to Valley Forge, or perhaps immediately after his arrival there, something inside Arnold had snapped. Seven months of unremitting disillusionment and physical agony had taken their toll. Perhaps the final nail in the coffin of his rectitude was the sight of his old comrades going off to war without him. Perhaps it was the continued silence of Betsy Deblois. Perhaps it was the odor of financial ruin wafting up from Hannah's account books. Or perhaps it was the visit he received at Valley Forge from his old friend John Dyer Mercier, the Quebec merchant whose support for the American invasion in 1775 had cost him his fortune and a term in a British prison. Mercier, exiled and nearly destitute, called to ask Arnold's help in finding employment "in some office in which he can be of service to his country and in some measure retrieve his losses." John Mercier was living proof of a stark reality: this war ruined people. Perhaps it was time for Benedict Arnold to start looking out for himself.

He now consciously severed any shred of devotion that had ever tied him to the cause of his country. Major surgery was not required; only a quick, painless snip to rid himself of an attachment that had once served his purposes and sanctified his actions, but which now appeared an encumbrance. It did not hurt, and the change was barely noticeable. Arnold had no need to alter his rhetoric or his public actions, which were always convincing. The only difference was inside himself, where the purely cosmetic function of his patriotism could finally be acknowledged.

Without batting an eye, Arnold took the loyalty oath now required of all Continental Army officers:

> I Benedict Arnold Major General do acknowledge the United States of America to be Free, Independent and Sovereign States, and declare that the people thereof owe no allegiance or obedience to George the Third, King of Great Britain; and I renounce, refuse and abjure any allegiance or obedience to him; and I do swear that I will, to the utmost of my power, support, maintain and defend the said United States against the said King George the Third, his heirs and successors, and his or their abettors, assistants and adherents, and will serve the said United States in the office of Major General which I now hold, with fidelity, according to the best of my skill and understanding.

He knew that it was not worth the paper it was written on (less perhaps; the army was very short of paper in 1778). Arnold did not yet contemplate treason, only larceny. But he did, from this moment, begin to commit treason of another sort, against his own best self.

Chapter 13

"AN INSATIABLE THIRST FOR RICHES"

JUNE-SEPTEMBER 1778

More than three thousand Philadelphia Loyalists abandoned their homes to accompany the departing British army into exile in New York. This massive exodus took nearly a month, which gave the city's soon-to-be commandant plenty of time to make his preparations to fleece the city.

When a merchant named Robert Shewell appeared at Arnold's Valley Forge headquarters to request a pass for his ship *Charming Nancy* to sail from Philadelphia loaded with "salt, linens, woolens, glass, nails, loaf sugar and tea etc."—all rare commodities in wartime America, bound to fetch a handsome price in any Continental port— Arnold complied, despite the fact that Congress was on the verge of placing an embargo on all shipping lying at the city's wharves pending an investigation of each vessel's cargo and the political leanings of its owner. Robert Shewell's political leanings were extremely suspect—two days after his conference with Arnold, he was publicly challenged on the parade ground at Valley Forge "by some officers who knew him, or knew his character" and expelled from the camp— but Benedict Arnold did not care. He granted the pass and invested forthwith in a number of trading vessels belonging to Shewell and his partners (one was christened *General Arnold*), culminating in August with the purchase of one quarter of the cargo of *Charming Nancy* herself, then lying in the Continental port of Egg Harbor, New Jersey.

Arnold and his new aide-de-camp David Franks concocted another potentially lucrative scheme whereby Franks, who expected to enter Philadelphia a day or two ahead of his commandant, would ferret out and begin to buy up "European and East-India goods in the city of Philadelphia to any amount," and to keep Arnold's participation in the purchases a secret even from "his most intimate acquaintance." The market in such scarce merchandise would be strictly regulated once civil authority was restored in the city, but in the meantime, Franks could use his position to lay hands on as many goods as possible for his general to peddle when the price was right.

The plan was aborted when Pennsylvania Congressman Joseph Reed called on Arnold during his first morning in the city, June 19, to insist that he temporarily close all shops and sign an official proclamation that "all persons having European, East or West-India goods, iron, leather, shoes, wines and provisions of every kind" should turn them over to the town major "in order that the quartermaster, commissary and clothier generals may contract for such goods as are wanted for the use of the army." Reed was a powerful man—scion of a prominent Philadelphia family, a London-educated lawyer and a former adjutant to General Washington—and he was not to be denied. Arnold closed the shops, signed the proclamation and quietly rescinded his instructions to David Franks.

This was only a minor setback, since the above-mentioned clothier general, James Mease, was already in Arnold's pocket. Mease, his deputy William West, Jr., and Benedict Arnold signed a secret compact on June 23 to sell any goods purchased by the clothier general's office for the use of the army and subsequently found unnecessary "for that purpose . . . for the joint equal benefit of the subscribers"— in other words, to buy at low army prices, sell high on the private market and pocket the difference.

An even more ambitious plot hatched in Arnold's brain when, in mid-July, a French fleet arrived in American waters and took a position off the entrance to New York harbor. Anticipating an early attack on British-held Manhattan Island, Arnold entered into a secret agreement with John Livingston (brother-in-law of the late Richard Montgomery) to buy up goods in New York City "to amount of ten, twenty or thirty thousand pounds sterling . . . salt and nails in particular, [and] every kind of dry goods," and have them "carted to some out-of-way places in the middle of town" until the Continentals recaptured the city, when Arnold would use his military position to "grant a protection" for the goods and share in the mammoth profits.

None of these financial schemes was precisely against the law, or rather, none was against any precise law. Freedom of trade was the cornerstone of the independent United States of America, and the Congress was neither willing nor able to curb any individual constituent's inalienable right to feather his nest. Before the war, smuggling had been regarded as a patriotic act; now, the ex-smugglers saw no reason to begin drawing fine lines between legal and illegal trade. Laissez-faire was their most sacred precept, and the Congress did not dare to tamper with it.

Some individual congressmen, however, argued that just because an action was legal did not mean that it was right. "How difficult is it," queried Henry Laurens, the new president of Congress, "for a rich or covetous man to enter heartily into the Kingdom of Patriotism?"; and a New Hampshire member declared, "He who increases in wealth in such times as the present must be an enemy to his country, be his pretentions what they may." Along with the commander in chief, they deplored the "speculation, peculation and . . . insatiable thirst for riches" that flourished in wartime America.

Benedict Arnold had no use for such niceties, although he was sufficiently aware of them to insist that John R. Livingston agree, in writing, that if their secret plan became public, "whatever misfortune both or either of our characters may suffer [as a result], every support and assistance shall be given them, by each other."* In the absence of a personal ethical code, Arnold fought for only one right: his own, to cover his retreat and make sure he would not go down alone.

Long before any of his financial eggs had time to hatch, Arnold began to spend lavishly on the temptations offered by the country's most urbane and cultured metropolis. Philadelphia high society barely paused to catch its breath between the round of festive farewell parties for the British and the whirl of events that marked the return of Congress and the American army. "We have a great many balls and entertainments," Mrs. Robert Morris reported to her mother, "[and] even our military gentlemen here are too liberal to make any distinctions between Whig and Tory ladies—if they make

---

*General Washington did not attack New York, the British remained there for another five years and nothing came of the Arnold-Livingston scheme.

any, it's in favor of the latter, such, strange as it may seem, is the way those things are conducted at present in this city. It originates at headquarters," i.e., with commandant Benedict Arnold.

Arnold moved into the old Penn mansion, an elegant brick edifice on High Street occupied most recently by the British commander in chief, and began to entertain. His official guest list included ambassadors, congressmen and local politicians, and his unofficial list was aimed at Philadelphia high society. After more than two years of army life, Arnold seized eagerly on every luxury and social perquisite his position offered. In this self-indulgent mood, he preferred women dressed in silk to those clad in Quaker black, and he cared not a fig for their politics. His guests were served excellent food and fine wine, with a liveried footman behind each chair. His two aides-de-camp, the foppish David Franks and New York aristocrat Matthew Clarkson, featured prominently in Arnold's social life, and his sister Hannah came from New Haven (with seven-year-old Harry) to serve as hostess. Arnold dwelt in splendor at home and abroad, driving through Philadelphia's cobblestone streets in an elegant coach-and-four.

His conspicuous pursuit of the high life inevitably drew down on his head the wrath of the man who became largely responsible for the return of civil authority to Philadelphia after the British occupation: Congressman Joseph Reed. Reed personified the bitter resentment and fear that had festered in Philadelphia's Whig population during its nine-month exile, and he and his political cohorts returned to the city determined to ferret out anything that smacked of Toryism. On a more personal level, they resented the gaiety and luxury of high society, which jarred their wartime (and, in many cases, Quaker) sensibilities and reminded them of the worst aspects of the British occupation.

According to Reed and his ilk, the physical damage inflicted on their city during the occupation was nothing compared to the moral devastation wreaked upon its citizens, particularly "the females . . . [who had taken up the] new [London] fashions . . . the most absurd, ridiculous and preposterous you can conceive. . . . Their caps exceed any of the sarcastic prints you have seen, and their hair is dressed with the assistance of wool, etc., in such a manner as to appear too heavy to be supported by their necks . . . many people do not hesitate in supposing that most of the young ladies who were in the city with the enemy and wear the present fashionable dresses have purchased them at the expense of their virtue. It is agreed on all hands that the British officers played the devil with the girls."

At the Mischianza, a splendid fête held just before the British left town, dashing enemy officers dressed as medieval knights (the Knight of the Blended Rose, the Knight of the Burning Mountain and so forth) had jousted before the ladies, some of whom were garbed in scandalously exotic Turkish costumes designed by the dashing British Captain John André, who had also masterminded the "regatta, tilts and tournaments, carousel, processions through triumphal arches, dancing, exhibition of fireworks, music and feast." Philadelphia had never seen anything like it, and after the departure of Captain André and his fellow officers, the local girls languished and pined for the silks and ribbons, the flowers and decorations, the banquets and pageantry, indeed for the whole past year of "halcyon days, forever dear," when gallant redcoats ruled the town and "all was frolic, all was gay."

As a result, many of the returning Whigs—particularly those who advocated the simpler style of living of the city's large Quaker population—came to view any indulgence in merriment or display of luxury as an indication of secret British sympathies, which added a dangerous dash of puritanical fervor to an already bubbling stew of political distrust and animosity. In addition to the usual confiscations of Tory property, several houses of suspected Tories were attacked by gangs, and a sort of vigilante group called the Patriotic Society was formed "to support each other in disclosing and bringing to justice all Tories within their knowledge." One of its founding members was Joseph Reed.

In this highly charged atmosphere, even the most tactful and sensitive commandant was bound to get singed. Benedict Arnold got cremated. Apparently blind to the danger, he unrepentantly reveled in his role in high society and entertained whomever he pleased. In short, he became a prominently placed, brightly colored moving target which inevitably came into the sights of Joseph Reed.

(It must be reported that Arnold's expansiveness was not entirely squandered on himself. Dr. Joseph Warren, the Boston radical who had commissioned him to capture Ticonderoga in May 1775, had been killed one month later at the battle of Bunker Hill. During the intervening three years, Congress had voted funds to educate only the oldest of Warren's three orphaned children. Arnold now attempted to persuade them to include the other two children. "If they decline it," he wrote to the children's guardian, Mercy Scollay, "I make no doubt of a handsome collection by private subscription. At all events I will provide for them in a manner suitable to their birth and the grateful sentiment I shall ever feel for the memory of my friend." He sent Miss Scollay $500 to clothe the younger son "handsomely" and enter him in the best school in Boston. This uncharacteristic altruism sprang from two sources, first and foremost the trauma of his own aborted education, which remained strong in his soul. But he also seized on the cause of the Warren children as a means of challenging Congress. "To a generous mind," he wrote Miss Scollay after six months of congressional inaction, "there can be no greater reward than the agreeable reflection of having protected those innocents from the affliction of poverty, and rearing them up to usefulness *when deserted by their ungrateful country.*")

Arnold's new life was extremely expensive, and unfortunately none of his financial chickens had yet produced an egg. *Charming Nancy* offered the greatest hope, but in early July Arnold learned that she had been captured off the coast of New Jersey by an American privateer and claimed as an enemy prize. (The taking of prizes by both privateers and navy vessels was standard practice, with the crews traditionally sharing in the profits.) *Charming Nancy*'s captain hastened to protest that she was an American ship rather than an enemy; but the New Jersey Court of Admiralty, after considering Robert Shewell's questionable politics, might well deem her an enemy and award both ship and cargo to the captors. This would be a disaster for Arnold on two fronts: the loss of the money, and also his own reputation, which would suffer if Shewell were legally declared an enemy by the court. He wrote a letter to New Jersey Judge John Imlay requesting him to ensure the safety of the ship until the case could be heard and vouching for Robert Shewell's good character and "upright intentions."

Restless and anxious, Arnold suddenly wanted to be out of Philadelphia. *Charming Nancy* was not the only reason. The fact was that, for all its perquisites, the job of commandant was fiercely frustrating. The military commandant in Philadelphia was expected to cooperate with both the Congress of the United States and the Supreme Executive Council of the State of Pennsylvania, two bodies currently locked in a titanic battle over precedence and jurisdiction. Not only did their interests diverge, their orders were frequently contradictory.

The underlying problem was that Congress, lacking any power of taxation, was utterly dependent on the goodwill of the several states for money, men and matériel to carry on the war. This meant that large and populous states like Pennsylvania had enormous leverage, and in the name of states' rights their leaders could challenge congressional directives and ignore congressional rulings with virtual impunity. Congress was not entirely blameless; too often its resentment and frustration boiled over into petty bickering and personal invective, and too seldom did it stand its ground in the name of a higher, common goal. In short, when the two sides weren't wrangling over power and responsibility, they were trumpeting about respect and dignity, often in a highly unrespectable and undignified manner.

It did not help that the Supreme Executive Council of the State of Pennsylvania also served as Congress's landlord. The two bodies met on different floors of the Pennsylvania State House (now called Independence Hall), which had served the British as a prison and hospital and been left by them "in a most filthy and sordid condition." By midsummer, Congress and the Council were back in their quarters, and the charges of fraud, chicanery, bias and arrogance (some of which were true) once again reverberated up and down the grand staircase. Congress and the Pennsylvania Council fought over every detail of civil and military administration, transforming the most mundane issues into cosmic do-or-die questions of principle. In the process, vast opportunities were lost and a fair number of men got torn to bits.

Benedict Arnold was one of them. Already a controversial figure before he reached Philadelphia, he was distrusted by powerful men on both sides of the states' rights controversy. As Philadelphia commandant, he was obliged to please everybody and doomed to please nobody. For a man with no talent for politics, it was sheer hell.

It was also extremely frustrating for a military man. A single example will suffice. When the British left Philadelphia in June and crossed New Jersey into New York, General Washington's army shadowed them all the way. (On June 28, at the battle of Monmouth, Continental regulars for the first time traded bayonet charge for bayonet charge with their British counterparts—Steuben's drills paying off.) By mid-August, with the British bottled up on Manhattan Island and the French fleet off Sandy Hook, the commander in chief was poised to attack the city. He ordered Arnold to transfer to the main army all the Continental troops then posted in Philadelphia, first replacing them with Pennsylvania militia. Quick action was crucial, and Arnold immediately sent a formal request to the Supreme Executive Council to call up the militia. The Council replied by sending Arnold a copy of a new state law requiring that all requests for militia come directly from Congress. His request to Congress for the requisite order was referred to the Board of War. *Two weeks later,* the board approved the request and Congress forwarded its report to the Pennsylvania Council—by which time General Washington had been forced to cancel the attack on New York for lack of manpower.

Little wonder that Benedict Arnold grew restless in Philadelphia. He longed for combat; but despite his best efforts, the muscles in his leg still refused to carry his weight, and he could neither stand nor sit a horse. He conceived of a way out: a congressional appointment to "command of the navy, to which my being wounded would not be so great an objection." He wrote to General Washington, ostensibly asking for advice but in effect requesting his endorsement. In response, the commander in chief protested his ignorance "in marine matters" and expressed a vague wish that "abilities like yours may not be lost to the public." Arnold's naval career died aborning.

Frustrated at every turn, and with his cash position deteriorating with each expensive day, Arnold entered into yet another highly speculative, highly questionable financial conspiracy. A Connecticut sailor named Gideon Olmstead called at headquarters in mid-September to ask Arnold's help in obtaining justice for himself and three companions who had been impressed into service aboard the British sloop *Active* and had seized the ship from her nine-man crew off the New Jersey coast. As they headed into port with their prize, a Pennsylvania State privateer came alongside, escorted them into Philadelphia and claimed the *Active* and her cargo for the state. Olmstead and his fellows naturally protested, and the case was now scheduled to be heard by the Pennsylvania Court of Admiralty, hardly a disinterested body.

The sailor and the commandant immediately struck a secret deal whereby Arnold, in exchange for a one-half interest in the *Active* and her cargo, pledged to pay Olmstead's legal fees and to apply what political pressure he could on his and his fellows' behalf. Arnold further agreed that once the case was won, he would return his shares after deducting the amount of his loan, plus interest: his first venture into the realms of shylocking and influence peddling.

His willingness to cross this line, and to enter into such a financially doubtful and politically perilous scheme, is easily explained: sometime during the weeks leading up to Gideon Olmstead's visit, Arnold had met and fallen in love with eighteen-year-old Margaret Shippen, a Philadelphia belle from the upper reaches of high society. In the first flush of love, he persuaded her family that he had "acquired something handsome." It was now imperative to make good on his boast.

The Shippen family had been prominent in Philadelphia society, finance and politics for four generations. Peggy's father, Edward Shippen, Jr., was a London-educated lawyer who had declared at the beginning of the war that the duty of every "moderate thinking man [was to] remain silent and inactive." Suspected of Toryism and forbidden by the Pennsylvania Council to travel beyond the borders of the state, he had moved his family to the country for the duration, restoring them to their handsome "double bay house, lavishly furnished," on Fourth Street only after the British entered the city. Peggy and her sisters had attended the many gay parties and entertainments given by the dashing redcoats and become thoroughly Anglicized in their manners and dress, if not in their politics.

Nearly twenty years Arnold's junior, Peggy was everything he wanted in a wife: young, pretty, vivacious and solidly upper class. A delicious combination of the provocative and the complaisant, she appeared at the same time both docile and sensual. Finally, she was extremely adept in the ancient female art of permitting the men in her life to believe that they were always right.

Philadelphia society found the May-December courtship diverting—"Cupid has given our little general a more mortal wound than all the host of Britons could," Mrs. Robert Morris wrote to her mother—and even Peggy's intimate circle assumed an air of amused detachment. "The gentle Arnold, where is he, how does he, and when is he like to convert our little Peggy?" her sister's friend Elizabeth Tilghman wrote to inquire. "They say she intends to surrender soon. I thought the fort would not hold out long. Well, after all, there is nothing like perseverence and a regular attack."

Arnold "la[id] close siege" to Miss Shippen throughout the autumn and into winter. He was as deeply in love as he was capable of being; but unsurprisingly, this did not mean that he knew, or even sensed, Peggy's true nature. (Neither did she, for that matter.) All he knew was that she satisfied every facet of his desires: social, sexual and emotional. What Arnold needed was a woman to admire him, to accept and support him unquestioningly and to sanction all his thoughts and actions—in other words, a young and inexperienced girl. When he found her, he fell quickly and passionately in love and pursued her with an all-consuming ardor.

His craving for such affection, such devotion, was so intense that the objects of his affection were virtually interchangeable. At least one of his ardent love letters to Peggy Shippen was a verbatim transcription (for more than half of its 513 words) of a letter he had written to Betsy Deblois five months before.

"Twenty times have I taken up my pen to write to you, and as often has my trembling hand refused to obey the dictates of my heart," he wrote to Peggy in September, as he had written to Betsy in April. "A union of hearts is undoubtedly necessary to happiness," he continued, but give me leave to observe that true and permanent happiness is seldom the effect of an alliance founded on a romantic passion, where fancy governs more than judgment. Friendship and esteem, founded on the merit of the object, is the most certain basis to build a lasting happiness upon, and where there is a tender and ardent passion on one side, and friendship and esteem on the other, the heart (unlike yours) must be callous to every tender sentiment if the taper of love is not lighted up at the flame . . .

"Consult your own happiness," he enjoined in peroration, "and if incompatible, forget there is so unhappy a wretch, for may I perish if I would give you one moment's inquietude. . . . Whatever my fate may be . . . my latest breath will be to implore the blessing of heaven on the idol and only wish of my soul."

Peggy Shippen deserved better, although nobody, including herself, suspected that yet.

MARGARET SHIPPEN

Pencil drawing by Captain John André, 1778.

Courtesy of the Yale University Art Gallery.

Chapter 14

"I AM NOT TO BE INTIMIDATED"

OCTOBER 1778-MAY 1779

Arnold's courtship of Edward Shippen's daughter confirmed his image in certain circles as "a pert Tory." Joseph Reed and his vigilantes refocused their sights accordingly.

Their opening gun in what proved a protracted and virulent war was fired on the morning of October 5, when a young Pennsylvania militia sergeant appeared in Arnold's office to complain of mistreatment at the hands of aide-de-camp David Franks. While on guard duty at headquarters, the sergeant reported, he had been ordered by Franks to fetch a barber to dress his hair. It was only after obeying the order that he realized that the errand did not become the dignity of a freeman and militia volunteer and decided to lodge a protest with his commandant.

It is impossible to believe that the protest originated with the young sergeant or that Benedict Arnold was not aware of its source: the sergeant's father, Timothy Matlack, secretary to the Pennsylvania Council and a close political ally of Joseph Reed.* Characteris-

---

*Matlack was a lapsed Quaker, having been expelled from the Society of Friends, reportedly for gambling.

tically, Arnold refused to heed the danger, and he dismissed the sergeant with some tart observations on military discipline and obedience.

Later that day he received a letter from the young man's irate parent. "The severity of military discipline [in cases] where no important end is to be answered by it must make every freeman feel!" Matlack wrote. "At a time when you were one of the militia," he queried, "what would have been *your* feelings had an aide of *your* commanding officer ordered *you* to call *his barber*? . . . Freemen will be hardly brought to submit to such indignities." And lest Arnold miss the point, Matlack reminded him that "it is upon [the militia's] *will* more than upon the force of *any law* we are to depend for their assistance in the time of need."

If ever a situation called for tact and forbearance, this was it; but Matlack's sermon was more than Benedict Arnold—the Continental Army's most renowned commander of militia—could bear. "I have served a whole campaign under the command of a gentleman who was not known as a soldier until after I had been some time a brigadier," he recounted (in total disregard for the truth: Horatio Gates had served as a combat officer in Virginia before Arnold ever left Norwich). "My feelings were hurt . . . [and] the event proved unfortunate to me, but I have the satisfaction to think I rendered some service to my country." As for young Matlack's so-called dignity, "the respect due to the citizen is by no means to be paid to the soldier any further than his rank entitles him to it. . . . [As] an orderly sergeant," Arnold elucidated, "it is his duty to obey every order of my aides . . . as mine, without judging of the propriety of them . . . [with this as his] consolation, that it is a sacrifice he pays to the safety of his country."

The safety of the country, Matlack shot back, depended more on the spirit of its citizen-soldiers than on Major Franks's coiffure, and unless Arnold could assure him that no further indignities would be offered, he would consider it his duty to withdraw his son from the militia and "to acquaint my fellow citizens of my reasons for so doing." "I am not to be intimidated by a newspaper," Arnold roared in response, adding that "disputes as to the rights of citizens and soldiers in conjunctures like the present may be fatal to both."

The battle lines were drawn, and the war between Arnold and the Reed-Matlack faction—a war fueled by social snobbery as well as politics—commenced. That old Philadelphia hand Silas Deane described the context in a letter to his son. Civil life in the capital city after the British occupation, he explained, was dominated by a "contest . . . between the respectable citizens of fortune and character . . . and the people in lower circumstances and reputation, headed by leaders well qualified for their business and supposed to be secretly supported by" the Supreme Executive Council of the State of Pennsylvania. Council Secretary Timothy Matlack was one of those whom Peggy Shippen's uncle Joseph called "violent, wrongheaded people of the inferior class." The feelings were mutual: Secretary Matlack naturally distrusted and loathed the Shippens and their ilk.

Matlack's cohort, Joseph Reed, was by birth, education and marriage a member of the upper class; but once he was elected president of the Pennsylvania Council in December 1778, he became, willy-nilly, the leader and champion of the hoi polloi. His feelings on this subject were probably mixed: although he prided himself on remaining aloof from high society—the Peggy Shippen set—he also may have resented being excluded, particularly by the arriviste Benedict Arnold.

Reed's simmering resentment boiled over on the November evening when Arnold entertained a particularly large gathering of "Tory ladies [and] the wives and daughters of persons proscribed by the state and now with the enemy at New York." What Reed found "extraordinary" about the occasion was that the execution by hanging of two Quaker Loyalists—a sentence that the Pennsylvania Council had imposed over the protests of many prominent citizens—was scheduled for the following morning. But Reed's patriotic indignation may also have contained a strong strain of social pique: he and his wife had recently moved next door to Arnold, and they had a good view of the party to which they were not invited.

The timing of the party was a deliberate affront to the political and social sensibilities of Joseph Reed; but Benedict Arnold, enraptured with his new life at the top and intoxicated by the elegant Miss Shippen, did not care. Utterly unrepentant for his way of life and his secret larcenies (or attempted larcenies), he almost seemed to be defying Reed to find him out. He had always been a risk-taker, but his behavior now began to verge on the suicidal.

For example, in October, when *Charming Nancy* narrowly escaped destruction during a British raid on Egg Harbor (John André, the erstwhile *beau idéal* of Philadelphia girlhood, was among the raiding party), Arnold persuaded the reluctant army quartermaster at Philadelphia, John Mitchell, to send a train of army wagons to bring the ship's cargo to Philadelphia, where it was sold for the benefit of himself and his partners. The use of public wagons for private purposes was marginally legal, and Arnold promised to pay all expenses; but at the very least it was subject to misinterpretation. As John Mitchell said later, Arnold put enormous pressure on him to provide the wagons, and "I conceived it as my duty to oblige him as my superior officer in everything in my power."

On the very day he learned of the British raid on Egg Harbor, Arnold wrote an illegal pass for a citizen of Philadelphia, Miss Hannah Levy, to travel into British-held New York City to collect "a sum of money which the British officers owed her when they left Philadelphia." He had no authority to issue the pass—that power resided exclusively with the State of Pennsylvania—but he was obviously anxious to get a message into Manhattan. Miss Levy left Arnold's office carrying a slip of paper with the name of "a gentleman in New York" from whom she was to receive "commands" for General Arnold. (The gentleman, whose name was Templeton, presumably had something to do with Arnold's business speculations in the city.)

Miss Levy, being refused passage through the lines by an alert Continental sentry, returned to Philadelphia and applied again to Arnold. Without revealing the history of his illegal pass, he applied on her behalf to the Pennsylvania Council. Their response revealed how careless he had been: Miss Levy was a suspected British sympathizer. Her friendship with a man who had recently been arrested for attempting to smuggle into New York a letter "inimical to the safety and liberties of the United States" explained why she had not applied to the Council for her pass in the first place. Even more embarrassing to Arnold, her "inimical" friend was the cousin and namesake of his aide David Franks.

The moment Reed became president of the Pennsylvania Council, he and Council Secretary Timothy Matlack began to wield their investigative and prosecutorial powers as weapons in their war against Arnold. They drew first blood by means of an anonymous letter to the *Pennsylvania Packet,* printed a few days after Arnold had secretly agreed to finance Gideon Olmstead's appeal of a Pennsylvania Admiralty Court decision awarding him and his fellows only one quarter of the prize money from the *Active* sloop. "It is whispered that some gentlemen of high rank, now in this city, have introduced a new species of champerty [promoting a lawsuit in order to share illegally in its proceeds], by interesting themselves in the claim of the sloop *Active,*" the letter said. "If this be so, there can be no doubt but that the contract is in itself void; and that the seamen are not bound to fulfil it."

Two days later they struck again in the *Packet*'s letter column. "To stand at the door of any man, be he ever so great, and when there liable . . . at the whim and caprice of any of his suite to be ordered on the most menial services, piques my pride and hurts my feelings most sensibly," the anonymous "Militia Man" wrote. "I cannot think that the commanding officer [in Philadelphia] views himself exposed to any real danger in this city. From a public enemy there can be none; from Tories, if any such there be amongst us, he has nothing to fear, they are all remarkably fond of him; the Whigs, to a man, are sensible of his great merit and *former* services, and would risk their lives in his defence."

Former services, indeed. The letters were certainly insulting; but the new devil-may-care Arnold ignored them. Gone was the hair-trigger sensibility of his former days; gone, too, was the habitual gush of eloquence in his own defense. Even when a friend at Continental headquarters, General Nathanael Greene, warned him that Reed was attempting to destroy his reputation among General Washington's military family, Arnold appeared untroubled. "The history you allude to is short," he informed Greene. "Some gentlemen . . . were offended with my paying a polite attention to the ladies of this city without first discovering if they were Whigs at *bottom*. Those gentlemen who avow such illiberal sentiments I shall treat with the contempt which I think they deserve by taking no notice of them."

As Reed's campaign emerged into the open, Congress could not afford to openly take the side of their finest fighting general against the powerful State of Pennsylvania. Instead, they offered Arnold indirect encouragement by voting to pay him $8,000 on his back accounts. (Arnold promptly requested a paroled British prisoner going into New York City to send him various expensive personal items, including new glass for the windows of his carriage.) One member reported that "every man who has a liberal way of thinking highly approve[s Arnold's] conduct"; but he acknowledged at the same time that the commandant remained "very unpopular [among the] men of power in Congress."

Neither did Arnold's opinion of Congress improve. "The great Council of the Nation," he wrote Nathanael Greene, "[is] distracted and torn with party and faction, the public credit lost and debt accumulated to an . . . incredible sum, the currency daily depreciating,* and Congress if possible depreciating still faster." The members of General Washington's headquarters staff agreed; and the commander in chief himself, after a visit to Philadelphia in December,

---

*The Continental dollar had plummeted in eight months from one-third to one-tenth its face value.

wrote to his friend Benjamin Harrison that "the common interests of America are mouldering and sinking into irretrievable (if a remedy is not soon applied) ruin, [while Congress is mired in] idleness, dissipation and extravagance. . . . Party disputes and personal quarrels are the great business of the day," the commander in chief reported, "whilst the momentous concerns of [the country] are but secondary considerations and postponed from day to day, from week to week." Many of his most experienced officers "from absolute necessity are quitting the service," he continued, "and the more virtuous few rather than do this are sinking by sure degrees into beggery and want. . . . And yet an assembly, a concert, a dinner or supper (that will cost three or four hundred pounds) will not only take men off from acting in but even from thinking of this business. . . . This is not an exaggerated account," the commander in chief declared, concluding, "I feel more real distress on account of the present appearances of things than I have done at any one time since the commencement of the dispute."

Washington was particularly horrified by "those murderers of our cause, the monopolizers, forestallers, and engrossers," and he encouraged his former aide Joseph Reed to "hunt them down as the pests of society and the greatest enemies we have. . . . I would to God that one of the most atrocious in each state was hung in gibbets, up on a gallows five times as high as the one prepared by Haman—No punishment, in my opinion, is too great for the man who can build his greatness upon his country's ruin." Reed did not need the commander in chief's urging to hunt down Philadelphia's premier monopolizer, forestaller and engrosser: he was already hot on the trail of Benedict Arnold. And Washington himself, during his sojourn in the city, cannot have failed to notice the luxurious life that the commandant was leading and to wonder how he was paying for it.

A highlight of the social season was the December wedding of Peggy Shippen's sister Betsey. According to one of the twenty-five bridesmaids, Betsey's prenuptial "quakes and tremblings and a thousand other quirks" succeeded in "frightening poor Peggy . . . into a solemn oath, never to change [her] state"—an assessment that perhaps tells us more about Peggy's histrionic talents than it does about her friend's acuity. The eighteen-year-old Miss Shippen was a consummate actress, capable of playing to perfection the innocent, docile, decorative, giddy young girl that her friends, her family and her society expected to see. But beneath the surface, she was an ardent young woman, and even as she giggled and squealed with her girlfriends over her sister's impending loss of virginity, and convinced them all that she was frightened to death, she found herself deeply attracted by her passionate, experienced suitor, General Benedict Arnold.

As for Arnold, the longer he courted Peggy, the more he wanted her. Not only was she beautiful and desirable, she also had a way of making him feel like the man he had always claimed to be. As reflected in Peggy's eyes, he appeared heroic and always in the right, and soon her likeness of him became the cornerstone of his house of mirrors. The fact that this image was just as distorted as the other mirrors in his inner house did not occur to him, in part because he did not wish to see the truth and in part because the skillful Miss Shippen did not let him see it. She brought him the peace that comes from complete self-justification, and he could no longer conceive of living without her.

In the end, Peggy Shippen permitted herself to be "Burgoyned" by Benedict Arnold, and shortly after her sister's marriage she agreed to a conditional engagement. The conditions were financial: Mr. Shippen insisted on a generous prenuptial settlement, and Arnold's financial desperation became even greater. Peggy was finally his for the taking, but where was he to find the wherewithal to take her? The answer came from an unlikely source, Philip Schuyler, who wrote that the State of New York wished to reward Arnold for his conduct at Saratoga and to solicit his suggestions for a suitable gift. It was a mouth-watering invitation. New York could offer him—and he in turn could offer Peggy—something that Pennsylvania could not provide: a landed estate, and a title to go with it.

Since early colonial days, huge tracts of undeveloped land called manors had been offered by the Province of New York to anyone who pledged to settle the land within a specified period of time. A title, "lord of the manor," came with the purchase, together with a set of manorial privileges and customs straight out of the Middle Ages—the quarter sale, quitrents and days' riding (unpaid work on manor projects), for example. The title was never invoked by the men who had a right to it, including Philip Schuyler, but the privileges were in regular use.

The image of manor lordship captivated Arnold, and he informed General Schuyler that he desired to become a citizen of New York if he could "obtain a tract of any consequence"—Kingsland, for instance, the 130,000-acre estate in the Mohawk Valley that had been confiscated from the Tory heirs of Sir William Johnson, or perhaps Philip Skene's magnificent estate at the head of Lake Champlain. Expecting to "establish a settlement of officers and soldiers who have served with him in the present war," Arnold promised to settle at least one family—"tenants in fee simple"—on every thousand acres within four years of the cessation of hostilities. The lure of instant aristocracy was irresistible to the former apothecary's apprentice. Lord of the Manor, on a social par with Philip Schuyler and George Washington, with Peggy at his side—for a moment he almost believed that in America, anything was possible.

While awaiting Schuyler's reply, Arnold received an unexpected windfall: the Congressional Commissioner of Appeals overturned the decision of the Pennsylvania Admiralty Court and awarded the entire *Active* prize money to Gideon Olmstead and his partners. But the apparition of wealth quickly faded. Citing a technicality in state law, the Pennsylvania court refused to recognize the ruling. They put the sloop and cargo on the auction block and pocketed the proceeds, in direct violation of a congressional injunction obtained at the eleventh hour by a frantic Major General Arnold. In response to this challenge, Congress lamely appointed a committee to conduct an inquiry, and, when it was completed, tabled the report. Arnold was livid. He knew what the postponement meant: that the report would die and he would never get his money. He was quite correct.

Desperate and short of cash, he borrowed £12,000 from a French shipping agent named Jean Holker (offering a piece of the *Active* as collateral, which Holker wisely refused), paid his most pressing bills, petitioned the commander in chief for a short leave and prepared for a long and arduous midwinter journey to Poughkeepsie to settle the matter of his estate with the New York Assembly. When his departure plans were made public, Joseph Reed struck.

During the weeks since the *Pennsylvania Packet* had printed the letter from "Militia Man," Reed and Timothy Matlack had been busy amassing evidence against the Philadelphia commandant. Having ferreted out the stories of Miss Levy's pass and the journey of the army wagons to Egg Harbor, Reed demanded an official explanation. "I am at all times ready to answer [for] my public conduct to Congress or General Washington, to whom alone I am accountable," Arnold responded loftily. Joseph Reed was not to be bluffed. He filed an official complaint with Congress for "the indignity offered to us upon this occasion . . . by one of their officers" and demanded that Arnold be stripped of command and detained in the city "until the charges against him are examined." Lest anyone miss the point, Reed also requested the Pennsylvania delegation in Congress to demand a roll call on any matter concerning Arnold, "that in our correspondence with our sister states we may have an opportunity to show them how far their delegates in Congress do or do not manifest a disposition to support the authority of civil government."

Congress was helpless, and although many of its members would have liked nothing better than to use the occasion to put Joseph Reed in his place, they could not afford to offend the president of the Pennsylvania Council. Instead, they offended Benedict Arnold by appointing a committee to cooperate with Reed's council in an investigation into his conduct as commandant.

The wagon master on the Egg Harbor trip, one Jesse Jordan, chose this moment to come to Philadelphia from his home in Chester to collect his pay. Calling at headquarters in person, he presented Arnold with a payroll for the two weeks that he and his fellow wagoneers had been absent from their homes. Since Arnold's only defense against a charge of improper conduct was to show that the wagons had not been called up specifically for his private use, he informed Jordan that he would pay only for the eight days that the wagons were actually in transit between Philadelphia and Egg Harbor.

Philadelphia quartermaster John Mitchell, whose only desire was to distance himself from the whole affair, protested. "Mr. Jordan is entitled to pay from the day he left home," he informed his commandant, "and as he was not employed in public service, but sent to you on his arrival, it is but just he should be paid by the person who employed him; but," Mitchell added, covering himself for all eventualities, "if you order I should pay him any part of the time . . . I will obey your order."

On the very evening that Mitchell wrote this letter, Jesse Jordan testified before the Pennsylvania Council. Among the other details he furnished to his eager listeners was the fact that Mitchell had never told him that goods in Egg Harbor were privately owned. (Had he known, Jordan righteously informed the Council, he would have refused the duty.) The Council promptly advanced Jordan £450 on account and advised him to bring action against General Arnold for his wages.

Arnold, still confident that evasion and bluffing would keep the situation under control, departed for Poughkeepsie on the morning of February 3. He carried with him a letter from the president of Congress, John Jay, to New York Governor George Clinton:

> Allured to our state by the excellency of its constitution [Arnold was no fool; Jay himself had written the New York State Constitution], the respect he has for many characters in it . . . and the views he has of forming a settlement in it conducive

to her interest and beneficial to the state, [General Arnold] intends to lay before the Legislature certain propositions to which I hope attention will be paid. . . . I wish . . . that in treating with him they may recollect the services he has rendered his country and the value of such a citizen to any state that may gain him.

As his carriage waited to cross the Delaware River at Bristol Ferry, a rider galloped up from the direction of Philadelphia and handed Arnold a copy of eight formal charges filed against him that morning by the Pennsylvania Council: one, permitting a ship belonging to persons of "disaffected character" to sail from Philadelphia in violation of the congressional embargo; two, making private purchases while the shops in Philadelphia were officially closed; three, "imposing menial offices upon the sons of freemen of this state"; four, purchasing shares in the *Active* at "a low and inadequate price" and causing a dispute between the Council and Congress; five, ordering army wagons to transport private goods; six, granting Miss Levy an illegal pass; seven, adopting "an indecent and disrespectful manner" toward the Council; and eight, "discourag[ing] and neglect[ing] . . . [persons] who have adhered to the cause of their country [while displaying] an entirely different conduct toward those of another character." Timothy Matlack's covering letter informed Arnold that copies of the charges had been sent to Congress, to General Washington and to the governing bodies of the thirteen states.

Arnold proceeded at once to his first planned stopover, Continental Army headquarters at Middlebrook, New Jersey. If he could get General Washington to support him publicly, he thought he might be able to put out the fire. The commander in chief received him with the "greatest politeness" (as Arnold wrote to Peggy, who had known Washington since childhood) but offered little comfort, advising Arnold only to ask Congress for a court-martial to clear his name. Washington's heart must have sunk at the thought of public disgrace falling on the head of a man the army needed so badly. Arnold's tactical acuity and flair for battle put him in a class by himself; he was one of the best, if not *the* best fighting general at Washington's disposal. Nevertheless, his honor, and the honor of the service, demanded that he undergo a trial, and if he were found guilty, he would have to resign his commission.

Arnold lingered at headquarters for several days, trying to decide whether to return to Philadelphia immediately or to proceed to Poughkeepsie as planned. Peggy's silence made the decision for him.

"Six days' absence without hearing from my Peggy is intolerable," he wrote to her in terrible suspense. Was it possible that the public charges had made her falter? "My Dearest Life," he pleaded,

> Never did I so ardently long to see or hear from you as at this instant. . . . Heavens! What must I have suffered had I continued my journey, the loss of happiness for a few dirty *acres*. I can almost bless the villanous roads, and more *villainous men* who oblige me to return.
>
> I am heartily tired with my journey, and almost so with human nature. I daily discover so much baseness and ingratitude among mankind that I almost blush at being of the same species, and could quit the stage without regret was it not for some few gentle, generous souls like my dear Peggy, who still retain the lovely impression of their Maker's image. . . . Let me beg of you not to suffer the rude attacks on me to give you one moment's uneasiness; they can do me no injury. . . . 'Til [we are reunited], all nature smiles in vain, for you alone, heard, felt and seen possess my every thought, fill every sense, and pant in every vein.

He rushed back to Philadelphia, where Peggy put all his fears to rest. She seemed to love him more than ever, and had persuaded all her family and friends to rally to his cause. "I think all the world are running mad," one of her sister's former bridesmaids wrote. "What demon has possessed the people with respect to General A____d? He is certainly much abused. Ungrateful monsters, to attack a character that has been looked up to, in more instance than one, since this war commenced; but, however, I have not a doubt of his now clearing himself with honor. Poor Peggy, how I pity her; at any rate, her situation must be extremely disagreeable. She has great sensibility, and I think it must have been often put to the trial." But the trial only demonstrated Peggy's mettle. In the ensuing weeks when Joseph Reed seemed bent on destroying Arnold, she provided confirmation and sympathy; when Congress failed him, she stood firm; and when all of Philadelphia whispered rumors of his misconduct, her love and loyalty never wavered.

Congress promptly granted Arnold's request for a court-martial and appointed a committee to prepare the charges under the chairmanship of the distinguished Maryland jurist William Paca. When, at Joseph Reed's insistence, the Pennsylvania delegation presented a motion on the floor to remove Arnold from command (Peggy's great-uncle William Shippen cast the only dissenting vote), Congress postponed consideration to some unspecified future date, leaving Arnold dangling and strengthening his conviction that they would never appreciate or do right by him. Unfortunately, during his absence at headquarters, Hannah Levy had testified before a committee of Congress about the secret note Arnold had given her to carry into New York. She could identify neither the recipient nor the subject of the correspondence, but the story gave comfort to Arnold's enemies and greater credence to the accusations of Joseph Reed.

The question was, would William Paca's committee recommend a court-martial on all or only some of the eight charges? Arnold was accused of six substantive actions and two political attitudes. The latter (numbers seven and eight on the list of charges: exhibiting disrespect to the Council and favoring Tories over Whigs) would be difficult to establish and easy to refute, if necessary. It was the other six—granting illegal passes to Miss Levy and to *Charming Nancy,* making purchases while the shops were closed in Philadelphia, investing improperly in the *Active* sloop, permitting David Franks to send a militia sergeant on a menial errand and, most dangerous of all, appropriating the army wagons to fetch his and Robert Shewell's goods in Egg Harbor—that posed a threat, largely because he was guilty of all six, by design if not by execution. (He was guilty of a good deal more besides, but Joseph Reed had not found out about the secret agreements with John R. Livingston and Clothier General Mease.)

Arnold viewed the charges quite coolly, as matters that needed to be brought under control. He told himself, as he told Peggy and the rest of the world, that they were trumped up by "a set of unprincipled, malicious scoundrels who have prostituted their honor and truth for the purpose of gratifying their private resentment against an innocent person." To acknowledge his own culpability never occurred to him, and his conscience was not bothered because he had none. His defensive style, therefore, is best described as ducking and weaving. It ranged from threats and attempted manipulation of potential witnesses to the promulgation of lofty pronouncements of outraged honor and innocence. What he never did, because he couldn't, was to address the charges directly and to establish his innocence beyond the shadow of a doubt by force of evidence.

Arnold first tackled the problem of John Mitchell, the Philadelphia quartermaster whose fear of involvement in the Egg Harbor affair had distilled into sheer panic. Shortly after his return to the city, Arnold summoned Mitchell to headquarters and insisted that he write a statement of the entire sequence of events, particularly noting the fact that Arnold had offered to pay Jesse Jordan for the time of the trip. When Mitchell refused, Arnold reached into his desk drawer and produced a certificate written by himself, which he permitted Mitchell to carry home for further study before signing. Instead, Mitchell took it straight to Joseph Reed, who deemed it a "colorable, unfair state[ment]" and advised him not to sign it.

At this juncture, Arnold learned that during his absence from the city, Mitchell had clumsily altered the entries in his office memorandum book to make it appear that the wagoneers had received their orders exclusively from Arnold. Once the memorandum book was in the hands of the Council, the alterations were discovered and Mitchell was forced to confess. Arnold promptly submitted to the *Pennsylvania Packet* a transcript of Mitchell's earlier testimony, exonerating them both of any wrongdoing. The *Packet* printed it in a special edition, along with Arnold's call for "Jesse Jordan to call [at headquarters] for the pay of his brigade of wagons, if the President and Council of the State will permit him."

Four days later the *Packet* published a letter signed "T.G." (a.k.a. Timothy Matlack, who had recently opened a correspondence with Arnold's old enemy John Brown) containing a list of the thirteen charges that Brown had leveled against Arnold two years before, which included, it will be remembered, personal responsibility for the spread of smallpox in the northern army, attempting to make "a treasonable . . . escape . . . to the enemy" and plundering the merchants' goods at Montreal.

Arnold promptly protested to the *Packet* that Congress had exonerated him of each and every charge, and he added the observation, "Envy and malice are indefatigable. Where they have not invention enough to frame new slanders . . . they will call in the feeble aid of old calumnies." "T.G.'s" response was printed within the week: "It will require that some faith be exercised by the next generation before they can believe that Congress really acquitted you of those charges . . . without hearing *the evidence against you. . . .* [The only argument] in favor of this decision by Congress [is] the improbability that any one man was ever guilty of so many crimes. . . . When I meet your carriage in the street, and think of the splendor in which you live and revel . . . and of the purchases you have made, and compare these things with the decent frugality necessarily used by other officers of the army, it is impossible to avoid the question, From whence have these riches flowed, if you *did not plunder Montreal?*"

Ironically, in the same edition of the *Packet* there appeared a reprint from the New York City Loyalist paper *Royal Gazette* characterizing Benedict Arnold as "an officer more distinguished for valor and perseverance than any commander in [the Continental] service. . . . [Having] been styled another Hannibal, but losing a leg in the service of the Congress, the latter, considering him unfit for any further exercise of his military talents, [have permitted him] to fall into the unmerciful fangs of the Executive Council of Pennsylvania, Mr. Joseph Reed, President." Somebody in the country, it appeared, recognized Arnold's merits and appreciated the sacrifices he had made, even if that somebody was the enemy.

Meanwhile, the preparation of charges for Arnold's impending court-martial had become the latest bone of contention between Congress and the Pennsylvania Council. Joseph Reed accused William Paca, chairman of the congressional committee, of deliberately suppressing evidence. Paca, a highly respected jurist, challenged Reed to prove the charge and, in turn, accused Reed of insolence and arrogation of power. Reed declared that the Council would no longer cooperate, and Paca proceeded without him.

Congress further muddied the waters by resuscitating the case of the *Active,* granting the entire ship's prize to Arnold's protégés— and then promptly backing off. Instead of suing the state for recovery of the money, they appointed a committee—chaired by the long-suffering William Paca—to explore the matter, and a month later tabled the committee's recommendation that Congress pay Gideon Olmstead and charge the amount to the State of Pennsylvania. Meanwhile, Reed retaliated by informing the Board of War that Pennsylvania would furnish no additional militia to the Continental cause as long as Benedict Arnold remained in command.

On March 17, the Paca court-martial committee recommended that Arnold be tried on two of the Pennsylvania Council's eight charges: appropriating army wagons to transport private goods, and "imposing menial offices upon the sons of freemen of this state." The remaining six they deemed either unprovable or outside the purview of a court-martial. Arnold immediately requested that Congress take up the matter quickly and "relieve me by a speedy decision . . . [thus alleviating] the cruel situation in which I am placed by the persecution of my enemies." He wanted it over. His new life with Peggy beckoned; he wished to start it with a clean slate.

His craving for her was greater than ever. During these past difficult weeks, her charms had enlivened him and her unexpected strength had sustained him. He had to have her. He acquiesced in abandoning the plan to settle in the Mohawk Valley (Peggy and her family had undoubtedly cooled on the idea, after the gruesome

Cherry Valley massacre). Instead, he somehow scraped together £16,240 (probably from his percentage of Gideon Olmstead's one-quarter share of the *Active* sale, plus the loan from Jean Holker) to make the down payment on a magnificent ninety-six-acre estate overlooking the Schuylkill River a few miles from the center of Philadelphia.

Mount Pleasant, a graceful stone mansion in the Georgian style, had been built before the war by an eccentric Scotsman named John McPherson, the inventor of the vermin-proof bed. (McPherson's son had been killed at Richard Montgomery's side in Quebec in 1775.) Recognized even by the dour John Adams as "the most elegant seat in Pennsylvania," it boasted porticos and pediments, high-ceilinged salons, sweeping lawns, orchards and an imposing entrance through an allée of trees. Mount Pleasant was currently occupied on a long lease by Don Juan de Miralles, the Spanish ambassador to the United States, but Arnold did not intend to move in anyway. Within hours of closing on the property, he signed it over to Peggy as a dower, to be divided on her death among all his children.

Edward Shippen was satisfied, and Arnold and Peggy set the date: April 8, less than three weeks away. Peggy would move into Arnold's house on High Street after the wedding. Acquiring Mount Pleasant had been a simple prenuptial business transaction; but it is impossible not to imagine that Arnold harbored dreams of one day reigning as master there. Like the image of manor-lordship in New York, it represented everything he had learned to want, and it had the advantage of being located near the country's most sophisticated city, and in the midst of his wife's grand friends, rather than at the verge of a savage frontier wilderness.

Three days before closing on Mount Pleasant, Arnold wrote to General Washington resigning as commandant of Philadelphia. He had obtained the commander in chief's permission to do so several months before, but "the villainous attacks made on my character by the President and Council of this state . . . made it necessary for me to continue in the command until their charges were cleared up. . . . A committee of Congress having reported in my favor, that objection ceases." His ostensible motive was to give his leg time to recover its strength; seventeen months after being wounded at Freeman's farm, he still could not walk without crutches. "As soon as my wounds will permit, I shall be happy to take a command in the line of the army," he promised the commander in chief. But he also wanted time with Peggy, to make order out of his chaotic life, and to make plans for their future.

Less than two weeks before the wedding, Arnold remained in suspense about how Congress would act on the Paca report. "I am still held up to the public as a most notorious criminal," he complained to John Jay, noting that as long as Congress failed to rule on the charges, the "calumniators, employed and supported by persons in power . . . [feel free to spread] their insinuations and false assertions through these United States to poison the minds of my virtuous countrymen and fellow citizens, and to prejudice them against a man whose life has ever been devoted to their service, and who looks on their good opinion and esteem as the greatest reward and honor he can receive. . . . Thus circumstanced," he explained, "I cannot be charged with undue impatience for soliciting an immediate decision . . . [and trust that Congress] will relieve me from a situation the cruelty of which is beyond my power to express." Beneath this lofty rhetoric, the practical Arnold was arranging for his two aides, David Franks and Matthew Clarkson, to transfer to the Southern Department, well out of subpoena range.

On April 3, Congress, declaring itself "highly sensible of the importance and services of the State of Pennsylvania" and unwilling to countenance "any disrespectful and indecent behavior of any officer of any rank . . . to the civil authority of any state in the union," ordered the commander in chief to court-martial Arnold on *four* charges, the two William Paca had recommended plus two that his committee had deemed "fully explained, and the appearance they carry of criminality fully obviated by clear, unquestionable evidence": issuing the pass to *Charming Nancy* and purchasing goods while the shops were closed.

Arnold fell into a stunned silence. Until now he had not really believed that Congress would throw him to the wolves. He had still uttered no protest when, on the fine spring morning of April 8, he and Peggy were married in her parents' drawing room with Arnold leaning on an orderly's arm throughout the service.

During his week-long honeymoon, Arnold drew closer both to Peggy and to the other object of his affections: his bright and shining public persona, the Patriot-Hero, to whom he had wedded himself some three years earlier. It now appeared to be in imminent danger of being ripped to shreds, and the country that had bestowed it on him seemed to have turned its back. The fact that his own felonious activities had attracted the wolves in the first place meant nothing to him. Arnold had no difficulty ignoring his own culpability; it was one of his most consistent attributes.

During these days of blissful intimacy with his beautiful, young and affectionate wife, Arnold conceived a way out of all his difficulties—a plan so bold, and yet so simple, it took one's breath away. The logic was indisputable: if the Congress—if America—had truly abandoned him, perhaps he should return the favor; if the country in whose cause he had suffered so much was truly incapable of appreciating his talents and granting his heart's desire—a secure fortune and a secure status in a secure society—then perhaps he should offer his services to a country that could. The idea of a fresh start in the new arena had always been alluring to Arnold; and if it was true that "successful and fortunate crime is called virtue," he would enter that new arena with his honor and virtue intact.

Once the subject was broached between Arnold and his bride, a flood of speculations followed. It is difficult to know exactly how they envisioned their life after a British victory in the war, but it is easy to imagine that Arnold's self-delusion and Peggy's immaturity combined to create a rosy picture. And the thought of revenging himself on his tormentors—Joseph Reed, Timothy Matlack, John Brown and the Congress of the United States—was extremely sweet.

On the other side loomed the appalling risk; but Arnold had always been a risk-taker, and Peggy quickly proved one as well. In fact, she began to display a kind of daring and resourcefulness that would have startled anyone who knew her: little Peggy Shippen, the bad, bold traitoress. Her audacity was a delicious secret between her husband and herself that deepened their intimacy and strengthened the ties that bound them together.

Although Arnold had not entirely committed himself by the time he and Peggy emerged from their honeymoon, the uncharacteristic tone of sweet reason in which he addressed the president of Congress on April 16 is evidence that beneath the surface a seismic shift had occurred: "I cannot but testify my surprise that a court-martial should be ordered to try me for offences some of which the committee of Congress [have already dismissed; but,]" he remarked mildly, "if Congress have been induced to this measure for the public good and to avoid a breach with this state, however hard my case may be, and however I am injured as an individual, I will suffer with pleasure until a court-martial can have an opportunity of doing me justice by acquitting me of those charges a second time."

His apparent calm was soon shattered. First, he was informed by General Washington that his court-martial, having been scheduled for May 1, would have to be postponed until June 1 to give time for David Franks and Matthew Clarkson to return from the South to testify. Joseph Reed himself had demanded their presence and, in the same letter, informed the commander in chief, regarding the charge of misusing army wagons: "Such is the dependence of the army upon the transportation of this state, and such the feelings of the people upon this sort of duty, that should the court treat it as a light and a trivial matter . .·. we fear it will not be practical to draw forth wagons in future, be the emergency what it may."

On May 5, just as Arnold was sitting down to respond to General Washington's letter, an even deadlier threat appeared in the form of an invitation from Timothy Matlack to attend the following morning when the Pennsylvania Council would hear testimony from a Colonel John Fitzgerald regarding the "instructions given by you to Major David S. Franks, one of your aides, to purchase in the City of Philadelphia European and East-India goods to any amount . . . and directing him not to communicate the same even to his most intimate friends." It was a terrible shock. Arnold had no idea what Fitzgerald knew or even who he was, except for the fact—smugly reported by Matlack— that he had once served as aide-de-camp to General Washington. If Fitzgerald could testify to his conspiracy with Franks, it would all be over. The Patriot-Hero would be unmasked, and all his tormentors would be vindicated.

Arnold pulled himself together just long enough to write a polite letter to Colonel Fitzgerald asking him to call after giving his testimony before the Council. He did not even respond to Timothy Matlack's invitation; obviously, he would not attend the Council. It was when he began to compose his letter to General Washington that the emotional dam burst. "As Congress have stamped ingratitude as a current coin, I must take it," he blurted, adding in a bizarre aside, "I wish Your Excellency for your long and eminent services may not be paid in the same coin. I have nothing left but the little reputation I have gained in the army," he continued. "Delay in the present case is worse than death. . . . I want no favor, I ask only for justice"—he was nearly delirious by now—"Let me beg of you, Sir . . . If Your Excellency thinks me criminal, for Heaven's sake let me be immediately tried and, if found guilty, executed."

He did not wait for an answer. Within the next forty-eight hours, Arnold sent an emissary into New York bearing an offer of his services to the British.

Chapter 15

"CONSCIOUS OF MY OWN INNOCENCE"

MAY 1779-JULY 1780

Arnold's treason did not demand that he switch allegiance, since he had no deep allegiance to either side. It is therefore not surprising that his first order of business in approaching the British was to find out how much his services would be worth.

His emissary was Joseph Stansbury, a purveyor of fine china to Philadelphia society and a staunch Loyalist with access to British intelligence. Peggy may well have proposed Stansbury's name to her husband; she almost certainly suggested the man he should seek out in New York: Captain John André, her friend from the "halcyon days, forever dear" of the occupation, who now served as personal aide to the British commander in chief, Sir Henry Clinton.

Stansbury's overture was carefully orchestrated by Arnold. At his initial meeting with Captain André, which took place in New York on May 10, 1779, he first elicited a firm guarantee that the British intended to pursue the war. The entry of France into the conflict had already forced the diversion of men and ships to the West Indies; with a new war looming in Europe, Parliament might well decide that the good of the empire at large demanded relinquishing the thirteen colonies. Benedict Arnold cared nothing for the good of the British Empire, and he had no intention of exerting himself for the losing side. He could tell the British how to win the war—even win it for them—but first he needed to know if they had the will to do so.

Captain André responded with "the strongest assurances . . . that no thought is entertained of abandoning" the war. He was quite wrong: a substantial proportion of the House of Commons already considered it not only necessary but desirable to sacrifice the thirteen colonies, although they had yet to convince the king or his colonial secretary, George Germain. In André's circle, however—the isolated society of Loyalist refugees and British Army officers crowded together on Manhattan Island—the notion of abandoning America was anathema. Captain André believed that the British would stay the course because he had to believe it. The same was true of Benedict Arnold.

Having obtained this guarantee, Stansbury quickly got to the point: the cash value of General Arnold's apostasy. Here Captain André was far less specific. British "liberality [would be] evinced," he promised "Monk" (Arnold's code name, after General George Monk, who, in the previous century, had been rewarded with a dukedom for turning against Oliver Cromwell's Commonwealth in favor of the restoration of the monarchy), "in the very first instance of receiving" intelligence. If the information should lead to "the seizing [of] an obnoxious band of men . . . the generosity of the nation [would] exceed even his most sanguine hopes." This was all very well, but André named no figure, and in fact, the grander his promises became, the less convincing they sounded. At least the captain offered some insurance: should Arnold's "manifest efforts be foiled and, after every zealous attempt flight be at length necessary, the cause in which he suffers will hold itself bound to indemnify him for his losses and receive him with the honor his conduct deserves."

Arnold received Captain André's memorandum of the meeting from Stansbury's hand on or about May 20 and was instantly released from the doldrums. It was done; he had offered himself and they had accepted; his way was now clear. To a man of Arnold's insecurities, being accepted is never a given. He needed to be needed, and the moment he knew the British wanted him, he became his own man again, with a hazardous but clearly defined task that demanded every ounce of his energy and intelligence.

Within the week he had dispatched his first report, couched, as per André's instructions, in the terms of an ordinary business communication with certain passages in cipher (*Bailey's Dictionary*,

21st edition, to be the key, "three numbers make a word, the first is the page, the second the line, the third the word*"): "General W[ashington] and the army move to the North [Hudson] River as soon as forage can be obtained. Congress have given up Ch[arleston, South Carolina] if attempted. They are in want of arms, ammunition and men to defend it. Three or four thousand militia is the most that can be mustered to fight on any emergency." Claiming to have access to congressional secrets "from a member," Arnold also offered the following political items: "No measure taken to prevent the depreciation of money, no foreign loan obtained, France refused to become surety, no encouragement from Spain."

The fact that this information might result in capture or death for some of his old comrades in arms was irrelevant to Arnold. This was business. "As life and everything is at stake," he declared, "I will expect some certainty: my property here secure and a revenue equivalent to the risk and service done." He was also anxious to establish "a mutual confidence" with the British commander in chief, and he suggested that if Sir Henry would reveal his plans for the coming campaign, "he should never be at a loss for intelligence."

It was preposterous to ask General Clinton to confide in him, but Arnold was anxious to let the British know that he was no ordinary spy. He longed for Sir Henry to acknowledge his stature and treat him with the deference he felt he deserved. If the British commander wanted him to remain where he was for the time being, gathering intelligence and preparing for a substantial coup, he would comply, although he preferred the notion of a general's commission in the British Army. But he would not be treated as Clinton's servant.

Sir Henry promptly put him in his place. "H[is] Excellency," Captain André reported, "cannot reveal his intentions as to the present campaign nor can he find the necessity of such a discovery." On the contrary, the captain pointed out, since Arnold himself had initiated the correspondence, it was up to him to deliver whatever services his new masters desired. "Join the army," André enjoined,

---

*As an alternative, André suggested interlining an apparently innocent epistle with invisible writing "to be discovered by a process, F is fire, A acid"; or "the lady [Peggy] might write to me with one of her intimates. She will guess who I mean, the latter remaining ignorant of interlining." He subsequently wrote a draft of a letter to Peggy's friend Margaret Chew and marked it "A" for acid, but for some reason never interlined or sent it. (A conservator at the University of Michigan has examined the original letter under a microscope and confirmed that the paper fibers between the lines have not been disturbed.) André was an enthusiast who relished the details of the spymaster's craft.

"accept a command, be surprised, be cut off. . . . It is services of this nature, or intelligence having evidently led to such strokes, which S[ir] H[enry] C[linton] looks for." His wages for delivering a corps of five or six thousand men would be "twice as many thousand guineas."

Twelve thousand guineas buys a lot of pride-swallowing. And there was an additional reason why Arnold did not take offense and end the correspondence: in his eyes, and in the eyes of his wife, he had committed himself. He would not turn back. It was a matter of honor.

Typically, Arnold had already begun to weave a complicated web of self-justification for his treason. At its center was an empty space where the word *treason* should have been written. No sooner had Arnold decided to turn his coat than he began to see it as a patriotic act. Surely it was in America's best interests to remain within the empire, he argued, without blinking an eye at the reversal; and if, through his brave and righteous efforts, he saved his countrymen from radicalism and brought about a British victory, men of good sense on both sides of the Atlantic would recognize and reward him as a hero.

Preening before this new reflection in his house of mirrors, Arnold also kept a sharp eye on the bottom line. His chillingly practical side now focused itself on three tasks: cashing in his assets against the day his new masters ordered him in, manipulating his role in the army to increase the value of his services, and protecting himself against the immediate threat of his court-martial.

Colonel John Fitzgerald called on Arnold, as requested, after giving his testimony before the Pennsylvania Council. It was even worse than Arnold had feared: Fitzgerald had lodged in the same house as David Franks in Philadelphia on the night of the British withdrawal, and had chanced to see two open papers that Franks had left lying on the parlor windowsill, one of them in Arnold's handwriting instructing Franks to make secret purchases of scarce goods in Philadelphia, "for payment of which the writer would furnish Major Franks with the money."

This explained why Joseph Reed had suddenly become so anxious for David Franks to testify at the court-martial, and Arnold's fertile brain began to fabricate ways in which he and Franks could explain Colonel Fitzgerald away. Now that he knew the worst, now that he had severed all ties to the cause and army of the United States, he was entirely free to manipulate his relationships as well as the truth, and from this moment on, his lying became more brazen and more cynical than ever before.

The closer he was to Continental headquarters, the more valuable his intelligence would be. Arnold therefore set about regaining General Washington's confidence, which had been badly shaken by the charges themselves and by the hysterical tone of Arnold's recent letter. "I feel my situation truly delicate and embarrassing," the commander in chief had responded. "I beg you to be convinced I do not indulge any sentiments unfavorable to you . . . and I am sure you wish me to avoid even the semblance of partiality." Regarding Arnold's guilt or innocence, Washington only promised to "cautiously suspend my judgment until the result of a full and fair trial shall determine the merits of the prosecution." In retrospect, Washington's failure to read Arnold may appear naïve; but the commander in chief was an essentially fair man whose own painful experience with backbiters and rumor mongers had taught him never to prejudge others. Arnold's record indicated nothing but the most fervent devotion to the cause of their country. But it is also probably true that Washington's insight into Arnold may have been deflected by his desperate need for Arnold's military talents.

The court-martial was scheduled to open at Continental headquarters in Middlebrook, New Jersey, on June 1. Arnold worked hard to prepare himself and was eager to have it over with. He accepted an invitation to lodge at the quarters of his friend Quartermaster General Nathanael Greene. Despite a close friendship with Joseph Reed, Greene was appalled at Arnold's situation. "It is a very discouraging circumstance to officers in public service," he wrote to Silas Deane, "to see that years of hard duty, constant fatigue and perpetual danger can be so soon forgotten, as we find it can in the instance of General Arnold, and that a little error, either real or imaginary, is sufficient to erase the very remembrance of the most important services. I wish America may not become famous for ingratitude. . . . I am persuaded the General will be able to acquit himself with honor. However, should he be found blameable on some little matters, his services and sufferings have been sufficient to wipe away a multitude of error."* Arnold could only hope that Greene's sentiments were shared by the officers of the court.

The first day went well, with Arnold conducting his own defense in a spirited fashion. (According to eighteenth-century court-martial procedures, he was permitted to examine witnesses and to give a closing statement but not to testify.) That very evening, however, news reached Middlebrook that British troops under the personal

---

*Greene also invited Timothy Matlack to lodge at his quarters, but Matlack, "from a regard to the General's feelings, declined it."

command of Sir Henry Clinton (with Captain André at his side) had captured the Continental forts at Stony Point and Verplanck's Point, the terminals of an important Hudson River crossing known as King's Ferry (see map, page 199). General Washington was utterly dependent on the ferry for supplies and communications from New England; without it, his men would starve. The main army prepared to march north immediately, and Arnold's court-martial was indefinitely postponed. Disappointed though he was, the trip had not been entirely unfruitful. Shortly after reaching home, Arnold sent Captain André several new items of intelligence he had picked up in the Continental camp.

He remained in suspense for more than a month, with no word from the British or from General Washington. Restless and anxious, he informed André that Sir Henry's offers were "not equal to his expectations" and demanded ten thousand pounds for his services. But he also continued to furnish useful intelligence concerning troop strengths, supplies and the current assignments of several prominent Continental generals. Arnold also gave himself a promotion: the former "Monk," a mere duke, now became "Gustavus," after Gustavus Vasa, who led Sweden to independence and was elected king. André also had a new code name, "John Anderson," but he was occasionally referred to as "Lothario" by one of the couriers.

On July 19, all the bells in Philadelphia chimed in celebration of the recapture of Stony Point by Continental troops under the command of Anthony Wayne. Arnold and General Washington exchanged terse letters regarding the resumption of the court-martial. "You must be sensible that I cannot fix with precision on any day," the commander in chief explained, "[as] the movements of the enemy will govern ours," adding, "You will have heard of our success at Stony Point; as I am extremely busy, I shall not trouble you with a detail of the affair."

In early August, Arnold finally heard from New York. "Real advantage must appear to have arisen from the expenditure" of so much money, Captain André explained. "Would you assume a command and enable me to see you I am convinced a conversation of a few minutes would satisfy you entirely." Meanwhile, he requested a particular item: "an accurate plan of West Point, with . . . an account of what vessels, gun boats or gallies are in the North [Hudson] River."

West Point, an American post in the Hudson River Highlands, was designed to protect King's Ferry and also to block enemy access to the upper Hudson Valley. Arnold was not surprised at Clinton's interest in the post, but he was unable to furnish any information.

West Point, he explained to André, was undergoing extensive alterations according to a secret plan known only to General Washington
and the engineers. He did promise, however, to "join the army in
about three weeks," visit the Point, make a drawing of the new works
and "contrive an interview" with André. What he did not tell the
captain was that he was unfit to accept a command, having not sat
a horse since the battle at Freeman's farm nearly two years before.
His wounded leg had recovered most of its strength, but it had healed
several inches shorter than the other, and he walked only slowly and
carefully, with a lift in his shoe.

The negotiations seemed to have reached an impasse: Arnold
refused to make his move until the British made a firm offer, and the
British refused to do so until they saw what his move would be.
Captain André tried another tack, a friendly and apparently guileless
letter to Peggy offering to purchase for her in New York "capwire,
needles, gauze, etc." for her millinery, "from which I hope you would
infer a zeal to be further employed." He did not receive an answer.

It was a frustrating and anxious August. Arnold put his house in
New Haven on the market, but nobody made an offer. He filed for
reimbursement of his table expenses while commandant in Philadelphia, but Congress, deeming the figures "extravagant indeed," refused to pay. He finished collecting depositions and vouchers for his
public expenditures in Canada in 1776 and submitted them to Congress, which referred the whole matter to the Treasury Board, whose
president, Congressman Elbridge Gerry of Massachusetts, Arnold
suspected of bias. He began to spread rumors about town that Gerry
was attempting to influence the board against him. Gerry, who was
highly respected among his colleagues for integrity, met Arnold one
day in the foyer of the State House and denied the accusation to his
face. Arnold refused to accept his word, and thus antagonized the
man who, to a large degree, controlled his financial fate.

As the hot and humid Philadelphia summer cooled into autumn,
a rash of public protests against food shortages and high prices broke
out in the streets. Tempers were short, anti-Loyalist sentiment
reached new heights and even Joseph Stansbury found it prudent to
slip out of town for a few weeks. On October 4, a riot broke out in
front of the home of James Wilson, a conservative lawyer whose
courtroom defense of a number of prominent Loyalists had earned
him a reputation as a Tory sympathizer. A street mob "armed with
bars of iron and large hammers" forced their way into the house in
which Wilson and a number of his friends had barricaded themselves.
In the melee that followed, several were killed and many wounded.

At this juncture, the "pert Tory" Benedict Arnold rode up in his carriage, and the crowd began to throw stones. Arnold's coachman beat a fast retreat, with some of the mob in pursuit.

Arnold reached home unhurt but extremely angry. (Peggy, who was four months' pregnant, was no doubt terrified.) He requested Congress to send "twenty men with a good officer" to protect him from "the mob of lawless ruffians [who] attacked me in the streets and threaten my life now. . . . As there is no protection to be expected from the authority of the state for an honest man, I am under the necessity of requesting Congress to order me a guard of Continental troops. This request I presume will not be denied to a man who has so often fought and bled in defence of the liberties of his country."

The new president of Congress, Samuel Huntington, returned a stiff note the same day informing Arnold "that his application ought to be made to the executive authority of the State of Pennsylvania, in whose disposition to protect every honest citizen Congress have full confidence, and highly disapprove the insinuations of every individual to the contrary." Arnold quickly backtracked. He did not doubt the "disposition" of Pennsylvania to protect him, he assured Huntington, only its "abilities"; but he went on to threaten that if he did not succeed in obtaining a guard "and am again attacked, self-preservation will induce me to defend myself to the last extremity, and I hope the Honorable Congress will not think me chargeable for the consequences."

Within the week, Arnold reopened his correspondence with the British by means of a demure little note from Peggy: "Mrs. Arnold presents her best respects to Captain André, is much obliged to him for his very polite and friendly offer of being serviceable to her . . . [and] begs leave to assure Captain André that her friendship and esteem for him is not impaired by time or accident." There was no reply. Six weeks later, at the beginning of December, Arnold sent Joseph Stansbury to New York with an extensive and detailed report on the state of Continental arms, an indirect plea for reassurance—"Some insect of your place hath written the President of Congress that the October packet has arrived [from London and] . . . that your officers look very blue"—and a peremptory challenge: "Tell me if you wish to have a useful hand in [the Continental] army and to pay what you find his services merit."

Before there was time to receive a reply, Arnold learned that his court-martial would reconvene on December 20. The Continental Army's winter camp was situated on the hillsides and in the hollows surrounding the village of Morristown, New Jersey. "The sufferings of the poor soldiers can scarcely be described," Dr. James Thacher wrote in his journal that winter (the same Dr. Thacher who had attended Arnold in the Albany hospital after the battle on Bemis's Heights). "So enfeebled from hunger and cold as to be almost unable to perform their military duty or labor in constructing their huts . . . they are badly clad and some are destitute of shoes. . . . It is a circumstance greatly to be deprecated," the doctor observed, "that the army, who are devoting their lives and everything dear to the defence of our country's freedom, should be subjected to such unparalleled privations while in the midst of a country abounding in every kind of provisions."*

Major General Robert Howe called the court to order in a chamber in Norris's Tavern at ten A.M. on the morning of December 23. The Judge Advocate read the charges, and Arnold pleaded not guilty. He had labored diligently to prepare himself for the trial, and he conducted his defense brilliantly throughout. His cross-examination of hostile witnesses was particularly effective: young Sergeant William Matlack folded completely and conceded every point made by the implacable Arnold, and his father was forced to admit that he could neither prove that Arnold had known about the alterations in the quartermaster's memorandum book nor that Robert Shewell (the owner of *Charming Nancy*) was a politically "disaffected" person.

After Colonel Fitzgerald's deposition was read, Arnold placed David Franks on the stand and led him through an inspired recitation that almost—but not quite—explained Fitzgerald away. When he entered Philadelphia in June 1778, Franks explained, he had been on the verge of resigning from the army, and the instructions to purchase goods were part of a plan for Arnold to help him set up in business. Later, Franks swore, Arnold said that he would have to withdraw the offer because the purchases were "incompatible" with the mercantile laws then in force in the capital. But in any case, the whole issue was moot because Franks had changed his mind about resigning.

Arnold expected to put John Mitchell on the stand immediately after the four-day New Year's holiday; but Mitchell failed to appear and the court was forced to adjourn to await his arrival. Peggy, who had sent a servant around to Mitchell's office, wrote to her husband,

---

* The winter of 1779–80 was the most severe in a hundred years. New York harbor froze to a depth of eighteen feet, which permitted some enterprising Americans to escape from their prison ships and make their way to shore on foot. One group walked all the way across Long Island Sound to Connecticut.

"I never wanted to see you half so much. You mention Sunday for your return [but] I will not flatter myself I shall see you even then, if you wait for Colonel Mitchell." The reluctant quartermaster finally appeared on January 19, after receiving a direct order from the commander in chief and the Board of War.

Predictably, Mitchell was difficult to pin down. On the one hand he acknowledged that Arnold had repeatedly offered to pay for the Egg Harbor wagon trip; on the other, he said that wagons *were* needed for the army at the time of Arnold's request, but that he felt he could not refuse "without incurring his displeasure as command-ing officer." His entire two-day testimony was so fraught with hedg-ing and backpedaling that by the time he stepped down, the facts of the case were more obscure than ever.

On Friday, January 21, nearly a month after the trial had begun, Arnold took the floor to make his closing statement. "When an accusation is made," he began, "I feel it a great source of consolation to have an opportunity of being tried by gentlemen whose delicate and refined sensations of honor will lead them to entertain similar sentiments concerning those who accuse unjustly and those who are justly accused. In the former case, your feelings revolt against the conduct of the prosecutors, in the latter against those who are de-served objects of a prosecution. Whether those feelings will be di-rected against me or against those whose charges have brought me before you will be known by your just and impartial determination of this case."

Thus launched, he slipped into high gear with a lengthy recita-tion of his services to the nation, complete with written testimonials to his valor from General Washington and the Congress, whose "au-thority," he pointed out, "will be thought *at least equal* to that of those who have spoken and written and published concerning me in a very different manner."

He then addressed each charge in turn. Issuing the pass to *Charming Nancy*, he acknowledged, was probably "an error judg-ment," but he denied any conscious wrongdoing. His treatment of Sergeant Matlack was based on the principle of military discipline, a point he could expect every man in the room to approve.

In addressing the other two charges, where the facts were ranged more formidably against him, he defended himself by attacking. The Pennsylvania Council, from "passion and envy," had created the problem of the army wagons out of whole cloth, he suggested, and then egged Jesse Jordan on "that they might have some pretence for instituting an action." As for John Fitzgerald's depostion, Arnold scornfully asked the court to judge whether the colonel's "manner of procuring a sight of the paper . . . was not a gross violation of the confidence subsisting between gentlemen. . . . I will not say it was a disgrace to the character of a soldier and gentleman. I will leave it to the gentleman's own feelings which (if he is not callous) will say more to him than I can possibly do on the subject. . . . On the honor of a gentleman and soldier, I declare to gentlemen and soldiers, that the charge is false."

Arnold was in full cry, and as his lies grew more outrageous, his language became more ornate. *If,* he declared, the charge of purchasing goods in Philadelphia was true, "I stand confessed in the presence of this honorable court the vilest of men; I stand stigmatized with indelible disgrace, the disgrace of having abused an appointment of high trust and importance to accomplish the meanest and most unworthy purposes. The blood I have spent in defence of my country will be insufficient to obliterate the stain.

"[I was] one of the first that appeared in field [to fight for my country]," he declared in conclusion, "and from that time to the present hour have not abandoned her service. . . . My conduct from the earliest period of the war to the present time has been steady and uniform. . . . Conscious of my own innocence, I have looked forward with pleasing anxiety to the present day, when, by the judgment of my fellow soldiers, I shall (I doubt not) stand honorably acquitted of all the charges brought against me, and again share with them the glory and danger of this just war."

This, from a man who had been transmitting intelligence to the enemy for the past eight months.

Three days passed. In a trial in which so few hard facts could be established, the verdict depended entirely on whom the court chose to believe. Arnold, whose view of the world encompassed no gray areas, had attempted to set up a stark choice for the court: to believe either Joseph Reed or Benedict Arnold. But there *were* gray areas, where probity rather than strict legality was the issue. Even if, for example, the owner of *Charming Nancy* was a loyal patriot, was it not improper for Arnold to issue a pass for a ship in which he personally owned an interest? Again, even if he had offered to pay for the use of the army wagons, was it not unbecoming for the Philadelphia commandant to put pressure on a junior officer to furnish them? Most telling of all, even if David Franks was telling the truth about the secret agreement, was it wise for the commandant of a recently liberated city to issue a blanket permission for secret purchases of scarce goods? These were questions of judgment, prudence and—to use one of Benedict Arnold's favorite words—rectitude. It never occurred to him to ask them.

On January 26, the court found Arnold guilty of a single charge: granting an illegal pass to *Charming Nancy*. In the matter of the wagons, while they discovered no attempt on his part to "defraud the public nor injure or impede the public service," they did deem his request for the wagons "imprudent and improper . . . considering the delicacy attending the high station in which the general acted, and that requests from him might operate as command." On the other two charges he was acquitted. The recommended sentence was an official public reprimand from the commander in chief.

Arnold could not stomach it. He had expected to be acquitted with honor on all counts—just as his friend Philip Schuyler and so many other officers had been. The fact that he was actually guilty as charged, the fact that he had been exonerated only because Joseph Reed lacked proof, was irrelevant to him. (Poor Reed: he had sensed all along that Arnold was a liar, a cheat and a Tory, but he laid hands on the proof only when Arnold was out of his reach.) Arnold could not bear the shame of a sentence that appeared extremely lenient to everyone except himself. He rushed back home to the waiting arms of the one soul in all the world who recognized his sense of hurt and loss and comforted him accordingly.

Together, they reaffirmed their commitment to the deliverance of their country to the enemy. There would be no more doubts, no more hesitation. Until they heard from Major André (who had recently been promoted, and now served as Sir Henry Clinton's adjutant with sole responsibility for British intelligence), they would concentrate their energies on increasing Arnold's market value.

Still unfit to take a command in the army, Arnold addressed the commander in chief with a proposition: "As I wish to render my country every service in my power," he wrote, "I have offered the Board [of Admiralty] to take the command of [a naval expedition] . . . to embark probably at New London by the middle of April for a [voyage] of about two months . . . provided it is agreeable to Your Excellency and the men can be spared from the army." A fleet of several frigates with four hundred men aboard would be a fine prize to offer to General Clinton.

Ironically, Washington's inability to cooperate was the direct result of intelligence that Arnold had passed to the British the previous spring: Charleston, South Carolina, was currently under siege by a large British force. General Washington, forced to dispatch a large detachment from the main army to reinforce the Charleston garrison, was unable to spare a single man for Arnold's naval expedition. (General Clinton captured Charleston by assault on May 12.)

Arnold was disappointed, but he had an alternative project, suggested perhaps the previous summer by Major André himself. As everyone knew, the fortifications at West Point in the Hudson River Highlands were currently being redesigned and hardened under General Washington's personal supervision in order to prevent a British fleet from sailing upriver as it had in 1777. Whoever controlled West Point controlled both the upper Hudson River and King's Ferry. With the main British force in South Carolina, the Point was under no immediate threat. As a backwater command, it would be eminently suitable for a general who was temporarily *hors de combat*. And it should fetch a magnificent price.

While Arnold and Peggy were plotting, Congress inadvertently extinguished any lingering doubts they might have had. On February 12, 1780, it voted to confirm the verdict of Arnold's court-martial and to order General Washington to issue a reprimand—a task that the reluctant commander in chief waited two months to perform. Two days later, on February 14, the committee that had been considering Arnold's Canadian accounts, pleading a case overload, recommended that the matter be returned to the Treasury Board, whereupon Treasury handed it back to the commissioners of the Chambers of Accounts, who had already ruled against Arnold ten months before.

Arnold lodged a vigorous protest, claiming that one of the commissioners, "with . . . whom [I have] had several disputes," had stolen a voucher that supported his claims. An investigation revealed that the voucher in question had been noted as missing by the accused man himself, shortly after *Arnold* had taken all the papers home for a few days to study them. The accusation fizzled (the thief, if there was a thief, has never been identified), but Arnold's impetuosity had once again earned the enmity of a man who had a great deal of power over his financial future.

The Treasury Board did comply with his request to consider the accounts themselves. Two months later, on April 27—a year to the day after he had first submitted his accounts—they recommended that Congress grant the full amount minus £2,500 (the deduction including the amount of the missing voucher, which, Treasury determined, may never have existed at all, "all the testimonies relating thereto amounting to no more than very vague and light presumptions"). Worse yet, they recommended that Congress delay payment until all Arnold's accounts could be "reexamined by the Commissioners of Accounts at Albany . . . and [subjected to] such corrections and amendments as they shall report."

That could take a year, and Arnold didn't have a year. Desperate, he lashed out at former Treasury Board chairman Elbridge Gerry, asking Congress to consider "how far Mr. Gerry's conduct . . . can be justified upon the principles of honor or equity, or how far his instructions and influence have operated in occasioning the disputes which have arose on the settlement of my accounts." Again, he had mistaken his target. Gerry categorically denied any bias and invited Arnold "to produce his evidence, if any he has, that I ever gave 'private instructions' of any kind to the Commissioners. . . . The assertion I declare on my honor to be an untruth." There was no question whom Congress would believe, General Benedict Arnold, whose public censure they had just ordered, or the unimpeachable Elbridge Gerry. Once again, Arnold had stamped his foot and detonated a land mine.

Congress did debate the five-month-old motion to pay Gideon Olmstead and his companions the full amount of the sale of the *Active* sloop and to send the bill to the State of Pennsylvania—and then voted it down. (Arnold never got another penny. The *Active* case was finally decided in favor of Olmstead *et al.* by the United States Supreme Court in 1809, eight years after his death.) And on April 6, two days before the Arnolds' wedding anniversary, General Washington included in his general orders for the day the reprimand that Congress had demanded. He did not let Arnold off lightly, adding to the pro forma recitation a personal rebuke: "The Commander in Chief would have been much happier in an occasion of bestowing commendations on an officer who has rendered such distinguished services to his country as Major General Arnold; but in the present case, a sense of duty and a regard to candor oblige him to declare that he considers his conduct in the instance of the permit [for *Charming Nancy*] as peculiarly reprehensible, both in a civil and a military view, and in the affair of the wagons as 'imprudent and improper.' "

From this moment, George Washington was regarded by Arnold as a personal enemy. To deliver up to the British his pride and joy, West Point, would be sweet revenge indeed.

Arnold sent Joseph Stansbury into New York—exactly a year after his first trip—with a blunt offer for General Clinton: "Mr. Moore" (Arnold's new code name) would arrange the capture of a major Continental military prize, identity unspecified, for a fee of £10,000 cash and command of a battalion in the British Army. Both General Clinton and Major André were absent in South Carolina, but André's stand-in, Captain George Beckwith, sent assurances that he would apprize General Clinton of the offer promptly on his return "and in the meantime will be happy in cultivating the connection and in giving Mr. Moore every testimony of his regard."

The delay and uncertainty were maddening, but Arnold's craving for revenge bore him over every obstacle. West Point was his only object, and the commander in chief his only means of getting it. He and Peggy (who in March had given birth to a son, Edward Shippen Arnold) presumed on their intimacy with General Philip Schuyler and his wife to plant the notion of West Point in the general's mind, and after Schuyler returned to Continental headquarters, Arnold followed up with a friendly letter: "When I requested leave of absence of His Excellency General Washington for the summer, it was under the idea that it would be a very inactive campaign. . . . The prospect now seems to be altered, and there is a probability of an active campaign, in which, though attended with pain and difficulty, I wish to render my country every service in my power; and with the advice of my friends am determined to join the army, of which I beg you will do me the favor to acquaint his Excellency General Washington, that I may be included in any arrangement that may be made."

Schuyler's reply was encouraging. No commander for West Point had yet been chosen; but General Washington had "expressed himself with regard to you in terms such as the friends who love you could wish . . . [he] dwelt on your abilities, your merits, your sufferings, and on the well earned claims you have on your country, and intimated that as soon as the arrangements for the campaign should take place that he would properly consider you. I believe you will have an alternative proposed, either to take charge of an important post with an honorable command, or your station in the field. . . . If the command at West Point is offered it will be honorable, if a division in the field you must judge whether you can support the fatigue, circumstanced as you are."

A few days later, Arnold received from Washington himself a brief, businesslike communication requesting him to find a Philadelphia printer "whose secrecy and discretion may be depended on" to make five hundred copies of a proclamation to the inhabitants of Canada. "The importance of this business will sufficiently impress you with the necessity of transacting it with every possible degree of caution," the commander in chief warned. Arnold agreed: the proclamation clearly signaled that an invasion of Canada was in the offing. He found a printer, obtained a proof and promptly mailed it off to Continental headquarters for approval, with a coded copy to British headquarters in New York.

Arnold now turned his attention to cashing in. He set off for

Connecticut in order to expedite the sale of his New Haven house and to request the state assembly to take up the cudgels on behalf of Gideon Olmstead and his fellow Connecticuters. Along the way he planned two important stops: Continental headquarters at Morristown, and West Point. He sent a detailed itinerary into New York, with the expectation of being intercepted along the way by a courier who would carry the latest intelligence swiftly back to British headquarters.

Arnold arrived at Morristown on June 12. Morale in the Continental camp, never robust, had been devastated by the loss of Charleston. After a harrowing winter, nearly everybody, from the highest staff officer to the lowliest foot soldier, was angry at their fellow countrymen for their lack of support. "Why don't you reinforce your army, feed them, clothe and pay them?" a colonel wrote to his brother at home. "Why do you suffer the enemy to have a foothold on the continent? You can prevent it. . . . You don't deserve to be free men. . . . I despise my countrymen," he proclaimed in despair. "I wish I could say I was not born in America. I once gloried in it, but am now ashamed of it. . . . The insults and neglects which the army have met with from the country beggars all description. It must go no farther; they can endure it no longer."

This was the voice Benedict Arnold heard as he listened to the men at Morristown; but there was another voice that he ignored. "Not a single complaint have I heard," a humble private wrote to his father. "Everyone seems willing to wait for a compensation till his country can grant it to him without injuring herself, which happy time we expect is near at hand." And Dr. Thacher, who was perhaps more intimately acquainted with the men's privations than anyone in camp, noted in his journal that "the heroic fortitude with which our officers and soldiers support their distresses proclaims their fidelity and intrinsic merit . . . it is to be ascribed to their patriotism and to a sense of honor and duty that they have not long since abandoned the cause of their country."

After a lengthy conference with the commander in chief, Arnold was able to furnish General Clinton with details regarding the summer campaign: the attack on Canada would consist of "three or four thousand rebels" marching against Quebec while "the Marquis Fayette with two or three thousand will go from Connecticut River to St. Jean and Montreal." In addition, a French fleet consisting of six "ships of the line, several frigates and a number of transports with six thousand troops" was expected to arrive off Rhode Island within the month. The second item was true, but ironically it backfired: about two weeks later, Sir Henry Clinton, in order to protect Manhattan from the French fleet, called off an attack on the main army at Morristown and withdrew his army from New Jersey, taking the pressure off General Washington and giving him considerable freedom of movement. As for the Canadian expedition, it was a total fabrication devised by generals Washington and Lafayette to mask their real intention, a joint Franco-American offensive against Clinton's army in New York. There is no evidence to suggest that Washington suspected Arnold. Only a few officers of his innermost circle knew about the Canadian ruse; the rest were told what Arnold was told.

A month later, Washington again resorted to "disinformation" (as it is known today) with excellent results: with Clinton poised to move in force against the French in Rhode Island, the commander in chief kept him in New York by planting evidence of an imminent Continental attack on the city. Major John André, who took such delight in playing at spymaster, could have learned something from Washington, who recognized spying for the deadly serious business that it is.

Arnold also informed the British that he expected shortly to receive the command of West Point—his own little fabrication, designed to goad Sir Henry Clinton into making a firm offer. George Washington had no intention of giving a stationary command to his best fighting general, whose leg was so far improved that the commander in chief hoped to see him in the field before the summer was over.

On June 15, Arnold paid a visit to Major General Robert Howe, the commandant of West Point. Howe had served as the president of Arnold's court-martial; yet the two enjoyed an intimate friendship. (Given Arnold's tendency to hold grudges, one has to suspect that he feigned friendship with Howe in order to learn more about his command.) After two days of inspecting the fortifications and two evenings of congenial conversation, Arnold sent a detailed report to Major André: "The Point is on a low piece of ground comparatively to the chain of hills which lie back of it. The highest, called Rocky Hill, which commands all the other works . . . [is] defenceless on the back, and I am told the English may land three miles below and have a good road to bring up heavy cannon to Rocky Hill. This redoubt is wretchedly executed . . . and might be taken by assault by a handful of men." His analytical skills were just as acute as ever: this was the very plan that he and Major André would agree on three months hence.

After a financially frustrating sojourn in Connecticut, Arnold returned to Philadelphia by the first week of July, where Peggy greeted him with good news. During his absence, she had been focusing her considerable charms on that perennial ladies' man, New York Congressman Robert R. Livingston, Jr., a wealthy Hudson Valley landowner who wielded great power in Congress and—more to the point—at headquarters with his close friend, General George Washington. (He was also the brother of Arnold's secret business partner, John R. Livingston.) Under Peggy's spell, Robert Livingston had written to the commander in chief inquiring if the command of West Point "might not be most safely confided to General Arnold, whose courage is undoubted, who is the favorite of our militia, and who will agree perfectly with our governor." Washington's response, no doubt confided to Peggy by her admirer, promised West Point to Arnold "if the operations of the campaign are such as to render it expedient to leave an officer of his rank in that command."

Arnold now embarked on the delicate task of convincing the commander in chief that, notwithstanding past performance, he would be perfectly happy with an inactive command. So sure was he of succeeding that he sent word into New York that he was "to take command of West Point immediately on the [French] fleet's arrival, or at any rate in the course of this month" and promised to provide detailed drawings of the fortifications and to devise a plan "that you might take it without loss." First, however, he insisted on a personal "interview with [a] proper officer, as nothing further can be done without it"—without, that is, a firm promise of adequate remuneration.

Four days later he wrote again, a letter so full of unmitigated falsehood and wishful thinking that it had to be the work of a desperate man: "I have accepted the command at West Point. . . . The mass of the people are heartily tired of the war and wish to be on their former footing. They are promised great events from this year's exertion. If disappointed, you have only to persevere and the contest will soon be at an end. The present struggles are like the pangs of a dying man, violent but of a short duration." There was no prevarication, however, when it came to money: "[I] most seriously wish an interview . . . as life and fortune are risked by serving His Majesty . . . a compensation for services [must be] agreed on and a sum advanced for that purpose."

The day after dispatching this letter, July 13, Arnold finally received a letter from Major André, the first in nearly a year. It was both inadequate and insulting. Sir Henry Clinton, it appeared, had been checking Arnold's intelligence against other sources for authenticity. Satisfied on that point, he now suggested that Arnold betake himself to some forward Continental post "which a flag of truce could reach and where you might be supposed to be detained by sickness," and there await Sir Henry's emissary. The notion of West Point was interesting, the major acknowledged, but as for money, "General [Clinton] trusts that in the same confidence in which you communicate with him you will rely on his promise that upon effectual cooperation you shall experience the full measure of the national obligation."

Arnold was furious. Major General Benedict Arnold would not act the flunky, coming and going at Sir Henry's command and cooling his heels at some remote outpost awaiting a British emissary. He countered brashly, by disdaining to discuss Clinton's arrangements for the meeting and upping the ante to "£10,000 sterling, to be paid to me or my heirs in case of loss"; £500 a year "in lieu of the pay and emoluments I give up"; and a £20,000 bonus for delivering up the Point. "I expect a full and explicit answer," he snapped, but added as bait, "the 20th I set off for West Point. A personal interview with an officer that you can confide in is absolutely necessary."

Arnold no longer had any room to maneuver: he had to make good on his boast, by convincing George Washington to give him West Point. Before he left for headquarters, Arnold and Peggy determined that all communications between him and British headquarters would have to pass through Philadelphia and be forwarded by her—a dangerous and time-consuming route, but one that would have to do until Arnold could establish a new system of couriers from West Point. Collecting some advance pay from Congress to outfit himself for the field, he arrived on horseback at Washington's headquarters on the west bank of the Hudson River at the end of July.

There ensued over the next several days a preposterous sequence of events in which all of Arnold's hopes were dashed to the ground and then, at the last moment, raised up again. When he reached headquarters, General Washington was preparing to make a feint against New York in order to pin General Clinton in the city and prevent his attacking the exposed French position in Rhode Island. If the ruse failed and Sir Henry sailed for Rhode Island anyway, Washington planned to draw the weakened New York garrison into the field and give battle, in anticipation of which he conferred on Major General Benedict Arnold the signal honor of command of the left wing of the army.

Frantically, Arnold dispatched a warning to Clinton not to take the bait, but it arrived too late (after traveling the roundabout route through Philadelphia). Ironically, however, another reversal brought Arnold what he wanted. The American commander in chief, with Clinton's forces entrenched on Manhattan Island, established his army on the west bank of the Hudson near the landing of Dobbs Ferry to await events. With no major military operations on the horizon, he finally acceded to General Arnold's expressed desire on August 3 by granting him the inactive command of West Point.

Arnold's sense of triumph was tempered only by the fact that, after fourteen months of hard bargaining, he still did not know what the British would pay for it.

Chapter 16

THE *VULTURE*
AUGUST 5-SEPTEMBER 25, 1780

Benedict Arnold arrived at his new headquarters near West Point on August 5 in a driving rainstorm. He ruled as commandant for a total of fifty-two days—glorious, heady, dangerous, demanding, self-willed days, days in which he felt totally engaged and alive and in charge of his own destiny; perhaps the best days of his life.

After all the months of uncertainty and disappointment, Arnold's way was clear. He had not felt so sure of himself since the afternoon nearly three years before when he had ridden alone into battle on Bemis's Heights in defiance of Horatio Gates's orders. Now he rode alone again, in defiance of the United States of America and all who served her.

The money, it appeared, was secondary. What counted most was to start over again, clean. The American Patriot-Hero was dead; long live the British Patriot-Hero: to this concept he was totally committed. As always, Arnold desired money not so much for itself as for the respect that it implied and the prestige that it conferred. A man's salary bespoke his worth. This also meant, unfortunately, that until the British put a monetary value on him, Arnold would remain in personal limbo. But he would not turn back.

What was extraordinary was his absolute conviction that purity would spring from treachery; that his past, his own, old self, would be consumed by the same flames that destroyed the independent United States of America, and that out of the ashes would arise the ideal Arnold, the hero, the man he saw reflected in his wife's eyes.

About sixty miles north of New York City, the Hudson River leaves the broad plains of Westchester and Rockland counties and enters the mountains of the Hudson Highlands. In the eighteenth century, the sailing reach through the Highlands was known as Martyrs' Reach, because ships that had cruised north under full sail through Tappan Zee and Haverstraw Bay (see map, page 199), on entering the Highlands, were suddenly checked, baffled and thwarted by fickle winds and the serpentine curves of the river as it threads its way among the mountains. Toward the northern end of the Highlands loomed the severest test of all: the ninety-degree bend around a high promontory known as West Point, where heavy vessels were obliged to adjust their sails (often radically) to negotiate the turn and accomodate the wind. With all hands fully occupied in the rigging, a ship might lie helpless in the water for a number of minutes, vulnerable to attack from either side of the narrow strait.

It was for this reason that West Point was chosen in April 1778 as the site for a new defensive chain to be stretched across the river. Only five months previously, just before the decisive battle on Bemis's Heights, a British fleet had rammed and broken the chain at Fort Montgomery and sailed north in support of General Burgoyne. (The fleet withdrew to New York after his surrender.) At West Point, General Washington and engineer Thaddeus Kosciusko reasoned, enemy vessels would lack the momentum to break the chain, and during the time their sails were down they would be sitting ducks for shore batteries on either side of the narrow strait.

The inviolability of the new chain—which was six hundred yards long and kept afloat on heavy wooden rafts—and of the West Point fortifications designed to protect it was a constant preoccupation of the commander in chief, whose army would be starved out in short order if the British gained control of the Hudson River crossings, particularly King's Ferry.

But West Point also had a topographical flaw: high hills to the rear that made it vulnerable to an attack by land. To compensate for this fault, Kosciusko designed a series of defensive rings, each intended to protect the one below and all intended to protect the chain itself (see map inset, page 199). Dominating the outermost ring, 750

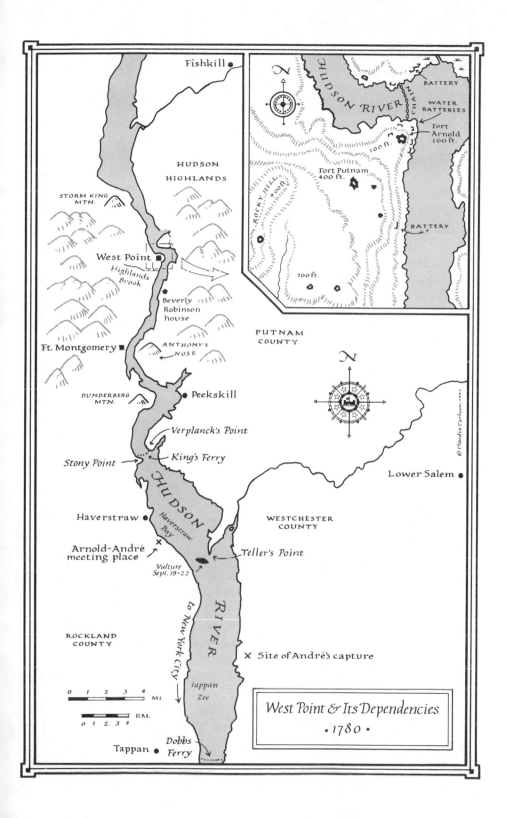

Fishkill

HUDSON HIGHLANDS

STORM KING MTN.

West Point

Highlands Brook

Beverly Robinson house

Ft. Montgomery

ANTHONY'S NOSE

DUNDERBERG MTN.

Peekskill

Verplanck's Point

Stony Point — King's Ferry

HUDSON

Haverstraw

Haverstraw Bay

Arnold-André meeting place

Teller's Point

Vulture Sept. 19-22

ROCKLAND COUNTY

RIVER

to New York City

Tappan Zee

Tappan

Dobbs Ferry

PUTNAM COUNTY

N

Lower Salem

WESTCHESTER COUNTY

X Site of André's capture

o 1 2 3 4 MI.
o 1 2 3 4 KM.

West Point & Its Dependencies
· 1780 ·

N

HUDSON RIVER

CHAIN

BATTERY

WATER BATTERIES

Fort Arnold 100 ft.

100 ft.

Fort Putnam 400 ft.

ROCKY HILL

900 ft.

BATTERY

700 ft.

© Claudia Carlson, 1993

feet above the river, was the redoubt on Rocky Hill. According to Kosciusko's plan, this redoubt's hundred or so defenders would bear the brunt of an initial attack, hold out long enough for the alarm to be raised in the neighborhood and then fall back on Fort Putnam, three hundred feet below, which was designed to withstand a siege of at least ten days, plenty of time for reinforcements to arrive and force the enemy to withdraw. All the while, the principal fort, which stood on the Point below, overlooking the water batteries and the chain itself, would remain safe. This fort, which all the others were designed to protect, was appropriately named Fort Arnold, after the hero of Saratoga.

The plan had its flaws—for example, it was based on the assumption that the British would not be able to bring cannon up Rocky Hill to bombard Fort Putnam from above—but it passed the acid test: the British obviously preferred the risk of buying West Point from General Benedict Arnold to the risk of mounting an assault.

But lack of money and manpower often subvert the best-laid plans, and, as Arnold himself had seen the previous spring, the half-finished fortifications at West Point were in dire condition. The redoubt on Rocky Hill was completely open on the back, Fort Putnam's walls were broken and crumbling and Fort Arnold itself had been largely destroyed by fire. When Arnold took over in August 1780, the post's entire garrison consisted of fifteen hundred "ungovernable [and] undisciplined" Massachusetts militia, whose wanton behavior better became "a wild Tatar's camp" (in one Continental Army officer's view) or "a bawdy house" than a military post.* "Everything is wanting . . . in this poverty-struck place," Arnold complained to Quartermaster General Timothy Pickering shortly after his arrival. "There is not a tent or any kind of camp equipage at the post, and it is with great difficulty that sheds can be made to cover the troops who are, in general, exposed to the inclemency of the weather, with only one camp kettle to 80 or 100 men. . . . Without these supplies, the garrison will be in a wretched uncomfortable situation next winter, the works in a ruinous and, by next spring, defenceless condition and great part that is done will be to do over again."

Arnold, of course, expected West Point to be in British hands long before "next spring," and his sole aim as commandant was to

---

*One example of Arnold's disciplinary style is instructive. When a wagon master at West Point was found guilty of using army wagons to transport private goods and sentenced to reimburse the army for the trip, Arnold, warning that "the lenity of the court-martial [would fail to deter] like offences in the future," ordered the court to review its sentence. He subsequently approved an added sentence of "twenty stripes laid on [the offender's] bare back."

weaken the fortress while appearing to strengthen it. He was therefore neither surprised nor disappointed when the quartermaster failed to furnish the requisitioned supplies; and Pickering's anguished excuse—"I am unhappy to inform you that I have not yet received one farthing of money for any purpose whatever, nor can get any, there being none in the treasury"—only confirmed his conviction that he was on the winning side.

Within hours of his arrival, Arnold had obtained the latest inventories of manpower, armaments and supplies at the post and secretly transmitted them to Peggy to forward to British headquarters, via Stansbury and his couriers. He then began to issue a flood of orders regarding every element of his command, from sentry posts to bakeries, from the jail to the hospital. Troop and artillery deployments attracted his particular attention, as did signal guns and the disposition of cavalry units, all of which befitted a commandant and surprised no one familiar with his style of leadership.

While Arnold took charge with his usual flair and efficiency, General Washington was encamped with the main army near Tappan, at the western landing of Dobbs Ferry. His men, too, were devoid of bread, tents, shoes and ammunition, and by the middle of August the commander in chief was forced to dismiss all new militia arrivals because he could not feed them. "There has never been a stage of the war in which the [army's] dissatisfaction has been so general and so alarming," the commander in chief declared to Congress, and he warned that "if something satisfactory be not done, the army (already so much reduced in officers by daily resignations as not to have a sufficiency to do the common duties of it) must either cease to exist at the end of the campaign, or it will exhibit an example of more virtue, fortitude, self-denial and perseverance than has perhaps ever yet been paralleled in the history of human enthusiasm."*

Congress responded by refusing to grant back pay to the officer

---

* Arnold received a particularly poignant appeal in early September from a foot soldier who had served under him in Canada and had subsequently lost his farm in the Champlain Valley when General Burgoyne captured Ticonderoga. Now, his letter explained, he had brought his family to Fishkill "expecting to draw some provision for them, as I understood that it was tolerated," but the quartermaster at Fishkill had refused him. "Honored Sir," the soldier wrote to his old commander, "if it is consistent either by the customs of the army or my needy circumstances to give me an order to draw provision for my wife and two boys (the oldest of which is in his twelfth year), as I am ordered to camp, and have no money to buy, and to beg I am ashamed, it will in some measure relieve the needy and much oblige, Honored Sir, your devoted and most humble servant, Gamaliel Painter." Arnold immediately ordered the assistant quartermaster at Fishkill to supply the family.

corps, calling instead for "patience and self-denial, fortitude and perseverance, and the cheerful sacrifice of time, health and fortune . . . virtues which both the citizen and the soldier are called to exercise, while struggling for the liberties of their country." "A truly Presbyterian sermon," Benedict Arnold scoffed in forwarding the resolution on to his friend Samuel Parsons (the Connecticut assemblyman who had financed the expedition against Ticonderoga in 1775 and who now commanded troops in western Connecticut and reported to Arnold). Parsons responded, "I think I have made great demonstrations of patience and self-denial . . . in giving it two or three readings before I stamped it into the dust." But his assessment diverged from that of his commandant at a crucial point: although "the wretches who have crept into Congress are almost below contempt," Parsons declared, "the cause of country I will never forsake . . . [and] the virtues of our General will ever attach us to his fortunes."

Unfortunately, the virtues of General Washington did not weigh so heavily with the French, whose resolve in pursuing the war in North America was rapidly draining into the waters of the Caribbean, whose rich island colonies were so crucial to France's economic well-being and to that of its ancient enemy, Great Britain. Washington was counting heavily on the arrival of the second division of the French fleet to reinvigorate his army's morale and inspire support throughout the country; but in the absence of healthy morale and solid support, the French might well abandon him. The commander in chief had little hope of producing a coup such as Trenton or Saratoga. All he could do was pray his allies would stay the course, and also take every precaution to avert a military disaster that would give them excuse not to. It was for this reason (among others) that he chose Tappan as the site for his summer encampment: it put the main army in range of West Point, the "Gibraltar of America," whose loss would surely trigger a French withdrawal.

The irony cannot have been lost on Benedict Arnold: the American hero who lured the French into the war by winning Saratoga would also strike the blow that would drive them away.

Arnold's command included West Point's "dependencies," which stretched along the Hudson River from King's Ferry to Fishkill and eastward into Westchester County. Serving under him was a distinguished group of senior officers, all former comrades in arms well known to him—and all marked for sacrifice as part of his plot, a thought which apparently concerned him not at all. In command at King's Ferry was Colonel James Livingston, who had fought in Arnold's division at Saratoga;* the chief officer in Westchester was another old comrade, Colonel Elisha Sheldon; and the commandant of the garrison at West Point itself was John Lamb, the tough artillery colonel who had lost an eye at Quebec and survived to fight at Arnold's side at Ridgefield.

Deceiving these men required considerable finesse. In order to siphon off manpower and slow down repair work on the fortifications at West Point, for example, Arnold ordered a number of work parties out into the countryside to gather supplies. John Lamb's one good eye saw clearly that "if such drafts as are called for are made from the garrison we shall neither be able to finish the works that are incomplete nor . . . defend those that are finished"; but he lacked the imagination for treachery and never questioned his general's motives. Lamb was also appalled at the dearth of artillery at the Point, and he concluded that an enemy attack "would not, in my opinion, be a very arduous undertaking in the present state of this garrison, and this state the enemy will not long be ignorant of. . . . I am not apt to conjure up phantoms nor to anticipate disagreeable events, but I do not like the present situation of matters here."

Keeping track of this far-flung command required an enormous amount of organization and paperwork, and it was with high satisfaction that Arnold welcomed the arrival on August 13 of Richard Varick, whom he had invited to serve as secretary. Varick, it will be remembered, had distinguished himself as General Schuyler's amanuensis and later, after Schuyler was relieved of command in the Northern Department, as the general's spy in the camp on Bemis's Heights. His efficiency was excelled only by his predilection for gossip, which had done much to fan the flames of the Schuyler-Gates feud and to bring to a head Gates's quarrel with Benedict Arnold. Varick had retired from the army at the end of the Saratoga campaign in order to resume his legal studies, and was persuaded to reenlist only after a personal appeal from Arnold himself, who added as an extra inducement that "as [West Point] has the appearance of a quiet post, I expect Mrs. Arnold will soon be with me."

Arnold's satisfaction at being served by two of his most ardent admirers, Varick and aide-de-camp David Franks, was short-lived. The problem was a simple one: both men were accustomed to being in his confidence, and at West Point they were not. It took them hardly any time to realize that he was holding out on them and to

*He was also distantly related to John R. Livingston, Arnold's erstwhile partner in attempting to fleece the city of New York.

learn to resent it. Arnold tried to ignore their complaints—in his view, both aide and secretary were there to be used and sacrificed, just like all his other old comrades who happened to be on the scene—but he had to be particularly careful not to arouse their suspicions. As tension in the office mounted, his wall of secrecy grew higher and stronger. Nobody was allowed inside that wall, except his wife.

Only to Peggy could he speak the secrets of his heart and the preoccupations of his mind; only from her could he seek approval and confirmation. Without her, he was more alone than he had ever been; and no doubt the twenty-year-old new mother, playing her customary role of ingenue among her family and friends in Philadelphia, felt even more isolated than he. They longed to be together, to share the working out of their perilous plot.

Unfortunately, Arnold's sister, Hannah, seemed determined to come to West Point as well with eight-year-old Harry. Hannah had followed and served her brother for virtually all of her thirty-eight spinster years, keeping his house, tending his businesses, taking second place to his wives and caring for his motherless children. Now Arnold did not want her, which he managed to convey in such a tactless manner that Hannah was moved to retaliate. "As you have neither purling streams nor sighing swains at West Point, 'tis no place for me," she responded to his "ill-nature[d]" letter, "nor do I think Mrs. Arnold will be long pleased with it, though expect it may be rendered dear to her (for a few hours) by the presence of a certain chancellor, who, by the by, is a dangerous companion for a particular lady, in the absence of her husband. I could say more than prudence will permit," she continued remorselessly, "I could tell you of frequent private assignations and of numberless billet doux, if I had an inclination to make mischief, but as I am of a very peaceable temper I'll not mention a syllable of the matter." Hannah's arrow missed its mark: Arnold was well aware of Peggy's flirtation with Chancellor Robert R. Livingston of New York—whom she had deliberately used to obtain the command of West Point for her husband—and he eagerly awaited her arrival, sans Hannah.

"Lover-like, [Arnold] torment[ed] himself with a thousand fancied disasters" that might occur on Peggy's journey from Philadelphia with the infant Edward. "You must by all means get out of your carriage in crossing all ferries and going over all large bridges to prevent accidents," he instructed her. "Bring your own sheets to sleep in on the road to avoid dirty ones and to prevent disagreeable apprehensions and perhaps something worse . . . [also] your own tea and sugar, some meats, tongues or ham, and send [one] of your light horsemen early every morning to have dinner provided for you." He even suggested that she "put a feather bed in the light wagon which will make an easy seat, and you will find it cooler and pleasanter to ride in when the roads are smooth than a closed carriage."

He also made careful preparations for her comfort at West Point, enlisting local farmers to provide fresh milk, meat and vegetables for the household and frantically attempting to buy a new bed. (A "feather bed of inferior quality" finally arrived, all the way from Connecticut, just before Peggy herself did.) "No sensations can bear a comparison with those arriving from the reciprocity of concern and mutual felicity existing between a lady of sensibility and a fond husband," he wrote to his friend Robert Howe in an expansive, anticipatory mood. "I myself had enjoyed a tolerable share of the dissipate joys of life, as well as the scenes of sensual gratification incident to a man of a nervous constitution; but when set in competition with those I have since felt and still enjoy, I consider the time of celibacy in some measure misspent."

Against Howe's advice, Arnold had chosen to establish his family and his headquarters not at West Point itself but across the river at the country seat of Beverley Robinson, a Loyalist now with the British in New York. The Robinson house was a spacious, rambling, clapboard structure, set in bucolic splendor amid orchards and pastures on a high plateau above the Hudson River, two miles downstream from West Point. There, surrounded by the hundred men of Arnold's life guard, Peggy and six-month-old Edward would be safe during the British attack.

A hundred feet below the house, at the bottom of a steep wagon track, lay the dock where Arnold's barge was stationed, an elegant and comfortable affair with seats and awnings, manned by eight oarsmen and a coxswain who stood ready at any moment to transport Arnold up to the Point (a trip of no more than ten minutes) or anywhere else along the river. Nevertheless, General Howe warned Arnold, "I look upon any officer [at Robinson's] . . . as exposed . . . [and] I leave it to you to determine whether, should accident happen, you will be held accountable." Of course, an "accident" was precisely what Arnold intended, so he thanked Howe for his concern but firmly declared that "at present, I apprehend no danger in these quarters, which are the most convenient for an invalid."

Once established at the Robinson house, Arnold seldom visited West Point. There was too much to do at headquarters, satisfying the demands of his disparate, far-flung post as well as fulfilling his own secret agenda. The duplicity came quite naturally to a man who had always lived in a house of mirrors, especially one whose facility for masquerade was sustained by a good memory and an excellent grasp of detail. In addition to cashing in all his personal assets (wherein he failed miserably), making preparations for Peggy's arrival and gathering intelligence for the British, Arnold had one overwhelming goal: to establish a secure means of communicating directly with Major André.

He had not heard from the major for months, and the suspense of not knowing Sir Henry Clinton's response to his latest demands—£20,000 pounds for West Point, £10,000 in case of failure, plus an life annuity of £500—was excruciating. A letter from André had arrived in Philadelphia, but Peggy had no secure means of forwarding it to him. He must find a courier.

He had to be extremely careful, of course, and for the first time in his career (and for all the wrong reasons), Arnold became deeply concerned with avoiding any appearance of impropriety. For example, he took the precaution of asking General Washington to clarify his authority to issue passes and flags, hoping to employ innocent civilian couriers if all else failed. (The two terms were used interchangeably, although, strictly speaking, a flag was a document permitting military personnel to approach or cross enemy lines and a pass granted similar permission to civilians.) The commander in chief's answer was disappointing: passes could be authorized only by the governor of the State of New York, whose written permission Arnold must seek if he desired to send someone toward British lines in Westchester or into New York.

But a wealthy local landowner, Joshua Hett Smith, informed Arnold that the governor had given Robert Howe, his predecessor, blanket permission to send into Manhattan any women and children who desired to join their Loyalist husbands there, "sound policy," Smith observed, "as it took so many mouths from us to feed and landed the enemy with them." Arnold chose to believe it because he wanted to, and also because he was assiduously cultivating Joshua Smith's friendship. Smith was uniquely positioned to be of service: as a longtime member of the community, he knew the local cast of characters and had already proffered the names of potential intelligence sources; as the brother of William Smith, the Royal Chief Justice of New York and one of Sir Henry Clinton's closest advisers, he had powerful contacts in the city; and as a dodgy, unctuous sort of person, he might well prove willing and able to perform services that another man might balk at. Arnold was prepared to use Smith

if the need arose, and he opened to him the hospitality of the Robinson house and paid frequent visits on the Smith family at Belmont,
their elegant mansion on the heights above the village of Haverstraw
overlooking Haverstraw Bay.

But Richard Varick distrusted Joshua Smith, and he persuaded
Arnold to verify his assertion concerning passes for women and children. When the governor of New York confirmed what the commander in chief had said, that only the state could issue passes,
Arnold brushed aside the implication that Joshua Smith had lied to
him. Richard Varick did not, however, and, unbeknownst to Arnold,
he wrote a letter to the governor's aide inquiring about Smith's "real
political character. . . . The General thinks well of Smith," Varick
explained; "I must confess that the conduct of the family will not
permit me to do so." While awaiting a reply, Varick, in true Bemis's
Heights style, began to rail against Smith as "a damned Tory and
snake in the grass" to anyone who would listen.

Meanwhile, his commandant was left dangling, with no way of
learning his value to his new British masters.

In mid-August, the American army in the Southern Department,
under the personal command of Horatio Gates, suffered a devastating defeat at Camden, South Carolina. Arnold received a report of the
battle from Nathanael Greene, who disdainfully observed that Gates,
in fleeing the bloody field, had been "obliged to retreat 180 miles
before he thought himself safe." Gates's "conduct on this occasion
has in no wise disappointed my expectations or predictions," Arnold
replied. Secretly, of course, he rejoiced: Camden would set the Continental cause reeling; the loss of West Point would knock it over and
out. At this juncture, General Washington received word that the
French fleet was bottled up in the harbor at Brest by a British block-
ade and would not reach American shores in the foreseeable future.

To a council of his officers, the commander in chief outlined the
situation: with the British navy operating freely in American waters,
the southern army had ceased to exist and the main army stood to
lose nearly two thirds of its manpower when enlistments expired on
January 1, leaving about six thousand regulars to face a British force
of some ten thousand men stationed in New York City. In view of
these stark realities, General Washington inquired, presumably without irony, what the goals of the current campaign should be. He sent
a memorandum of the meeting to Arnold and solicited his opinion as
a senior officer.

In his reply, the traitor explored the various alternatives with his
usual thoroughness and accuracy, and concluded that "no offensive

operations against the enemy can with prudence be undertaken this fall . . . without a decided superiority by sea," adding, with considerable irony, that everything could be turned around in an instant "from the fluctuating situation of our affairs, which may be totally changed in a short time by a variety of circumstances which may happen." Having dispatched his answer to the commander in chief, he prepared to send Washington's summary to General Clinton in New York. Unfortunately, he still had no means of getting it there.

Finally, on the afternoon of August 24, with "hail as big as musket balls" pelting the windows of the Robinson house, Arnold received Major André's long-awaited letter via secure courier from Peggy. Sir Henry Clinton agreed to pay £20,000 for the delivery of West Point, but refused to guarantee anything should the plot fail. As the major put it, "Services done are the terms on which we promise rewards." Arnold was both disappointed and angry. He had been denied the fruits of his honest efforts too many times in the past not to demand surety now; more significantly, the major's lofty tone rankled. There was but one solution: a face-to-face meeting with Major André to secure both payment and plot—and to establish, once and for all, Major General Benedict Arnold's dignity and consequence.

Fortuitously, within the next week not one but two unwitting couriers to New York presented themselves in Arnold's office. The first was William Heron, who appeared on the hot, humid afternoon of August 29 with a letter of introduction from Samuel Parsons and a request for a pass to meet an acquaintance at the British lines near Kingsbridge, on the northern end of Manhattan Island, in order to collect a debt. (Arnold had boasted to Parsons that he had the commander in chief's permission "to grant flags at discretion," which was clearly not the case.) Arnold thought quickly, and then invited Heron to stay for dinner and the night before proceeding on his journey.

The following morning, when Heron called at the office for his pass, Arnold—who had clearly underestimated how long it took to disguise his handwriting—kept him waiting for nearly an hour. Finally he emerged carrying a business letter with a broken seal addressed to "Mr. John Anderson, Merchant" of New York and signed "Gustavus." The letter, he explained, was from a personal friend, and he had personally opened and read it to make certain its contents were harmless; now, he hoped, Heron's friend at Kingsbridge would be willing to deliver it to Mr. Anderson.

To Arnold's relief, Heron accepted the letter and went on his way. "Mr M[oo]re flatters himself that in the course of ten days he will have the pleasure of seeing you," the letter read; "I expect to [write to you more] fully in a few days and to procure an interview with Mr. M. when you will be able to settle your commercial plan I hope agreeable to all parties. . . . He expects when you meet that you will be fully authorized from your house [and] that the risks and profit of the co-partnership may be fully and clearly understood."

Three days later, when another opportunity presented itself, Arnold was better prepared. A Mrs. Mary McCarthy, carrying a pass from the governor of the state, came to headquarters with her children to request an escort into New York City. Arnold sent her downriver in style, accompanied by a lieutenant, a sergeant and seven privates—and carrying a sealed letter addressed on the outside to the royal governor of New York, General James Robertson. Inside, however, the letter was addressed to Major André, and it instructed him to come to Continental headquarters at Lower Salem in Westchester County in civilian disguise under the name "John Anderson."

The sheer gall of it was astonishing: if André was caught behind American lines traveling in disguise, he would be tried as a spy rather than a prisoner of war, and probably hanged. General Clinton would never permit his adjutant to run such a risk—which was exactly why Arnold proposed it: as a means of instructing his new masters to treat him with respect. Major André would come to meet Major General Arnold on Arnold's turf and terms, and if General Sir Henry Clinton did not like it—but there, unfortunately, the argument fell apart. Clinton seemed to sense that Arnold had burned his bridges, and that no matter how hard he bargained he would not go back.

To preserve his pride, Arnold tried to pretend this was not true. But at some level, he sensed it, and even as he told himself that the British wanted him more than he wanted them, he took extensive pains to ensure against being rejected. He began to closet himself away for hours at a time writing detailed accounts of the fortifications, troop deployments and artillery dispositions at West Point to hand over to Major André at their meeting, not because the major needed the information (he could easily memorize the assault plan Arnold had devised), but because Benedict Arnold wanted his exertions to be documented. That carrying the papers would multiply Major André's peril a hundredfold simply did not matter to Arnold. Nothing mattered, except his own security. If the plot failed, he would not be denied his just rewards.

Arnold had dispatched David Franks to Philadelphia to escort Peggy on her journey to the Robinson house. Her prompt arrival was critical: once he met with Major André, the attack on West Point could not be far behind. Now he alerted Westchester commander Elisha Sheldon to expect the early appearance at his headquarters at Lower Salem of an unnamed civilian bringing valuable intelligence from New York.

Two days later, September 9, he was startled to receive a puzzled note from Sheldon enclosing a letter he had received from a man he had never heard of: John Anderson. "I am told my name is made known to you," Anderson/André had written to Sheldon; "I will endeavor to obtain permission to go out with a flag which will be sent to Dobbs Ferry on Monday next, the 11th, at 12 o'clock, when I shall be happy to see Mr. G [another name unfamiliar to Sheldon]. Should I not be allowed to go, the officer who is to command the escort, between whom and myself no distinction need be made, can speak on the affair. . . . I shall rather risk that than neglect the business in question or assume a mysterious character to carry on an innocent affair."

Arnold was both furious and unnerved at André's carelessness in naming names, hinting at disguises and intimating that Sheldon's commandant planned a secret meeting with a British Army officer. Fortunately, Sheldon seemed more baffled than suspicious. Unfortunately, the message from Sir Henry Clinton was unmistakable: Major André would not venture behind American lines in civilian disguise. The meeting would take place in neutral territory (the eastern terminus of Dobbs Ferry was held by the British, the western terminus by the Americans), and André, "the officer . . . between whom and myself no distinction need be made," would wear his regimentals.

"You must be sensible my situation will not permit my meeting or having any private intercourse with [a British] officer," Arnold responded, repeating his insistence that André come to Lower Salem "by stealth. If you can do it without danger on your side," he added, "I will engage you shall be perfectly safe here." He then wrote to Colonel Sheldon: "if Mr. Anderson . . . should find means to come to your quarters, I wish you to send an express to let me know, and send two or three horsemen to conduct him on the way to meet me, as it is difficult for me to ride so far. If your health will permit, I wish you to come with him. I have promised him your protection and that he shall return in safety."

But once again, Sir Henry Clinton had Arnold right where he wanted him, having scheduled the rendezous at Dobbs Ferry on such short notice that Arnold would have to take the risk of showing up, no matter what. He could vent his frustration in his letter to Major

André if he wished, but he had no way to send it and no power to refuse the meeting.*

Just before noon on September 11, as Arnold's barge cautiously approached Dobbs Ferry, a swift British gunboat suddenly appeared from the eastern shore, bore down on him and opened fire. Arnold's coxswain swung the rudder and increased the cadence, and the oarsmen sprinted to safety at the American blockhouse on the western shore. Arnold was utterly confounded. Had it been a trap, or merely an unforeseen blunder? If General Clinton had failed to instruct the British river patrols to let his barge through, did it mean the meeting was off? All afternoon he paced the shoreline, searching the river for a sign from Major André and wondering what to do. He dashed off a note to General Washington, whose headquarters was only three miles away, explaining his presence: "I came here this morning in order to establish signals to be observed in case the enemy came up the river." Then he waited. Finally, toward sunset, he reembarked for the long pull back to headquarters.

On the opposite shore, he learned much later, another man also paced all afternoon, searching the river for a sign and finally returning to his headquarters in disappointment: Major André, who dared not approach in the absence of a clear signal that Arnold dared not give.

Back at Robinson's, Arnold learned that Elisha Sheldon, whose trust he had so carefully cultivated, had been arrested for fraud and removed from command pending a court-martial (he was eventually acquitted). His replacement, a Lieutenant Colonel John Jameson, whom Arnold did not know, had not yet reached Lower Salem, and in the interim, Major Benjamin Tallmadge of the Westchester dragoons served as commander. Arnold quickly wrote to Tallmadge requesting that if John Anderson, "a person I expect from New York, should come to your quarters . . . [you will] give him an escort of two

---

*A final note on the subject of couriers: Arnold realized from Major André's letter to Colonel Sheldon that the letter he had sent via Mary McCarthy had gotten through. What he did not realize was that William Heron, whose suspicions had been aroused by the oddly broken seal and Arnold's fumbling explanations, instead of giving the letter to his man in New York, had sent it to their mutual friend Samuel Parsons. Parsons casually read it, deemed it a harmless commercial message and promptly forgot about it.

Ironically, William Heron turns out to have been a double agent whose trip to New York was for the purpose of conferring with British intelligence. His duplicity was never suspected, and after the war he dwelt peacefully in Redding, Connecticut, was twice elected to the Connecticut Assembly and died in his bed in 1819.

horsemen to bring him on his way to this place . . . [and] if your business will permit, I wish you to come with him."

What Arnold did not know was that Major Tallmadge's role as a dragoon major was only a cover for his real assignment as overseer of General Washington's extensive secret service. In other words, Arnold had unwittingly asked one spymaster to escort another to his headquarters. Tallmadge had recently received a report from his most reliable agent inside New York City (Robert Townsend, code name "Culper, Junior") that a highly placed American traitor was about to produce a momentous coup; so although he had no reason to suspect Arnold, he no doubt scrutinized the commandant's request more closely than he might otherwise have done, and committed the name John Anderson to memory.

On September 14, three days after his narrow escape at Dobbs Ferry, Arnold again embarked on his barge and headed south, this time for a rendezvous with Peggy at Joshua Smith's house in Haverstraw. Happy and relieved as he was to see her, he did not lose sight of a new and urgent mission. The experience at Dobbs, which he did not care to repeat, had finally convinced him that Sir Henry Clinton was not going to permit his adjutant to travel in civilian disguise all the way to Arnold's headquarters at the Robinson house. He had therefore devised an alternative scheme: André would travel by boat, and the meeting would take place at Haverstraw, in the parlor where he and Peggy now took their tea with Mr. and Mrs. Joshua Hett Smith.

Smith's sycophantic eagerness to oblige the great General Arnold made it easy to gain his cooperation. He would, he assured the commandant, be delighted to row to Dobbs Ferry after dark a few nights hence to bring a mysterious civilian intelligence agent back to the house to meet with Arnold; he would be happy to get his family out of the way so that the general and his visitor could talk in complete privacy; and he would, of course, make sure that the visitor was safely delivered back to Dobbs Ferry.

On the sparkling-clear autumn morning of September 15, Arnold, Peggy, baby Edward and David Franks embarked on Arnold's barge and headed north. After passing through King's Ferry and coming around the thousand-foot hump of Dunderberg Mountain, the little barge came under the guns of Fort Montgomery, where Peggy got her first glimpse of the Robinson house gleaming in its high meadow above the river three miles ahead. Behind it rose the distinctive shape of Sugarloaf Mountain, and beyond it on the opposite shore stood Fort Arnold, with Storm King Mountain looming in the background. The Highlands' "diversified scenery of wild mountains, craggy precipices and noble lofty cliffs" was, according to a contemporary of Peggy's, both "truly romantic" and claustrophobic—depending, perhaps, on one's state of mind upon entering it.

Peggy's arrival smoothed over the tension in the household between Arnold and his two aides, although it continued to fester beneath the surface. When Richard Varick told Franks that their general had recently been corresponding "in a mercantile style to a person in New York whose fictitious name was John Anderson, to establish a line of intelligence of the enemy's movements," Franks recognized "Anderson" as the name of a man Arnold had contacted from Philadelphia. Although they could not prove it, the two apparently began to suspect Arnold, not of treason, but of intending to trade illegally with New York "under the sanction of his own command and through the rascal Smith." (If anyone knew about Arnold's proclivities toward illegal trade it would be David Franks.)

Before Arnold could send his latest proposal for a meeting into New York (he had found a courier, whose identity is still unknown), he received a confidential letter from General Washington requesting a special guard to be sent to King's Ferry the following evening, September 17, to cover the commander in chief's crossing with his suite. Washington planned to spend the night in Peekskill en route to Hartford for a secret conference with the French general and admiral. Arnold responded immediately that he would attend the general in person, and then scribbled a hasty postscript in cipher to Major André informing him of Washington's plans. He cannot have imagined that André would receive the news in time to organize an abduction of the commander in chief; more likely, he was warning the major to delay his trip upriver until the special security had disappeared.

Before departing for King's Ferry on the seventeenth, Arnold presided at mid-afternoon dinner in the spacious dining room of the Robinson house. Among the company were Mr. and Mrs. Joshua Hett Smith—on their way to Fishkill, where, it appeared, Mrs. Smith and the children were to spend a few days with relatives—Richard Varick, David Franks and John Lamb with some of his West Point officers. During the meal, Arnold was handed a note from Colonel Livingston at King's Ferry enclosing a letter delivered by a flag from the British sloop *Vulture*, which was newly anchored off Teller's Point. Arnold read the letter, blanched, and quickly stuffed it into his pocket: it was from the owner of the house, Beverley Robinson, ostensibly asking to meet with Arnold to inquire about his property; but it carried a secret message. "I did intend in order to have your

answer immediately to have sent this by my servant, James Osborn
. . ." Robinson had written. James Osborn, as Arnold well knew, was
the name of Joseph Stansbury's courier inside New York City: Beverley Robinson was upriver on Major André's business.

With his one, all-seeing eye, John Lamb noticed and appraised
his old friend's agitated response to the letter he had just received.
It was from Beverley Robinson, Arnold hastily explained; he wished
to have an interview; how did Colonel Lamb think he should respond? Tell Robinson to address his request to the governor of New
York, Lamb replied quite correctly. Or, better yet, show the letter to
General Washington that evening and follow his instructions.

It was excellent advice which Arnold was obliged to take. After
dinner, he traveled down to King's Ferry, where he met the commander in chief and the members of his suite, including the Marquis
de Lafayette, Alexander Hamilton and Henry Knox, and crossed with
them to Peekskill. General Washington, appalled at Beverley Robinson's tactlessness in requesting an interview with a Continental officer, forbade Arnold to meet him. He then informed Arnold that he
wished to visit West Point on his return from Hartford and would
probably spend the night at the Robinson house the following Saturday, September 23. Arnold replied with appropriate cordiality; but
something in his manner may have troubled General Washington,
who sent orders to Tappan to his second-in-command, Nathanael
Greene, to move the main army north in order to protect West Point
more closely.

Arnold returned home the following morning to find Richard
Varick still fuming over Joshua Hett Smith's presence at dinner the
day before. The secretary was extremely touchy; but when he raised
objections to the friendly tone of a letter Arnold dictated to Beverley
Robinson, Arnold mildly told him to alter it in any way he found
proper. The letter was irrelevant. Arnold retired to his private office
to write another letter to Robinson, proposing a new scheme based
on the presence of the *Vulture* in Haverstraw Bay: "I expect his
Excellency General Washington to lodge here on Saturday night
next," Arnold wrote; "I shall send a person to Dobbs Ferry or on
board the *Vulture* on Wednesday night the 20th instant, and furnish
him with a boat and flag of truce. . . . I think it will be advisable for
the *Vulture* to remain where she is until the time mentioned . . .
[when I] make no doubt . . . the gentleman in New York . . . will be
permitted to come." He placed the letter, together with a copy of his
latest to Major André, in a sealed envelope addressed to Royal Chief
Justice William Smith (to indicate that Smith's brother Joshua would

be the bearer of the flag) and slipped it into the envelope containing Varick's sanitized letter to Beverley Robinson.

A polite reply from Robinson was delivered the following day: "[I] am sorry . . . that it is not thought proper to allow me to see you, my business being entirely of a private nature. . . . I shall wait here [on board the *Vulture*] until tomorrow afternoon if, upon your reconsidering my request I may be permitted to see you, shall be glad to have notice of it in the morning—at any place you please." The message was clear: Major André would come to Arnold tomorrow, from the *Vulture*. He had won.

Wednesday, September 20, dawned gray and rainy. Joshua Smith called on his way home from Fishkill and agreed to fetch his mysterious passenger from the British warship that night. Arnold wrote a pass permitting "John Anderson" to enter and leave the American lines at Haverstraw, and Smith pocketed it and departed, happy at the prospect of avoiding the long pull to Dobbs.

The day passed slowly. During the afternoon a report was received from Colonel Livingston: a brisk firing of muskets had been heard from the direction of *Vulture*'s anchorage. Hours passed, but no explanation followed. Arnold and Peggy ate their dinner and eventually retired. Incredibly, Arnold did not go to Haverstraw that night: Major André, in civilian disguise behind American lines, was apparently intended to cool his heels at Smith's house until morning, when the American major general would deign to visit him.

At dawn the eagerly awaited message arrived from Smith. The trip to the *Vulture* had not taken place, two of Smith's tenants having refused to be impressed as oarsmen. In a fury, Arnold jumped on his horse, rode down the steep track to the dock and ordered his bargemen to row him to Stony Point. There he was intercepted by a note from Colonel Livingston enclosing two letters from the *Vulture*. The first was from Beverley Robinson: "I have been greatly disappointed in not seeing Mr. Smith at the time appointed. . . . I can now make a final settlement with him as my partner . . . arrived here last night." The other was from the captain of the *Vulture* ostensibly protesting an incident in which one of his boats was fired on without provocation, but the contents were irrelevant: the note was in the familiar handwriting of John André.

Riding by horse the short distance from Stony Point to Haverstraw, Arnold could clearly see the *Vulture* riding at anchor across the bay off Teller's Point. He strode into Smith's house and demanded to see the tenants who had refused their master's service the night before. Two extremely reluctant countrymen were ushered in, the brothers Joseph and Samuel Colquhoun. Did they not love their country? inquired the hero of Saratoga. The trip he wished them to take was in her service, and if they refused he would be forced to regard them as unfriendly to the cause. After lengthy argument and much hesitation, Samuel reluctantly agreed to make the trip that night and departed to inform his wife. He returned promptly: Mrs. Colquhoun had induced him to change his mind. He would not go. More argument ensued, laced with flattery, sips of whiskey and promises of extra rations (fifty pounds of flour, Joseph Colquhoun said later, "but I never saw it."). Eventually, and inevitably, they bowed to the will of their master and his powerful military friend. Toward midnight, as they set off with Smith for the creek where their boat was tied, Arnold himself handed them strips of sheepskin with which to muffle the oars.

The night was crystal-clear but moonless. Arnold, guided by one of Smith's slaves, set off on horseback for the chosen landing place, a secluded dock lying at the bottom of a wagon track off the King's Highway, about two miles south of Haverstraw. Arnold and the slave rode silently through the sleeping village, into the thick woods and down the wagon road to the dock, where they dismounted. The slave tied their horses and then returned to Smith's house on foot, leaving Arnold alone.

Tiny waves lapped against the shore, and the *Vulture*'s riding lights appeared very close in the cool, clear air. About one o'clock, a rowboat emerged from the darkness with a man wrapped in a dark cloak sitting in the stern. Arnold stood beneath the trees at the edge of the narrow beach as they disembarked. Joshua Smith joined him briefly and then returned to the beach. The hooded figure approached and entered the woods: Major John André and Benedict Arnold were face-to-face at last.

The meeting got off to a bad start when André categorically refused to mount the extra horse and ride back to Smith's house, his commander in chief having forbidden him to enter American lines. Neither, Arnold realized, had he followed his instructions regarding disguise; beneath his cloak, the major was wearing his regimentals. There was nothing to be done. Making themselves as comfortable as possible, the two exchanged social pleasantries and then began to confer in the chilly midnight woods.

André accepted without question Arnold's plan for the attack on West Point, and the initial phase of their conversation passed quickly and smoothly. Predictably, it was when the subject turned to money that the difficulty arose. Major André had doubtless been instructed not to promise anything in case of failure; but Major André had never met a man as adamantine on the subject of money as Benedict Arnold. Some three hours later, still deep in negotiation, they realized that dawn was imminent. It was too late to row the major back to his ship in safety. Reluctantly, André mounted the extra horse and set off with Arnold for Haverstraw, leaving Smith and the Colquhoun brothers to return by water.

The day would be warm and pleasant, but a chilly predawn mist still hung over the village of Haverstraw as they approached the American sentry post. Arnold answered the guards' challenge with a password and led his visitor past the lines, through the village and up the heights to Belmont.

Dismounting, the two men got their first good look at one another: André was slender, graceful, handsome and appeared younger than his thirty years; Arnold was nearing forty, stocky, solid and crippled. Arnold ordered a servant to bring breakfast, and then led the major up to a room on the second floor from which they could view the length and breadth of placid, windless Haverstraw Bay under the early sun, with *Vulture* looking small and very far away at her anchorage across the water. Behind her, the flats of Westchester County were just emerging from the misty light; and to the south the grotesquely shaped bumps and ridges of Long Clove Mountain dropped down toward the bay at just the spot where the major had landed.

Suddenly, the boom of cannon reached their ears, and from the window they saw flashes and heavy smoke arising from the *Vulture*. She was being fired on from Teller's Point—impossible, Arnold thought, there was no cannon at Teller's Point—but it was nonetheless true. The intrepid James Livingston, offended by the persistent presence of a British warship near his post, had hauled a howitzer and a small mortar down from Verplanck's Point the evening before and opened up on *Vulture* at dawn. At Livingston's request, John Lamb sent a few rounds of ammunition from West Point, although he complained that "firing at a ship with a four-pounder is, in my opinion, a waste of powder." For once, John Lamb was wrong.

At slack tide, the sloop sat helpless in the water, firing her six-pounders ineffectually while taking "six shot in the hull (one of which was between wind and water) and three through the boats on the booms, the standing and running rigging shot away in many different places [and] two of the iron stanchions on the gangways broke." After half an hour, Arnold and André saw her longboats launched, and soon *Vulture* was towed out of range, her sails unfurled and she headed south, disappearing from their view around the hump of Long Clove Mountain.

André, already angry and unnerved at finding himself stranded behind American lines, became extremely agitated. Arnold did not seem to care. Perhaps he liked the idea of punishing the major for holding out in their negotiations over money; whatever the reason, he foolishly left André and the question of his safe return up to the judgment and ingenuity of Joshua Hett Smith. Before departing for home, Arnold wrote out passes to cover two possibilities. The first permitted Smith to go "with a boat and three hands and a flag to Dobbs Ferry," where the major could be put aboard the *Vulture;* the other allowed Smith and "John Anderson" to pass through the American lines in Westchester County on the overland route to New York.

André strongly objected to the latter, partly because it would mean traveling in civilian disguise, and partly because Westchester was a no-man's land, infested by bands of renegades who roamed at will robbing travelers and terrorizing the local inhabitants, some of them loosely aligned with the Continental cause and some with the Tories, but none subject to the control and discipline of either army. Given the importance of his errand, the major correctly rejected the route as too risky. Arnold not only failed to appreciate that argument, he augmented the peril to them both by insisting that André carry with him the papers and plans of West Point that he had prepared for General Clinton. It was this total collapse of judgment that confirms Arnold's fixation with establishing his worth to the British. In tactical affairs, he was not usually so careless.

Arnold was back at the Robinson house by mid-morning. He had much to tell Peggy; and she, too, had news. First of all, General Washington's visit had been postponed for a few days. Second, during Arnold's absence, David Franks and Richard Varick had solemnly entreated her to influence her husband to break off his friendship with Joshua Hett Smith, which, Peggy announced, she had agreed to do. Arnold was not concerned; he had to see Smith only once more, to receive his report on Major André's safe return to his lines, and then the connection could be severed without a backward glance. Finally, in his office he read a piece of news that made his heart surge: American intelligence inside New York City reported the embarkation of a large detachment of the British Army, destination unknown. He had done it. Within a few days, West Point would be in Sir Henry Clinton's hands, and he and Peggy would enter their new life as honored subjects of the British crown.

The next day, Saturday, September 23, dawned fair and warm.

Joshua Smith arrived toward midday to report that he had taken Major André overland through Westchester County, lending him one of his old coats as a disguise ("crimson broadcloth [with] vellum buttonhole[s] and bound with Prussian binding"). After crossing King's Ferry in the evening, they had spent an uncomfortable night in a farmhouse and purchased breakfast—just a few hours ago—from a countrywoman near Pines Bridge, after which Smith left the major to make his own way to the British lines a few miles farther on. Everything had gone smoothly, and by now André was doubtless in New York reporting to General Clinton.* Well pleased, Arnold invited Smith to stay for dinner before departing for Fishkill to rejoin his family.

Richard Varick hit the roof. He picked a quarrel with Smith at the dinner table, infuriating Arnold and provoking a row that became so heated that Peggy had to beg them all to stop. The meal was finished in uneasy silence. After seeing Smith out, Arnold stormed into his office to confront his two aides. Varick cursed Smith as "a damned rascal, a scoundrel and a spy"; Arnold responded that "if he *asked the Devil to dine with him, the gentlemen of his family should be civil to him";* and Franks vowed that he would have thrown something more than words at Smith if he had been at anyone else's table. I am "always willing to be advised by the gentlemen of [my] family," Arnold shouted back, "but *by God* [I will] not be dictated to by them," whereupon Franks stormed from the room and departed for Newburgh on an official errand.

Later that evening, Varick approached Arnold with a letter he had just received from an aide to the governor of New York confirming the fact that Joshua Smith had told a bald-faced lie about the passes, and adding the aide's personal opinion that Smith's "loose character [did not] entitle [him] to the fullest confidence." By this time, Arnold had gained control of his temper. Realizing that Varick must be placated for a few more days, while Joshua Smith was now expendable, he all but apologized to his astonished secretary for "treating [him] with such cavalier language" and gave him a solemn promise never to visit Smith again. Later that evening, when Varick came down with the flu and began to spike a high fever, Peggy appeared at his bedside with tea "and paid me the utmost attention in my illness."

*The slave who had guided Arnold to the dock on the night of the twenty-first also accompanied Smith and André across King's Ferry on the twenty-second. He was never called upon to testify.

Sunday was warm and humid, with thundershowers in the afternoon. Word came from General Washington that he would arrive at Robinson's in time for breakfast the following morning. Would the British attack come in time to capture him? The muggy weather blew out, and Monday dawned fair and cool, a beautiful Hudson Valley day. Arnold rose early and descended to his office, leaving Peggy to breakfast in their bedroom. Richard Varick, whose bedroom was part of the office suite, was still very ill with fever. A message arrived from the commander in chief: he was pausing to inspect several redoubts on the east bank of the river and requested that Arnold begin breakfast without him. Arnold and the messenger duly repaired to the table.

During the meal, Arnold was handed two dispatches from Colonel John Jameson in Westchester. "[I am sending you under escort] a certain John Anderson taken going into New York," read the first. "He had a pass signed with your name. He had a parcel of papers taken from under his stockings which I think of a very dangerous tendency. The papers I have sent to General Washington." Arnold tore open the second dispatch: Jameson had rescinded his original order sending André up to West Point, keeping him a prisoner at his headquarters instead.

Tucking the papers into his pocket, Arnold excused himself and mounted the stairs. His announcement to his wife cannot have been gentle: the papers had been sent to General Washington, who was practically on their doorstep; he must seize the instant to make his escape. They heard footsteps on the stairs, and then a knock at the door; it was David Franks announcing that the commander in chief was "nigh at hand. . . . In great confusion," Arnold burst through the door and down the stairs, shouted for his horse and rode pell-mell out the gate and across the road, heading for the steep path down to the river and his waiting barge.

The horse stumbled and lurched as Arnold spurred him down the track. At the dock, his startled bargemen handed him aboard and hastily pulled out into the river, heading north toward West Point. Breathless from his ride, Arnold ordered them to reverse course. He would try to reach the *Vulture;* it was his only hope.

Luckily, the tide was flowing out, and the rowers' rapid cadence made the barge slide quickly through the water. As they approached Fort Montgomery, Arnold could see clearly through his spyglass the Robinson house sitting in pristine splendor amid the splashes of autumn color—peach and apricot and gold—in the surrounding woods. There was no sign of unusual activity about the house, nor of a horse galloping down the highway on that side of the river. Half an hour later, the barge curved around Anthony's Nose and the Robinson house disappeared from view. Arnold turned his face downriver.

Skirting the side of Dunderberg, with Peekskill Bay to port, the oarsmen pulled hard for King's Ferry. Stony Point lay dead ahead, sticking out boldly from the western shoreline. As they approached, Arnold could see the members of the garrison going about their routine duties at the landing. An hour after leaving Robinson's dock the barge rounded Verplanck's Point, affording Arnold his first glimpse into Haverstraw Bay. If the *Vulture* was not there, they would have to keep going until they found her. But how long could the men keep up their grueling pace? And how long did he have?

Wide-open Haverstraw Bay, a different world from the hemmed-in Highlands, glinted and gleamed on that dazzling autumn day. On the western shore, above the village, Joshua Hett Smith's Belmont reflected the light of the blazing sun; and in the center of the bay, anchored well out of range of Teller's Point, lay the *Vulture*. As the barge pulled in under her guns, Arnold affixed a white handerkerchief to his sword as a signal—far from the triumphant entrance into his new life that he had planned, but entirely fitting under the circumstances.

It was 11:30 A.M., ninety minutes since leaving Robinson's dock. Climbing aboard the ship—Tom Paine later described it as "one vulture . . . receiving another"—Arnold was greeted by Beverley Robinson demanding to know where Major André was. A single sentence in reply from Arnold, and the ship sprang into action. Arnold ordered his bargemen to come aboard and invited them to join him in the British service. All refused and were made prisoners of war. (Two of the nine turned out to be British deserters; their fate is unknown.)

Robinson quickly wrote a letter to General Washington protesting the detention of Major André as a "violation of flags and contrary to the custom and usage of all nations" and demanding his immediate release. It was sent by boat to Verplanck's Point, together with two letters written by Benedict Arnold. The first was addressed to General Washington and is given here in its entirety:

On board the Vulture Sept 25th 1780

Sir,

The heart which is conscious of its own rectitude cannot attempt to palliate a step which the world may censure as wrong. I have ever acted from a principle of love to my country, since the commencement of the present unhappy contest between Great Britain and the colonies; the same principle of love to my country actuates my present conduct, however it may appear inconsistent to the world, who very seldom judge right of any man's actions.

I have no favor to ask for myself; I have too often experienced the ingratitude of my country to attempt it. But from the known humanity of your Excellency I am induced to ask your protection for Mrs. Arnold from every insult and injury that the mistaken vengeance of my country may expose her to. It ought to fall only on me. She is as good and as innocent as an angel and is incapable of doing wrong. I beg she may be permitted to return to her friends in Philadelphia or to come to me, as she may choose. From your Excellency I have no fear on her account, but she may suffer from the mistaken fury of her country. I have to request that the enclosed letter may be delivered to Mrs. Arnold and she permitted to write to me.

I have also to ask that my clothes and baggage, which are of little consequence, may be sent to me. If required, their value shall be paid in money.

I have the honor to be with great regard & Esteem

> Your Excellency's most obedt hle servt
> B Arnold

N.B. In justice to the gentlemen of my family, Colonel Varick and Major Franks, I think myself in honor bound to declare that they, as well as Joshua Smith Esq. (who I know is suspected) are totally ignorant of any transaction of mine that they had reason to believe was injurious to the public.

The lie had come full circle. A new myth was in the making, although its author was the same old Benedict Arnold—Patriot and Hero.

The second letter, also given in its entirety, reflects a much more confused state of mind. It probably broke his heart:

Thou loveliest and best of women,

> Words are wanting to express my feelings and distress on your account, who are incapable of doing wrong yet are exposed to suffer wrong.* I have requested his Excellency Gen-

*Arnold knew that General Washington would read the letter before permitting Peggy to have it.

eral Washington to take you under his protection and permit you to go to your friends in Philadelphia—or to come to me. I am at present incapable of giving advice. Follow your own intentions. But do not forget that I shall be miserable until we meet. Adieu—kiss my dear boy for me. God almighty bless and protect you, sincerely prays

> Thy affectionate and devoted,
> B. Arnold.

P.S. Write me one line if possible to ease my anxious heart.

As the *Vulture* weighed anchor and headed south, Arnold finally had time to catch his breath; more time than he wished, perhaps. Did he worry about his wife, or was he too preoccupied with his own loss? His magnificent plot had failed, he told himself, through no fault of his own. The British would therefore reward him, *must* reward him, for an honorable effort, for the risks he had taken and for the sacrifices he had made in entering their service. He was, after all, Major General Benedict Arnold, the hero of Quebec and Saratoga, and almost-hero of West Point.

The view from the *Vulture*'s deck was dazzling. To the north, the mountains of the Hudson Highlands glimmered in the sun. (What was happening at the Robinson house at this very moment? Was Peggy being questioned, was she suspected?) Beyond the Highlands lay the upper Hudson Valley: Saratoga, Ticonderoga and Valcour Island. A hero is a hero forever, after all, and the British had always valued Benedict Arnold's martial prowess more highly than had the American rebels. A hero's welcome no doubt awaited him in New York.

But would he ever see his wife again? She was the only creature in the world who had ever completely satisfied his craving for devotion and confirmation. Would she come to him? As the light of evening faded into dark, *Vulture* passed under the formidable cliffs of the western palisades, a noble entrance into New York harbor and the rest of Benedict Arnold's life.

Chapter 17

"A LOOKING-GLASS WORLD"

SEPTEMBER 26 -DECEMBER 20, 1780

The following morning, September 26, Arnold came face-to-face for the first time with the temperamental, hypersensitive, invidious, erratic recluse who served as commander in chief of British forces in North America, Sir Henry Clinton. The meeting was awkward at best. General Clinton had counted heavily on the capture of West Point to end the war and redound to his own greater glory, so he was bitterly disappointed to hear that Arnold's plot had failed. The news that John André was in the hands of the enemy sent him into an emotional tailspin. The adjutant's amiable manners and affectionate disposition had penetrated Clinton's defenses and won his lonely heart. Unable to tolerate the thought of losing him, the commander in chief promptly summoned his advisers to organize a full-scale campaign to obtain Major André's release. Nothing else mattered, not even a hero's welcome for Major General Benedict Arnold, who was expected to put his shoulder to the wheel just like everybody else.

That very evening, at the commander in chief's request, and under the supervision of Royal Chief Justice William Smith, Arnold composed a formal memorandum stating the legal argument for André's release:

I apprehend a few hours must return Major André to your Excellency's orders, as that officer is assuredly under the protection of a flag of truce. . . . I commanded at the time at West Point, had an undoubted right to send my flag of truce for Major André, who came to me under that protection, and having had my conversation with him, I delivered him confidential papers in my own handwriting to deliver to your Excellency. Thinking it much properer he should return by land, I directed him to make use of the feigned name of John Anderson, under which he had, by my direction, come on shore, and gave him my passports to pass my lines to go to the White Plains on his way to New York . . . all of which I then had a right to do, being in the actual service of America, under the orders of General Washington and commanding general of West Point and its dependencies.

This mixture of half-truth, wishful thinking, logical perversity and gall was dispatched to General Washington at Tappan. No answer could be expected for several days, and meanwhile, Arnold was installed in a comfortable house at 3 Broadway, next door to headquarters, and introduced to the members of Clinton's staff.

His welcome was scrupulously polite but unmistakably cool. As a failed traitor he could hardly have expected better; as the instrument of Major André's downfall he might have gotten much worse, for the major was a universal favorite, cherished by all his acquaintance for his "excellent understanding . . . [his] elegance of mind and manners," his eloquence, his modesty and his affectionate nature.

It was perfectly clear to André's friends in New York that the major was in jeopardy because of Benedict Arnold's carelessness. Arnold, of course, would never recognize that uncomfortable truth, nor did he ever acknowledge an uglier fact that the major's friends were ignorant of: that he had deliberately placed a spy's noose around John André's neck for reasons that had nothing to do with the mission. It was never essential to their plot for the major to travel behind American lines, to assume a civilian disguise or to carry the plans in his stocking—the three actions that legally distinguished him as a spy rather than as a prisoner of war. All three had been forced on him by Benedict Arnold, solely in order to defy General Clinton and thereby demonstrate who had the upper hand. Now the major had been caught, and the traitor sensed, too late, that if André died he would be lost as well.

General Washington's reply to the memorandum reached New York on September 30. "Major André was taken under such circumstances as would have justified the most summary proceedings against him," Washington informed General Clinton. "I determined, however, to refer his case to the examination of a board of general officers," which included Nathanael Greene, the Marquis de Lafayette, Baron von Steuben, Robert Howe, Samuel Parsons and Henry Knox. During the proceedings, which had taken place the previous day, Major André confessed "with the greatest candor . . . 'that it was impossible for him to suppose that he came on shore under the sanction of a flag,' " which left the board no choice but to sentence him to death as a spy.

A ripple of shock and dismay spread through British headquarters, but Arnold scarcely felt it, being engulfed in a tidal wave of his own. In the same packet with General Washington's letter had been a note to him from Peggy announcing her decision to go to Philadelphia and live under the protection of her family.*

His anguish was stifled in a burst of activity. Clinton ordered the preparation of a new round of appeals and legal opinions, to be delivered to General Washington in person by the royal governor of New York, James Robertson. Arnold duly composed a set of variations on the same theme: "Mr. John Anderson . . . was the name I had requested Major André to assume . . . at my particular and pressing instance he exchanged [his uniform] for another coat. I furnished him with a horse and saddle and pointed out the route by which he was to return . . ." But his inner turmoil overflowed onto the page in a savage peroration. "If, after this just and candid representation of Major André's case, the Board of General Officers adhere to their former opinion," he wrote, "I shall suppose it dictated by passion and resentment; and if that gentleman should suffer the severity of their sentence, I shall think myself bound by every tie of duty and honor to retaliate on such unhappy persons of your army as may fall within my power . . . and I call heaven and earth to witness that your Excellency will be justly answerable for the torrent of blood that may be spilt in consequence."

Arnold also requested Governor Robertson to carry a personal note from him to the American commander in chief: "I take this opportunity to inform your Excellency that I consider myself no longer acting under the commission of Congress. . . . At the same time, I beg leave to assure your Excellency that my attachment to the true interest of my country is invariable, and that I am actuated by

---

*Peggy's active participation in her husband's treason was not discovered until the 1930s, when a researcher in the British Headquarters files happened upon the Arnold-André treason correspondence.

the same principle which has ever been the governing rule of my conduct in this unhappy contest." In a way it was true: his conduct had been consistently governed by the principle of self-interest.

Robertson disembarked at Dobbs Ferry on the morning of October 1, but General Washington refused to meet with him. Recognizing from the outset the delicacy of Major André's case, the American commander in chief had insisted on the strictest adherence to military law, which precluded his entertaining an appeal from the British governor. Courtesy demanded that he send his second-in-command, Nathanael Greene, to greet Robertson, however; and if those two gentlemen chose to stroll along the river shore at Dobbs for a time in earnest conversation, nobody could fault them for it.

Robertson found Greene polite, attentive and unyielding. On reading Arnold's mea culpa, for example, he pointedly remarked that he found Major André's courtroom confession more credible than the traitor's avowals; and when Robertson offered to obtain the release of any of General Washington's—or indeed General Greene's—particular friends in exchange for André, he replied that the only person they might accept in exchange would be Benedict Arnold. (Obviously, General Clinton could not turn Arnold over to the Americans, much as he might have liked to, nor could he accept an offer that Arnold is alleged to have made to give himself up for Major André, an offer he was perfectly safe in making.)

The following day, October 2, passed slowly at headquarters in New York. Toward evening, Governor Robertson returned without any news. He had lingered at Dobbs an extra night in hopes of the major's release, but all he and his staff had gleaned upriver was the sorry saga of his capture—by all accounts a tragedy of errors, many of them André's.

Approaching the British lines near Tarrytown, the major had been accosted at gunpoint by three armed irregulars and had completely lost his head. Instead of simply showing them General Arnold's pass, he had first tried to determine if they were Whig or Tory sympathizers (equally possible in that part of Westchester). In the process, he was gulled into identifying himself as a British officer, whereupon the three searched him and discovered the incriminating papers. André offered bribes for his release—first his gold watch and horse, and then a hundred guineas—staggering bribes that alerted the men to his significance and induced them to deliver him to Colonel John Jameson at Continental headquarters in Westchester.

(André, of course, had had no need to determine the men's political allegiance. Good Whigs would have honored General Arnold's pass and sent him on his way, while Tories would have turned him in to the British. The three irregulars' names were Paulding, Williams and Van Wart, and it has been suggested that their motive in stopping André in the first place was robbery. If so, they hit the jackpot. Each of the three was awarded a lifetime annuity of $200 [a goodly sum in 1780] and personally presented by General Washington with a silver medal inscribed on one side "Fidelity" and on the other, *"Vincit amor patriae."*

Jameson was completely befuddled by the appearance of "John Anderson" traveling in the opposite direction from the one his commandant had led him to expect—i.e., toward New York, instead of away from it—and carrying plans of West Point's fortifications in that same commandant's familiar handwriting. Jameson (whom one historian has characterized as "less than brilliant . . . and [with] the disposition of an army mule") responded with stupendous inconsistency: he dispatched the suspicious papers to General Washington and sent Anderson himself to the man who had written them.

Shortly after André and his escort had departed for the Robinson house, however, Major Benjamin Tallmadge happened to stop at Jameson's headquarters on a routine patrol. The spymaster instantly put two and two together and persuaded the colonel to call back "Anderson"; he failed, however, to dissuade Jameson from reporting the incident to General Arnold, who was thereby warned in time to make his escape.

Major André, his hopes of salvation dashed by the return to Jameson's headquarters, broke down under the strain and wrote an affecting but foolish confessional to General George Washington: "The person in your possession is Major John André, adjutant-general to the British Army. . . . What I have as yet said concerning myself was in the justifiable attempt to be extricated," he explained, adding proudly, "I am too little accustomed to duplicity to have succeeded. I beg your Excellency will be persuaded that no . . . apprehension for my safety induces me to take the step of addressing you, but that it is to rescue myself from an imputation of having assumed a mean character for treacherous purposes or self-interest, a conduct incompatible with the principles that actuate me as well as with my condition in life." André was a romantic who truly believed that he could treat with traitors without engaging in treachery, and encourage dishonor while keeping his own honor bright. He was also a naïf who had no business operating behind enemy lines, and he was about to pay for it.

The major's indiscretions and miscalculations meant little to the friends who waited anxiously in New York for news of him. Sir Henry Clinton rode an emotional roller coaster between hope and despair. "As they have delayed it so long I do not think they will proceed to extremities," he wrote to his sisters. "Washington seems a moderate man." In one breath he professed not to mind the failure of the plot, and in the next cried out, "Good God, what a coup manqué . . . had it succeeded all agree it would have finished the rebellion immediately." Surely, he told himself, "the defection of one of the best generals they have at this time has thrown them into great confusion and . . . the ice once broke, many will follow [Arnold's] example . . . [surely] the object was a great one [and], as far as depended upon me, every precaution was taken." The poor man suffered at once the agonies of grief and guilt, of fear for his adjutant's life and anxiety about his own career.

On the morning of October 5, the major's personal servant, who had joined his master at Tappan, returned to New York to announce that André had been hanged three days before at high noon in the presence of the officers and men of the Continental Army. He had behaved throughout the ordeal with characteristic grace and generosity. "Most elegantly dressed in his full regimentals," the major had marched more than a mile from his prison to the place of execution "with as much ease and cheerfulness of countenance as if he had been going to an assembly room," saluting the mounted Continental officers that lined his route and with a particularly courteous bow to the members of the board that had condemned him. After climbing the scaffold—an army wagon placed under a tree in the middle of a field—he tied his own handkerchief around his eyes "with perfect firmness, which melted the hearts and moistened the cheeks . . . of the throng of spectators. The rope being appended to the gallows, he slipped the noose over his head and adjusted it to his neck," asking all present to "bear me witness that I meet my fate like a brave man."

"When I saw him swinging under the gibbet," Benjamin Tallmadge wrote, "it seemed for a time as if I could not support it." Tallmadge, having been André's constant companion during his detention, had become "so deeply attached to [him] that I can remember no instance where my affections were so fully absorbed in any man." Even General Washington, unable for reasons of policy to grant André's wish to be shot like a soldier, sent the major breakfast from his own table every morning during his captivity. In short, as Alexander Hamilton noted, "in the midst of his enemies he died universally esteemed and universally regretted."

In New York a great howling arose, led by Sir Henry Clinton.

"The horrid deed is done," he wrote to his sisters; "W[ashington] has committed premeditated murder. . . . I feel beyond words to describe." Safely returned, André no doubt would have been roundly criticized for his blunders; martyred, he ascended to the angels— leaving Benedict Arnold to bear all the blame for his destruction, at least as far as his new commander in chief was concerned.

Like everybody else in New York, but for different reasons, Arnold was deeply affected by the news of André's death. He heard an echo in the banging of the major's coffin lid: the sound of a door slamming in his own face. Had André lived, he might have received from the British a generous reimbursement for services rendered, and also perhaps some sympathy for his situation and respect for "the rectitude of his intentions." Now, whatever he got would be grudgingly given. "Could Arnold have been suspended on the gibbet erected for André, not a tear or a sigh would have been produced, but exultation and joy would have been visible on every countenance." The words were Continental Army Dr. James Thacher's, but the sentiment was clearly shared by Arnold's new allies.

Still, General Clinton had to go through the motions, and on October 9 he bestowed on Arnold the rank of brigadier general in His Majesty's army (a demotion from his former rank, which Arnold had to swallow) with authority to raise his own regiment. Arnold badly needed the pay; but of course he needed much, much more. So, less than two weeks later, in the absence of any sign from the commander in chief, he wrote what was probably the most tactless letter of his career.

"In the conference which I had with Major André," Arnold asserted, "he was so fully convinced of the reasonableness of my proposal of being allowed ten thousand pounds sterling for my services, risk, and the loss which I should sustain in case a discovery of my plan should oblige me to take refuge in New York . . . that he assured me 'though he was commissioned to promise me only six thousand pounds sterling he would use his influence and recommend it to your Excellency to allow the sum I proposed.' . . . No sum of money," Arnold hastened to add, "would have been an inducement to have gone through the danger and anxiety I have experienced . . . [nevertheless I am confident] that you will not think my claim unreasonable when you consider the sacrifices I have made." Clinton's response was swift and to the point—he remitted Arnold a draft for £6000.*

Another man, seeing in the stern rebuff a pattern for the future,

---

*When Eleazer Oswald learned of the transaction, he wrote to John Lamb that their old comrade had proven himself "as base a 'prostitute' as this or any

might have collapsed in despair; but Arnold, blessed with neither sympathetic imagination nor an accurate self-image, stood firm. He willed himself not to see the stark image in the mirror: a man dressed in red regimentals with gold braid and epaulets, standing alone in an empty background. His inner mirror reflected a different image. It was not blind courage that sustained him, but courageous blindness; and no matter what the General Clintons of this world thought of him, no matter how many John Andrés died and went to heaven, Benedict Arnold would be a Patriot-Hero in a just cause, because he himself would have it so.

Wrestling the truth to the ground and bending it out of shape is hard work, but Arnold received assistance from an unlikely source: William Smith, the brother of Joshua Hett Smith and Royal Chief Justice of the Province of New York. Smith, a prominent member of New York's prewar provincial elite, had begun his tenure as Chief Justice nearly twenty years before and retained his loyalty to king and country at the commencement of the revolution. The basis of his otherwise unlikely rapport with Benedict Arnold was that each man had a personal investment in a British victory so immense as to bankrupt his sense of reality.

The line that Smith espoused dovetailed perfectly with Arnold's. Observing the same fact—that many Americans were sick of the war and disenchanted with Congress—both drew the erroneous conclusion that the vast majority of their countrymen wished to renounce independence and return to the British Empire. Their second error was to believe that the dire (and very real) difficulties facing the rebel army would prove insurmountable. Like Arnold, William Smith was blind to the human forces that would finally surmount them: the spirit and determination of men like George Washington, Nathanael Greene, Henry Knox, Samuel Parsons, Eleazer Oswald, John Lamb, Daniel Morgan and John Brown, true patriot-heroes who understood what they were fighting for and preferred to die rather than yield.

Arnold and Smith were not alone in their stubborn unperceptiveness. Many Englishmen, including prominent generals, admirals and members of Parliament, still adhered to the official line from

---

other country ever nurtured to maturity," adding sadly, "Happy for him and for his friends it had been, had the ball which pierced his leg at Saratoga been directed through his heart; he then would have finished his career in glory."

Benjamin Franklin took a larger view: "Judas sold only one man, Arnold three millions. Judas got for his one man thirty pieces of silver, Arnold not a halfpenny a head. A miserable bargain!"

Buckingham Palace: that the war could and would be won. (Even George Washington presumably doubted the event from time to time.) But the most fervent believers of all, because they had the most at stake, were the thousands of Loyalist refugees, three thousand from Philadelphia alone, who had fled their homes and livelihoods early in the war for the safety of New York City, where they now lived under British protection, at British sufferance and in some cases on British charity. Isolated from all that was familiar (and, in many cases, from all who were dear), desperately anxious about their futures, insular, claustrophobic and increasingly paranoid, they lived in what has been accurately described as a "looking-glass world," where reality was skewed to suit the needs and fancies of its inhabitants. Because their needs and fancies coincided so perfectly with those of Benedict Arnold, he gratefully embraced their fantasies and stepped into their world as into a refuge.

William Smith, although he did not care much for the traitor personally, agreed to collaborate with him on a series of major public statements in order to hasten the inevitable dissolution of the rebel war effort that they both believed had been precipitated by his defection. Their first joint literary effort, "General Arnold's Address to the Inhabitants of America on his Joining the British Army," appeared in the pages of the *Royal Gazette* two days after Arnold received his commission as brigadier. Thanks to Smith's smooth legal argumentation, the address is extremely cogent; it is also utterly mendacious.

"When I quitted domestic happiness for the perils of the field," its central proposition begins, ". . . a redress of grievances was my only object and aim; however, I acquiesced in a step which I thought precipitate, the Declaration of Independence. . . . I lamented therefore the impolicy, tyranny and injustice" of Congress's failure to accept the 1778 British peace proposals, "but continued to be guided in the negligent confidence of the soldier . . . [until Congress accepted] the insidious offers of France . . . the enemy of the Protestant faith." (According to the Loyalist line, the alliance between Catholic France and the American rebels was part of an anti-Protestant Papist plot.) The moment the French alliance was signed, the address continues, "[I] determined to retain my arms and command for an opportunity to surrender them to Great Britain . . . for a purpose in my opinion as grateful as it would have been beneficial to my country."

But if Smith composed the principal theme, the coda was vintage Arnold: "I pray God to give [my countrymen] all the lights requisite to their own safety before it is too late; and with respect to that herd of censurers, whose enmity to me originates in their hatred to the principles by which I am now led . . . they may be assured that, conscious of the rectitude of my intentions, I shall treat their malice and calumnies with contempt and neglect."

Two weeks later, the second Arnold-Smith collaboration appeared in the *Gazette* under the title "Proclamation by Brigadier General Arnold to the Officers and Soldiers of the Continental Army who have the real interest of their country at heart, and who are determined to be no longer the tools and dupes of Congress and of France." Offering rank and good wages to those who volunteered for the American Legion, as his regiment was called, Arnold declared himself ready "to lead a chosen band of Americans to the attainment of peace, liberty and safety . . . and with them to share in the glory of rescuing our native country from the grasping hand of France as well as from the ambitious and interested views of a desperate party among ourselves, who, in listening to French overtures and rejecting those from Great Britain, have brought the colonies to the very brink of destruction."

The propaganda put out by Arnold and Smith may have persuaded its authors, but it had little effect on its intended targets. General Washington declared himself "at a loss which to admire most, the confidence of Arnold in publishing, or the folly of the enemy in supposing that a[ny] production signed by so infamous a character will have any weight with the people of these states."

The commander in chief's confidence in his fellow citizens was partly based on his own successful propaganda efforts. Within hours of Arnold's escape from the Robinson house on September 25, Washington—who was at the time uncertain of the scope of the plot and fearful of an imminent attack on West Point—declared in a bold address to his army that the timely discovery "affords the most convincing proof that the liberties of America are the object of divine protection" and that her "enemies, despairing of carrying their point by force, are practicing every base art to effect by bribery and corruption what they cannot accomplish in a manly way. Great honor is due to the American army that this is the first instance of treason of the kind where many were to be expected from the nature of the dispute," Washington proclaimed, "and nothing is so bright an ornament in the character of the American soldiers as their having been proof against all the arts and seduction of an insidious enemy." By the end of the day, "treason of the blackest dye" (as Washington called it) had been turned on its head, and everybody from Nathanael Greene down to the lowliest foot soldier was confidently congratulating himself for being on the same side as the Almighty. On the battlefield of propaganda, William Smith had met his match.

As for Arnold, the less the world believed his new great lie, the more fervently he espoused it, especially after his former disguise as a Patriot-Hero was stripped away by his angry countrymen. The seizure of his papers by the Philadelphia authorities revealed all the evidence of his malfeasance in office: the written agreement with clothier General James Mease to sell army goods on the open market, the correspondence with John R. Livingston concerning secret purchases in New York City and the documentation of his financial involvement in the *Active* sloop. The *Pennsylvania Packet* regaled the public with details of Arnold's "baseness and prostitution of office and character," and all his enemies, from John Brown to Joseph Reed, were fully vindicated.*

Peggy, too, came under attack when the letter she had received from Major André on August 1779, offering to buy millinery supplies in New York, was made public. The *Packet* darkly remarked "on the fallacious and dangerous sentiments so frequently avowed in this city that female opinions are of no consequence in public matters," and the Supreme Executive Council opened an investigation.

Meanwhile, Richard Varick and David Franks had testified at their respective court-martials (which they requested, and by which they were fully exonerated) that Arnold had stolen public goods intended for the poverty-stricken garrison at West Point and sold them for his own benefit. They could not prove the charge—and indeed, their urgent desire to distance themselves from their former commandant colored their entire testimony; but the officers of the court accepted the allegations as fact, and the published transcripts of the trial directed public attention to the *"base peculations . . .* of the late General Arnold."

Once his probity and dignity had been revealed as a sham—and once the plot against West Point had fizzled—the American public vented its relief in laughter. In nearly every village and town in the United States, Arnold effigies were paraded through the streets and publicly hanged, burned or otherwise dispatched to the cheers of the populace. In Philadelphia, "The Rogues' March" accompanied the festivities, while in New Milford, Connecticut, "the hissing explosion of a multitude of squibs and crackers . . . graced his exit." Arnold

---

*John Brown barely had time to gloat. He was killed in an Indian ambush on October 19 (his thirty-sixth birthday) on his way up the Mohawk River to relieve General Schuyler, who was resisting an enemy foray from Canada.

might have borne their vilification, being quite inured to it, but their mirth and derision were insupportable.

He had nothing left—except his great new lie, which now became etched in stone: that Benedict Arnold was not a traitor but a true patriot who had plotted with the enemy only in order to rescue his beloved country from the clutches of Catholic France. It was the lie of a lifetime—and the rest of his life would be devoted to the Sisyphean task of proving that it was true.

Holding his new image before him like a shield, Arnold fought more desperately than ever to wrest from the British the just rewards of his treachery. If Sir Henry Clinton stood in the way, he would outflank Sir Henry, a maneuver that William Smith enthusiastically applauded and assisted. Like most of his fellow Loyalists, Smith blamed the commander in chief's passivity for the military stalemate in America. Given their high level of expectation and anxiety, it is not surprising that the Loyalists failed to appreciate Sir Henry's many difficulties—severe shortages of manpower, equipment and supplies, for example—or that Smith condemned Clinton as "a procrastinator . . . a trifler . . . [and] very unfit for his station."

In a series of letters and memoranda to Lord George Germain, the British secretary of state for the colonies and a key adviser to King George III, Arnold presented a rosy vision of the imminent triumph of British arms and outlined a two-level strategy for winning the war that, not coincidentally, ran directly counter to the strategy of General Clinton.

First, he declared, General Washington must be forced into a general battlefield engagement—the very thing the Continental commander in chief had been judiciously avoiding for the past four years. This could be brought about, Arnold suggested, by collecting new recruits and supplies on a sweep through the southern states and then attacking the main Continental Army with an overwhelming force; or, alternatively, by capturing West Point, cutting off Washington's supplies and forcing him to fight or starve.

His second argument was equally cogent. Arnold urged Germain to offer any man who defected from the Continental Army reimbursement for the entire amount of his back pay. "Their whole arrears," Arnold calculated, would "not amount to the expense of [carrying on] the war for a few months," and each man "taken from the rebel army and added to ours is as two men imported from Europe"—a potent argument at a time when British military resources were stretched so thin that, in the words of one English historian, "the misdirection of a single ship might mean disaster." If an additional bounty of fifteen or twenty guineas were offered, Arnold declared, "I have not the least doubt of being able to recruit two or three thousand men [in the American Legion] in a short time."

In summary, Arnold argued, "money, properly applied in America, may with some prove a more formidable argument than arms." Clearly, his strategic instincts had not deserted him; but neither had his obtuseness concerning the human heart. "A title offered to General Washington," Arnold suggested, "might not prove unacceptable."*

For himself, Arnold modestly requested a promotion to major general and assignment to "a command in which I can, by my conduct, testify to His Majesty my sincere attachment to his person and interests and atone for any errors that I may have been guilty of heretofore. . . . In the fullest confidence of his clemency, I most cheerfully cast myself at his feet, imploring his royal grace and protection."

What Arnold still did not realize—and never would—is that nobody trusts a traitor, not even the supposed beneficiaries of his treachery. In England, of course, the word *traitor* would never have been used if his plot against West Point had succeeded. In the words of the old couplet,

> Treason doth never prosper—what's the reason?
> If it doth prosper, none dare call it treason.

But his plot had failed; and though the British felt an obligation to see to his basic needs and to go through the obligatory social motions, they would never offer him their friendship or their trust, let alone the high command in America he so obviously sought.

Early on the morning of October 21, a young Continental Army sergeant-major, mud-spattered and out of breath, was escorted through the door of Sir Henry Clinton's headquarters. Identifying

---

*Arnold also wrote a personal invitation to Major Benjamin Tallmadge "to join me with as many men as you can bring over with you. . . . As I know you to be a man of sense, I am convinced you are by this time fully of opinion that the real interest and happiness of America consists in a reunion with Great Britain. . . . I will only add that the English fleet has just arrived with a very large reinforcement of troops." Tallmadge later recalled being "mortified that my patriotism could be even suspected by this most consummate villain. I took the letter, however, to General Washington, who consoled me abundantly on the occasion."

himself as John Champe of "Light-Horse Harry" Lee's famous Virginia cavalry division, he recounted a hair-raising tale of his escape from the Americans and announced his desire to defect. "Rather above the common size, full of bone and muscle, with a saturnine countenance, grave, thoughtful and taciturn," Champe was an impressive personage who regaled Sir Henry with "the spirit of defection which prevailed among the American troops in consequence of Arnold's example" and expressed his firm conviction that "some of [Washington's] best corps would leave him." Clinton spent more than an hour with the young man before turning him over to Arnold, who promptly accepted him as a volunteer in his regiment.

The appearance of John Champe represented to Arnold both a vindication of his past actions and the wave of the future. He was wrong on both counts: the defection was a sham. Champe's real mission in New York was to kidnap Arnold and deliver him alive to General Washington to stand trial. "No circumstance whatever shall obtain my consent to his being put to death," the commander in chief had stipulated in approving the plot. "The idea which would accompany such an event would be that ruffians had been hired to assassinate him. My aim is to make a public example of him." Within days of his arrival, Champe had familiarized himself with Arnold's routine and formulated an intricate plan to abduct the traitor during his nightly stroll in the garden behind 3 Broadway and row him across to New Jersey.

Meanwhile, the wave of the future failed to crest. By the beginning of December—some seven weeks after John Champe's arrival, and after thirteen semiweekly appearances of the "Proclamation by Brigadier General Arnold to the Officers and Soldiers of the Continental Army" in the *Royal Gazette*—enlistments in the American Legion stood at eight officers, three sergeants, twenty-eight common soldiers and one drummer. (A year later the grand total had risen to 212.)

Toward the end of October, every other preoccupation faded temporarily into the background with the arrival of news that Peggy had been banished from the State of Pennsylvania. She reached New York with baby Edward in mid-November,* pale, exhausted and preoccupied, a very different personage from the eager young conspirator Arnold had left behind at the Robinson house two months before.

---

*Eighteenth-century women lived under the protection of their husbands or their fathers; there was no other choice.

Little wonder: Peggy had lived for the past eight weeks in a state of continuous terror for her own fate and shock at the revelations of her husband's malefactions.

What had saved her was playacting, especially during the hours immediately following her husband's departure from the Robinson house on September 25. Before going onstage, however, she cleaned out the wings, searching the bedroom for every scrap of paper that had to do with the plot, including all her own letters from Philadelphia, and burning the lot. Then, toward noon (about the time her husband reached the *Vulture*), she disarranged her flimsy negligee, mussed up her long hair, opened her throat and began to scream.

Her maid and David Franks answered the summons first, followed closely by Richard Varick, who jumped from his sickbed at the first cry. Varick's temperature soared at the sight of lovely Peggy in "her morning gown with few other clothes remain[ing] on her, too few," he vividly recalled, "to be seen even by a gentlemen of the family." She grabbed Varick's hand and pleaded "with a wild look, *'Colonel Varick, have you ordered my child to be killed?'*" then fell down at his feet "with prayers and intreaties *to spare her innocent babe.*" Carried to bed, she "burst into pitiable tear and exclaimed . . . [that her husband was] 'gone forever, *there, there, there,* the spirits have carried [him] up there, they have put hot irons in his head.'"

Eventually, she grew calmer and asked to see General Washington, whom she had known since childhood. When the commander in chief entered the room, however, Peggy shrieked hysterically, "That is not General Washington, that is the man who was going to assist Colonel Varick in killing my child." "One moment she raved, another she melted into tears; sometimes she pressed her infant to her bosom and lamented its fate." In short, as the susceptible young Alexander Hamilton put it, "All the sweetness of beauty, all the loveliness of innocence . . . and all the fondness of a mother showed themselves in her appearance and conduct." Naturally, when Washington learned of Arnold's treason several hours later, he never suspected her of complicity; and when he and Hamilton saw her the following morning, they accepted her profession of total amnesia regarding the previous day's events. "Her sufferings were so eloquent," Hamilton wrote to his fiancée, Elizabeth Schuyler, "that I wished myself her brother, to have a right to become her defender."

Artful though it was, Peggy's portrayal of madness was based on genuine emotional turmoil. Being barely out of her teens, she had probably never contemplated the possibility of failure, let alone of being left in mortal danger to fend for herself. Given her terror and perplexity, the performance was a triumph that transfixed its entire audience, including the future first president of the United States and his secretary of the treasury. Having beguiled all those powerful patriots, she was wise not to break the spell. She chose to go to her family in Philadelphia rather than join the traitor in New York, and every man in sight fell all over himself making certain that she traveled in comfort, safety and style.

By the time she reached her father's house, however, Major André's letter had been discovered and the public outcry had commenced, led by the strident voices of Joseph Reed and the Supreme Executive Council. Dry-eyed and silent, Peggy took to her bed in "a kind of stupor." Her family scoffed at the notion of "so delicate and timorous a girl as poor Peggy being in the least privy or concerned in so bold and adventurous a plan," and Edward Shippen appealed directly to the Council not to return his daughter to "the hands of so bad a man, [lest] her mind . . . in time be debased and her welfare, even in another world, endangered by his example." At her father's urging, Peggy promised, if permitted to remain, to cut off all correspondence with her husband for the duration of the war; but to no avail. The Supreme Executive Council, finding her very presence "dangerous to the public safety," exiled her for the duration of the war.

Edward Shippen escorted his favorite daughter as far as the Hudson River shore opposite Manhattan Island, where they bade their final, tearful farewells. Within the hour, she was with her husband.

And what were the Arnolds to make of one another, now that the ground beneath them had shifted forever? Peggy's girlish adoration for her heroic husband had undoubtedly been tempered by exposure to his venality, which was the talk of all Philadelphia during the weeks of her stay. She had expressed a desire to remain there, away from him. Could he ever forgive her for deserting him when he needed her most? Perhaps he sympathized to some degree with her present turmoil, uncertainty and state of exhaustion, and perhaps he even praised her for her resourcefulness and courage. At the very least, in his presence she could stop feigning innocence: only her husband knew how shrewd and daring the real Peggy Arnold was. And finally, one must remember the strong physical attraction between these two. Whatever the nature of their reunion, Peggy became pregnant within two weeks of her arrival in New York.

But a fundamental shift had occurred beneath the surface, based on the fact that Peggy now had a much firmer grasp on reality than Arnold did. Watching her oldest friends turn their backs had broken her heart, but it had also opened her eyes. She now knew the meaning of the word *treason*. Her husband clearly did not.

True to her upbringing and her class, Peggy now embarked on her greatest role: that of the unalterably loyal and adoring wife. It did not come as naturally as it had before, because she knew better; but she hid her new knowledge from everyone, including her husband, giving the invariable impression of total adherence to his opinions, desires, standards and directions while slowly but surely beginning to nurture her own.

The Arnolds took their place in Loyalist society, attending dinner parties, theaters, concerts and dancing assemblies in the company of Governor Robertson, Sir Henry Clinton and William Smith and his wife. For many reasons, though, idle, claustrophobic Loyalist New York was not for Benedict Arnold. He longed for action and a chance to prove himself, and less than two weeks after Peggy's arrival he was given it.

Due to the stalemate in the mid-Atlantic states, the British had shifted their attention to the south, where they hoped to demonstrate their strength and resolve by conquering and securing South Carolina as a base on which to build Loyalist support throughout the colonies. The British commander in chief in the south was the able and energetic General Charles Cornwallis, who had just suffered a humiliating defeat at King's Mountain, South Carolina, and who now faced a formidable new opponent: Nathanael Greene, who had recently been given command of the Continental southern army and was on his way to the Carolinas with the elite corps of Daniel Morgan and "Light-Horse Harry" Lee.

Crucial to success in the south was maintaining control of Chesapeake Bay, whose access from the sea was commanded by the town of Portsmouth, Virginia (see map, page 244). The British garrison there had recently been obliged to march out in support of General Cornwallis, leaving the town virtually defenseless. Arnold's orders were to repossess the town and harden its fortifications.

Once the expedition was announced by General Clinton, rumors buzzed throughout New York of British officers who refused to serve under the new brigadier. They remained largely rumors, thanks to the example of men like Lieutenant Colonel John Graves Simcoe, commander of a Loyalist regiment of horse and foot known as the Queen's Rangers, who agreed without hesitation to join the expedition. The Rangers embarked for Virginia with black and white feathers attached to their horses' bridles, a sign of mourning for Simcoe's closest friend, John André. During the dark days of André's captivity, Simcoe and his Rangers had volunteered to try to rescue him; now, with enormous good grace, they agreed to serve under the command of the man who was widely blamed for his death.

Arnold's detachment consisted of about seventeen hundred men: his own American Legion (brought up to fighting strength with a large infusion of Loyalist volunteers), Simcoe's Rangers, a company of Hessians and one regiment of British regulars under the command of Lieutenant Colonel Thomas Dundas. His orders were to man and fortify Portsmouth and then to remain there to defend it against all comers. General Clinton left room for a single improvisation: if, *before* entering Portsmouth, Arnold saw "a favorable opportunity of striking at any of the enemy's magazines" along the James River, he was "at liberty to attempt it provided it may be done without much risk." It was a small gift with strings attached. "Previous to your undertaking any operation of consequence," General Clinton stipulated, Arnold was to consult both lieutenant colonels Simcoe and Dundas, "officers of great experience and much in my confidence."

On the evening of December 20, with all his troops embarked (including a deeply chagrined John Champe, who had not had time to spring his trap), Arnold joined the fleet of forty-two sail off Sandy Hook, boarded the commodore's flagship *Charon* and sailed on the evening tide with a fair wind.

Chapter 18

"A LIFE OF JOBS"

DECEMBER 1780 -DECEMBER 1781

The open ocean was a welcome relief after the stifling atmosphere of New York, especially with the tantalizing prospect of battle in the offing. Not since his voyage to the mouth of the Kennebec River five years before had Arnold ridden the deep swells of the Atlantic. Although he sailed now under a different flag and in a different direction, his inner direction had changed very little. The old craving to establish a secure position for himself was stronger than ever. Possessing and fortifying Portsmouth was the least of his concerns; he still had to possess and fortify himself.

Six days out from New York, gale-force winds separated the fleet, and by the time it reassembled off the Virginia capes four days later, half the cavalry horses and a number of heavy guns had been lost. Coming to anchor in Hampton Roads, Arnold immediately landed scouts, who returned with the news that the road to Richmond was open. (Virginia Governor Thomas Jefferson, having inexplicably ignored General Washington's warning of an impending invasion, now waited a fatal three days after Arnold's fleet had entered the capes before calling up his militia.) With the way clear for a daring and dramatic strike at the American magazines near the Virginia capital, Arnold set off to demonstrate to the British Army the skill and daring of its new brigadier.

The landscape of the Virginia tidewater did not encourage comparison with the triumphs of Arnold's past. The shoreline of the James River is unremittingly flat, the air heavy and dank. Here are no imposing Hudson River Highlands, no spectacular Adirondacks or Green Mountains, not even the high stony bluffs of Arnold's boyhood home of Norwich, where his earliest battles had been fought. Even the vibrant winter colors of burnt-orange earth and dark-green pine trees seem to dissipate in the soft atmosphere.

On New Year's Eve morning, the army headed up the James in a makeshift fleet of small river-going vessels. Beating against a strong headwind, they passed the junction with the Chickahominy and gained the middle reaches of the river. Drawing in toward shore on the evening of January 3 at the plantation of Flowerdew Hundred ("Hundred" is the term applied to plantations established by the Virginia Company in the early seventeenth century; Flowerdew Hundred was named after Temperance Flowerdew, the wife of its first proprietor), the ships received several rounds of artillery fire from a hidden American battery. Simcoe's Rangers were put ashore and soon surprised and captured the small enemy fort. As Arnold stepped ashore, an American patrol suddenly emerged from the woods a short distance away. Realizing they were outnumbered, they quickly scuttled back into hiding, but it was a close call: there could be no doubt whatsoever about the fate of Benedict Arnold if he were captured by the Americans. (The story goes that shortly after arriving in Virginia, Arnold interrogated an American prisoner who was not aware of his identity. Asked what the local farmers would do if they captured General Arnold, the man replied that they would first cut off the leg wounded at Saratoga and bury it with honor, then hang the rest.)

The following morning, the fleet pushed upriver to the magnificent plantation of Westover, where they were cordially welcomed by the proprietor, Mary Willing Byrd, the widow of a prominent Virginia Tory and a cousin to Peggy Arnold. While the troops disembarked for the thirty-five-mile march to Richmond, Arnold was entertained in Mrs. Byrd's red brick mansion overlooking Westover's magnificent gardens, fields and lawns. He set off again at the head of his men in mid-afternoon in a driving rainstorm, and reached the broad plain before Richmond the following morning at eleven o'clock.

Massed in front of the small riverfront village were its defenders,

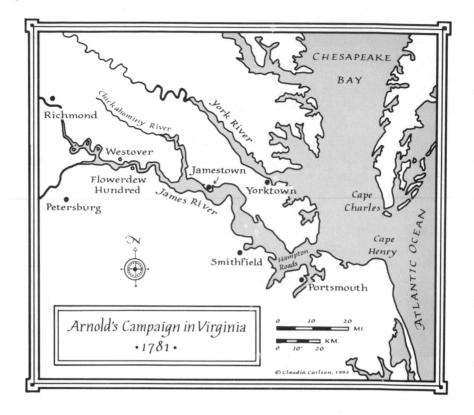

Arnold's Campaign in Virginia
· 1781 ·

© Claudia Carlson, 1993

some 250 Virginia militia, many of them without guns. Arnold, with more than 800 well-armed troops, ordered his men to parade with "as great an appearance as possible . . . [so] that a more skillful enemy than those who were now reconnoitering would have imagined the numbers to have been double." The maneuver may have fooled any American scouts who were looking on from the surrounding woods; but it also set off ghostly echoes of Arnold's defiant parade before Quebec in 1775. That had been a real war for high stakes: Arnold's gallant Kennebec veterans really had been outnumbered, and their brave show of strength was all that stood between them and certain destruction—stark contrast to the present instance, when Richmond's defenders simply melted into the soft tidewater landscape and Arnold's men walked into town.

The merchants of Richmond refused to respond to Arnold's offer of one-half the going price for the goods in their warehouses without first consulting Governor Jefferson. Jefferson, who had taken refuge across the river, declined to treat with "the parricide Arnold," so warehouses, shops and magazines were put to the torch, along with "a printing press and types . . . also purified by the flames." Meanwhile, Colonel Simcoe's Rangers rode upriver to destroy the American foundry at Westham. Simcoe and his men returned a few hours before dawn, and Arnold promptly ordered them to join immediately in the withdrawal downriver, silencing Simcoe's objections with another echo from the past. "If General Tryon and Sir William Erskine had marched two hours sooner from Danbury [in 1777]," he declared, "they would have met with no opposition; and if they had delayed it much longer, they would have found it absolutely impossible to have regained their shipping."

The march back to Westover took nearly two days, in a torren tial rain that turned the roadbed into a bog of stiff red mud. The exhausted army reembarked and dropped downriver, raiding storehouses and magazines along the way. They disembarked again at Smithfield, and Arnold, with enemy forces gathering on all sides, ordered a forced march through swamps and across flooded streams to Portsmouth, which the army entered unopposed on January 20.

Welcome news awaited him: the Continental Army's Pennsylvania Line had staged a successful mutiny over lack of pay. "This event," Arnold crowed to Sir Henry Clinton, "will be attended with happy consequences. We anxiously wait in expectation of hearing that the malcontents have joined His Majesty's army in New York." Instead, when Clinton sent out two secret emissaries to treat with the Pennsylvanians, the mutineers, "despis[ing] a treachery and meanness like that of Benedict Arnold," turned them over to their superiors, who hanged them as spies. The mutineers then negotiated their differences with Congress, after which about half of them reenlisted.

For weeks, Arnold kept his men hard at work constructing new fortifications at Portsmouth and making preparations for a possible siege. He put on a fine show of industry, but beneath the surface he grew restless and discontented, and he begged General Clinton to return him to New York, "as a life of inaction will be very prejudicial to my health."

By the middle of February, however, Portsmouth was in imminent danger. General Cornwallis's army, having suffered more than nine hundred casualties in a devastating defeat at Hannah's Cowpens, South Carolina, began to limp north toward Virginia, with Nathanael Greene and Daniel Morgan (the victor at Hannah's Cowpens) in hot pursuit. With his southern flank newly exposed, Arnold learned that one third of the British fleet had been lost in a severe storm at its main anchorage at Gardiner's Bay, Long Island, severing his lifeline to the north. As if on cue, three French warships appeared off Cape Henry on February 13, lingered a week unchallenged and then withdrew; and a few days later, British intelligence reported that a major expedition against Portsmouth, led by the Marquis de Lafayette, was massing in Maryland for embarkation at the head of Chesapeake Bay.

At this juncture, Arnold lost the cooperation of his naval counterpart, Captain Thomas Symonds, commodore of the fleet that had brought him to Virginia. The two commanders had agreed during the voyage that any prizes taken on the expedition, whether on water or land, would be shared equally between the army and the navy. (Prize money—the proceeds from sales of captured enemy goods and ships—was a crucial source of supplementary income to officers and men in the eighteenth-century military services.) But after a large number of lucrative prizes was captured on the James River during January, Symonds's officers balked and demanded they all be turned over to the navy. In the process of appealing the matter to General Clinton, Arnold managed to offend Symonds so egregiously that the commodore refused to take his ships up Chesapeake Bay to intercept Lafayette's transports. Arnold sneered when Captain Symonds "alleg[ed] that he has orders to keep the ships in shoal water, which I believe he is heartily inclined to do whenever he thinks there is danger." He stepped up the pace of construction at Portsmouth, and Colonel Simcoe reported that "the garrison is in great spirits, full of confidence in the daring courage of General Arnold."

On March 16, the British fleet, which had risen Phoenix-like from the devastation at Gardiner's Bay, engaged the French fleet off Cape Henry in a two-hour battle involving sixteen ships of the line, mounting a total of more than six hundred cannon. The following morning, before the outcome of the battle was known, General Lafayette appeared before the works at Portsmouth with his army. He withdrew after a brief skirmish, waiting to learn the outcome of the battle. If the French won, Portsmouth was apparently doomed, along with its commander, whom Lafayette would surely take pains to capture alive. But Portsmouth and Arnold were saved by the British fleet, which entered Chesapeake Bay the next day in triumph.

With it came a letter to Arnold from Lord George Germain. Ignoring entirely Arnold's request for a promotion, the colonial secretary blandly reported that the king had been "graciously pleased to express his satisfaction in demonstrations you have given of the sincerity of your return to your allegiance . . . [and has given] Sir Henry Clinton his royal approbation of the rank he has given you in the army under his command and of his having appointed you to raise a corps."

But General Clinton had acceded to one of Arnold's requests by sending an officer to replace him as commander at Portsmouth, Major General William Phillips, a veteran of the mid-century European wars who had also fought at Saratoga. Phillips was full of praise for Arnold's "ability, activity and zeal," but no amount of praise could hide the fact that, having been superseded, there was little for Arnold to do. Clinton had not ordered him back to New York, however, so he accompanied General Phillips on an expedition up the James River.

With Portsmouth secure, the two generals spent the last two weeks of April raiding Continental storehouses along the river, capturing enemy shipping and burning mills and warehouses. On their way back to Portsmouth at the beginning of May, they received urgent orders from Lord Cornwallis to take possession of Petersburg and await him there with supplies, his army being in a "very critical situation."* Arnold rode into Petersburg at the head of his troops on May 9, with General Phillips riding behind in a carriage desperately ill with fever. By the time Cornwallis arrived, Phillips had died. Arnold promptly suffered an attack of gout in both hands and both feet. He was put aboard a ship heading for New York, where he arrived on June 10 in acute physical agony.

His welcome was colder than ever: General Clinton had learned about Arnold's letter to Lord George Germain deprecating his conduct of the war. Arnold realzied by now that his further advancement might well depend on Sir Henry's goodwill, so he quickly backpedaled. "My opinion with respect to the operations against the posts in the Highlands was founded upon a belief that [a] reinforcement of six thousand men . . . would arrive in America early in the spring. . . . Had the reinforcements arrived . . . the Highlands would probably have been the first object of the army," he wrote to Germain a week after

*Cornwallis's army had been badly bloodied by Nathanael Greene at Guildford Courthouse, North Carolina, on March 15, suffering nearly twice as many casualties as the Americans. Cornwallis himself was among the wounded.

In marching north, the British general was deliberately disobeying Sir Henry Clinton's express order to hold South Carolina. He had been emboldened by Lord George Germain's increasing reliance on his advice, as opposed to Sir Henry's, and was obviously angling for Clinton's job.

his return to New York. "I find my letter has given umbrage; I am extremely sorry for it, as I meant not to condemn men or measures but to communicate intelligence."

The letter did nothing to assuage Clinton's anger (much as he may have enjoyed seeing Benedict Arnold roll over and wag his tail). He not only dismissed Arnold's arguments in support of an attack on West Point, he also tortured the brigadier by assigning him a series of menial administrative chores around headquarters. In addition, Arnold was called upon to furnish the royal governor of Canada with the names of American sympathizers in Quebec. "From the resentment he has discovered at the fate of Major André," the governor opined to General Clinton, "as well as the change of his political ideas . . . [he] will not hesitate to [furnish] every information in his power by which a discovery may be made." Arnold reluctantly furnished six names, one of them Père Hoguet, the Superior of the Jesuits.

New York was full of gossip about the feud between the army and navy over the James River prizes. One officer of the garrison wrote to a friend that Arnold "has hurt himself by discovering too much fondness for *cash*. . . . If he is attached to the latter, as is represented, he is no loss to the cause he has deserted and eventually he can be no acquisition to us." Worse yet was the speculation over the American Legion, which had returned from Virginia reduced by desertions and casualties to barely ninety men. "[Arnold has] gained a loss," another officer prattled; "if they had stayed [in Virginia] any longer, they would all have run away."

For this he had deserted George Washington and the cause of his country. The frantic effort to clean his slate had been utterly fruitless. The corridors of British headquarters were just as full of backbiting and backstabbing as the halls of Congress; and the British Benedict Arnold was even worse off than the American, reduced in rank, property and reputation. He could not escape from sordidness and lying because he could not escape from himself. All he could do was cling to the lies, plunging deeper and deeper into self-delusion and ultimate despair.

His wife, who was seven months' pregnant at the time of his return, had been experiencing something of a triumph during her husband's absence. "Amazingly improved in beauty and dress, having really recovered a great deal of that bloom she *formerly* possessed but *did not* bring in with her," a former Philadelphia Loyalist acquaintance noted, she had appeared at a headquarters ball "a star of the first magnitude, and had every attention paid her as if she had been Lady Clinton." Peggy began to pay formal calls on all the prominent Loyalist ladies, and although some of them shunned her at first, they finally gave in to her charm and good manners. After all, one of the last holdouts explained, "She is *a Philadelphian.*"

The arrival of nearly three thousand fresh Hessian mercenaries at the beginning of August failed to inspire Sir Henry Clinton to action. William Smith dubbed the commander in chief "the whimsical knight . . . all misery . . . [and prone to] such gusts of passion that no gentleman of spirit and independency will long continue in his family." On August 28, however—the same day on which Peggy gave birth to a second son, named after royal governor James Robertson—events conspired to stir Sir Henry: a fleet arrived from the West Indies carrying three regiments of regulars, and the French fleet departed Rhode Island, leaving the entire New England coast open to the British.

Arnold was ordered to lead a raid against American shipping in the harbor at New London, Connecticut, twelve miles from his boyhood home. But even as his men were embarking, New York was electrified by the news that General Washington had broken camp at Tappan and was on the way to Virginia with the main army, leaving West Point vulnerable to attack. General Clinton, however, refused to consider a move against the Highlands, and there was even talk of aborting the New London raid. Arnold moved swiftly, and before the commander in chief had time to change his mind his troops were ready to sail. At five A.M. on September 4, exactly seven days after the birth of his son, he sailed from Whitestone under a full moon with a fresh wind from the southwest.

The raid on New London was a technical victory for the British and a personal disaster for Benedict Arnold. He did what he set out to do, destroying more than a dozen American privateers in the harbor (although an equal number escaped upriver) as well as several warehouses full of Continental stores. But in the course of the action, the town of New London was consumed by fire and more than eighty Americans were massacred inside the walls of Fort Griswold *after* the fort had been surrendered—events for which Arnold the Traitor was inevitably blamed.

In order to accomplish his mission, Arnold had to secure two military targets at the outset: New London itself, on the west side of the river, and Fort Griswold, which commanded the harbor from a high hill on the opposite shore (see map, page 250). Griswold, reportedly undermanned and underarmed, promised to be the easier task,

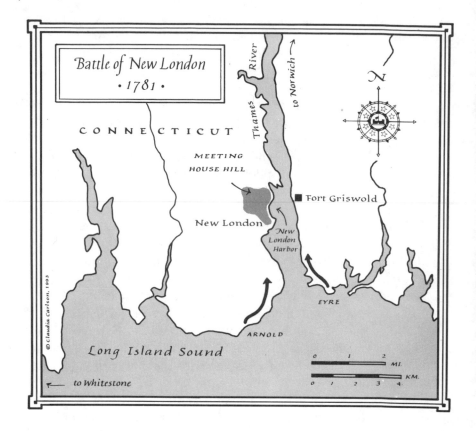

so Arnold assigned it to one of his junior officers, Lieutenant Colonel Edmond Eyre, while he himself led the main body of troops against New London. The two detachments, about eight hundred men each, were put ashore on opposite sides of the Thames estuary at about ten A.M. on September 6. By noon, having easily overrun New London's defenses, Arnold's men commenced the business of destruction while their commander climbed to the top of Meeting House Hill to survey the progress of the operation.

At his feet lay the town he had known since childhood, its once-peaceful streets now filled with armed soldiers and frightened civilians. Plumes of smoke rose up from several points where the burning had begun, and from his vantage point Arnold could clearly hear the pop of musket fire and the human cries of battle. Beyond the town lay the broad harbor, which was filled with little rowboats bearing New London's defenders across the water to reinforce Fort Griswold. Several large American privateers were already in flames; but others had managed to set sail and move upriver, aided by a favorable wind and protected by the guns of Fort Griswold, which was still in American hands.

Griswold stood on its high hill directly across from Arnold's vantage point. Through his spyglass he could see that the fort was much more heavily fortified than he and Colonel Eyre had been led to expect. Even if Eyre captured it within the next hour, he would not be able to prevent the escape of the American privateers. Arnold quickly dispatched an order canceling the assault, but it came too late. As he watched through his spyglass, the first line of Hessians and Loyalists (there were very few British regulars on the expedition) made its way up the long hill under heavy fire and began to scramble down into the deep ditch surrounding the fort. "Here the coolness and bravery of the troops were very conspicuous," Arnold noted later, "as the first who ascended the fraise [sticks mounted in the wall of the ditch on the side nearest the fort] were obliged to silence a nine-pounder, which enfiladed the place on which they stood, until a sufficient body had collected to enter the works, which was done with fixed bayonets."

The first assault was repulsed, and amid the smoke Arnold could see the men fall back and regroup. Again and again they flung themselves against the high stone walls of the fort, again and again they were thrown back. Only after forty minutes of terrible slaughter did they get over the top, after which Arnold could see no more.

Suddenly the town beneath his feet rocked with a huge explosion: one of the warehouses set afire by Arnold's men turned out to be full of gunpowder. The flames spread rapidly, and soon much of the town was burning. Arnold ordered his troops to begin withdrawing toward their ships, which proved much more difficult than he had anticipated. Militia, which had been gathering in the neighborhood all day, harassed his men in their retreat with exceptional tenacity and viciousness. He soon learned why.

After his men had gone over the walls of Fort Griswold, the American troops inside the fort, outnumbered four to one, had still refused to surrender. Finally, after a brief but bloody period of hand-to-hand fighting, the American commander, Colonel William Ledyard, determining that further resistance was futile, approached his enemy counterpart in the time-honored tradition and proffered his sword in surrender. Unfortunately, this officer was not Lieutenant Colonel Eyre, who had been wounded, nor was it second-in-command Major William Montgomery, an extremely popular officer who had been thrust through by a spear on the walls. It was a third gentleman, identity unknown, who took Ledyard's sword and used it to run him through. A junior American officer who was standing by quickly drew his sword and thrust it into the offending enemy commander, and was bayoneted in return. This series of appalling actions triggered a massacre in which the American garrison was butchered virtually to a man.

In the aftermath, both Arnold and General Clinton denied that a massacre had occurred; but nobody believed them, and nearly everybody—British as well as American—blamed Arnold the Traitor. Once again New York buzzed with rumors of misconduct, and this time much of the gossip originated with his own men. Some of them criticized him for spending the day at the top of Meeting House Hill, well apart from the battle and the danger; others held him personally responsible for the burning of New London. Most telling of all, perhaps, some of his officers accused him of falsifying the casualty figures. Arnold's official report listed 44 dead and 127 wounded, but many who were there gave a figure between 400 and 500, calling it *"a Bunker Hill expedition"* and muttering that if Arnold were given command again, General Clinton "will be able to make but few more expeditions." The point is not whose figures are more accurate; the point is that Benedict Arnold was an officer who no longer inspired the respect and trust of his men.

Rumors of massacre and heavy casualties deepened the sense of impending gloom in New York City. All eyes now turned anxiously toward Virginia, where the French fleet had beaten a British squadron off the capes, entered Chesapeake Bay and begun to land men and equipment at Jamestown. General Cornwallis, dug in at Yorktown, was now caught between the French and the Continental Army (which was approaching from the north), with no means of escaping or being resupplied. General Clinton resolved to relieve Cornwallis, even at the risk of losing New York, and headquarters began to bustle with plans and embarkations. Benedict Arnold, however, was put to work again pushing papers; he would not be part of the Virginia operation.

Furious and frustrated, Arnold determined to go around the commander in chief again, this time in person. Lord George Germain had asked for his thoughts on the war; if he went to England and spoke to the colonial secretary face-to-face, he might be able to rescue both the war and his own career. Sir Henry refused to grant permission for the trip, and Arnold continued to languish at headquarters. Then, on October 24, New York learned that General Cornwallis had surrendered his army and his sword before Yorktown.

A few days later, Arnold was walking past city hall when he spied a "pasquinado" (lampoon) suggesting that Cornwallis had been sacrificed to Benedict Arnold's envy. He ripped it from the door and hurried on. Two days later, he appealed again in person to General Clinton for permission to go to England, and Clinton finally complied. With the help of William Smith, Arnold began to prepare material for what they hoped would be detailed interrogations by Lord George Germain, the leaders of Parliament and the king. Lord Cornwallis, free on parole, arrived in New York on his way to England. His views concurred entirely with Arnold's. If their arguments prevailed, London might stiffen its resolve, replace Sir Henry Clinton with a more aggressive general and win the war.

Although he fully expected to return to America in the spring, Arnold brought his family with him to England. New York, perhaps, was no longer safe; and by now he may have sensed that they could never make their home in America, no matter how the war turned out. On the evening of December 8, Peggy and the children boarded a civilian packet while Arnold, in company with Lord Cornwallis, sailed with the same fleet aboard *Robuste,* under the protection of the Royal Navy's guns. His mission in England was crystal-clear: to persuade the government to reinvigorate the war effort by committing the money, ships and manpower necessary to win. This was more than a military and political effort on Arnold's part; it was a matter of life and death. If the British won the war, Benedict Arnold's deeds would be vindicated and his stature affirmed. If they lost, he would be nothing.

Chapter 19

"A PHILOSOPHER
IN MY OWN DEFENSE"

1782-1791

A few weeks later, standing beside King George III's chair, Arnold told his sovereign and Colonial Secretary George Germain exactly what they wanted to hear: that an overwhelming majority of Americans earnestly desired "a renewal of the royal government and the reunion of the empire." So far, he explained, these loyal Americans had remained silent out of fear, but the moment the British demonstrated both the will and the ability to protect them, they would act on their convictions by driving out of power the radical Whig minority responsible for pursuing the war.

At Germain's request, Arnold spelled out his arguments in a thirty-two-page memorandum, in which he dismissed Yorktown as "a French victory" that would prove fatal only if it persuaded the government in London to abandon the war. If, on the other hand, Parliament were to send an enterprising commander, a fleet and fifteen thousand men to America in the spring, Arnold promised total victory in a single campaign, and he offered to "evince my attachment to His Majesty and my country by taking an active part in it."

But he had come too late. Power to pursue the war in America ultimately rested not with the king and the colonial secretary but with Parliament, where a majority had already put in motion the mechanisms necessary to end the war by granting independence to the United States of America. Germain was forced to resign as secretary for the colonies a few days after receiving Arnold's memorandum, and within the month Parliament formally voted to abandon the war. The king reluctantly replaced the prowar ministry of Lord North with a proindependence government headed by Lord Rockingham, who dispatched envoys to meet with American ambassador Benjamin Franklin in Paris to establish terms for the peace.

Arnold refused to accept it. When Sir Guy Carleton, his old opponent on Lake Champlain, sailed for New York to replace Sir Henry Clinton as commander in chief, Arnold begged to go with him. "I am convinced that Mr. Washington will not be able to collect a very formidable army this spring," he wrote Carleton, "and I hope the recruits from hence . . . will give your Excellency a very decided superiority over [him]." The new colonial secretary, Lord Shelburne, "has very politely promised me his friendship and has hinted his wishes to have me go to New York," Arnold claimed, "but it is opposed (as I apprehend) by some one or more of the gentlemen in administration. . . . [I] hope soon to have the matter reduced to a certainty, whether I am to go or not. He has assured me that my detention in England shall not in the least affect my pay or corps."

It was all wishful thinking. Carleton sailed without him, and three months later, when Shelburne was elevated to prime minister after the sudden death of Lord Rockingham, it became clear that he had no intention of sending Arnold to America. The peace negotiations in Paris had officially begun. The war in America was over.

All doors began to close against him. A series of letters signed "R.M." appeared in the *General Advertiser and Morning Intelligencer* protesting Arnold's reception at court and describing him as "a mean mercenary, who, having adopted a cause for the sake of plunder, quits it when he is convicted of that charge." Arnold's vaunted courage, the writer asserted, came more from "the brandy bottle [than from] his heart. He does not at least seem to feel himself bold in this country, or else he would not patiently put up with all the personal reflections that are cast upon him." Although Arnold had been convicted of horse thievery in England before the war, "R.M." claimed, "he stands [not] so much chance of being hanged here as he does in America . . . [and] as to hanging, he ought not so much to mind it. He thought the risk of it was but a trifle for his friend Major André to undergo."

Major André again. All England was dissolved in tears over the death of General Clinton's handsome, romantic, youthful, innocent adjutant, largely thanks to the recent publication of a *Monody on Major André,* written by a popular poetess named Anna Seward, a.k.a. "The Swan of Litchfield." It commences as follows:

> Loud howls the storm! the vex'd Atlantic roars!
> Thy Genius, Britain, wanders on its shores!
> Hears cries of horror wafted from afar,
> And groans of Anguish, mid the shrieks of War! . . .
> O'er his damp brow the sable crape he binds,
> And throws his victor garland to the winds; . . .
> With one pale hand the bloody scroll he tears;
> And bids his Nation blot it with their tears;
> And one, extended o'er the Atlantic wave,
> Points to his André's ignominious grave! . . .

The king had granted Major André's mother a gift of £1000 plus an annual pension and had created his brother Sir William André, baronet. His Majesty also commissioned the famous designer Robert Adam to create a marble monument to the major, which was being installed in the south aisle of Westminster Abbey at the time of the Arnolds' arrival in London. Its inscription reads:

Sacred to the Memory
of
MAJOR JOHN ANDRÉ
who raised by his Merit at an early period of Life
to the rank of Adjutant General of the British Forces in America,
and employed in an important but hazardous Enterprise
fell a Sacrifice to his Zeal for his King and Country
on the 2nd of October A D 1780
Aged 29*
universally Beloved and esteemed by the Army in which he served
and lamented even by his
FOES,
His gracious Sovereign KING GEORGE the Third
has caused this Monument
to be erected.

*He was thirty, but twenty-nine sounds so much younger and purer. The error was typical of the romanticizing (both inadvertent and intentional) that went on around Major André's memory.

Benedict Arnold, however, inspired another sort of public verse:

> Our troops by Arnold thoroughly were banged,
> And poor St. André was by Arnold hanged;
> To George a rebel, to the Congress traitor,
> Pray, what can make the name of Arnold greater?
> By one bold treason, to gain his ends,
> Let him betray his new adopted friends.

Arnold could at least pretend to rise above such mortifications. What threatened to sink him was the prospect of financial embarrassment. With the formal cessation of hostilities, Arnold's army pay was reduced by two-thirds, as was that of his underage sons, Richard and Henry, to whom (according to standard practice) he had granted commissions in the American Legion. (Richard had joined his father in England, and in order to forestall his going on half-pay, Arnold had offered to bring him to America to commence active service, "though he is but twelve years old and can be of little use." Henry, who had been promised a lieutenancy, was now nine.) His only additional source of income was the £5,000 he had left from the money Sir Henry Clinton had given him in New York. Finally, on the day before the fall of the North government, he was granted his long-awaited reward from King George III: an annual royal pension of £500 to Margaret Arnold, "wife of our trusty and wellbeloved Brigadier General Benedict Arnold ['trusty and wellbeloved' was the standard phrase] . . . to continue payable during our pleasure." The wellbeloved general himself received "for his services" a one-eighth share of the James River prize money.

Arnold's and Peggy's combined incomes would henceforth total about £750 a year, a respectable sum, but not nearly enough to cut a dash in London society. Worse yet, his sons, denied the gentleman's education that he himself had been denied, would sink into apprenticeship or worse, a thought that Arnold found intolerable.

Within a month of Lord Shelburne's succession to the post of prime minister, Arnold called at his office with a proposal to build and outfit a privateer at government expense, sail it at his own expense and then turn it over to the navy at the end of the war. Shelburne was too busy to see him. Arnold next sent the proposal to Colonial Secretary Thomas Townshend with a covering letter: "Permit me, Sir, to say that from the sacrifices I have made of country, friends, fortune and prospects . . . I think I have a just claim to [government's] protection and support; and the aid which I now solicit . . . is much less than I have sacrificed for her. . . . [I ask only] a chance of making some provision for my family, which is numerous and expensive, nor have they any other provision at present. . . . If my proposal is accepted," he added, "I wish not to preclude myself from joining the army whenever my services are wanted." He never received an answer.

With growing desperation, Arnold applied for compensation as a Loyalist refugee, claiming £16,125 for his confiscated property in America* and an additional £9,050 for lost Continental Army half-pay, land grants and disability benefits. "[I] was third in command in the American army," he attested, and firmly "in the confidence and esteem of [my] country." Arnold also claimed an extra £20,000, the amount of money that had been rewarded by the southern states at the end of the war to Nathanael Greene, commander in chief of the Southern Department—a post that Arnold said he had turned down when General Washington offered it because of "loyalty and engagements with Sir Henry Clinton." Total compensation due: £45,175. Whether or not the commissioners saw through his lies, they informed him that there would be no compensation given for personal property, and Arnold withdrew his claim.

After two and a half fruitless years, Arnold abandoned his petitions to government and tried to get a job. He called on George Johnstone, a newly elected director of the British East India Company, to ask his influence in obtaining a high command in the company's private army. Johnstone listened carefully and then asked Arnold to send him a detailed account of his "political conduct" in the American war. Much encouraged, Arnold went home to comply.

His letter, dated the following day (July 18, 1784), offers several new variations on the old familiar theme. "During every period of the war," he claimed, "I disclaimed any idea of independence or a separation from Great Britain . . . nor did I consent to join the British army until I had received the most unequivocal and positive assurances from Sir Henry Clinton that Great Britain had given up every idea of taxing America . . . nor did I, previous to my joining the British Army,

*Only Mount Pleasant had been saved from confiscation, after Edward Shippen argued that it really belonged to his daughter and her children. Shippen purchased Arnold's life interest from the government in 1784 in vain effort to generate some income for Peggy by renting the estate. He sold it for her in 1792.

Joseph Stansbury also applied for compensation as a Loyalist, but was refused. "He seems at no time to have been true to his allegiance," the commissioners commented, "and however you may like the treason it is impossible to approve the traitor."

make any terms for myself"—a whopping lie and a stupid one, since Johnstone could easily check the facts with Sir Henry himself. "Unconnected and unsupported, having nothing to recommend me but my poor abilities as a soldier," Arnold pleaded, "I will notwithstanding venture to tender my services to the East India Company, provided I am honored with your approbation and patronage, without I shall give up any idea of the matter. I am sensible, sir, it is a favor I have no right to ask or expect. My wish is to serve the company faithfully and make some provision for a numerous family is the only apology I can make for the request."

Three days later he received his answer. It told him exactly what he needed to hear but could never accept: "Under an unsuccessful insurrection all actors are rebels. Crowned with success, they become immortal patriots. A fortunate plot holds you up as the savior of nations, a premature discovery brings you to the scaffold or brands your fame with dark and doubtful suspicions. . . . It is inglorious in a great mind who has taken a leading part to retire until the scene is settled," Johnstone observed, "and in the multiplied difficulties in which the most virtuous may be environed, he must trust his conscience for the rectitude of his conduct and appeal to the honor of his life to prove that the general good was his motive. Although I am satisfied of the purity of your conduct, the generality do not think so. While this is the case, no power in this country could suddenly place you in the situation you aim at under the East India Company."

Several months later, a Londoner wrote to his wife in the country, "I saw General Arnold the other day at Court. . . . His name was called over, and he passed in a hurry; he is taken very little notice of. . . . His lady was not there. . . . By all accounts she is an amiable woman, and was her husband dead [she] would be much noticed."

In the autumn of 1785, nearly four years after reaching London, the forty-four-year-old Arnold took a job as supercargo on a ship headed for the British colony of New Brunswick. He was back to square one.

Accompanied by his sixteen-year-old son, Richard, Arnold arrived at Saint John, New Brunswick, toward the end of 1785 in the middle of a December gale. He was suffering a violent gout attack when his ship ran aground at the entrance to the harbor (victim of an inept pilot and the notorious tides in the Bay of Fundy), and had to be carried into town on a litter.

New Brunswick was perhaps the only place in the world where Benedict Arnold could be certain of a welcome: more than half of

Saint John's twelve thousand citizens were American Loyalist refugees, many of them veterans of his own American Legion, whose discharge pay had included land grants in New Brunswick. The economy of the new colony (which had only recently been separated from Nova Scotia) was sluggish, but a burgeoning population offered good investment opportunities, and Arnold decided to stay long enough to amass some capital. He set up a store near the Saint John waterfront, built a small house, acquired a mistress, purchased a commercial wharf and began to look for profit-making ventures.

The thousands of hastily constructed, raw wooden houses that sprawled along the Saint John docks and climbed the steep hills above the harbor sheltered a population in trauma. The Loyalists had never imagined, even after Yorktown and the commencement of peace negotiations, that their sovereign would grant independence to the American colonies. When the terms of the treaty were made public in August 1782, however, independence was far less of a shock than the fact that His Majesty had failed to elicit from the United States of America any guarantee for the persons and properties of its Loyalist citizens. "This information struck me as the loss of all I had in the world," William Smith wrote, and the Loyalist community gave way to "universal despair and frenzy."

Those who had managed to rescue some cash from the wreckage made their way to England; the rest repaired to British colonies in Canada, the West Indies or—as a last resort—New Brunswick. One young Loyalist mother remembered that on arriving in Saint John she had climbed to the top of a hill with her baby to watch the fleet depart. As the last "sails disappear[ed] in the distance," she wrote, "such a feeling of loneliness came over me that, although I had not shed a tear through all the war, I sat down on the damp moss with my baby in my lap and cried."

By the time Arnold arrived, a nasty social split had developed in this tiny provincial society between the older residents, including the first Loyalist arrivals, and a small group of newcomers, mostly members of the Massachusetts gentry who had gone first to England and obtained royal administrative appointments in the new colony. These men—Solicitor General Ward Chipman, for example, and his friends Surrogate General Edward Winslow and Attorney General Jonathan Bliss—congregated with their wives and families in the area of town known as Upper Cove, where streets called King, Prince William and Germain threaded their way up the steep hills above the docks. Beneath them, in Lower Cove, on streets named Water and Dock, lived "the common people," whom Winslow deemed "insolent and rude." In a town where virtually everybody lived above the shop, the Upper Cove purveyors of dry goods, gunpowder and books looked down on the Lower Cove dealers in lumber and nails, while the Lower Covers in turn resented their snobbery and the political plums their social position had procured.

Although from necessity Arnold lived and worked along the docks, he managed to insinuate himself into the society of Upper Cove. Chipman and the others initially resisted the overtures of the notorious General Arnold, but his manners and connections soon earned him a welcome in their drawing rooms.

Spending his only capital (the £6000 that Sir Henry Clinton had awarded him in 1781), Arnold bought a lumberyard and shipyard, half interest in a trading sloop and dozens of building lots in Saint John and Fredericton, New Brunswick's second city. Within weeks of his arrival he commissioned construction of "an entire new and most noble ship" named *Lord Sheffield*. "Her timbers," the Saint John *Royal Gazette* trumpeted, "are altogether white oak, and [she] is allowed to be as well constructed a vessel as any ever built in America . . . [General Arnold's] laudable efforts to promote the interest of this infant colony have, during his short residence, been very productive to its commercial advantage, and as such deserve the praises of every will wisher to its prosperity."

But the launching of *Lord Sheffield* marked both the beginning and the end of Arnold's glory in New Brunswick. As the ship was being outfitted for her maiden voyage, the builder set every tongue in the province wagging with a public charge that Arnold had reneged on their contract. Arnold insisted that he had merely deducted from the fee the amount the builder himself had agreed to forego if the ship were not delivered on time, while the builder claimed (but could not prove) that the delays had all been caused by last-minute changes made by Arnold himself.

Treachery and greed: the accusations, whether justified or not, would eventually have been sloughed off by any other man. They stuck to Arnold like burrs. Turning his back on them—and on his pregnant mistress (her identity is unknown; she bore a son, John Sage, in 1786)—he sailed on *Lord Sheffield*'s maiden voyage to the West Indies. From thence, the ship returned to Saint John and Arnold took a packet to London to fetch his wife and children.

Peggy had been alone for a year, "torn from almost everybody that is dear to me . . . in a strange country, without a creature near me that is really interested in my fate." She had three young children to tend (baby Sophia Matilda had been born shortly before her father's departure for New Brunswick), as well as all her husband's business, including an expensive and vexatious lawsuit brought by John Holker, the French consul in Philadelphia, to recover the £12,000 he had loaned Arnold in 1779. One of her brothers had died, and she worried lest her mother, "being untrained in the school of adversity," should crumble under "this very heavy trial. . . . Yet I hope she will consider the many blessings by which she is surrounded and endeavor to support herself." As for herself, Peggy wrote to her father, "I find it necessary to summon all my philosophy to my aid." It was becoming more and more apparent that "philosophy" (in the sense of equanimity and mental diligence) was one of Peggy's strongest attributes.

After her husband arrived and took charge, Peggy became pregnant almost immediately and the British government was applied to for "interference and protection" from the Holker lawsuit. "The government ought either to stop the proceedings against me, defend the cause at the public expense, or pay the money," Arnold insisted, citing "the sacrifices I have made and the services which I have rendered." Lest these sacrifices and services have been forgotten during the nearly six years since the end of the war, Arnold requested a testimonial from the only man who could document them, Sir Henry Clinton, who was now living in London in semiretirement.

"Having on many occasions received the most illiberal and unmerited abuse in consequence of the decided part I had taken in the late American War, which has been imputed to mercenary rather than to the just motives," he wrote to Clinton in May 1787, "for the satisfaction of my family and friends I may hereafter think it necessary to appeal to the public in justification of my conduct. As you, dear sir, are the principal person who can form a just judgment of my motives . . . I beg you will have the goodness to say . . . that I acted from principle and that my conduct was perfectly disinterested."

Sir Henry replied in his habitually laconic fashion within the week. "Had I not been persuaded that the negotiation you opened with me . . . arose solely from principle and a conviction of your error, I certainly should not have paid that regard to it I did. . . . My ideas of your services while you acted with the King's troops have been already communicated to the Secretary of State. I am no longer in a situation either to notice or reward them. But I sincerely hope that it will not be long before your conduct may be fully elucidated to your satisfaction, and the motives which influenced it better known than you seem to think them at present." Arnold's appeal for government intervention went unanswered, and he was eventually obliged to pay Holker £900 out of his pocket.

Arnold returned to Saint John with his family nearly a year after he had left it, in July 1787. He rented a house on King Street, Upper Cove, where Peggy arranged the furnishings she had brought from England: blue damask sofas and chairs, card tables, desks, chandeliers, "an elegant set of Wedgewood gilt ware, two table sets of Nankeen china, a variety of glassware [and] a terrestrial globe." The couple did not intend to remain in Saint John any longer than necessary—neither of them fancied little ponds—but Peggy quickly set about making life as pleasant as possible by making friends with the Upper Cove ladies. The family doubled within a few months: Arnold's sister Hannah and fifteen-year-old Henry joined them, and in September Peggy gave birth to George Arnold, who she determined would be her last child.

When George was two, he and his mother went to Philadelphia to see her family. As Peggy had predicted, the visit was a mixture of joy and sorrow. Welcomed by her parents, sisters and few close friends, she was shunned by many others; and when she left after six months, she knew she would never see any of them again. "How difficult is it to know what will contribute to our happiness in this life," she wrote to her sister from Saint John in July 1790, shortly after her return. "I had hoped that by paying my beloved friends a last visit, I should insure to myself some portion of it, but I find it far otherwise. The[ir] affectionate attention . . . has greatly increased my love for them, and of course my regret at this cruel, dreadful separation."

During her absence, many of Arnold's investments in New Brunswick had turned sour (ironically, Saint John's financial boom did not occur until ten years after Arnold left, when a thriving trade in timber, furs and fish earned it the appellation "the Liverpool of America"), and he had become involved in a staggering number of petty lawsuits: his old flamboyance and pugnacity reduced to spasms of litigation. The most serious was a suit for slander he had filed against an erstwhile business parter, who had publicly accused him of torching his Lower Cove store in order to collect the insurance. Ward Chipman, who served as Arnold's attorney in the case, deemed the charge "one of the most hellish plots that ever was laid for the destruction of a man," and the jury found in his favor. The judge, however, registered his dissent by awarding Arnold damages of only twenty shillings, and the citizens of Saint John expressed their feelings by burning Arnold in effigy in the middle of the night in front of his King Street house, with Peggy and the children looking on. Little ponds, it appeared, were even more difficult to hide in than large ones.

Both Arnolds were desperate to return to London, but it was more than a year before he could raise enough capital to finance the trip. During this period of profound uncertainty, Peggy fell into a deep depression. Its immediate occasion is easy to identify—the burning-in-effigy must have been terrifying—as is its underlying cause: the prospect of a life, permanently separated from her beloved family, in a far-off country, with a man who had no future. Peggy had outgrown her husband, acquiring a firm grip on reality even as his slipped away entirely. She accepted the fact that he had betrayed her (in a small town like Saint John, she was bound to learn about his illegitimate son), but she never again referred to him as "the best of husbands."

By the time they sailed for England in December 1791, Peggy's depression had begun to lift. Although she would never again be truly happy except in her children, her continuing education in the "school of adversity" endowed her with greater and greater strength as the years went by. She never succumbed to bitterness, and she never failed to support her husband. Her support was all he had during the long, dark years to come.

Chapter 20

"IIER EVER DEAR
AND SORROWED HUSBAND"

1792-1801

In January 1792, as Arnold made his way back to England, his former commander in chief, George Washington, passed the midpoint in his first term as president of the United States. Alexander Hamilton served the administration as secretary of the treasury, and Henry Knox was secretary of war. Daniel Morgan, on the other hand, had retired to his 250,000-acre estate in Virginia, where he was in the process of building a mansion called "Saratoga." Meanwhile, in New York City, Arnold's erstwhile secretary, Richard Varick, was serving the third of his eleven consecutive terms as mayor, while his cohorts from Saratoga days, Matthew Clarkson and Henry Brockholst Livingston, held positions of prominence in the city's business and social communities.

Two of Arnold's old nemeses had fared less well: Joseph Reed was dead, and Timothy Matlack was in debtors' prison, having lost his job as secretary to the Pennsylvania Council because of irregularities in his accounts.

Arnold's British counterparts had all achieved glory: Lord Cornwallis, having served with distinction as governor-general of India, was on the verge of being created Marquis Cornwallis; Sir Guy Carleton, now Lord Dorchester, served as governor of Quebec; and General John Burgoyne rested in a hero's grave near John André in Westminster Abbey.

Benedict Arnold spent his fifty-first birthday nursing an attack of gout in the cabin of a ship that rolled and heaved its way across the Atlantic in a violent winter storm. Safe in London, he created a storm of his own.

On the morning of May 31, 1792, James Maitland, Earl of Lauderdale, rose to his feet in the House of Lords to denounce a former political ally, the Duke of Rutland, for "apostasy from principles." The duke had recently received an important command in the army, and in the course of his remarks, Lauderdale remarked off-handedly that "if apostasy could justify promotion, [the Duke] was the most fit person for that command, General Arnold alone excepted." Apostasy: the one charge that Arnold could not let stand. He had spent the last ten years trying to prove that he was *not* an apostate, not a turncoat, not a traitor; now he demanded from the earl a public apology.

Lauderdale complied, but in language insufficiently specific for Arnold. After several weeks of negotiations, during which Arnold's obduracy never softened, the two men met with their seconds on a dueling ground near London. Reaching their positions, both stood motionless for a moment, then Arnold raised his pistol and fired. The bullet missed its mark. Arnold stood his ground, waiting for Lauderdale to fire, but the earl refused, saying he had no enmity toward Arnold. Arnold's second, Lord Hawke, then inquired if the earl would apologize, but Lauderdale refused.

For a number of confused minutes, the two seconds scurried back and forth between their principals. Finally, Lauderdale stepped forward with a formal declaration "that he did not mean to asperse [Arnold's] character or wound his feelings, and was sorry that General Arnold or any other person should be hurt at what he had said." Arnold pronounced himself satisfied, "provided that their seconds as men of honor would say that he ought to be so," which they promptly did.

Arnold returned home to find Peggy in her room, so distraught that "for some hours [her] reason was despaired of." For weeks she had remained "perfectly silent on the subject" of Lauderdale, lest she "unman [her husband] and prevent his acting himself." Arnold, who felt completely vindicated, basked in the congratulations of their friends; but *The Times* reported that Lauderdale had neither fired *nor apologized,* leaving its readers with the impression that nothing had been concluded.

Arnold wrote cheerfully to Jonathan Bliss, his friend and business agent in Saint John, "our reception [in England] has been very pleasant. . . . The little property that we have saved from the hands of a *lawless ruffian mob* and *more unprincipled judges* in New Brunswick is perfectly safe here, as well as our *persons from insult,* and though we feel and regret the absence of the friends we had there, we find London *full as pleasant!* and I cannot help viewing your great city as a shipwreck from which I have escaped." But his private anxiety was intense. With a wife, seven children and a sister to support, his "little property" did not go very far.

Arnold had spent virtually all his treason earnings on worthless investments in New Brunswick, so that now his and Peggy's only sources of income were her royal pension and his half-pay as a brigadier, both of which would cease on their respective deaths, leaving their children penniless. Fortunately, Peggy had persuaded her husband to leave the pension untouched during their sojourn in New Brunswick, and it had been accumulating, she told her father, "in the Funds, in the name of *my* agent, for which *I* am credited on his books [original emphasis]." Now she wished to invest her nest egg for the children's educations. Interest rates in Philadelphia were much higher than in London, so Peggy asked her father to invest for her there. This led to a spirited correspondence between father and daughter that lasted many years. Peggy was extremely well informed on financial and political matters, and although she always seemed to defer to her father's judgment, she usually got her way in the long run.

Arnold had no such resources. His only hope was to renew his appeal for compensation for the loss of his American properties and emoluments, and less than four months after his return to London, he addressed an appeal directly to Prime Minister William Pitt. "From my private fortune and the high rank I held in the American army, I was amply provided for," he wrote, "[and] no officer of my rank stood in higher estimation in the States or had fairer prospects of ease, honor and independence . . . [having since then] experienced the most unmerited and mortifying abuse not only from my own countrymen but from many persons in England . . . I now find myself deprived of my fortune and rank, and so far from being able to provide for and educate a numerous family of six sons and one daughter, that it is barely in my power to support them decently."

On learning that Pitt intended to consult with Sir Henry Clinton, Arnold again applied to his former commander in chief, repeating the claim that Major André had promised him "a much greater sum than I have received. . . . As I wish to be as little burdensome as possible to government," he continued, "I have no objection to any employ[ment] either civil or military that I can with propriety accept; and as no person is so capable of judging of my abilities in the latter as yourself, I have no doubt that you will mention me to Mr. Pitt as you think I deserve." Clinton did not even bother to reply, sending instead a verbatim copy of the letter he had written five years before: "My ideas of your services while you acted with the King's troops have been already communicated to the Secretary of State. I am no longer in a situation either to notice or reward them."

After weeks of silence, Arnold called on the prime minister at his office in Whitehall and twice at his home, but was always informed that Pitt was out. Finally, four months after lodging his appeal, he was summoned for an interview. (Pitt's dilatoriness is explained—at least in part—by the fact that he had more important things on his mind, the French revolutionary government having recently imprisoned Louis XVI and declared war on the Hapsburg Empire. Even as he and Arnold sat down to talk, Paris was awash with blood from the September Massacres.) The prime minister, Arnold reported to Peggy, was "surprised at the small sum I had received and seemed inclined to do something for me." He asked Arnold what he required; the answer was £25,000 to provide for his family and allow him to live in "the style of the first people of America, by whom I was respected and beloved and among whom I had many friends."

They waited for two months, without receiving any word. Peggy ventured to write to Sir Henry Clinton.

> Surrounded by a numerous little family, without the means of educating and supporting them in a style at all equal to what the former part of my life promised, and our scanty income being dependent upon our lives . . . you will not be surprised that every maternal feeling is awakened and that I am deeply interested in General Arnold's present application to Mr. Pitt, the favorable event of which will no doubt in a great measure depend upon your representations of his conduct. From your justice I have everything to hope—May I presume to solicit your friendship?

A few days later, they were ecstatic to learn that Clinton had told the prime minister that £6000 was far from adequate payment for

Arnold's services, or indeed for Peggy's, which had been "very meritorious." But another six months of silence ensued (again, not surprising: Great Britain was once again at war with France). Peggy became ill, her ankles swelling so that she could barely walk. Arnold wrote Pitt a whole series of letters and memoranda, including a request to be appointed governor of Dominica, West Indies. Finally, on July 20, 1793, more than a year and a half since his return from New Brunswick, Arnold got his answer in the form of a king's warrant establishing pensions of £100 per annum for each of Peggy's four children.

Arnold did not break. Instead, at the age of fifty-three, he prepared himself to go to sea again. Moving his pregnant wife and children into a more modest house in Queen Ann Street, he sailed on a trading ship for the West Indies in the spring of 1794, coming to anchor in the harbor at Point-à-Pitre, Guadeloupe, just before the town was recaptured by the French fleet in heavy fighting. Imprisoned aboard a French ship, he was questioned by a representative of the Robespierre government. Under the shadow of the guillotine (this was the summer of the Reign of Terror in Paris), he was understandably unwilling to identify himself and gave a false name: Anderson—the same name that John André had used.

Making his escape from the ship by night, Arnold managed to reach the safety of a British fleet anchored off another part of the island. The British commander in chief, Sir Charles Grey, gave him a job as victualer to the army and also sought his advice on strategy—or at least Arnold claimed he did. One of Grey's junior officers saw it differently, reporting later that Arnold asked for "a command as senior brigadier general, and . . . fastened himself on to Grey with a tenacity which the General's undisguised disgust was powerless to shake."

Sir Charles did offer Arnold's son Henry a lieutenant's commission, which his father declined. Henry had come down to the islands to serve as Arnold's assistant, "but until I can trust him with money, and be assured that he will not squander it away and think himself above giving an account of it," Arnold wrote to a business acquaintance, "I will treat him like a stranger and not as a son. I wish to God he would have a little sense and prudence." Henry's behavior was perfectly understandable to any parent who has ever survived a twenty-one-year-old male child; but Arnold simply threw up his hands and sent him back to his aunt Hannah in New Haven. (Richard was also living with Hannah, while Benedict, Jr., had commenced a career in the British Army.)

By the time Arnold returned to England in July 1795, Peggy was "very much an invalid." Her principal symptom was edema, which she treated "with a plan of abstinence, which is the only one recommended to me by an eminent physician whom I have consulted. He orders me to eat not one half my usual quantity of food," she wrote to her father, "and to lessen my drink in the same proportion. . . . I am to take no kind of medicine and never fatigue myself with exercise." Arnold may well have been correct in ascribing her condition to mental and emotional distress (which he called "nerves"): during his absence, she had given birth to a child, watched it die, learned of her own mother's death and become enmeshed in the details of her husband's tangled New Brunswick investments. But she had also found a new source of solace: her eldest son, Edward, who, at a remarkably steady and sensible fifteen years of age, had become his mother's mainstay and confidant.

All the younger children, Arnold boasted to Jonathan Bliss, "are placed at exceeding good schools where they improve very much [Peggy's prudence paying off]. Edward . . . will soon have the start of me in height and is a remarkably forward and fine boy. . . . James goes a cadet to Woolwich Academy under the patronage of Lord Cornwallis; I design him for an engineer." In short, he concluded complacently, "in this age of revolutions and the consequent horrors and devastations of war . . . there is great consolation to be drawn from our situations, which are comfortable but not sufficiently elevated to be the objects of envy and distinction. We therefore ought to be content, which is the greatest happiness to be expected in this world."

And he seemed content, but very briefly. The high point, perhaps, was his reception by the Standing Committee of the West India Planters and Merchants, who applauded an address he gave them and formally recommended to the government that he be sent back to the islands "in a military character. . . . [I] have agreed," Arnold told Bliss, "if my terms are complied with, in which case I shall soon leave England." Nothing ever came of it. Peggy loyally reported that the ministry was "extremely anxious for him to go . . . [but] were fearful of putting [him] over the heads of so many old general officers." Meanwhile, she ruefully acknowledged, "he has, by his trip to the west, gained more credit than money."

Arnold had borrowed £10,000 to victual the army in Guadeloupe. While the interest payments ate up his little income and wartime prices soared (bread and meat, for example, increased by as much as 40 percent in one year; presumably school tuitions did the same), the Treasury Board delayed, month after month, honoring his victualing invoices. Still, he did not break—even after learning of the death of his oldest son, Benedict Jr., of a fever while on active duty in Jamaica. "I have the consolation to hear that he was much respected and beloved by the officers of his acquaintance," the grieving father wrote to Jonathan Bliss, "and Lord Balcarres had promised him further promotion."*

In an act of feckless bravado, Arnold moved his family in the autumn of 1796 from their modest home in Queen Ann Street to a grand town house in Gloucester Place in the district of Marylebone, "London's newest and most fashionable center of aristocratic wealth, opulent residential development and artistic activity." Even as he filled his cellar with fine wine, he continued to dun the Treasury Board for payment of his victualing money. But the content and the tone of his appeals grew increasingly desperate.

He proposed to Prime Minister Pitt an expedition "to liberate Chile, Peru, and both Mexicos from the Dominion of Spain,"† commanded, of course, by himself. In the absence of a reply he wrote to the First Lord of Admiralty volunteering to command a small fleet of fire ships in the English Channel, to guard against a threatened invasion by Napoleon Bonaparte, the rising young French military genius. The First Lord promptly rejected the plan as inconsistent "with the rules and practice of the naval service," but he also took pains to point out that "there are many officers [already in the navy] who would most cheerfully carry through any enterprise which government might think it fit to offer them to undertake."

Fresh out of schemes, Arnold began to borrow heavily to invest in privateers—and Peggy's anxieties increased tenfold. "I am almost sick of the struggle to keep up an appearance," she confessed to her father, "however, [it] is absolutely necessary in this country to bring forward a young family," and she concluded ruefully, "Matrimony is but a lottery." Shortly after moving into the new house in Gloucester Place, she suffered "a violent attack in my head that . . . nearly proved fatal. . . . My spirits are much broken," she wrote to her father, "and I think I could be contented in a very humble retired situation; but to see my children's rising prospects blasted would fill me with the keenest anguish." Within the year she discovered that

---

*The same Balcarres whose redoubt Arnold had so persistently attacked during the second battle of Saratoga in 1777 (see page 138). Balcarres now served as royal governor of Jamaica.

†Spain was an ally of France in the current war.

she was pregnant again at the age of thirty-seven. A son was born in June 1798 and named William Fitch Arnold, in honor of one of Peggy's closest friends, an American Loyalist who lived with his sisters in nearby Portman Street.

When twenty-year-old Edward accepted Lord Cornwallis's offer of a cadetship in the engineering corps in India, his father bade him farewell with some advice: "Make yourself agreeable and useful to General Lake [the commander in chief, and] . . . form, if you can, an *intimate* acquaintance with his son, who is a captain and aide-de-camp. . . . I need not observe to you that great *civility* and *attention to everybody* will do more for you than most young men are aware of, and though I should despise you for being a sycophant, I would have you espouse the cause of any man who is spoken ill of in his absence, as far as you can do so with truth and propriety."

Peggy's advice was more succinct: "Nature has been bountiful to you as far as external appearance goes; a knowledge of life will convince you of the great utility of a conciliatory manner and an apparent wish to please and oblige." Edward was the only person on earth in whom she confided totally, and her heart sank at the thought of being separated from him.

Arnold's hopes soared when the Treasury Board voted to pay him £8,500 of his victualing money; but after a new anti-French war coalition was formed by Great Britain and Austria, he was told that no government funds were available to honor the order. One of his privateers captured a prize worth £25,000 and then lost it again, through the negligence of her captain. Peggy, who had tried to warn her husband against the captain's "too free indulgence in his bottle," wrote to Edward that the loss had sunk them deeper into debt than ever before. Arnold addressed another desperate appeal to Prime Minister Pitt, who managed to lose the letter and all the attached documentation.

It was the latter, perhaps, that finally broke Benedict Arnold's spirits: the realization that he was nothing but a man whose papers other men mislaid. His house of mirrors had shielded him from such knowledge for all these years; now, suddenly, its images shattered, and in their place he saw a failed husband, a failed father and a failed traitor. The sight proved the death of him.

Toward the end of 1800, Arnold's legs began to swell from "a general dropsy and a disease in the lungs," and "his difficulty of breathing was at times so great, particularly at night, that he could scarcely lay down . . . [a] sensation . . . always brought on by any agitation of mind." Peggy took him to the country, where he seemed to rally; but with his creditors finally at the end of their patience, and in the absence of any reply to his last, desperate appeal to Prime Minister Pitt, he and Peggy were forced to return to London to sell the lease of the grand house on Gloucester Place.

Within the week he took to his bed. "Strong symptoms of salivation appeared in his mouth, which soon extended to his throat, by which he was entirely disabled from swallowing or speaking." After suffering thus for three days Arnold died "without a groan" just after dawn on the morning of Sunday, June 14.

The Patriot-Hero was gone. Not the real Patriot-Hero, of course (who had been dead for nearly a quarter of a century, since that moment in the Continental camp at Valley Forge when he had consciously severed himself from the cause of his country and signed an oath of allegiance that was a lie) but the phantom Patriot-Hero, who had lived on as a shining image inside his creator's heart, sheltered from the truth by sheer willpower and courage. Finally, when the image cracked, the heart that had nurtured it cracked as well. It was a mighty heart.

PEGGY, AT LAST

The death notices were uniformly terse: "June 14 in Gloucester Place, Brigadier General Arnold, a person much noticed during the American War," was typical. The only sympathetic chord was struck in an editorial comment in the antigovernment *Morning Post,* which observed, "Poor General Arnold has departed this world without notice; a sorry reflection this for the Pitts . . . and other turncoats."

Peggy buried him in the basement crypt of the village church of Battersea, a new suburb across the Thames from London proper. Squat, foursquare, modest St. Mary's Church is a far cry from the soaring grandeur of Westminster Abbey, but it was a popular burial place for former American Loyalists, and it suited Peggy's frugal mood.

Her husband's will was just as unrealistic as his life had been. He had left all the appropriate bequests—to his sister, his three older sons and his illegitimate son, John Sage (whom Peggy referred to as "a young man in Canada": the fourteen-year-old lived with his three American brothers and their aunt Hannah in Upper Canada); but there was no money to honor them. What he left instead were debts, amounting to some £6,000, more than even the clear-eyed Peggy had imagined.

She entered a period of profound despair, in which "I fancied that nothing but the sacrifice of my life would benefit my children, for that my wretchedness embittered every moment of their lives; and, dreadful to say, I was many times on the point of making the sacrifice." Her memory and concentration deserted her, and she felt what she supposed "would be the sensations of anybody extremely drunk and very desirous of concealing their situation."

Doctors could not help her, so she undertook her own cure, resolving "to observe the medium between full and very low living, to keep regular and early hours, to mix with cheerful and rational society, to make the best of my little income, and to be thankful for the blessings yet left me, among the greatest of which is the uncommon excellence of my children."

The house in Gloucester Place and all its grand accoutrements were sold: furniture, pictures, wine cellar, carpets, even Arnold's clothing. She elicited £2000 of his victualing money from the Treasury Board, which tided her over and paid some of the debts. She applied for a royal pension for three-year-old William and resumed her correspondence with Jonathan Bliss in an attempt to salvage something from her holdings in New Brunswick. She even attempted to collect £750 which she and her husband had loaned her brother many years before; but, her father informed her, "he is not possessed of a single shilling." It was a cold, implacable parent who revealed his own "continual contributions" to keep her brother's family afloat without making a single gesture to do the same for her. (He did begin sending her money the following year.) "I will make no reflections upon the causes of your distress," he wrote, "it is of less consequence to account for misfortunes than to apply the most practicable means to alleviate them." He did issue a half-hearted invitation for Peggy to come to America with her "little lovely daughter," but he categorically excluded her sons, so she naturally declined.

Unfortunately, Peggy's own small investments, which had not been legally secured to her children, were also sacrificed to her husband's creditors. "There is little probability of anything being saved to the family out of the wreck," Peggy informed her oldest son in India. She suggested, gently but firmly, that in future he would have to "live within your pay," but enjoined him at the same time not to cut back so drastically as to "place yourself upon a footing inferior to your brother officers, as, in order to get on well, it is necessary to make a certain appearance. . . . But upon this subject I will not dwell,

convinced from my knowledge of your heart that you will not err."
Edward volunteered to undertake William's education, which his
mother declined; but she did accept when he gave over his royal
pension to Sophia and when James, who was serving in the army in
Gibraltar, did the same to Peggy for the younger children.

Six months after Arnold's death, Peggy moved into a "small, but
very neat house" at 32 Bryanston Street. She bought back a few
personal items from the estate (including, from "a little family
pride," the family silver) and purchased furniture from her servant,
"who is now a more independent woman than her mistress." Once
installed, she informed her Canadian stepsons, with justifiable pride,
"I have not a teaspoon, a towel or a bottle of wine that I have not paid
for." Within the year she had "collected from the wreck" of her
husband's estate enough money to "satisf[y] every *ascertained*
debt" and to honor the legacies to Arnold's older sons ("the only
thing," she told Edward, "that preserved them from utter ruin or
prevented their being thrown into a jail"). Hannah's legacy she undertook to pay herself, vowing that "while I have the means of pre-
venting it, I will never suffer the sister of my husband to want."

She began to "feel the disposition, as well as the propriety on
account of my children, of mixing with the world. . . . I must [do so]
. . . in a way not very gratifying to my vanity or the natural ambition
which, I confess, has often annoyed me; but I have the satisfaction
of knowing that I stand well with the world and that the change of my
circumstances can never be imputed to any imprudence of my own."
Meeting some rebuffs, she confessed to her son that she was hurt,
"but I trust I shall have philosophy enough to despise civilization
shown only to a carriage and good house, and to set a proper value
upon attentions shown me for myself only." In short, for the first time
in many years, Peggy felt "tranquil, serene and cheerful . . . exerting
myself to make the most of my little income, and surrounded by
friends who do not estimate me according to my present appearance.
. . . Misfortunes and other circumstances have made me lay castle-
building quite aside," she wrote to Edward; "but I sometimes flatter
myself that we may yet see happier days. Mine has been an eventful
life, and I may yet ascend nearer the top of the wheel."

In sixteen months Peggy had accomplished a miracle, but no
miracle could save her from what came next. She became increasingly aware that her memory was deteriorating, to the point where
her letters began to ramble and repeat. In the summer of 1803, her
doctors diagnosed "a complaint of the womb, which requires the
greatest care and attention to conquer, if it can ever be effected

. . . my complaint is quite local," she informed her sister, "as my general health was never better . . . [and I am] restored to a perfect serenity of mind and a degree of contentment that some time ago I thought it impossible for me ever to regain." She traveled to a friend's house in the country "in a coach so fitted out as to enable me to perform the whole journey lying down," and there spent a few weeks "quite at home . . . on my sofa, surrounded by a large and friendly family." But in her private moments, she "endeavor[ed] to prepare my mind for the worst, but when I reflect upon the unprotected state of my children, whose welfare so greatly depends upon my exertions for them, I am almost deprived of that fortitude so essential to my own support."

By autumn, a "very large tumor" had been discovered, "which broke and discharged an immense quantity. To prevent another is now the great object," Peggy wrote her father, "but I am not much encouraged to hope for success." In January she suffered a "violent attack [when] for nine days I lay with every appearance of a corpse, and as cold in the extremities as you ever felt. . . . Most violent remedies were used internally, with constantly applying cloths dipped in iced water to my body, without the effect of stopping the complaint, till exhausted nature worked her own cure."

She began to recover strength, but developed breathing difficulties. By the spring of 1804, her pain was so great that only opium brought relief. "My only chance," she wrote to her sister, "is from an internal operation, which it is at present dangerous to perform." Nevertheless, "I do not suffer my spirits to overcome me. I have much to be thankful for, most particularly for the very uncommon attention and kindness that I hourly experience from my numerous friends . . ."

By midsummer she was taking opium constantly. Her release came on August 24, three years and two months after that of her husband. When she died, she was forty-four years old.

Peggy was buried with Arnold in the crypt at St. Mary's, Battersea, after a funeral that she stipulated should be "as plain as is consistent with the situation of my family, avoiding superfluous expense."

In 1976, 172 years later, an American admirer of the Arnolds paid for a stained-glass window in their honor. Its inscription reads in part:

Beneath this church lie buried the bodies of Benedict Arnold, sometime general in the army of George Washington, and of

his faithful and beloved wife Margaret Arnold of Pennsylvania.
. . . The two nations whom he served in turn in the years of
their enmity have united in this memorial as a token of their
enduring friendship.

Twelve years later, Arnold finally received the promotion and
the title he had sought throughout the last grim twenty years of his
life. A historical plaque placed in 1988 on the house in Gloucester
Place is dedicated to

Major General Benedict Arnold, American Patriot.

At last. He would have been very pleased.

Acknowledgments

I owe a great debt of gratitude to all the following for help, encouragement, interest and hospitality:

In Connecticut: Ed Leonard, director of the Otis Library in Norwich; Mrs. Arthur Warner of Canterbury; Mr. and Mrs. Daniel McKeon of Ridgefield; Mary Sisco; Silvio Bedini; Alesandra M. Schmidt, reference librarian, and Paige A. Savery of the Connecticut Historical Society; Ms. Stark of Manuscripts and Archives at the Sterling Memorial Library, Yale University; Kaz Kozlowski of the Prudence Crandall Museum in Canterbury; Margaret Sax of the Watkinson Library at Trinity College; Josephine Harrell of the First Church of Christ, New Haven; Bill Stanley; Marilyn Cruthers; Gloria Beauchamp; Dee Longly of the Middlesex Historical Society; Jack Sanders of the *Ridgefield Press;* and the staffs of the Connecticut State Library, New Haven Colony Historical Society, Yale's Beinecke Library and Sterling Memorial Library, especially the very helpful keepers of the Benjamin Franklin Collection.

On Lake Champlain: Jim Carroll, Bob Carroll and Frank Pabst, boatmen supreme; Mr. and Mrs. J. Robert Maguire; Jane M. Lape, director of the Fort Ticonderoga Museum; Tim Titus of Crown Point State Historic Site; and Carol Greenough of Whitehall, New York.

On the Kennebec River: Duluth Wing and his wife, Betty, without whom I would never have made it; Jannice Baker; Karen and Crosby Milliman of the Reuben Colburn House in Gardiner, Maine, headquarters of the Arnold Expedition Historical Society; Robert A. Cunningham; and Jay Adams, curator of the Fort Western Museum.

In Quebec: M. Georges Henri Dagneau; Mme. Berubé and Michel Gagnon of the Quebec Tourism Bureau; and Bryan Leconte of Quebec Government House in New York.

In and around Philadelphia: Chief Historian David Dutcher and Historian Anna Coxe Toogood of Independence National Historical Park; Beatrice Garvan, former curator of Mount Pleasant; Elizabeth Carroll-Horrocks, manuscripts librarian at the American Philosophical Society; the staff of the Historical Society of Pennsylvania; Jane Unkefer; Addie Lou Caywood; Elaine Forman Crane, editor of the diaries of Elizabeth Drinker; and Lee Ellen Griffith of the Philadelphia Museum of Art.

At and around West Point: Colonel Jim Johnson of the West Point History Department; Marie T. Capps, manuscripts librarian, and Alan Aimone, military affairs librarian, of the United States Military Academy Library; David Meschutt, curator of art at the West Point Museum; John Scott of the Historical Society of Rockland County; Daina Dubitsky of Stony Point State Historic Site; and Bill and Myra Calabrese.

In Virginia: John Casey; W. W. Abbot, editor of the Papers of George Washington at the Alderman Library, University of Virginia; Ned Berkeley, director of Alderman's special collections; Donald R. Sutherland; Chris Kolbe of the Archives Division at the Virginia State Library; Charles Carter of Shirley Plantation; John Ingram, research librarian at Colonial Williamsburg; Mark Wenger, architectural historian at Colonial Williamsburg; Carolyn Weekly, director of the Wallace Gallery in Williamsburg; John Selby of the College of William and Mary; Virginius Hall of the Virginia Historical Society; Deborah L. Sisum of the National Portrait Gallery in Washington, D.C.; Fred M. Darden; Malcolm Jamison; Caroline Dowdey; Margaret Cook; and Alice C. Hanes, curator of the Portsmouth Naval Shipyard Museum.

In England: Mr. and Mrs. Vere H.C. Arnold; Peter William Arnold; Derrick Langford; the staffs of the Public Record Office, the London Library, the University of London Library, the India Office Library, the Newspaper Library (British Library) and the Archives and Local History Section of the Marylebone Library; Jim Parker of the National Register of Archives; Brenda Ralph Lewis; Fred Hammond, the verger of St. Mary's Battersea; André Deutsch; and Richard Mortimer, Keeper of the Muniments at Westminster Abbey.

In Saint John, New Brunswick: Jackie Ringuette; Barbara A. Malcolm and the staff of the Saint John Regional Library; Carol Rosevear, Gary Hughes and Janet Bishop of the New Brunswick Museum; Linda Baier of the Harriet Irving Library at the University of New Brunswick; Mary Peddle; and J. Vincent Saunders.

Everywhere else: Galen Wilson, former archivist of the Clements Library at the University of Michigan (the lemon juice experiment was the highlight of the entire project); James T. Flexner; Peter Arnold; AFIO members Russ Bowen, Walter Pforzheimer, Mike Speers and especially Ed Thompson; Joe Goulden; Joe Blotner; Nick and Ellen Delbanco; Peter Partner; John R. Alden; Bill Gekle; John Spicer; Codman Hislop; Charles B. MacDonald; Philip N. Cronenwett of the Dartmouth College Library; Ralph A. Pugh of the Chicago Historical Society; Bill Ward of Saratoga National Historical Park; Dick Wiles of Bard College; Audrey Wallace; Elizabeth Singer Maule of the Maine Historical Society; Rita Matthews and Jackie Haley of Historic Hudson Valley; Robert I. Goler of the Fraunces Tavern Museum; Juliana D. Flower of the Yale University Art Gallery; Lieutenant Colonel Charles R. Shrader; Professor Roger Stiller; Professor Robert Norton; John J. Slonaker of the United States Army Military History Institute; Ed Skipworth of the Rutgers University libraries; Barbara J. Todd of the Litchfield Historical Society; John H. Rhodehamel of the Huntington Library in San Marino, California; Edward Park; Stacy F. Roth; Elizabeth Diamond of the National Archives of Canada; David J. Fowler of the David Library of the American Revolution; Bim Chanler; John Shelly of the Pennsylvania State Archives; Laurent Tailleur of the Archives of the Seminaire de Quebec; and the staffs of the Library of Congress Manuscripts Division, the National Archives, the Massachusetts Historical Society (especially Associate Librarian Peter Drummey), the Houghton Library of Harvard University, the American Antiquarian Society, the Vassar College Library, the New York State Library in Albany (particularly Chris Beauregard), the Rare Books and Manuscripts Division of the New York Public Library, the library at the New-York Historical Society and the Starr Library in Rhinebeck, New York.

My most particular thanks are reserved for last: Bill Emerson, Joe Furnas, Carl Brandt, Jon Karp (of Random House), Art Cohn and my agent, Jane Cushman, for careful readings and constructive comments; Camille Capozzi of Random House; and finally Kate Medina, who is, simply and forever, the best editor in the world.

Notes

In the interest of clarity, I have standardized spelling and punctuation in all direct quotations.

ABBREVIATIONS:

CHS: Connecticut Historical Society

Clinton: Clinton Papers, Clements Library, University of Michigan, Ann Arbor, Mich.

CO: Colonial Office Papers, PRO

Fitz *Writings:* George Washington, *Writings,* John C. Fitzpatrick, ed.

Force: *American Archives,* Peter Force, ed.

GWP: George Washington Papers, Library of Congress

HSP: Historical Society of Pennsylvania, Philadelphia

Houghton: Houghton Library, Harvard University, Cambridge, Mass.

Huntington: Huntington Library, San Marino, Calif.

LC: Library of Congress, Washington, D.C.

MHS: Massachusetts Historical Society, Boston

NBM: New Brunswick Museum, Saint John

NHCHS: New Haven Colony Historical Society

NYHS: New-York Historical Society

NYPL: Rare Books and Manuscripts Division, New York Public Library, Astor, Lenox and Tilden Foundations

PCC: Papers of the Continental Congress

PMHB: Pennsylvania Magazine of History and Biography

PRO: Public Record Office, Kew (London)

Proceedings: Benedict Arnold, defendant, *Proceedings of a General Court Martial of the Line.*

Roberts: Kenneth Roberts, *March to Quebec*

USCC: United States Continental Congress

USMA: Library of the United States Military Academy, West Point

INTRODUCTION (PAGES XIX–XXII)

PAGE

xx   "from a principle": Arnold to George Washington, Sept. 25, 1780, GWP.

xx   "Genius of War": Recollections of Captain E. Wakefield, in Reuben Aldridge Guild, *Chaplain Smith and the Baptists* (Philadelphia: American Baptist Publication Society, 1885), quoted in Commager, I, 581.

CHAPTER 1 (PAGES 3–8)

4   Arnold pew in First Church of Norwich: Perkins. The American pronunciations are "Nor-witch" and "Thaymes."

4   "Nobody can be": Hannah Arnold (mother) to Arnold, Mar. 9, 1752, HSP.

5   Norwich Burying Ground: the Arnold family headstones are still there, except for those of the two Benedicts (father and brother), which were presumably destroyed by the townspeople of Norwich in 1780 in a spontaneous act of outrage at their namesake's treason.

5   "It is with": Hannah Arnold (mother) to [Rev. James Cogswell], n.d., HSP.

5   "Be dutiful to": Hannah Arnold (mother) to Arnold, Apr. 12, 1754, Personal Miscellaneous Papers, Benedict Arnold, NYPL (photostat).

5   "Deaths are multiplied": Hannah Arnold (mother) to Arnold, Aug. 13, 1753, *Historical Magazine,* Vol. IV, No. 1 (Jan. 1860), 18.

6   "My dear": Hannah Arnold (mother) to Arnold, Sept. 10, 1753, Huntington.

PAGE

15 Forbes's vendetta: Arnold to Captain Dobson and to Mssrs. McKenzie and Campbell, Arnold Collection, NHCHS; Arnold to Captain McCormick, HSP; all Jan. 1771.

16 Arnold house on Water Street, New Haven: Arnold agreements with Hezekiah Bassett and Job Smith, Jan. 1772, Arnold Collection, NHCHS; "Old New-Haven House," *New-York Daily Tribune,* June 12, 1902, 6; Arnold to Enoch Brown, June 25, 1780, HSP. A glass slide of the house is in Special Collections, USMA, West Point, N.Y.

16f. Arnold's letters to his wife during the 1773–1774 voyage: Aug. 26, 1773, and July 17, 1774, Miscellaneous Manuscripts, Huntington; Oct. 5 and 7, 1773, HSP; Jan. 21, 1774, *Magazine of History,* II, 259. There are additional letters in Arnold Collection, NHCHS.

17f. Organization of Second Company Governor's Foot Guards: Petition to Connecticut Assembly, Mar. 2, 1775, New Haven Military Collection, NHCHS (transcript); Thomson.

18 Events of April 22, 1775: Gipson, 337f., and *Program for Foot Guard Day: 2nd Company of Governor's Foot Guards.* This program, written for the two-hundredth anniversary of the Foot Guards, never mentions the name of the unit's original commanding officer.

CHAPTER 3 (PAGES 20–38)

20 Foot Guards' Covenant, April 24, 1775: Force 4, II, 383f.

25 Arnold visits Skenesboro in 1774: Arnold's testimony, 1787, Commission of Enquiry into the Losses and Services.

25 "to rank according": Edward Mott to the Massachusetts Congress, May 11, 1775, Force 4, II, 557f.

25 "Shockingly surprised" and "club . . . their fire-locks": Edward Mott to Massachusetts Congress, May 11, 1775.

26f. Taking of Ticonderoga: Report of Lt. Jocelyn Feltham to General Gage, June 11, 1775, in Commager, 100ff.; also see Ethan Allen to Albany Committee, May 11, 1775, Force 4, II, 606, and John Brown's report to the Continental Congress, Minutes of May 20, 1775, Force 4, II, 623f.

27 "The sun seemed": Ethan Allen.

27 "was most rigidly": Report of Lt. Feltham, 102.

28 St. Jean: Arnold and his contemporaries referred to the British outpost at the outlet of Lake Champlain by three different names—St. Jean, St. John and St. John's. To avoid confu-

sion, this book will employ modern nomenclature: St. *Jean* for the outpost in question and St. *John* for the city in New Brunswick in which a later chapter is set. (St. John's, Newfoundland, does not appear in the story at all.)

28 "Committee of War": Committee at Ticonderoga to the Massachusetts Congress, May 10, 1775, Force 4, II, 556.

28 "[Ethan] Allen" and "buried in the ruins": Arnold to Massachusetts Committee of Safety, May 11, 1775, Force 4, II, 557.

29f. "with their fusees": Arnold, "Regimental Memorandum Book," 366f.

30 "immediate assistance": Allen to Albany Committee of Correspondence, May 11, 1775, Force 4, II, 606; and May 12, 1775, *Magazine of American History,* Vol. XIV, No. 3 (Sept. 1885), 319.

31f. Expedition to St. Jean: Arnold, "Regimental Memorandum Book," 367f.; Arnold to Massachusetts Committee of Safety, May 19, 1775, Force 4, II, 645; Arnold to Continental Congress, May 29, 1775, Force 4, II, 734; Letter from Ticonderoga to a Gentleman in Hartford, May 23, 1775, Force 4, II, 686.

33 "I have had intimations": Arnold to Massachusetts Committee of Safety, May 19, 1775.

33 "[if] I had but": Allen to Continental Congress, May 29, 1775, Force 4, II, 733.

33 "make a stand": Arnold to Massachusetts Committee of Safety, May 23, 1775, Force 4, II, 694.

33 "out of twenty-six": Arnold to Connecticut Assembly, May 23, 1775, Force 4, II, 840.

33 "every man within": Arnold to Captain Noah Lee, May 23, 1775, Force 4, II, 841.

33 "seamen, gunners": Arnold to Albany Committee, May 22, 1775, Force 4, II, 839f.

33 "critical situation": Barnabas Dean to Silas Deane, June 1, 1775, Deane, "Correspondence," 246ff.

34 "Colonel Arnold has": Barnabas Deane to Silas Deane, June 1, 1775, Deane, "Correspondence," 246ff.

34 "hunted with": Allen to Connecticut Assembly, May 26, 1775, Force 4, II, 713f.

34 "indubitable evidence": Resolution of Continental Congress, May 18, 1775, USCC *Journals,* II, 55f.

PAGE

34f.   "Ticonderoga is the key": Arnold to USCC, May 29, 1775, Force 4, II, 734f. The settlers of the Champlain Valley later wrote Arnold a letter expressing their "gratitude and thankfulness for [your] uncommon vigilance, vigour, and spirit . . . the humanity and benevolence which you have exercised towards the inhabitants . . . [and] your tenderness and polite treatment to such prisoners as have fallen into your hands. . . . By your vigilance and good conduct, we have been, under Providence, preserved from the incursions and ravages of an enraged enemy." In thanking them, Arnold declared that their "esteem and approbation . . . [are] more than an adequate recompense for the poor services and protection I have been happy enough to render you." Inhabitants of Champlain region to Arnold and Arnold's reply, July 3 and 4, 1775, Force 4, II, 1,087f.

35   "determined to join us": Arnold to Continental Congress, June 13, 1775, Force 4, II, 976f.

36   Altercation between Easton and Arnold, June 11, 1775: Arnold, "Regimental Memorandum Book," 373.

36n.   Easton lies about assault: Force 4, II, 1,085ff.

37   "It appears to me": Arnold to Spooner Committee, June 24, 1775, Force 4, II, 1,598f.

37f.   Mutiny of Arnold's men, June 24, 1775: Arnold, "Regimental Memorandum Book," 376; Mott to Jonathan Trumbull, July 6, 1775, Force 4, II, 1,592f.; Spooner Committee to Massachusetts Congress, July 6, 1775, Force 4, II, 1,596ff.; Spooner to New York Congress and to Trumbull, July 3, 1775, Force 4, II, 1,539ff.

CHAPTER 4 (PAGES 39–44)

39   "but for": Arnold to Silas Deane, July 10, 1775, Crossley Autograph Collection, LC.

40   "I dare not": Schuyler to Silas Deane, July 3, 1775, Burnett, I, 168 fn.

41   "anarchy and confusion": Arnold to Silas Deane, July 10, 1775, Crossley Autograph Collection, LC.

41   "with a pen-knife": Schuyler to Washington, July 18, 1775, Commager, I, 186f.

42   Arnold sends brigantine to Quebec: Arnold to James Price, July 25, 1775, Emmet Collection, NYPL.

44   "fall into our hands": Washington to president of Congress, Sept. 21, 1775, Fitz *Writings,* 3, 510.

CHAPTER 5 (PAGES 45–58)

45 "active woodsmen": Washington, General Orders, Sept. 5, 1775, Fitz *Writings,* III, 472.

45 "deep ash-colored": Henry, in K. Roberts, 301.

47 "The drums beat": Jesse Lukens to John Shaw, Jr., Sept. 16, 1775, quoted in Scheer, 115.

47 "taverns very plenty": Pierce, 653.

47 "the fleas": Senter, in K. Roberts, 197.

48 "Should any American": Washington to Arnold, Sept. 14, 1775, in Fitz *Writings,* III, 491ff.

48 "occasioned most": Senter, in K. Roberts, 198.

49 "seven or eight": Pierce, 654.

49 Hostile Mohawks on the Chaudière: Dennis Getchell and Samuel Berry to Reuben Colburn, Sept. 13, 1775, GWP.

50 "beat anyone": Barney.

50 "a man of": Henry, in K. Roberts, 303.

50 Shooting at Fort Western: Arnold to Washington, Sept. 25, 1775, GWP; same to same, Sept. 27, 1775, in K. Roberts, 67; Senter, in K. Roberts, 199; Stocking, in K. Roberts, 547; Thayer, in K. Roberts, 249. McCormick's sentence was confirmed by headquarters, but he died in prison before it could be carried out.

50f. Morgan refuses to take orders from Greene: Arnold to Washington, Sept. 5, 1775, Force 4, III, 960; Washington to Morgan, Oct. 4, 1775, Force 4, III, 946.

51 At Quebec in three weeks: Arnold to Washington, Sept. 25, 1775.

51 "up to their waists": Arnold to Schuyler, Nov. 27, 1775, in K. Roberts, 98.

51 Complaints about bateaux: Senter, in K. Roberts, 201; Barney; Thayer, in K. Roberts, 251.

51 "Now we are": Haskell, in K. Roberts, 474.

52 "dismal" and "a pane of": Thayer, in K. Roberts, 252, 250.

52 "Arnold's Hospital": Senter, in K. Roberts, 205.

52 "Balm of Gilead": Henry, in K. Roberts, 310f.

52 "spirit and industry": Arnold, in K. Roberts, 49f.

52 Stealing food: Barney.

52 "fine, deep river": Arnold, in K. Roberts, 50.

53 "passed the remainder": Arnold, in K. Roberts, 54.

53 "entirely overflowed": Thayer, in K. Roberts, 255.

53 "We had not contemplated": Morison, in K. Roberts, 516f.

PAGE

54   "a direful howling" and "fired with": Senter, in K. Roberts, 210, 213.

54   "the whole valley": Stocking, in K. Roberts, 553.

55   "inevitably have": Arnold, in K. Roberts, 60.

55   "those who have": Arnold to the Officers of the Detachment, Oct. 31, 1775, in K. Roberts, 80.

55   "made a general prayer": Dearborn, in K. Roberts, 137.

55   "up to [their] arm pits": Dearborn, in K. Roberts, 138.

55   Famine: in K. Roberts: Senter, 218, 216; Thayer, 258; Henry, 341f.

55f. "a vision": Senter, in K. Roberts, 219.

56   "very ghostly": Pierce, 674.

56   "terrible road": Senter, in K. Roberts, 222.

57   "fine ball": Pierce, 674.

57   "mortification": Thayer, in K. Roberts, 264.

CHAPTER 6 (PAGES 59–76)

60   "seemingly chilled": Henry, in K. Roberts, 351f.

60   "Screaming and dismal": Thayer, in K. Roberts, 264.

60   "fair, serene": Pierce, 676.

62   "pay the full value": Washington to Arnold, Sept. 14, 1775.

62   "fryed stakes": Pierce, 678.

62   Court-martials: Pierce, 678.

62   "the ground [being]": Stocking, in K. Roberts, 560.

63   "bottle of very": Pierce, 683.

64   "prodigious snowstorm": Thayer, in K. Roberts, 270.

64   "the voluntary love": Meigs, in K. Roberts, 192.

64   "I find Colonel Arnold's": Montgomery to Schuyler, Dec. 5, 1775, Force 4, IV, 188ff.

65   "the virtuous General": Thayer, in K. Roberts, 270.

65   Montgomery offers bounties: Montgomery to Schuyler, Dec. 5, 1775.

65   "to coax": Schuyler to Washington, Nov. 22, 1775, Force 4, III, 1,635.

65   "a little money": Montgomery to Schuyler, Nov. 20, 1775, Force 4, III, 1,684.

68   "rum, pork": Pierce, 688.

68   "wretched, motley": Arnold to Washington, Dec. 5, 1775, in K. Roberts, 101f.

68   "Maclean's banditti" and "Fortune often baffles": Montgomery to Schuyler, Dec. 5, 1775, Force 4, IV, 188ff.

69   "Who but": Letter from Unknown to a Gentleman in New York, Dec. 17, 1775, Force 4, IV, 296.

69   "never expected any other": Montgomery to Wooster, Dec. 16, 1775, Force 4, IV, 288f.

69   Officers in Lower Town: Pierce, 691.

69f. *Peggy:* Certificate of Freegift Arnold, June 15, 1776; Certificate of David Wooster, April 1777; Certificate of William Cross, Aug. 5, 1779; Certificate of John Taylor, Aug. 6, 1779; all PCC.

70   "as if the heavens": Pierce, 694.

70   "administering a spiritous": Senter, in K. Roberts, 228.

71   "agreeable to prescription": Senter, in K. Roberts, 229.

71   "skulking riflemen": Ainslie, 27.

71   "no man after having": [J. Danford] 184.

71   "lice, itch": Pierce, 694.

72   "great mortification": Montgomery to Schuyler, Dec. 26, 1775, Force 4, IV, 464f.

72   "famine-proof": Senter, in K. Roberts, 232.

72   "enraptured": Morison, in K. Roberts, 535.

72   "the fire": Stocking, in K. Roberts, 562.

73   "very drunk": Pierce, 701.

73   "signif[ied]" and "be wanted": Senter to Arnold and Arnold to Senter, Dec. 27, 1775, in K. Roberts, 231.

73   "The storm": Henry, in K. Roberts, 375.

73   "whole right flank": Stocking, in K. Roberts, 564.

73   "about midway": Senter, in K. Roberts, 234.

74   "under the continual": Arnold to Hannah Arnold (sister), Jan. 6, 1776, in K. Roberts, 108f.

75   "to be carried back": Senter, in K. Roberts, 233ff.

75   "either carry the Lower": Arnold to David Wooster, Dec. 31, 1775, in K. Roberts, 102f.

75   "awful voice": Morison, in K. Roberts, 538.

75   "Here we found": Meigs, in K. Roberts, 190.

76   "You can have no": Henry Caldwell to James Murray, June 15, 1776, in Scheer, 128.

76   "the most terrible": Pierce, 703.

76   "the nursery": "Further Accounts of the Unsuccessful Attack on Quebec," Jan. 17, 1776, Force 4, IV, 705f.

76   "I have no thoughts": Arnold to Hannah Arnold (sister), Jan. 6, 1776.

CHAPTER 7 (PAGES 77–85)

77 "before this": Washington to Arnold, Dec. 5, 1775, Fitz *Writings*, 4, 148f.

77f. "the notice": Arnold to Washington, Jan. 14, 1776, in K. Roberts, 113ff.

78 "struck an amazing": Arnold to Washington, Jan. 14, 1776.

78 "I pray God": Arnold to Wooster, Jan. 2, 4 and 5, 1776, in K. Roberts, 103ff.

78 "to lay on": Arnold to Continental Congress, Jan. 11, 1776, in K. Roberts, 109ff.

78 "plays sweetly": Samuel Hodgkinson to his parents, Apr. 27, 1776, PMHB, X (1886), 158ff.

78 "killed a boy": J. Danford, 227.

79 "to a man": Wooster to Schuyler, Jan. 5, 1776, Force 4, IV, 669.

79 Kennebec veterans refuse sentry duty: Haskell, in K. Roberts, 488f.

79 "to put the best": Arnold to Continental Congress, Jan. 11, 1776.

79 "much more anxious": Arnold to Schuyler, Feb. 10, 1776, Philip Schuyler Papers, NYPL.

79f. "at least five thousand": Arnold to Continental Congress, Jan. 11, 1776.

80 "The multiplicity": Arnold to John Hancock, Feb. 1 and 12, 1776, in K. Roberts, 119ff.

80 "our credit": Arnold to Silas Deane, Mar. 30, 1776, Force 4, V, 549f.

80 "is the public topic": Arnold to John Hancock, Feb. 1, 1776.

81 "impeach to Congress": Jeremiah Duggan Deposition, Aug. 1, 1776, Emmet Collection, NYPL.

82 "cold enough": quoted in Hatch, *Thrust,* 157.

82 "were sent into": Application of Josiah Sabin, in Dann, 19ff.

82 "able to hobble": Arnold to Washington, Feb. 27, 1776, in K. Roberts, 121ff.

82 Weather, Feb. and Mar.: Haskell, in K. Roberts, 491f.; [J. Danford], 201, 204.

82 "which fatigued" and "under almost as many": Arnold to Unknown, Mar. 26 and 28, 1776, Force 4, V, 512.

83 "generally in our favor": Arnold to Unknown, Mar. 26 and 28, 1776.

92　"if he were superseded": Notes of a conversation between Schuyler and Gates, June 30, 1776, Gates Papers, NYHS. Also see Schuyler to Washington, July 4, 1776, Force 4, VI, 1,199ff.; and Gates to Hancock and Gates to Washington, July 16, 1776, Force 5, I, 375f.

93　"stand upon punctilios": Schuyler to Washington, July 1, 1776, PCC.

93　"a mob": John Trumbull to his father, July 12, 1776.

93　"Everything about this army": Gates to Washington, July 29, 1776, Force 5, I, 650f.

94　Declaration of Independence: Although most Americans had been opposed to independence only twelve months before, by the summer of 1776 they had changed their minds, mostly thanks to British intransigence and also to the influence of Thomas Paine's *Common Sense.*

94　"a naval armament": Minutes of Council of War, July 7, 1776, Force 5, I, 233.

94　Skenesboro: Whitehall, New York, stands on the site today. A sign at the city limits proclaims it as "the birthplace of the United States Navy."

94　"General Arnold is very busy": Beebe, 341f.

95　"I think we shall": Arnold to Gates, July 24, 1776, Force 5, I, 563f.

95　"As there is no": Arnold to Schuyler, July 24, 1776, Letters and Papers of Benedict Arnold, NYHS.

95　"infinite satisfaction": Gates to president of Congress, July 29, 1776, Force 5, I, 649.

95　"overstrained zeal": Enoch Poor to Gates, Aug. 8, 1776, Force 5, I, 1,273. (Force gives the date as Aug. 6, which is incorrect.)

96　Poor to Arnold and Arnold to Poor re Hazen court-martial: PCC.

96　"contemptuous, disorderly" and Gates's dissolution of court: Copy of proceedings of Arnold's prosecution of Col. Hazen, August 1776, Shober Collection, HSP.

96　"obliged to act": Gates to president of Congress, Sept. 2, 1776, Force 5, I, 1,267f.

96　"grossest abuse": Arnold to Gates, Aug. 7, 1775 (one of two on this date), Gates Papers, NYHS.

97　"B.A. and sent": Testimony of General John Sullivan, Report of Congressional Committee to inquire into the causes of the miscarriages in Canada, July 30, 1776, PCC.

98   "prudent": USCC *Journals,* V, 780.

98   "Many reports": Samuel Chase to Arnold, Aug. 7, 1776, Force 5, I, 810f.

CHAPTER 9 (PAGES 99–111)

100   "Sir, I know": Wynkoop to Arnold, Aug. 17, 1776, Force 5, I, 1,275.

100   "You surely must be": Arnold to Wynkoop, Aug. 17, 1776, Force 5, I, 1,275f.

100   Gates-Schuyler exchanges re Jacobus Wynkoop: Gates to Schuyler, Aug. 18 and 20, 1776, Force 5, I, 1,218, 1,277; Schuyler to Gates, Aug. 20 and 25, 1776, Force 5, I, 1,083, 1,277.

100   "I believe the": Arnold to Gates, Aug. 19, 1776, Force 5, I, 1,277.

100n.   Congress fails to act on Wynkoop: USCC *Journals,* XIV, 544.

101   "several large": Arnold to Schuyler, July 30, 1776, Force 5, I, 680.

101   "maintain possession": Gates's orders to Arnold, Aug. 7, 1776, GWP.

101   "a violent": Arnold to Gates, Aug. 31, 1776, Force 5, I, 1,266f.

102   *"four hundred"*: "Diary of Joshua Pell, Jr., an Officer of the British Army," *Magazine of American History,* Vol. II, Part 2, 45, in Morgan, 661.

102   "vastly superior": Arnold to Schuyler, Sept. 9, 1776, Philip Schuyler Papers, NYPL.

102   "putrid, intermitting": Beebe, 346.

102   "a watch coat": Arnold to Gates, Sept. 8, 1776, Gates Papers, NYHS.

102   "on the bows": Arnold to Gates, Sept. 7, 1776, Gates Papers, NYHS.

102   "attacked by": Arnold to Gates, Sept. 7, 1776.

102   "wretched motley": Arnold to Gates, Sept. 18, 1776, Force 5, II, 481f.

103   "a good seaman": Gates to Arnold, Sept. 5, 1776, Force 5, II, 186f.

103   "an able seaman": Gates to Schuyler, Aug. 18, 1776, Force 5, I, 1,218.

103   Intelligence from British deserter: Deposition of Thomas Day, Sept. 12, 1776, PCC (copy).

103   "with utmost": Gates to Arnold, Sept. 12, 1776, Force 5, II, 302f.

103 "designed to mount": Arnold to Gates, Sept. 18, 1776.

103 "with a working": Mahan, 152.

103 "there is a": Arnold to Gates, Sept. 15, 1776, Force 5, II, 531f.

105 "very severe": Arnold to Gates, Oct. 1, 1776, Force 5, II, 834f. Also see Gates to Arnold, Sept. 26, 1776, Force 5, II, 555f.

105 "Where [supplies]": Gates to Arnold, Oct. 3, 1776, Force 5, II, 860f.

105 "It appears to me": Arnold to Gates, Oct. 7, 1776, Force 5, II, 933.

105 "for an opportunity": Arnold to Schuyler, Oct. 7, 1776, Philip Schuyler Papers, NYPL.

105 "on a retreat": Waterbury to John Hancock, Oct. 24, 1776, PCC.

106n. British naval officers' squabble after Valcour: Capt. Thomas Pringle to Secretary of the Admiralty, Oct. 15, 1776, Force 5, II, 1,069f; John Starke *et al.*, "An Open Letter to Captain Pringle," *Bulletin of the Fort Ticonderoga Museum,* Vol. I, No. 4 (July 1928), 14ff.

106 "general and," "a very hot," "was hulled," "which I believe" and "upwards of": Arnold to Gates, Oct. 12, 1776, GWP.

107 "the cannon": "Journal of Captain George Pausch," Morgan, 1,259.

108 "to push forward": Waterbury to Hancock, Oct. 24, 1776, PCC.

108 "sails, rigging": Arnold to Schuyler, Oct. 15, 1776, Force 5, II, 1,079f.

109 "Exceedingly fatigued": Arnold to Schuyler, Oct. 15, 1776.

109 "beautiful strong": Lt. Col. Israel Shreve to his brother, Aug. 26, 1776, PMHB, XXVIII, 114f.

110 "dangerous impression": Autobiography of Colonel John Trumbull, Oct. 14, 1776, Morgan, 1,261f.

110 "The fleet has acted": Norton, Oct. 15, 1776.

110 "No man ever": Thacher, *Military Journal,* 65.

110 "life and spirits" and "he would be in": Baldwin, Oct. 16, 1776.

110 "free and": Gates to Schuyler, Oct. 24, 1776, Force 5, III, 575.

110 "Simple man": extract of a letter from Ticonderoga, Oct. 27, 1776, Force 5, II, 1,267.

111 "The whole camp": Captain John Lacey, "Memoirs," PMHB, XXV, 510ff., quoted in Commager, I, 225f.

111 "the countenance": Dodsley's (London) *Register* for 1777, 6, quoted in Spears, 281.

CHAPTER 10 (PAGES 112–125)

112 "You must have heard": Gen. William Maxwell to Gov. William Livingston, Oct. 20, 1776, William Livingston Papers, MHS.

112f. Waterbury's complaint: Waterbury to John Hancock, Oct. 24, 1776, PCC.

114 John Brown's charges against Arnold: Petition to Gen. Gates, Dec. 1, 1776, Force 5, III, 1,158f.

114 "an aspersion of": Court of Inquiry on a Complaint of Col. Moses Hazen against Gen. Arnold, Dec. 2, 1776, Gates Papers, NYHS.

115 "take such measures": Washington to Arnold, Dec. 14, 1776, GWP.

115f. "We have it yet": Arnold to Samuel Chase, Feb. 12, 1777, J.S.H. Fogg Autograph Collection, Maine Historical Society.

116 "beautiful . . . straight": "A Love Affair of Benedict Arnold," 76.

116 "the heavenly Miss Deblois": Arnold to Mrs. Knox, Mar. 4, 1777, Henry Knox Papers, MHS (transcript from the original).

116 "Congress have doubtless" and "Every personal injury": Arnold to Washington, Mar. 11, 1777, GWP.

118 "Surely a more": Washington to Richard Henry Lee, Mar. 6, 1777, Fitz *Writings,* 7, 251f.

118 "I cannot . . . help": Arnold to Gates, Mar. 25, 1777, Gates Papers, NYHS.

119 "avoid Mr. Arnold": *Journal of Col. Stephen Kemble,* quoted in McDevitt, 47.

120 "appeared in one": Gen. Selleck Silliman to Gov. Trumbull, April 1777, in Ridgefield *Press,* Oct. 14, 1976.

120 "through a shower": (New Haven) *Connecticut Journal,* Apr. 30, 1777, quoted in Moore, *Diary,* I, 424.

121 "running full": (New Haven) *Connecticut Journal,* Apr. 30, 1777, 425.

121 "Expos[ing] himself": Hugh Hughes to Horatio Gates, May 3, 1777, Gates Papers, NYHS.

121 "The militia": Arnold to Brig. Gen. Alexander McDougall, Apr. 28, 1777, GWP.

121 "Conscious of": Arnold to Hancock, May 20, 1777, PCC.

PAGE
122 "a variety of": USCC *Journals,* VIII, 382.
122n. "The liberty of the press": Arnold to Jeremiah Wadsworth, May 30, 1777, Jeremiah Wadsworth Papers, CHS.
122 "properly caparisoned": USCC *Journals,* VII, 372f.
124 "If General Arnold": Washington to Hancock, July 10, 1777, PCC.
124f. "The duty": Arnold to Hancock, July 11, 1777, PCC.
125 "waiv[e] all": Washington to Schuyler, July 18, 1777, Fitz *Writings,* VIII, 427.
125 "high satisfaction": Schuyler to Washington, July 22–23, 1777, PCC.

CHAPTER 11 (PAGES 126–139)

126 "We are daily insulted": Arnold to Washington, July 27, 1777, GWP.
126 "infernal savages": Arnold to Gates, Aug. 5, 1777, Gates Papers, NYHS.
126 "unaccountable panic": Schuyler to Washington, Aug. 1, 1777, PCC.
127 "in a condition": Arnold to Washington, July 27, 1777.
127 "a few days": Arnold to Gates, Aug. 5, 1777.
127 "conducted almost": James Lovell to William Whipple, Burnett, II, 445.
127f. "reasoning upon this": Henry Laurens to John Rutledge, Aug. 12, 1777, Burnett, II, 448.
128 "grew furious": report of Gen. Barry St. Leger to Gen. Burgoyne, quoted in Marshall and Peckham, 42.
128 Han-Yost Schuyler: see Thacher's *Military Journal,* William Hull's *Revolutionary Services* and William L. Stone's *Life of Joseph Brandt.*
129 "Our people": Arnold to John Lamb, Sept. 5, 1777, Lamb Papers, NYHS.
130 "Placed . . . in": Arnold to Gates, Sept. 22, 1777, Gates Papers, NYHS.
130 "a little spirit": Varick to Schuyler, Sept. 12, 1777, Philip Schuyler Papers, NYPL.
131 "a view of": Journal of Lt. Thomas Blake, in Kidder, 33f.
131 "so dense": Diary of a soldier at Saratoga, quoted in Ludlam, 288.
133 "heroically, like": Varick to Schuyler, Sept. 19, 1777, Philip Schuyler Papers, NYPL.

PAGE

133 "infuriated by": Recollections of Captain E. Wakefield, quoted in Commager and Morris, I, 581.

133 "most formidable": Fortescue, III, 235, 410.

133 "who had something more" and "one of the": Dearborn, *Revolutionary War Journals,* 106, 107.

133 "the field . . .": Warren.

135 "Face of Clay": Henry Brockholst Livingston to Schuyler, Sept. 26, 1777, Philip Schuyler Papers, NYPL.

135 Varick's fight with Gates: Varick to Schuyler, Sept. 19 and 22, 1777, Philip Schuyler Papers, NYPL.

135 "the day dawned": Eyewitness report quoted in Ludlam, 289.

135 "a general Whooray": Baldwin, 121.

135 "thirteen cannon": Boardman, Sept. 21, 1777.

135 "three cheers": Warren.

135 Indians in the Continental camp on Bemis's Heights: Boardman, Sept. 21, 1777; Warren, Sept. 25, 1777; Baldwin.

136 "Colonel Morgan's": Thaddeus Cook, *Orderly Book*, Sept. 22, 1777.

136 "the general good behavior": Gates to Hancock, Sept. 22, 1777, Gates Papers, NYHS.

136 Arnold-Gates altercation, Sept. 22, 1777: Arnold to Gates, Sept. 22, 1777; Henry Brockholst Livingston to Schuyler, Sept. 23, 1777, Philip Schuyler Papers, NYPL; Wilkinson, I, 254.

137 "for his past service": Henry Brockholst Livingston to Schuyler, Sept. 24, 1777, Philip Schuyler Papers, NYPL.

137 "an advanced post": Henry Beekman Livingston to Robert R. Livingston, Oct. 1, 1777, Robert R. Livingston Papers, NYIIS.

137 "lest it should appear": Henry Brockholst Livingston to Schuyler, Sept. 26, 1777, Philip Schuyler Papers, NYPL.

137 "his grateful thanks": Bigelow, *Orderly Book,* and Thaddeus Cook, *Orderly Book,* Sept. 26, 1777.

137 "to sacrifice": Arnold to Gates, Oct. 1, 1777, Gates Papers, NYHS.

137 "The reason of": Livingston to Schuyler, Sept. 23, 1777.

138 "Perhaps his despair": Gates to Gov. George Clinton, Oct. 4, 1777, Gates Papers, NYHS.

138 "If Mr. Burgoyne": Dearborn, *Revolutionary War Journals,* 107.

138 "bewildered": Dearborn, *Journals,* 108.

PAGE

138 "a scene of": Wilkinson, I, 270.

139 "the very genius": Recollections of Captain E. Wakefield, quoted in Commager and Morris, I, 581.

139 "Magnificent, but": quoted in Furneaux, 240.

CHAPTER 12 (PAGES 140–147)

140 "thirty surgeons" and "his lady": Thacher, *Military Journal,* 112.

141 "bravery and": Varick to Schuyler, Oct. 30, 1777, Philip Schuyler Papers, NYPL.

141 Conway Cabal: The cabal eventually fizzled and Conway himself resigned from the army. In 1778, after being gravely wounded in a duel, he wrote a letter of apology to General Washington. He recovered and returned to his prewar home in France.

141 "a gentleman": Washington to Arnold, May 7, 1778, Fitz *Writings,* 11, 359f.

142 "The malice": Robert Troup to Gates, Feb. 19, 1778, quoted in Patterson, 263.

142 *"the greatest poltroon"*: Lafayette to Henry Laurens, Feb. 19, 1778, quoted in Idzerda, I, 296f.

143 "one whole shirt": Anthony Wayne, quoted in Elting, *Uniforms,* 72.

143 Mutiny in Poor's brigade: Hamilton to Washington, Nov. 10, 1777, Sparks, *Correspondence,* II, 32ff.

144 "Twenty times have I": Arnold to Elizabeth Deblois, Apr. 8, 1778, Winthrop Papers, MHS.

144 "You entreat me to": Arnold to Elizabeth Deblois, Apr. 26, 1778, Winthrop Papers, MHS.

145 "some loose splinters": Arnold to Washington, Mar. 12, 1778, GWP.

145 "Several Continental": (New Haven) *Connecticut Journal,* May 6, 1778.

147 "in some office": Arnold to Schuyler, June 12, 1778, PCC.

147 Arnold's loyalty oath, May 30, 1778: *Centennial USMA,* I, opposite 171.

CHAPTER 13 (PAGES 148–157)

148 "salt, linens": Arnold's pass for *Charming Nancy,* June 4, 1778, Timothy Pickering Papers, LC.

PAGE

148 Robert Shewell ordered out of camp, June 1778: Tench Tilghman to Joseph Reed, Apr. 5, 1779, in Fitz *Writings*, 14, 342 fn.

149 "European and": Deposition of Colonel Fitzgerald, Arnold, *Proceedings*, 10.

149 "all persons": Arnold, Proclamation, June 19, 1778, *Proceedings*, 10.

149 "for that purpose": Arnold-Mease-West Agreement, June 23, 1778, PCC.

149f. "to amount of" and "whatever misfortune": John R. Livingston to sundry merchants in New York, July 18, 1778, PCC.

150 "How difficult" and "He who increases": quoted in East, 196.

150 "speculation, peculation": Washington to Benjamin Harrison, Dec. 18 and 30, 1778, Fitz *Writings*, 13, 462ff.

150f. "We have a great many": Mrs. Robert Morris to her mother, PMHB, II, 162f.

151 "the females": "From a Late Philadelphia Paper," *Continental Journal and Weekly Advertiser* (Boston), July 30, 1778, quoted in Scheer and Rankin, 326f.

152 "regatta, tilts": Montresor's journal, quoted in Serle.

152 "halcyon days": quoted in Sargent, 167.

152 "to support each other": Whig association pledge, quoted in Scharf and Westcott, I, 387.

152 "If they decline it": Arnold to Mercy Scollay, July 15, 1778, Bigelow Collection, MHS.

153 "To a generous mind": Arnold to Mercy Scollay, Feb. 19, 1779, Miscellaneous Bound Collection, MHS.

153 "upright intentions": Arnold to John Imlay, July 10, 1778, Houghton.

154 "in a most filthy": Josiah Bartlett, quoted in Scheer and Rankin, 327.

154 Pennsylvania militia to replace Continental troops: Arnold to Matlack, Aug. 18, 1778; Matlack to Arnold, Sept. 18, 1778; Pickering to Arnold, Sept. 18, 1778, *Pennsylvania Archives*, VI, 708, 748, 749; Arnold to Laurens, Aug. 19, 1778, PCC; USCC *Journals*, XI, 816, and XII, 865; Arnold to Washington, Aug. 29, 1778, GWP.

155 "command of the navy": Arnold to Washington, July 19, 1778, GWP.

155 "in marine matters": Washington to Arnold, Aug. 3, 1778, GWP.

PAGE

155 "moderate thinking man": Edward Shippen, Jr., to Jasper Yeates, June 5, 1776, Dreer Collection, HSP.

156 "double bay house": Insurance appraisal of Shippen house, Dec. 20, 1791, Independence National Historical Park.

156 "Cupid has given": Mrs. Morris to her mother, no date, PMHB, II, 162f.

156 "The gentle Arnold": Elizabeth Tilghman to Elizabeth S. Burd, Jan. 29, 1779, Walker, XXV, 38.

156 "la[id] close siege": Edward Shippen, Sr., to Col. Burd, Jan. 2, 1779, Walker, XXV, 36.

156f. "Twenty times": Arnold to Margaret Shippen, Sept. 25, 1778, Walker, XXV, 30f.

CHAPTER 14 (PAGES 159–176)

159 "a pert Tory": Charles Stewart to Joseph Galloway, Dec. 1, 1778, *Historical Magazine,* V, No. 10, 296.

160 "The severity": Matlack to Arnold, Oct. 5, 1778, Reed Papers, NYHS.

160 "I have served": Arnold to Matlack, Oct. 6, 1778, Reed Papers, NYHS.

160 "to acquaint": Matlack to Arnold, Oct. 10, 1778, Reed Papers, NYHS.

160 "I am not to be": Arnold to Matlack, Oct. 12, 1778, Reed Papers, NYHS.

160f. "contest . . . between": Silas Deane to Simeon Deane, July 27, 1779, PMHB, XVII, 348f.

161 "violent, wrongheaded": Joseph Shippen, quoted in Klein, 164.

161 "Tory ladies": Reed to Nathanael Greene, Nov. 5, 1778, "The Lee Papers," 245ff.

162 "I conceived it": Mitchell testimony, *Proceedings,* 36.

162 "a sum of": Clarkson to Gen. William Maxwell, Oct. 3, 1778, PCC.

162 "a gentleman": Testimony of Hannah Levy, Feb. 6, 1779, PCC. Arnold later claimed that Templeton was in a position to provide intelligence concerning "the motions and designs of the enemy," but the business connection is more likely. See Arnold to Unknown, 1779, Reed Papers, NYHS, and Arnold to Matlack, Mar. 5, 1779, *Pennsylvania Archives,* VII, 223.

162 "inimical to the safety": USCC *Journals,* XII, 1,032.

162 "It is whispered": *Pennsylvania Packet,* Nov. 12, 1778.

PAGE

162f. "To stand at": *Pennsylvania Packet,* Nov. 14, 1778.

163 "The history you allude": Arnold to Greene, Nov. 10, 1778, Houghton.

163 Arnold orders carriage glass: Arnold to Lord Stirling, Oct. 29, 1778, Emmet Collection, NYPL.

163 "every man who has": John Cadwalader to Nathanael Greene, Dec. 5, 1778, NYHS *Collections,* III, 270f.

163 "The great Council": Arnold to Nathanael Greene. Nov. 10, 1788, Houghton.

164 "the common interests": Washington to Benjamin Harrison, Dec. 18 and 30, 1778.

164 "those murderers": Washington to Reed, Dec. 12, 1778, Fitz *Writings,* 13, 382ff.

164 "quakes and tremblings": Elizabeth Tilghman to Elizabeth Shippen Burd, Apr. 14, 1779, quoted in Walker, XXV, 40.

165 "Burgoyned": Elizabeth Tilghman to Elizabeth S. Burd, Apr. 14, 1779.

165 "obtain a tract": Arnold to Schuyler, Nov. 30, 1778, Schoff Collection, Clements.

165f. "establish a settlement": John Jay, James Duane, Francis Lewis and William Floyd to George Clinton, Feb. 3, 1779, Houghton; also see Arnold to Schuyler, Feb. 8, 1779, Philip Schuyler Papers, NYPL.

166 "I am at all times": Arnold to Supreme Executive Council, Jan. 25, 1779, *Proceedings,* 7.

166 "the indignity": Reed to Jay, Jan. 25, 1779, *Proceedings,* 7.

166f. "that in our correspondence": Reed to Pennsylvania delegates, Jan. 30, 1779, *Pennsylvania Archives,* VII, 174.

167 "Mr. Jordan is entitled": Mitchell to Arnold, Jan. 30, 1779, *Proceedings,* 33.

167f. "Allured to": John Jay to George Clinton, Jan. 31, 1779, Houghton.

168 Eight charges, Feb. 3, 1778: *Proceedings,* 5.

168f. "greatest politeness" and "Six days": Arnold to Margaret Shippen, Feb. 8, 1779, Reed Papers, NYHS.

169 "I think all the world": Elizabeth Tilghman to Elizabeth Burd, Mar. 13, 1779, Walker, XXV, 39.

170 "a set of unprincipled": Arnold to Washington, May 5, 1779, GWP.

171 "colorable, unfair": Mitchell statement, Feb. 26, 1779, *Pennsylvania Archives,* VII, 207f.

PAGE

171 "Jesse Jordan to call": *Pennsylvania Packet,* Evening Extra, Feb. 23, 1779.

171 First letter from "T.G.": *Pennsylvania Packet,* Feb. 27, 1779.

171 "Envy and malice": Arnold to the editor, *Pennsylvania Packet,* Mar. 2, 1779.

171 "It will require": "T.G." to Arnold, *Pennsylvania Packet,* Mar. 6, 1779.

172 "an officer more distinguished": New York *Royal Gazette,* Feb. 17, 1779, 3.

172 "imposing menial": *Proceedings,* 5.

172 "relieve me by": Arnold to Jay, Mar. 17, 1779, PCC.

173 "the most elegant": quoted on an historical marker at Mount Pleasant.

173 "the villainous attacks": Arnold to Washington, Mar. 19, 1779, GWP.

174 "I am still held": Arnold to Jay, Mar. 27, 1779, PCC.

174 "highly sensible of": USCC *Journals,* XIII, 413.

174 "fully explained": Report of Paca Committee, Mar. 17, 1779, PCC.

175 "successful and fortunate": Lucius Annaeus Seneca, *Hercules Furens.*

175 "I cannot but testify": Arnold to Jay, Apr. 16, 1779, PCC.

176 "Such is the dependence": Reed to Washington, Apr. 24, 1779, *Pennsylvania Archives,* VII, 337f.

176 "instructions given by you": Matlack to Arnold, May 5, 1779, *Pennsylvania Archives,* VII, 370.

176 "As Congress have": Arnold to Washington, May 5, 1779, GWP.

CHAPTER 15 (PAGES 177–196)

178 "the strongest assurances": André to Stansbury, May 10, 1779, Clinton.

179 "General W[ashington] and": Arnold to André, May 23, 1779, Clinton.

179 "H[is] Excellency": André to Arnold, mid-June, 1779, Clinton.

180 "for payment of": Fitzgerald deposition, May 7, 1779, Arnold, *Proceedings,* 10f.

181 "I feel my situation": Washington to Arnold, May 15, 1779, GWP.

181 "It is a very": Greene to Silas Deane, July 4, 1779, Miscellaneous Manuscripts, Huntington.

PAGE

181   Greene invites Timothy Matlack: Nathanael Greene to Reed, June 2, 1779, Reed Papers, NYHS.

182   "not equal to his": Stansbury to André, July 11, 1779, Clinton.

182   "You must be sensible": Washington to Arnold, July 20, 1779, GWP.

182   "Real advantage": André to Arnold, end of July, 1779, Clinton.

183   "join the army": Stansbury to André, 1779 (probably early Aug.), Clinton.

183   "capwire, needles": André to M. S. Arnold, Aug. 16, 1779, Sargent, 220, quoted in Van Doren, 454.

183   "extravagant indeed": John Fell's Diary, in Burnett, IV, 466.

183   "armed with bars": Allen McLane's Journal, Reed Papers, NYHS.

184   "twenty men": Arnold to president of Congress, Oct. 6, 1779, Burnett, IV, 476f. fn.

184   "that his application": USCC *Journals,* XV, 1,147.

184   "disposition": Arnold to Samuel Huntington, Oct. 6, 1779, Burnett, IV, 477 fn.

184   "Mrs. Arnold presents": M. S. Arnold to André, Oct. 13, 1779, Clinton.

184   "Some insect": Stansbury to Odell, probably Dec. 3, 1779, Clinton.

184f.   "The sufferings of": Thacher, *Military Journal,* 180ff.

185   "incompatible": *Proceedings,* 11.

186   "I never wanted": M. S. Arnold to Arnold, Jan. 4, 1780, Reed Papers, NYHS. (The letter is unsigned but clearly comes from Peggy.)

186   "without incurring": *Proceedings,* 36.

186f.   Arnold's closing statement: *Proceedings,* 40ff.

188   Court-martial verdict: *Proceedings,* 55.

188   "As I wish": Arnold to Washington, Mar. 6, 1780, GWP.

189   "with . . . whom": Arnold to Congress, Feb. 18, 1780, PCC.

189   Arnold charges theft of vouchers: Arnold to Huntington, Feb. 28, 1780, PCC.

189f.   "all the testimonies": Report of Board of Treasury, Apr. 22, 1780, USCC *Journals,* XVI, 393ff.

190   "how far Mr. Gerry's": Arnold to Huntington, May 12, 1780, PCC.

190   "to produce his evidence": Elbridge Gerry to president of Congress, May 18, 1780, PCC.

PAGE

190 "The Commander in Chief": Washington, General Orders, Apr. 6, 1780, Fitz *Writings,* 18, 222ff.

190f. Arnold's terms and Beckwith's response: Knyphausen's notes (May 1780), Clinton.

191 "When I requested": Arnold to Schuyler, May 25, 1780, Philip Schuyler Papers, NYPL.

191 "expressed himself": Schuyler to Arnold, June 2, 1780, Reed Papers, NYHS.

191 "whose secrecy": Washington to Arnold, June 4, 1780, Fitz *Writings,* 18, 476.

192 "Why don't you reinforce": Lt. Col. Ebenezer Huntington to Andrew Huntington, July 7, 1780, Ebenezer Huntington *Letters,* 87f., quoted in Scheer and Rankin, 376.

192 "Not a single complaint": Samuel Cogswell to his father, July 15, 1780, *Historical Magazine,* 2nd Series, VIII (Aug. 1870), 102.

192 "the heroic fortitude": Thacher, *Military Journal,* 180ff.

192 "three or four thousand": Arnold to Beckwith or André, June 12, 1780, Clinton.

193 "The Point": Arnold to Beckwith or André, June 16, 1780, Clinton.

194 "might not be most": Robert R. Livingston to Washington, June 22, 1780, in Burnett, V, 233f.

194 "if the operations": Washington to Robert R. Livingston, June 29, 1780, Fitz *Writings,* 19, 90ff.

194 "to take command": Stansbury to Beckwith or André, July 7, 1780, Clinton.

194 "I have accepted": Arnold to André, July 12, 1780, Clinton.

195 "which a flag": André to Arnold, [June–July 1780] Clinton.

195 "£10,000 sterling": Arnold to André, July 15, 1780, Clinton.

CHAPTER 16 (PAGES 197–223)

200 Complaints about militia at West Point: Major Sebastian Bauman to Alexander Hamilton, Aug. 13, 1780; Colonel William Malcom to Arnold, Aug. 12, 1780, quoted in *History of West Point,* 39f.

200 "Everything is wanting": Arnold to Timothy Pickering, Aug. 16, 1780, NYHS.

200n. "the lenity": Arnold to Udny Hay, Aug. 12, 1780, Jeremiah Wadsworth Papers, CHS; West Point Orderly Book, Aug. 14 and 26, 1780, NYHS.

PAGE

201 "I am unhappy": Timothy Pickering to Arnold, Aug. 28, 1780, GWP.

201 "There has never been": Washington, quoted in Boyneton, 89.

201 "if something satisfactory": Washington to president of Congress, Aug. 20, 1780, Fitz *Writings*, 19, 412.

201n. "expecting to draw": Painter to Arnold, Sept. 9, 1780, GWP.

202 "patience and self-denial": USCC *Journals*, XVII, 725.

202 "A truly Presbyterian": Arnold to Nathanael Greene, Aug. 23, 1780, GWP.

202 "I think I have": Samuel Parsons to Arnold, Sept. 5, 1780, GWP.

203 "if such drafts": John Lamb, quoted in Palmer, 259.

203 "would not, in my": John Lamb to Henry Knox, Aug. 8, 1780, Lamb Papers, NYHS.

203 "as [West Point]": Arnold to Varick, Aug. 5, 1780, Varick, 82.

204 "As you have neither": Hannah Arnold to Arnold, Sept. 4, 1780, Houghton.

204 "Lover-like": Hannah Arnold to M. S. Arnold, Sept. 10, 1780, Walker, XXV, 43.

204f. "You must by all means": Arnold's "Directions for Mrs. Arnold on her way to West Point," Houghton.

205 "feather bed": Inventory of Arnold's belongings left at the Robinson house, Dec. 6, 1780, Benedict Arnold Letters and Papers, NYHS.

205 "No sensations": Arnold to Robert Howe, Sept. 12, 1780, GWP.

205 "I look upon": Robert Howe to Arnold, Aug. 5, 1780, GWP.

205 "at present": Arnold to Robert Howe, Aug. 5, 1780, GWP.

206 "sound policy": J. H. Smith to Arnold, Aug. 13, 1780, GWP.

206f. Correspondence with Gov. George Clinton re passes: Arnold to J. H. Smith, Aug. 16, 1780; Arnold to Clinton, Aug. 17, 1780; Clinton to Arnold, Aug. 22, 1780; all GWP.

207 "real political character": Varick to Robert Benson, Aug. 24, 1780, Varick, 92ff.

207 "a damned Tory": Varick, 149.

207 "obliged to retreat": Nathanael Greene to Arnold, Sept. 7, 1780, Huntington.

207 "conduct on this": Arnold to Greene, Sept. 12, 1780, Huntington.

207f. "no offensive operations": Arnold to Washington, Sept. 14, 1780, Huntington.

PAGE

208 "hail as big": Benjamin Peabody Orderly Book, USMA, quoted in Palmer, 260.

208 "Services done": André to Arnold, probably July 24, 1780, Clinton.

208 "to grant flags": Arnold to Samuel Parsons, Aug. 16, 1780, GWP.

208f. Letter to "Mr. John Anderson, Merchant," Aug. 30, 1780, Clinton (transcript).

210 "I am told": André to Elisha Sheldon, Sept. 7, 1780, Clinton.

210 "You must be sensible": Arnold to André, Sept. 10, 1780, Clinton.

210 "if Mr. Anderson": Arnold to Sheldon, Sept. 10, 1780, GWP.

211 "I came here": Arnold to Washington, Sept. 11, 1780, GWP.

211f. "a person I expect": Arnold to Benjamin Tallmadge, Sept. 13, 1780, GWP.

212f. "diversified scenery": Thacher, *Military Journal,* 133.

213 "in a mercantile": Varick, 124f.

213 "under the sanction": Varick, 127.

213f. "I did intend": Beverley Robinson to Arnold, Sept. 17, 1780, GWP.

214 "I expect his Excellency": Arnold to Robinson, Sept. 18, 1780, Clinton.

215 "[I] am sorry": Robinson to Arnold, Sept. 19, 1780, GWP.

215 "I have been greatly": Robinson to Arnold, Sept. 21, 1780, Clinton (in Robinson to Clinton, Sept. 24).

216 "but I never": Joshua Hett Smith, "Trial," 5. Of the millions of words spoken and sworn to in the aftermath of Arnold's treason, the Colquhoun brothers strike me as the least self-serving and the most truthful.

216 Location of meeting place: Lavalette Wilson has provided the most likely argument for its exact location (see bibliography), despite the fact that the rock on which is carved "André the spy landed here Sept. 21, 1780" lies several hundred feet south of Wilson's chosen spot. The person who despoiled the rock was a better carver than historian: the bank that rises behind that particular stretch of beach is much too steep for a horse, or for the crippled Arnold on foot, to have negotiated.

217 "firing at a ship": Lamb to Livingston, Sept. 20, 1780, quoted in Leake, 258.

217 "six shot in": *Vulture* log, quoted in Sargent, 328 fn.

218 Secret British embarkation: Jameson to Arnold, Sept. 20, 1780; also see Greene to Washington, Sept. 21, 1780 (both GWP).

219 "crimson broadcloth": Joshua Hett Smith, *Narrative,* 100.

219 Argument at Robinson's, Sept. 23, 1780: Testimony of Richard Varick, David Franks and John Lamb: Varick, 128, 150f., 173ff.

219 "loose character": Robert Benson to Varick, Sept. 19, 1780, Varick, 98.

219 "treating [him]": Varick, 176f.

219 "and paid me": Varick to his sister, Oct. 1, 1780, in Varick, 191.

220 "[I am sending you]": dispatches from Jameson to Arnold and Jameson to Lt. Allen (André's escort), Sept. 23, 1780, Clinton.

220 "nigh at hand": Varick, 129f.

221 "one vulture": Thomas Paine, *The Crisis Extraordinary.* Arnold's oarsmen clocked an average speed of eight knots over the hour and a half, a remarkable feat even with the tide in their favor. Ironically, their effort was irrelevant. General Washington did not receive the incriminating papers and dispatch a horseman to chase Arnold until about four o'clock that afternoon.

221 "violation of flags": Robinson to Washington, Sept. 25, 1780, GWP.

221f. "Sir, The heart": Arnold to Washington, Sept. 25, 1780, GWP.

222f. "Thou loveliest and best": Arnold to M. S. Arnold, Sept. 25, 1780, James McHenry Papers, Manuscripts Division, LC, (copy in McHenry's handwriting; McHenry was secretary to General Washington).

CHAPTER 17 (PAGES 224–241)

225 "I apprehend": Arnold to Sir Henry Clinton, Sept. 26, 1780, GWP.

225 "excellent understanding": Alexander Hamilton to John Laurens, Oct. 11, 1780, Hamilton, II, 467. That these words of praise were written by a member of the enemy commander in chief's staff is indicative of André's wide appeal. After his death, Hamilton wrote to his fiancée (General Schuyler's daughter Elizabeth) that he wished himself "possessed of André's accomplishments for your sake; for I would wish to

charm you in every sense." (Oct. 2, 1780, Hamilton, II, 449).

225f.   "Major André was taken": Washington to Clinton, Sept. 30, 1780, GWP.

226   "Mr. John Anderson": Arnold to Washington, Oct. 1, 1780, Clinton.

226f.   "I take this opportunity": Arnold to Washington, Oct. 1, 1780, GWP.

228   Rewards for Paulding, Williams and Van Wart: USCC *Journals,* XVIII, 1,009f.

228   "less than brilliant": Bakeless, 285.

228   "The person in": André to Washington, Sept. 24, 1780, GWP.

229   "As they have delayed": Clinton to his sisters, Oct. 4 and 9, 1780, Clinton.

229   "Most elegantly": Tallmadge to Heath, Oct. 10, 1780, William Heath Papers, MHS.

229   "with perfect firmness": Thacher, *Military Journal,* 228.

229   "When I saw him": Tallmadge, 38f.

229   "in the midst": Hamilton to John Laurens, Oct. 11, 1780, Hamilton, II, 468.

230   "The horrid deed": Clinton to his sisters, Oct. 4 and 9, 1780, Clinton.

230   "Could Arnold have been": Thacher, *Military Journal,* 230f.

230   "In the conference": Arnold to Clinton, Oct. 18, 1780, Clinton.

230n.   "as base a 'prostitute' ": Oswald to John Lamb, Dec. 11, 1780, Lamb Papers, NYHS.

231   William Smith helps Arnold: Smith's brother Joshua was currently on trial at Tappan for complicity in Arnold's treason. He was acquitted for lack of evidence, but New York State jailed him anyway, as a precaution. After escaping in 1781, he made his way to New York and eventually to England.

231n.   "Judas sold": Benjamin Franklin to Marquis de Lafayette, May 14, 1781, Franklin and Franklin, 101f.

232   "looking-glass world": Mackesy, 511.

232f.   "General Arnold's Address": *Royal Gazette* (New York), Oct. 11, 1780.

233   "Proclamation by Brigadier General Arnold": *Royal Gazette,* Oct. 25, 1780.

233   "at a loss": Washington to president of Congress, Oct. 15, 1780, Fitz *Writings,* 20, 189.

PAGE

233 "affords the most convincing": Washington, General Orders, Sept. 26, 1780, Fitz *Writings,* 20, 94ff.

234 "baseness and" and "on the fallacious": *Pennsylvania Packet,* Sept. 30, 1780.

234 *"base peculations":* Varick, 165.

234 "the hissing explosion": Account of an anti-Arnold demonstration in New Milford, Connecticut, *Pennsylvania Packet,* Jan. 16, 1781. Also see Mrs. Henry Drinker "Journal," Sept. 30, 1780, and *Pennsylvania Packet,* Oct. 3, 1780.

235 "a procrastinator": William Smith, Dec. 21, 1780.

235f. Arnold's letters to Lord George Germain: Oct. 7, 1780, CO, PRO; and Oct. 28, 1780, Clinton.

235 "the misdirection of": Mackesy, 367.

236n. "to join me": Arnold to Tallmadge, Oct. 25, 1780, GWP.

236n. "mortified that": Tallmadge to Jared Sparks, Nov. 16, 1833, *Magazine of American History,* Vol. III, No. 12 (Dec. 1879), 754.

236 "Treason doth never": Sir John Harington (1561–1612), *Of Treason.*

237 "Rather above": Henry Lee, *Memoirs,* 396, 404.

237 "No circumstance whatever": Washington to Henry Lee, Oct. 20, 1780, GWP.

238 Peggy burns letters: None of the letters has been found, leading me to conclude that they were kept in the bedroom (rather than in the office, accessible to Richard Varick) and that Peggy destroyed them. From this day until the end of their lives, both she and her husband must have disposed of all their personal correspondence, as none has survived.

238 Peggy's hysteria: Richard Varick to his sister, Oct. 1, 1780, Varick, 191f; Alexander Hamilton to Elizabeth Schuyler, Sept. 25–26, 1780, Hamilton, II, 441. Also see Thacher, *Journal,* 472. It is unlikely that the hysteria was entirely out of her control. Although she had been known since childhood for emotional outbursts, those that are documented seem to have been timed in order to obtain something she wanted or to avoid something she didn't. This was her last and best.

239 "a kind of" and "so delicate": Edward Burd to Jasper Yeates, Oct. 5, 1780, in Walker, XL, 380f.

239 "the hands of": Edward Shippen to William Moore, Oct. 5, 1780, Personal Miscellaneous Papers, Benedict Arnold, NYPL (photostat of original).

239   "dangerous to": *Minutes of the Supreme Executive Council,* XII, 520.

241   "a favorable opportunity": Clinton to Arnold, Dec. 14, 1780, Clinton.

CHAPTER 18 (PAGES 242–253)

242   "A Life of Jobs": Thomas Paine, *The Crisis Extraordinary,* 187.

243ff.   Arnold's march from Westover to Richmond: The plantation next door to Westover was Berkeley, the home of Benjamin Harrison, a signer of the Declaration of Independence and a close friend of George Washington's. Berkeley is now open to the public, and its owner and promoter has cooked up a story of Arnold pausing on his way to Richmond and ordering his men to remove all the Harrison family portraits from the house and burn them on the front lawn. Exhaustive research has revealed no documentation whatsoever for this yarn, and common sense refutes it. In the first place, Arnold was in too much of a hurry to engage in a petty act of revenge against a man he didn't even know; second, if he wanted to harm Harrison, why not burn the whole house down?; and finally, the weather was much too wet for a bonfire.

244   "as great an appearance": Simcoe, 161.

245   Destruction of goods at Richmond: "Proposals by Brigadier General Arnold to the Inhabitants of Richmond and Manchester, Jan. 5, 1781," in Shackelford, 598; Jefferson to president of Congress, Jan. 10, 1781, PCC; Arnold to Clinton, Jan. 21, 1781, CO, PRO.

245   "If General Tryon": Simcoe, *Journal,* 164.

245   "This event": Arnold to Clinton, Jan. 23, 1781, Clinton.

245   "despis[ing] a treachery": John Sullivan to Chevalier de la Luzerne, Jan. 13, 1781, Burnett, V, 529ff.

245   "as a life of": Arnold to Clinton, Jan. 23, 1781.

246   "alleg[ed] that he": Arnold to Capt. Simon Kollock, Mar. 10, 1781, *Report on American Manuscripts,* II, 255.

246   "the garrison is in": Simcoe, *Journal,* 180.

247   "graciously pleased": Germain to Arnold, Dec. 7, 1780, CO, PRO.

247   "ability, activity": Phillips to Cornwallis, Apr. 8, 1781, Cornwallis Papers, PRO.

PAGE

247 "very critical situation": Cornwallis to Phillips, enclosed in Clinton to Germain, May 18, 1781, CO, PRO.

247f. "My opinion with": Arnold to Germain, June 25, 1781, CO, PRO.

248 Arnold furnishes names: Haldimand to Clinton, Nov. 16, 1780; Feb. 7, 1781; June 6, 1781; and Arnold memo, July 26, 1781; all in Skull, 307ff.; Arnold to Capt. John Smith, Aug. 24, 1781, Clinton.

248 "has hurt himself": Nathaniel Coffin to Unknown, June 20, 1781, PCC.

248 "[Arnold has] gained": Joseph Lee to Isaac Allen, June 10, 1781, PCC.

248f. "Amazingly improved": Shoemaker, n.d.

249 "She is *a Philadelphian*": Shoemaker, Sept. 21, 1781.

249 "the whimsical": William Smith, Aug. 1, 15 and 25, 1781.

251 "Here the coolness": Arnold to Clinton, Sept. 8, 1781, Clinton.

251f. Massacre at Fort Griswold: Admirers of British military tradition speculate that the massacre would never have occurred had the assault party been composed of British regulars, and they are probably correct. Arnold's Loyalist troops were perhaps the most likely to give way emotionally, since the men who had defended the fort with such unexpected tenacity were their own countrymen.

252 "*a Bunker Hill*": intelligence from New York, enclosed in Tallmadge to Heath, Sept. 23, 1781, Massachusetts Historical Society *Collections,* 7th Series, Vol. 5 (1905), 264f.

253 "pasquinado": William Smith, Nov. 3, 1781.

CHAPTER 19 (PAGES 254–264)

254 "A philosopher": "I have met with so much unmerited reproach from the world that it has taught me to become a philosopher in my own defence": Arnold to B. Goodrich, July 27, 1786, Arnold papers in private hands.

254 "a renewal of": Arnold to Germain, Feb. 3, 1782, Shelburne Papers, Clements.

255 "I am convinced": Arnold to Guy Carleton, May 13, 1782, Carleton Papers, PRO.

255 Letters from R.M. to *General Advertiser and Morning Intelligencer:* Feb. 9 and 22, 1782. "R.M." was a Welshman named Robert Morris.

PAGE

257 "Our troops": quoted in the *Pennsylvania Packet,* July 17, 1781.

257 "though he is but": Arnold to Carleton, Nov. 3, 1782, Carleton Papers, PRO.

257 "wife of our": King's warrant, Mar. 19, 1782, Treasury Papers, PRO.

257 "for his services": Welbore Ellis to Lords of the Treasury, Mar. 23, 1782, in Historical Manuscripts Commission, "American Manuscripts," II, 429.

257f. "Permit me, Sir": Arnold to Thomas Townshend, Aug. 27, 1782, J.S.H. Fogg Autograph Collection, Maine Historical Society, Portland.

258n. "He seems at no time": PRO, quoted in Taylor, p. 18 fn.

258 "[I] was third": Arnold, Memorial, Mar. 1784, Chatham Papers, PRO.

258 Arnold and the East India Company: Arnold to George Johnstone, July 18, 1784, and Johnstone to Arnold, July 21, 1784, in Isaac N. Arnold, "Something New," 314ff.

259 "I saw General Arnold": James H. Watmough to his wife, Feb. 5, 1785, PMHB, XXIX, 303.

260 "This information" and "universal despair": quoted in Bell, 11.

260 "sails disappear[ed]": quoted in Christopher Moore, 139.

260f. "the common people": Edward Winslow, quoted in Bell, 77.

261 "an entire new": *Royal Gazette* (Saint John), June 6, 1786.

261 "torn from almost": MSA to Edward Shippen, Mar. 6, 1786, Houghton.

262 Claims against Arnold's American estate: June 7, 1787, HSP; and n.d., Benedict Arnold Collections, NHCHS.

262 "interference and protection": Arnold to Unknown (probably Lord Sydney), Mar. 6, 1787, Myers Collections, Rare Book and Manuscript Division, NYPL.

262 "Having on many": Arnold to Clinton, May 22, 1787, Clinton.

262 "Had I not been": Clinton to Arnold, May 26, 1787, Clinton.

263 "an elegant set": Auction notice, *Royal Gazette,* Sept. 6, 1791.

263 "How difficult": MSA to Elizabeth Burd, July 5, 1790, HSP.

263 "one of the most": Stephen Sewell to Jonathan Sewell, n.d., quoted in Lawrence, *Judges,* 23.

263 Arnold burned in effigy: There is no firsthand documentation of this incident, but a letter written later by Arnold seems to confirm the legend that persists in Saint John to this day. See

Arnold to Jonathan Bliss, Feb. 26, 1792, Arnold Papers, NBM.

264 "the best of": MSA to Edward Shippen, Mar. 6, 1786, Houghton.

CHAPTER 20 (PAGES 265–273)

266 "apostasy from principles": Cobbett, XXIX, 1,518.

266 Lauderdale duel: statement of Lord Hawke (Arnold's second), July 2, 1792, Arnold Papers in private hands; statement of Lord Hawke, July 7, 1792, in Taylor, 77.

266 "for some hours: MSA to Edward Shippen, July 6, 1792, in Walker, XXV, 462.

266 "perfectly silent": MSA to Edward Shippen, June 26, 1792, in Walker, XXV, 460.

267 Report of duel: *The Times* (London), July 3, p. 4, col. 1.

267 "our reception": Arnold to Jonathan Bliss, Feb. 26, 1792, Arnold Papers, NBM.

267 "in the Funds": MSA to Edward Shippen, June 26, 1792.

267 "From my private": Arnold to William Pitt, May 28, 1792, Chatham Papers, PRO.

268 "a much greater sum": Arnold to Clinton, July 23, 1792, Clinton.

268 "My ideas of": Clinton to Arnold, May 26, 1787, Clinton.

268 "surprised at the": Arnold to Clinton, Oct. 17, 1792, Clinton.

268 "the style of": Arnold to Pitt, Sept. 8, 1792, Chatham Papers, PRO.

268 "Surrounded by": MSA to Clinton, Nov. 13, 1792, Clinton.

269 "very meritorious": Clinton memorandum, Nov. 14, 1792, Clinton.

269 Governorship of Dominica: Arnold to Pitt, Dec. 15, 1792, Chatham Papers, PRO.

269 "a command as": in Fortescue, IV, 376.

269 "but until I can": Arnold to Josiah Blakesley, Sept. 10, 1794, Arnold Collection, MSS 106, Whitney Library, NHCHS.

270 "very much an invalid": Arnold to Bliss, Sept. 5, 1795, Arnold Papers, NBM.

270 "with a plan of": MSA to Edward Shippen, May 2, 1796, in Walker, XXV, 465f.

270 "are placed at exceeding": Arnold to Bliss, Aug. 15, 1795, Arnold Papers, NBM.

270 "in a military character": Arnold to Bliss, Sept. 5, 1795.

PAGE

270 "extremely anxious for him": MSA to Bliss, Dec. 5, 1795, Arnold Papers, NBM.

271 "I have the consolation": Arnold to Bliss, Feb. 20, 1796, Arnold Papers, NBM.

271 "London's newest": Mackenzie, 15.

271 "to liberate Chile": Arnold Papers in private hands.

271 Arnold volunteers for fire ships: Arnold to Lord Spencer, Jan. 14, 1798; and Spencer to Arnold, Jan. 21, 1798 (both in Arnold Papers in private hands).

271 "I am almost sick": MSA to Edward Shippen, July 29, 1796, in Walker, XXV, 466.

271 "a violent attack": MSA to Edward Shippen, May 20, 1797, in Walker, XXV, 467f.

272 "Make yourself agreeable" and "Nature has been": Arnold and MSA to Edward S. Arnold, Sept. 7, 1800, BA and MSA Correspondence, NYPL.

272 "too free indulgence": MSA to Edward S. Arnold, Sept. 7, 1800, BA and MSA Correspondence, NYPL.

272 "a general dropsy": Ann Fitch to Edward Shippen, June 29, 1801, in Walker, XXV, 472.

272f. "his difficulty of" and "Strong symptoms": MSA to Edward S. Arnold, July 1, 1801, BA and MSA Correspondence, NYPL.

EPILOGUE (PAGES 275–279)

275 Death notices: quoted in Taylor, 26.

276 "I fancied": MSA to Edward Shippen, Autumn 1801, Walker, XXV, 474ff.

276 "he is not possessed": Edward Shippen to MSA, Nov. 10, 1801, in Walker, XXVI, 240ff.

276 "little lovely daughter": Edward Shippen to MSA, Aug. 10, 1801, in Walker, XXVI, 240.

276 "There is little": MSA to Edward S. Arnold, July 31, 1801, Taylor, 61f.

276f. "live within your pay": MSA to Edward S. Arnold, Nov. 17, 1801, in PMHB, XXIII, 192f.

277 Edward volunteers to educate William: MSA to Richard and Henry Arnold, Nov. 5, 1802, Walker, XXV, 481ff.; MSA to Edward S. Arnold, Oct. 16, 1802, Arnold Papers in private hands.

277 "small, but very neat": MSA to Edward Shippen, June 2, 1802, in Walker, XXV, 477.

PAGE

277 "a little family pride": MSA to Edward S. Arnold, Oct. 16–17, 1802, Arnold Papers in private hands.

277 "who is now": MSA to Richard and Henry Arnold, Nov. 5, 1802.

277 "I have not a teaspoon": MSA to Richard and Henry Arnold, Aug. 1803, in Walker, XXV, 489.

277 "collected from the wreck": MSA to Edward S. Arnold, Oct. 16–17, 1802.

277 "the only thing": MSA to Edward Shippen, Jan. 5, 1803, in Walker, XXV, 483ff.

277 "while I have": MSA to Richard and Henry Arnold, Nov. 5, 1802.

277 "feel the disposition": MSA to Edward Shippen, Jan. 5, 1803.

277 "but I trust": MSA to Edward S. Arnold, July 16, 1802, Arnold Papers in private hands.

277 "tranquil, serene": MSA to Edward S. Arnold, Mar. 20, 1803, Arnold Papers in private hands.

277f. "a complaint of": MSA to Elizabeth Burd, July 3, 1803, in Walker, XXV, 486f.

278 "endeavor[ed] to prepare": MSA to Richard and Henry Arnold, July 27, 1803, in Walker, XXV, 488.

278 "very large tumor": MSA to Edward Shippen, Nov. 2, 1803, in Walker, XXV, 490.

278 "violent attack": MSA to Elizabeth Burd, May 14, 1804, in Walker, XXV, 491f.

278 "as plain as": MSA will for her English property, Jan. 26, 1804, Houghton.

Bibliography

Abbatt, William. *The Crisis of the Revolution.* Tarrytown, N.Y.: William Abbatt, 1899.

Adams, Dr. Samuel. Diary. Rare Books and Manuscripts Division, New York Public Library.

"An Account of the late Gallant and unfortunate Major André, Aid-du-Camp to Sir Henry Clinton, and Adjutant General of the British Forces in America." *The Political Magazine,* Vol. I (1780), pp. 688f.

"Account of Major General Arnold, who has abandoned the Rebel Service, and joined our Army at New York." *The Political Magazine,* Vol. I (1780), pp. 690, 746–48.

Ainslie, Captain Thomas. *Canada Preserved.* Journal. Edited by Sheldon S. Cohen. New York: New York University Press, 1968.

Albany, N.Y. New York State Library. André Papers.

———. Miscellaneous Manuscripts.

Allen, Ethan. *A Narrative of Colonel Ethan Allen's Captivity.* Introduction by John Pell. New York: The Georgian Press, 1930 (originally published in 1779).

Allen, William. "Account of Arnold's Expedition." *Collections of the Maine Historical Society,* Vol. I (1831).

André, John. *Major André's Journal.* Tarrytown, N.Y.: William Abbatt, 1930.

[André, John, defendant] *Proceedings of a Board of General Officers, Held by Order of His Excellency General Washington, Commander in Chief of the Army of the United States of America, Respecting Major John André, Adjutant General of the British Army, September 29, 1780.* Philadelphia: Printed; Hartford: Reprinted by B. Webster, 1780.

Andreana, Containing the Trial, Execution and Various Matter Connected with the History of Major John André. Philadelphia: Horace W. Smith, 1865.

Ann Arbor, Mich. University of Michigan. William L. Clements Library. Clinton Papers.

————. Benjamin Gilbert Letter Book 1780–1783.

————. Miscellaneous Collection.

————. James S. Schoff Collection.

————. Shelburne Papers.

————. Simcoe Papers.

Annual Register, Vol. 24 (1781). London: J. Dodsley, 1800.

Arnold, Benedict. "Address to the Inhabitants of America on his Joining the British Army." *Royal Gazette* (New York), Oct. 11, 1780, p. 3.

————. Day Book 1777 [–1779]. Pennsylvania State Archives, Harrisburg.

————. "Journal of his Expedition to Canada" and "Letters Written during the Expedition to Quebec." In Kenneth Roberts, *March to Quebec* (see), pp. 45–123.

————. Journal, Sept. 15–Oct. 30, 1775. George Washington Papers. MSS. Division, Library of Congress, Washington, D.C. (The Arnold journal in the George Washington Papers is a "true copy" made by Eleazer Oswald and sent to Washington on Oct. 13, 1775. I have used it for the dates Sept. 15 to Sept. 27. After that, I have used the journal as printed in Kenneth Roberts's *March to Quebec,* which starts on Sept. 27 and is more complete.)

————. "Letters on his Expedition to Canada in 1775." *Collections of the Maine Historical Society,* Vol. I, pp. 447–98.

————. Papers of Benedict Arnold and Margaret Shippen Arnold, in private hands.

————. *The Present State of the American Rebel Army, Navy, and Finances. Transmitted to the British Government in October,*

1780. Edited by Paul Leicester Ford. Brooklyn, N.Y.: Historical Printing Club, 1891.

————. "Regimental Memorandum Book, Ticonderoga and Crown Point, 1775." *Pennsylvania Magazine of History and Biography,* Vol. VIII, pp. 363–76.

[————, defendant] *Proceedings of a General Court Martial of the Line, Held at Raritan, in the State of New Jersey, By Order of His Excellency George Washington, Esq. General and Commander in Chief of the Army of the United States of America, For the Trial of Major General Arnold, June 1, 1779.* Philadelphia: Francis Bailey, 1780.

Benedict Arnold in New Brunswick. St. John Free Public Library, 1983.

"Benedict Arnold's Letters to Nathaniel Shaw, Jr." The New London County Historical Society *Collections,* Vol. II (1933), pp. 120–24.

Arnold, Isaac N. *The Life of Benedict Arnold: His Patriotism and His Treason.* 2 vols. Chicago: Jansen, McClurg & Company, 1880.

————. "Something New of Benedict Arnold and his Descendants in England." *Magazine of American History,* Vol. X (July–December 1883), pp. 307–19.

"Arnold the Traitor, André the Sufferer." From the Tallmadge Manuscripts. *Magazine of American History,* Vol. III, No. 12 (December 1879).

Ashmun, Margaret. *The Singing Swan.* New Haven, Conn.: Yale University Press, 1931.

Bailey, James Montgomery, and Susan Benedict Hill. *History of Danbury, Connecticut.* New York: Burr Printing House, 1896.

Bakeless, John. *Turncoats, Traitors, and Heroes.* Philadelphia and New York: J. B. Lippincott Company, 1959.

Balch, Thomas, ed. *Letters and Papers Relating Chiefly to the Provincial History of Pennsylvania.* Philadelphia: Crissy & Markley, 1855.

Baldwin, Col. Jeduthan. *Revolutionary Journal 1775–1778.* New York: The New York Times & Arno Press, 1971 (originally published in 1906).

Bancroft, George. *Joseph Reed: A Historical Essay.* New York: W. J. Widdleton, 1867.

Banks, Charles E. Card index of Arnold's March to Quebec. Massachusetts Historical Society.

Barney, Samuel. *Diary 1775–1776.* Benedict Arnold Collection. New Haven Colony Historical Society.

Bartlett, Clifford A.H. "Historic Cannon Balls and Houses: The British

Invasion of Connecticut in 1777." *Magazine of American History,* Vol. XIX, No. 3 (March 1888), pp. 185–99.

Bedini, Silvio. *Ridgefield in Review.* Ridgefield, Conn.: Ridgefield 250th Anniversary Committee, Inc., 1958.

Beebe, Lewis. "Journal of a Physician on the Expedition Against Canada, 1776." *Pennsylvania Magazine of History and Biography,* Vol. LIX, pp. 321–61.

Bell, D. G. *Early Loyalist St. John.* Fredericton, N.B.: New Ireland Press, 1983.

Bergen, Jenifer, Trudy Caswell, Christine Mazzaferro, and Anthony Scuderi. "Raising the *Philadelphia.*" *Lake Champlain Horizons,* Vol. 1, No. 1 (June 1988), pp. 4–6, 12.

"Bethlehem During the Revolution." Extracts from the diary of the Moravian congregation of Bethlehem. *Pennsylvania Magazine of History and Biography,* Vol. XII, pp. 385–406.

Bielinski, Stefan, ed. *A Guide to the Revolutionary War Manuscripts in the New York State Library.* Albany: New York State American Revolution Bicentennial Commission, 1976.

[Bigelow, Col. Timothy?] *Orderly Book, August 12 to November 4, 1777.* Orderly Books Collection, American Antiquarian Society, Worcester, Mass.

Boardman, Oliver. "Journal." *Collections of the Connecticut Historical Society,* Vol. VII (1899), pp. 221–38.

Boatner, Mark Mayo. *Cassell's Biographical Dictionary of the American War of Independence: 1763–1783.* London: Cassell, 1973.

Boston, Mass. Massachusetts Historical Society. Bigelow Collection.

———. Boston Marine Society Papers.

———. Curtis Papers.

———. Endicott Collection.

———. C. E. French Collection.

———. C. Guild Autograph Collection.

———. William Heath Papers, 1774–1872.

———. Henry Knox Papers.

———. William Livingston Papers, 1695–1839.

———. Miscellaneous Bound Collection.

———. Miscellaneous Manuscripts.

———. Norcross Collection, 1751–1792.

———. Photostats, 1777–1780.

———. Timothy Pickering Papers.

———. Elisha Porter Papers, 1762–1822.

———. Revere Papers.

————. Richmond Autograph Collection.

————. Ridley Papers, 1754–1782.

————. Revolutionary Letters of Gen. John Sullivan, 1774–1780.

————. Theodore Sedgwick Papers.

————. Thaxter Papers, 1774–1791.

————. John Thomas Papers, 1724–1776.

————. David Townsend Papers, 1753–1829.

————. Waterston Autograph Collection.

————. Meshech Weare Papers, 1713–1786.

————. Winslow Papers, 1690–1782.

————. Winthrop Papers.

Boylan, Brian Richard. *Benedict Arnold: The Dark Eagle.* New York: W. W. Norton & Company, Inc., 1973.

Boyneton, Edward C. *History of West Point.* New York: D. Van Nostrand, 1863.

Bradford, Gamaliel. *Damaged Souls.* Boston and New York: Houghton Mifflin Company, 1922.

————. *Wives.* New York: Harper & Brothers, 1925.

Brinton, Crane. *A Decade of Revolution, 1789–1799.* New York: Harper & Row, 1963 (originally published in 1934).

Burd, Edward, to Jasper Yeates. Philadelphia, October 5, 1780, *Pennsylvania Magazine of History and Biography,* Vol. XL, pp. 380f.

Burgoyne, John. *A State of the Expedition from Canada.* New York: The New York Times & Arno Press, 1969 (originally published in 1780).

Burnett, Edmund C., ed. *Letters of Members of the Continental Congress.* 8 vols. Washington, D.C.: Carnegie Institution of Washington, 1921–1936.

Burnham, Rev. N. H. *The Battle of Groton Heights.* New London: E. E. Darrow, 1894.

Bush, Martin H. *Revolutionary Enigma: A Re-appraisal of General Philip Schuyler of New York.* Port Washington, N.Y.: Ira J. Friedman, Inc., 1969.

Cambridge, Mass. Houghton Library. Manuscripts Collection.

Carrington, Henry B. *Battles of the American Revolution.* New York: Promontory Press, 1974 (originally published in 1877).

Carson, Hampton L. "The Case of the Sloop 'Active.'" *Pennsylvania Magazine of History and Biography,* Vol. XVI (1892), pp. 385–98.

Caulkins, Frances Manwaring. *History of Norwich, Connecticut.* Published by the author, 1866.

Centennial of the United States Military Academy at West Point: 1802–1902. 2 vols. Washington, D.C.: Government Printing Office, 1904.

Chapin, Bradley. *The American Law of Treason.* Seattle: University of Washington Press, 1964.

Chicago, Ill. Chicago Historical Society. Manuscripts Collection.

"Circumstances respecting the Betraying of Major André." *The Political Magazine,* Vol. II (1781), p. 62.

"Circumstances respecting General Arnold." *The Political Magazine,* Vol. II (1781), pp. 291f.

The Clarksons of New York. New York: Bradstreet Press, 1876.

Clinton, George. *Public Papers.* 10 vols. New York and Albany: Wynkoop Hallenbeck Crawford Co., 1899–1914.

Cobbett, William. *The Parliamentary History of England, from the Earliest Period to the Year 1803,* Vol. XXIX (1791–1792). London: T. C. Hansard, 1817.

Coffin, Robert P. Tristram. *Kennebec, Cradle of Americans.* New York: Farrar & Rinehart, 1937.

Coffin, Victor. *The Province of Quebec and the Early American Revolution.* Madison, Wisc.: Published by the University, 1896.

Cohen, Sheldon S. *Connecticut's Loyalist Gadfly: The Reverend Samuel Andrew Peters.* Hartford, Conn.: The American Revolution Bicentennial Commission of Connecticut, 1976.

Cohn, Art. "An Incident Not Known to History: Squire Ferris and Benedict Arnold at Ferris Bay, October 13, 1776." *Vermont History,* Vol. 55, No. 2 (Spring 1987), pp. 96–112.

Collard, Edgar Andrew. "When Money Wasn't Worth a Thing." *The Gazette* (Montreal), November 24, 1984, p. B-2.

Commager, Henry Steele, and Richard B. Morris, eds. *The Spirit of Seventy-Six: The Story of the American Revolution as Told by the Participants.* 2 vols. Indianapolis and New York: The Bobbs-Merrill Company, Inc., 1958.

Commission of Enquiry into the Losses and Services of the American Loyalists. *Transcript of Manuscript Books and Papers, 1783–1790* (originals in Audit Office, Public Record Office), Vol. 45. Transcribed for the New York Public Library, 1900.

Connecticut Archives. Archives, History and Genealogy Unit. Connecticut State Library. Hartford, Conn.

The Connecticut Gazette. January 24, 31, and February 7, 14, 21, 1766.

Cook, Captain Thaddeus. *Orderly Book, September 6 to October 6, 1777.* Orderly Books Collection, American Antiquarian Society, Worcester, Mass.

Copp, John J. "Historical Sketch." In *The Battle of Groton Heights*. Groton Heights Centennial Committee, December 1879.

Crick, B. R., and Miriam Alman. *A Guide to Manuscripts Relating to America in Great Britain and Ireland*. London: Mansell Publishing, 1979.

Crockett, Walter Hill. *A History of Lake Champlain*. Burlington, Vt.: McAuliffe Paper Co., n.d.

Crofut, Florence S. Marcy. *Guide to the History and the Historic Sites of Connecticut*. 2 vols. New Haven, Conn.: Yale University Press, 1937.

Cutting, Nathaniel. "Journal of an Embassy to Algiers in 1793." *Historical Magazine*, Vol. IV, No. 9 (Sept 1860), pop. 262–65.

[Danford, J.] "Journal of the Most Remarkable Occurrences in Quebec, 1775–1776. By an Officer of the Garrison." *Collections of the New-York Historical Society*, 1880, pp. 175–236.

Dann, John C., ed. *The Revolution Remembered*. Chicago: The University of Chicago Press, 1980.

Davis, Matthew L. *Memoirs of Aaron Burr*. 2 vols. New York: Harper & Brothers, 1858.

"Deane Papers." *Collections of the Connecticut Historical Society*, Vol. XXIII (1930).

"Deane Papers." *Collections of the New-York Historical Society*, Vol. XXII (1899).

Deane, Silas. "Correspondence." *Collections of the Connecticut Historical Society*, Vol. II (1870).

———— to Simeon Deane, Philadelphia, July 27, 1779. *Pennsylvania Magazine of History and Biography*, Vol. XVII (1893), pp. 348–49.

Dearborn, Henry. "A Narrative of the Saratoga Campaign." *The Bulletin of the Fort Ticonderoga Museum*, Vol. I, No. 5 (Jan. 1929), pp. 2–12.

————. *Revolutionary War Journals of Henry Dearborn, 1775–1783*. Ed. Lloyd A. Brown and Howard H. Peckham. Chicago: The Caxton Club, 1939.

Decker, Malcolm. *Benedict Arnold, Son of the Havens*. New York: Antiquarian Press, Ltd., 1961 (originally published in 1932).

————. *Ten Days of Infamy*. New York: Arno Press, 1969.

Diamant, Lincoln. *Chaining the Hudson*. New York: Carol Publishing Group, 1989.

Dictionary of American Biography.

Dictionary of National Biography. London: Oxford University Press.

"Documents sur la Revolution americaine, 1775–1776: Papiers Arnold." *La Revue de L'Université Laval* (Quebec), Vol. II, Nos. 3–10 (Nov. 1947–June 1948), pp. 262–68, 544–48, 642–48, 742–48, 838–46, 926–34.

Dorr, William. *Diary of Arnold's Expedition, 1775–1776.* Original in Massachusetts Historical Society.

Dow, George Francis. *Fort Western on the Kennebec.* Augusta, Me.: Gannett Publishing Company, 1922 (reprinted by Friends of Fort Western, 1977).

Drinker, Elizabeth. *Diaries 1758–1807.* Drinker Papers. Historical Society of Pennsylvania, Philadelphia.

Drinker, Mrs. Henry. Extracts from the *Journal.* Ed. Henry D. Biddle. Philadelphia: J. B. Lippincott Company, 1889.

———. "Extracts from the Journal of Mrs. Henry Drinker of Philadelphia, from September 25, 1777, to July 4, 1778. *Pennsylvania Magazine of History and Biography,* Vol. XIII (1889), pp. 298–308.

"Duel." *The Times* (London), July 3, 1792, p. 4, col. 1.

Dwight, Timothy. *Travels in New England and New York.* 4 vols. Cambridge, Mass.: Harvard University Press, 1969 (originally published in 1821–1822).

East, Robert A. *Business Enterprise in the American Revolutionary Era.* New York: Columbia University Press, 1938.

Eaton, Arthur W.H. "The De Blois Family." *New England Historical and Genealogical Register,* Vol. LXVII (1913), pp. 6–21, 186–87.

Eckenrode, H. J. *The Revolution in Virginia.* Boston: Houghton Mifflin Company, 1916.

Eliot, Ellsworth, Jr. *The Patriotism of Joseph Reed.* New Haven, Conn.: Yale University Press, 1943.

Elting, John R. *The Battles of Saratoga.* Monmouth Beach, N.J.: Philip Freneau Press, 1977.

———. *Military Uniforms in America, the Era of the American Revolution.* San Rafael, Calif.: Presidio Press, 1974.

Everest, Allan S. *Moses Hazen and the Canadian Refugees in the American Revolution.* Syracuse, N.Y.: Syracuse University Press, 1976.

Fay, Bernard. *Revolution and Freemasonry, 1680–1800.* Boston: Little, Brown and Company, 1935.

Flexner, James Thomas. *The Traitor and the Spy: Benedict Arnold and John André.* Boston: Little, Brown and Company, 1975 (originally published in 1953).

Fobes, Simon. "Narrative of Arnold's Expedition to Quebec." In Kenneth Roberts, *March to Quebec* (see), pp. 571–613.

Foot Guard Day Program. Second Company Governor's Foot Guard. (Conn.) April 26, 1920.

For Want of a Horse. Ed. and with an introduction by Lt. Col. George F.G. Stanley. Sackville, N.B.: The Tribune Press Ltd., 1961.

Force, Peter, ed. *American Archives,* 4th and 5th Series. Washington: M. St. Clair Clarke and Peter Force, 1837–1853.

Ford, Corey. *A Peculiar Service.* Boston: Little, Brown and Company, 1965.

Ford, Worthington Chauncey. "Defences of Philadelphia in 1777." *Pennsylvania Magazine of History and Biography,* Vol. XVIII, pp. 1–19.

Fortescue, J. W. *A History of the British Army.* 14 vols. London: Macmillan and Co., Ltd., 1910–1920.

Foster, Raymond. "Shipbuilding in New Brunswick." Typed manuscript at New Brunswick Museum, St. John.

Franklin, Benjamin, and William Temple Franklin. *Memoirs of the Life and Writings of Benjamin Franklin.* London: Printed for Henry Colburn, 1818.

Franks, Rebecca, to Abigail Hamilton, Flatbush, N.Y., August 10, 1781. *Pennsylvania Magazine of History and Biography,* Vol. XXIII (1899), pp. 303–9.

Fredericton, N.B. University of New Brunswick. Library Archives. Benedict Arnold Papers.

Freeman, Douglas Southall. *George Washington.* 7 vols. New York: Charles Scribner's Sons, 1948–1957.

French, Allen. *The Taking of Ticonderoga in 1775: The British Story.* Cambridge, Mass.: Harvard University Press, 1928.

Frese, Joseph R., and Jacob Judd, eds. *Business Enterprise in Early New York.* Tarrytown, N.Y.: The Sleepy Hollow Press, 1979.

Frost, Samuel. *Orderly Book.* Massachusetts Historical Society, Boston.

Furneaux, Rupert. *Saratoga, the Decisive Battle.* London: George Allen & Unwin Ltd., 1971.

Gaine, Hugh. *Notebook, 1779–1781.* Library of Congress, MSS. Div.

Galloway, Grace Growden. "Diary Kept at Philadelphia from June 17, 1778, to July 1, 1779." *Pennsylvania Magazine of History and Biography,* Vol. LV, pp. 35–94.

General Advertiser, and Morning Intelligencer (London), Feb. 9, 18, 22, 23, 28, 1782.

Gerlach, Don R. "Philip Schuyler and 'The Road to Glory': A Question of Loyalty and Competence." *New-York Historical Society Quarterly,* Vol. XLIX, No. 4 (October 1965), pp. 341–86.

Gipson, Lawrence Henry. *Jared Ingersoll*. New Haven, Conn.: Yale University Press, 1920.

Gocek, Matilda A. *Benedict Arnold: A Reader's Guide and Bibliography*. Monroe, N.Y.: Library Research Associates, 1973.

Gottschalk, Louis. *Lafayette and the Close of the American Revolution*. Chicago: The University of Chicago Press, 1942.

Graham, James. *The Life of General Daniel Morgan*. New York: Derby and Jackson, 1856.

Griggs, Walter S., Jr. "Yankee Doodle's Undoing: Benedict Arnold's Raid on Richmond." *Richmond Guide* (Winter 1989–1990).

Hadden, Lt. James M. *A Journal Kept in Canada and Upon Burgoyne's Campaign in 1776 and 1777*. Albany, N.Y.: Joel Munsell's Sons, 1884.

Hall, Charles S. *Benjamin Tallmadge: Revolutionary Soldier and American Businessman*. New York: Columbia University Press, 1943.

———. *Life and Letters of Samuel Holden Parsons*. Binghamton, New York: Otseningo Publishing Co., 1905.

Hamilton, Alexander. *Papers*. Ed. Harold C. Syrett and Jacob Cook. New York: Columbia University Press, 1961–1987.

Hanover, N.H. Dartmouth College Library. Special Collections. Benedict Arnold's Expense Accounts, September 15–December 23, 1775.

———. Samuel Brown to Thomas Worthington, April 10, 1812.

Harris, William W. *The Battle of Groton Heights*. Revised and enlarged by Charles Allyn. New London: Charles Allyn, 1882.

Hartford, Conn. Connecticut Historical Society. American Revolutionary Letters.

———. Benedict Arnold Papers.

———. Silas Deane Letterbook.

———. Hoadley Collection.

———. Miscellaneous Manuscripts.

———. Peters Family Papers.

———. Rinsland Collection.

———. Jonathan Trumbull, Sr., Papers.

———. Jeremiah Wadsworth Papers.

Haskell, Caleb. "Diary at the Siege of Boston and on the March to Quebec." In Kenneth Roberts, *March to Quebec* (see), pp. 455–99

Hatch, Robert McConnell. *Major John André*. Boston: Houghton Mifflin Company, 1986.

———. *Thrust for Canada*. Boston: Houghton Mifflin Company, 1979.

Hayden, Rev. Horace E. "General Roger Enos, A lost chapter of Arnold's expedition to Canada, 1775." In Kenneth Roberts, *March to Quebec* (see), pp. 629–48.

Hayes, John T. *Connecticut's Revolutionary Cavalry: Sheldon's Horse.* Chester, Conn.: The American Revolution Bicentennial Commission of Connecticut, 1975.

Hazen, William. "The Chipman House." New Brunswick Historical Society *Collections,* No. 15 (1959).

Heath, Major General William. *Memoirs.* New York: The New York Times & Arno Press, 1968 (originally published in 1798).

Hempstead, Stephen. "Narrative." In *Narrative of Jonathan Rathbun.* 1840.

Henry, John Joseph. *Account of Arnold's Campaign Against Quebec, and of the Hardships and Sufferings of That Band of Heroes Who Traversed the Wilderness of Maine from Cambridge to the St. Lawrence, in the Autumn of 1775.* Albany, N.Y.: Joel Munsell, 1877 (originally published in 1812).

Hill, Ralph Nading. *Lake Champlain, Key to Liberty.* Woodstock, Vt: The Countryman Press, 1976.

Hiltzheimer, Jacob. *Diary.* American Philosophical Society Library, Philadelphia.

Historic Philadelphia. American Philosophical Society Transactions, Vol. 43, Part 1. Philadelphia, 1953.

Historical Manuscripts Commission (London). "American Manuscripts."

———. "Stopford-Sackville Manuscripts."

History of West Point. United States Works Progress Administration. United States Military Academy Library (transcripts). West Point, N.Y.

Hoadley, C. J. *Public Records of the State of Connecticut,* Vol. III. Hartford, Conn.: Press of the Case, Lockwood & Brainard Company, 1922.

Hodgkinson, Samuel, to his parents, Quebec, April 27, 1776. *Pennsylvania Magazine of History and Biography,* Vol. X (1886), pp. 158–62.

Holden, W. H. *Houses with a History in St. Marylebone.* London: British Technical and General Press, 1950.

Hughes, J. M. "Notes relative to the Campaign against Burgoyne." Massachusetts Historical Society *Proceedings* (February 1858), pp. 278–80.

[Hull, William] *Revolutionary Services and Civil Life of General William Hull.* Ed. Mrs. Maria Campbell. New York: D. Appleton & Co., 1848.

Hurst, James Willard. *The Law of Treason in the United States.* Westport, Conn.: Greenwood Publishing Corp., 1945.

Idzerda, Stanley J., ed. *Lafayette in the Age of the American Revolution.* 3 vols. Ithaca, N.Y.: Cornell University Press, 1977.

Jack, D. R., compiler. *Biographical Data Relating to New Brunswick Families, Especially of Loyalist Descent.* Typed manuscript on microfilm at St. John Library.

Jacobus, Donald Lines. *The Waterman Family.* 3 vols. New Haven, Conn.: Privately printed, 1939.

Jefferson, Thomas. *The Papers of Thomas Jefferson.* Ed. Julian P. Body. Vol. 4. Princeton, N.J.: Princeton University Press, 1951.

"John Brown's Attack, September 18, 1777." *The Bulletin of the Fort Ticonderoga Museum,* Vol. I, No. 1 (Jan. 1927), pp. 19–21.

Johnston, Henry P. "The Secret Service of the Revolution." *Magazine of American History,* Vol. VIII, No. 2 (February 1882), pp. 95–105.

Journal of the House of Lords, 1792.

Journal of the Principal Occurrences During the Siege of Quebec by the American Revolutionists under Generals Montgomery and Arnold in 1775–1776. Ed. W.T.P. Shortt. London, 1824.

Journals of Each Provincial Congress of Massachusetts in 1774 and 1775. Boston: Dutton and Wentworth, 1838.

Kidder, Frederic. *History of the First New Hampshire Regiment in the War of the Revolution.* Albany, N.Y.: Joel Munsell, 1868.

Klein, Randolph Shipley. *Portrait of an Early American Family: The Shippens of Pennsylvania Across Five Generations.* Philadelphia: University of Pennsylvania Press, 1975.

Kohler, Max J. "Colonel Davis S. Franks." *Magazine of History,* Vol. IV (July–Dec. 1906), pp. 63–72.

Kyte, George W. "A Projected British Attack Upon Philadelphia in 1781." *Pennsylvania Magazine of History and Biography,* Vol. LXXVI, pp. 379–93.

Lafayette, Marquis de. *Lafayette in Virginia.* Baltimore, Md.: The Johns Hopkins Press, 1928.

———. *The Letters of Lafayette to Washington, 1777–1799.* Ed. Louis Gottschalk. New York, 1944.

Larned, Ellen D. *Historic Gleanings in Windham County, Connecticut.* Providence, R.I.: E. L. Freeman & Sons, 1899.

Lawrence, J. W. *Footprints; or, Incidents in Early History of New Brunswick.* Saint John, N.B.: J. & A. McMillan, 1883.

———. *The Judges of New Brunswick and their Times.* St. John, N.B., 1907.

Leake, Isaac Q. *Memoir of the Life and Times of General John Lamb.* Albany, N.Y.: Joel Munsell, 1850.

Lee, Henry. *Memoirs of the War in the Southern Department of the United States.* New York: The New York Times & Arno Press, 1969 (originally published by University Publishing Company, New York, 1869.)

Lee, Major Henry. "Capture of Major André" (letter to Thomas Sim Lee, October 4, 1780). *Pennsylvania Magazine of History and Biography,* Vol. IV, pp. 61–65.

Lee, Richard Henry. *Letters.* Ed. James Curtis Ballagh. 2 vols. New York: The Macmillan Company, 1911.

"Lee Papers." *Collections of the New-York Historical Society,* Vol. III (1873).

Lewis, Brenda Ralph. "Benedict Arnold: An Epilogue." *Army,* Vol. 33, No. 1 (January 1983), pp. 46–52.

Lewis, Dennis. "Valcour, an Old Battle, a New Look." *Lake Champlain Horizons,* Vol. 1, No. 2 (July 1988), pp. 4–6, 12, 15.

Litchfield, Conn. The Litchfield Historical Society. Miscellaneous Collection.

———. Alice Wolcott Collection.

London, England. British Library. Add. MSS. Liverpool Papers.

London, England. Public Record Office. Audit Office Papers.

———. Chatham Papers.

———. Colonial Office Papers.

———. Cornwallis Papers.

———. Miscellaneous Papers.

———. Treasury Papers.

Lossing, Benson J. *Pictorial Field-Book of the Revolution.* 2 vols. New York: Harper Brothers, 1851–1852.

"A Love Affair of Benedict Arnold." *New England Historical and Genealogical Register,* Vol. XI (1857), pp. 75–76.

Ludlam, David M. "The Weather of Independence: Burgoyne's Northern Campaign." *Weatherwise* (October and December, 1976).

Luzader, John F. "The Arnold-Gates Controversy." *West Virginia History,* Vol. XXVII, No. 2 (Jan. 1966), pp. 75–84.

Mackenzie, Gordon. *Marylebone.* London: Macmillan, 1972.

Mackesy, Piers. *The War for America 1775–1783.* Cambridge, Mass.: Harvard University Press, 1964.

Maguire, J. Robert. "Dr. Robert Knox's Account of the Battle of Valcour, October 11–13, 1776." *Vermont History,* Volume XLVI, No. 3 (Summer 1978).

Mahan, Captain A. T. "The Naval Campaign of 1776 on Lake Champlain." *Scribner's Magazine,* Vol. 23 (January–June 1898), pp. 147–60.

Maidstone, England. Kent Archives Office. Letters from Benedict Arnold to William Pitt, 1794–1801.

Main, Jackson Turner. *The Social Structure of Revolutionary America.* Princeton, N.J.: Princeton University Press, 1965.

Marshall, Douglas W., and Howard H. Peckham. *Campaigns of the American Revolution, An Atlas of Manuscript Maps.* Ann Arbor, Mich.: University of Michigan Press, 1976.

Martin, James Kirby. "Benedict Arnold's Treason as Political Protest." *Parameters,* Vol. XI, No. 3 (September 1981), pp. 63–74.

Martin, James Kirby, and Mark Edward Lender. *A Respectable Army: The Military Origins of the Republic, 1763–1789.* Arlington Heights, Ill.: Harlan Davidson, Inc., 1982.

Martin, Joseph Plumb. *Private Yankee Doodle.* Boston: Little, Brown and Company, 1962 (originally published anonymously in 1830 as *A Narrative of Some of the Adventures, Dangers and Sufferings of a Revolutionary Soldier, Interspersed with Anecdotes of Incidents That Occurred Within His Own Observation*).

Massachusetts Historical Society. *Proceedings,* Vol. III (1855–1858). Boston: Printed for the Society, 1859.

Mastromarino, Mark A. " 'The Horrid Disposition of the Times': Charles City County, Virginia, and the American Revolution." *Charles City County, Virginia: An Official History.* Salem, W.Va.: Don Mills, Inc., 1989.

Maxwell, L.M.B. "General Benedict Arnold of Fredericton." *The Maritime Advocate and Busy East* (n.d.). In Benedict Arnold Papers, New Brunswick Museum.

———. *An Outline of the History of Central New Brunswick to the Time of Confederation.* Sackville, N.B.: The Tribune Press, 1937.

McDevitt, Robert. *Connecticut Attacked: A British Viewpoint, Tryon's Raid on Danbury.* Chester, Conn.: Pequot Press, 1974.

McFarland, Philip. *Sojourners.* New York: Atheneum, 1979.

McGroarty, William Buckner. "Captain Cameron and Sergeant Champe." *William and Mary Quarterly,* 2nd Series, Vol. 19, No. 1 (January 1939), pp. 49–54.

———. "Sergeant John Champe and Certain of his Contemporaries." *William and Mary Quarterly,* 2nd Series, Vol. 17, No. 2 (April 1937), pp. 145–75.

McKendry, William. *Journal.* Massachusetts Historical Society *Proceedings,* 2nd Series, Vol. II, pp. 442–78.

Meigs, Major Return J. *Journal of the Expedition Against Quebec, Under Command of Col. Benedict Arnold, in the Year 1775.* In Charles I. Bushnell, *Crumbs for Antiquarians,* Vol. 1. New York: Privately printed, 1864.

Melvin, James. "Journal of an Expedition to Quebec." In Kenneth Roberts, *March to Quebec* (see), pp. 431–54.

Miller, Charles E., Jr.; Donald V. Lockey; and Joseph Visconti, Jr. *Highland Fortress: The Fortification of West Point During the American Revolution, 1775–1783.* West Point, N.Y.: United States Military Academy, Department of History.

Minutes of the Provincial Council and Supreme Executive Council of Pennsylvania. 16 vols. Harrisburg: Theo Fenn & Co., 1838–1853.

Mitchell, Joseph B., and Edward S. Creasy. *Twenty Decisive Battles of the World.* New York: The Macmillan Company, 1964.

Montross, Lynn. *The Story of the Continental Army, 1775–1783.* New York: Barnes & Noble, Inc., 1967. (Originally published as *Rag, Tag and Bobtail.* New York: Harper & Row Publishers, Inc., 1952.)

Moore, Christopher. *The Loyalists.* Toronto: Macmillan of Canada, 1984.

Moore, Frank, ed. *Diary of the American Revolution.* 2 vols. New York: The New York Times & Arno Press, 1969 (originally published in 1858).

Morgan, William James, ed. *Naval Documents of the American Revolution.* Vol. 6. Washington, D.C.: Naval History Division, Department of the Navy, 1972.

Morison, George. "Journal of the Expedition to Quebec." In Kenneth Roberts, *March to Quebec* (see), pp. 501–39.

Morning Herald and Daily Advertiser (London), Feb. 12, 1782.

Morpurgo, J. E. *Treason at West Point: the Arnold-André Conspiracy.* New York: Mason/Charter, 1975.

Morton, Doris Begor. *Philip Skene of Skenesborough.* Granville, N.Y.: The Grastorf Press, 1959.

"Muster Rolls of New York Provincial Troops." *Collections of the New-York Historical Society,* Vol. XXIV (1891).

Nafie, Joan. *To the Beat of a Drum.* Norwich, Conn.: Old Town Press, 1975.

Namier, Sir Lewis, and John Brooke. *The House of Commons, 1754–1790.* London: History of Parliament Trust, 1964.

Naval Records of the American Revolution, Vol. 6. Ed. Charles Henry Lincoln. Washington: Government Printing Office, 1906.

Neilson, Charles. *Burgoyne's Campaign.* Albany, N.Y.: Joel Munsell, 1844.

Nelson, Paul David. *General Horatio Gates: A Biography.* Baton Rouge, La.: Louisiana State University Press, 1976.

New Brunswick, N.J. Rutgers University Libraries. Special Collections and Archives. Nathanael Greene Papers.

New Haven, Conn. New Haven Colony Historical Society. Benedict Arnold Collection.

———. Ingersoll Papers.

———. New Haven Military Collection, 1710–1945.

New Haven, Conn. Yale University. Beinecke Library. Benedict Arnold to Major General Nathanael Greene, West Point, September 12, 1780.

———. Benedict Arnold to Jacob Thompson, Philadelphia, March 16, 1780.

———. Sterling Memorial Library. Manuscripts and Archives. Roger Sherman Collection.

New-York Daily Gazette, Oct. 31, 1789.

New York, N.Y. The New-York Historical Society. Letters and Papers of Benedict Arnold.

———. Sebastian Bauman Papers.

———. Memorandum Book of Anthony Clarke.

———. Donald F. Clark Collection.

———. Horatio Gates Papers.

———. Lamb Papers.

———. Robert R. Livingston Papers.

———. McDougall Papers.

———. Allen McLane Papers.

———. Miscellaneous Manuscripts.

———. Joseph Reed Papers.

———. Steuben Papers.

———. Varick Papers.

———. West Point Orderly Book, Aug. 14–Oct. 9, 1780.

New York, N.Y. New York Public Library. Rare Books and Manuscripts Division. Benedict Arnold Papers.

———. Benedict Arnold and Margaret Shippen Arnold Correspondence.

———. Bancroft Collection. Philip Schuyler Letterbook, 1776–1788.

———. Emmet Collection.

———. Myers Collection.

———. Philip Schuyler Papers.

Nickerson, Hoffman. *The Turning Point of the Revolution.* Boston and New York: Houghton Mifflin Company, 1928.

North, James W. *The History of Augusta*. Augusta, Me., 1870.

Norton, Captain Ichabod. *Orderly Book of Colonel Mott's Regiment, 1776*. Fort Edward, N.Y.: Keating & Barnard, 1898.

Notes on a debate of the Phi Beta Kappa group at Harvard College Class of 1781 on whether or not Benedict Arnold was a traitor. Curtis Papers. Massachusetts Historical Society.

"Occupation of New York City by the British" (extracts from the diary of the Moravian congregation of New York). *Pennsylvania Magazine of History and Biography*, Vol. X, pp. 418–45.

"Old New-Haven House." *New-York Daily Tribune*, June 1, 1902, p. 6.

Olmsted, Gideon. *Journals*. Frederick Law Olmsted Papers. Library of Congress, MSS. Div.

Ottawa, Ontario, Canada. National Archives of Canada.

Paine, Thomas. *The Crisis Extraordinary*. Philadelphia, October 4, 1780.

Palmer, Dave Richard. *The River and the Rock: The History of Fortress West Point, 1775–1783*. New York: Greenwood Publishing Corp., 1969.

"Papers Relating to the Expedition to Ticonderoga, April and May, 1775." *Collections of the Connecticut Historical Society*, Vol. I (1860), pp. 163–88.

Park, Edwards. "Could Canada have ever been our Fourteenth Colony?" *Smithsonian*, Vol. 18, No. 9 (December 1987).

Parker, David W. *Guide to the Materials for United States History in Canadian Archives*. Washington, D.C.: Carnegie Institution of Washington, 1913.

Patterson, Samuel White. *Horatio Gates: Defender of American Liberties*. New York: Columbia University Press, 1941.

Peale, Charles Wilson. Autobiographical Notes. *Pennsylvania Magazine of History and Biography*, Vol. XVIII (1904), pp. 250–51.

Peckham, Howard Henry. *Treason of the Blackest Dye*. Ann Arbor, Mich.: The William L. Clements Library, 1958.

Pell, John. "The Revenge." *The Bulletin of the Fort Ticonderoga Museum*, Vol. I, No. 4 (July 1928), pp. 6–11.

Pennsylvania Archives. 1st Series. 12 vols. Philadelphia: Joseph Severns & Co., 1852–1856.

Perkins, Mary E. *Old Houses of the Ancient Town of Norwich*. Norwich, Conn.: 1895.

Peters, Samuel A. *A General History of Connecticut*. London: Printed for the author, 1782.

Peterson, Harold L. *Round Shot and Rammers*. Harrisburg, Pa.: Stackpole Books, 1969.

Philadelphia, Pa. American Philosophical Society. Benjamin Franklin Papers.

———. Thomas Jefferson Papers.

———. Shippen Family Papers.

Philadelphia, Pa. Historical Society of Pennsylvania. Balch Collection.

———. Charles Biddle Papers.

———. Cadwalader Collection.

———. Conarrol Papers.

———. Dreer Collection.

———. Etting Papers.

———. Edward Carey Gardiner Collection.

———. Gratz Collection.

———. Charles Hildeburn Collection.

———. Miscellaneous Collection.

———. Shober Collection.

———. Society Collection.

———. Stauffer Collection.

———. Wayne Papers.

Philadelphia, Pa. Independence National Historical Park. Miscellaneous manuscripts and materials.

Phillips, Fred H. "Benedict Arnold: Even the Loyalist City Burned His Effigy." *Evening Times Globe* (St. John, N.B.), July 15, 1970, p. 11.

Pierce, John. "Journal by the Advance Surveyor with Col. Arnold on the March to Quebec." Reprint from the 3rd ed. (1940) of Kenneth Roberts, *March to Quebec* (see title below).

Portland, Me. Maine Historical Society. J.S.H. Fogg Autograph Collection.

———. Miscellaneous Collection.

Potts, William John. "Du Simitière, Artist, Antiquary, and Naturalist, Projector of the First American Museum, with Some Extracts from his Notebook." *Pennsylvania Magazine of History and Biography,* Vol. XIII, pp. 341–75.

Princeton, N.J. Princeton University Library. Delafield Papers.

Program for Foot Guard Day: 2nd Company of Governor's Foot Guards. (No publishing information.)

[Rawle, Anna] "A Loyalist's Account of Certain Occurrences in Philadelphia after Cornwallis's Surrender at Yorktown." *The Pennsylvania Magazine of History and Biography,* Vol. XVI (1892), pp. 103–7.

Rawle, William Brooke. "Laurel Hill." *Pennsylvania Magazine of History and Biography,* Vol. XXXV, pp. 385–414.

Raymond, Rev. William Odber, ed. *Winslow Papers, A.D. 1776–1826.* St. John, N.B.: The New Brunswick Historical Society, 1901.

Records of the Council of Safety and Governor and Council of the State of Vermont. 8 vols. Montpelier, Vt.: J. & J. M. Poland, 1873.

Reed, William B. *Life and Correspondence of Joseph Reed.* 2 vols. Philadelphia: Lindsay & Blakiston, 1847.

Report on American Manuscripts in the Royal Institution of Great Britain. 4 vols. London, 1904–1909.

Riddell, William Renwick. "Benjamin Franklin's Mission to Canada and the Causes of its Failure." *Pennsylvania Magazine of History and Biography,* Vol. XLVIII, pp. 111–58.

Roberts, Allen E. *Freemasonry in American History.* Richmond, Va.: Macoy Publishing & Masonic Supply Co., Inc., 1985.

Roberts, Kenneth, ed. *March to Quebec.* New York: Doubleday, Doran & Company, Inc., 1938.

Roberts, Robert B. *New York's Forts in the Revolution.* Rutherford, N.J.: Associated University Presses, 1980.

Robinson, Charlotte M. "The Pioneers on King Street." New Brunswick Historical Society *Collections,* No. 14 (1955).

Rockwell, George L. *The History of Ridgefield, Connecticut.* Harrison, N.Y.: Harbor Hill Books, 1979 (originally published in 1927).

Rogers, Ernest E., ed. *Sesquicentennial of the Battle of Groton Heights and the Burning of New London, Connecticut.* New London, 1931.

Royal Gazette (New York), Feb. 17, 1779; Oct. 11, 21, 25, 1780.

Rush, Benjamin. *Autobiography.* Ed. George W. Corner. Princeton, N.J.: Princeton University Press, 1948 (written 1800–1813).

Rush, Richard. *Occasional Productions, Political, Diplomatic, and Miscellaneous.* Philadelphia: J. B. Lippincott & Co., 1860.

St. John, N.B. The New Brunswick Museum. Benedict Arnold Papers, 1783–1802 (Odell Collection).

———. Benedict Arnold Accounts, 1791.

———. Ward Chipman Correspondence.

———. T. T. Odber Collection.

———. Odell Papers.

———. Simond, Hazen and White Papers.

San Marino, Calif. Huntington Library. Miscellaneous manuscripts.

Sargent, Winthrop. *The Life and Career of Major John André.* Tarrytown, N.Y.: William Abbatt, 1902.

Scharf, J. Thomas, and Thompson Westcott. *History of Philadelphia, 1609–1884.* 3 vols. Philadelphia: L. H. Everts & Co., 1884.

Scheer, George F., and Hugh F. Rankin. *Rebels and Redcoats.* Cleveland and New York: The World Publishing Company, 1957.

Seidensticker, Oswald. "Frederick Augustus Conrad Muhlenberg, Speaker of the House of Representatives, in the First Congress, 1789." *Pennsylvania Magazine of History and Biography,* Vol. XIII, pp. 184–206.

Selby, John E. *The Revolution in Virginia.* Williamsburg, Va.: The Colonial Williamsburg Foundation, 1988.

Sellers, Charles Coleman. *Benedict Arnold, the Proud Warrior.* New York: Minton, Balch & Company, 1930.

Senter, Isaac. *Journal.* New York: The New York Times & Arno Press, 1969 (originally published in 1846).

Sereisky, Jean E. "Benedict Arnold in New Brunswick." *Atlantic Advocate,* Vol. 53 (March 1963), pp. 33–43.

Serle, Ambrose. *American Journal.* New York: The New York Times & Arno Press, 1979.

Seward, Anna. "Monody on Major André." Boston: W. Spotswood and C. P. Wayne, 1798 (4th American edition).

Shackelford, George Green. "Benedict Arnold in Richmond, January, 1781." *Virginia Magazine of History and Biography,* Vol. 60, No. 4 (Oct. 1952), pp. 591–99.

Sherman, Andrew M. *Historic Morristown, New Jersey: The Story of Its First Century.* Morristown, N.J.: The Howard Publishing Company, 1905.

Shippen, Nancy. *Her Journal Book.* Ed. Ethel Armes. Philadelphia: J. B. Lippincott Company, 1935.

Shoemaker, Rebecca. *Journal, July 7, 1781–February 18, 1782.* Albany, N.Y. New York State Library. Miscellaneous Manuscripts.

Silliman, Gen. Selleck, to Governor Trumbull, April 1777. Transcript at the Ridgefield *Press,* Ridgefield, Conn.

Simcoe, Lt. Col. J. G. *Military Journal.* New-York: Bartlett & Welford, 1844 (originally printed privately by the author, 1787).

[————] *Remarks on the Travels of the Marquis de Chastellux in North America.* London: G. and T. Wilkie, 1787.

Skull, G. D. "General Sir Frederick Haldimand in Pennsylvania." *Pennsylvania Magazine of History and Biography,* Vol. VIII, pp. 300–309.

Smith, J.E.A. *The History of Pittsfield (Berkshire County), Massachusetts.* 2 vols. Boston: Lee and Shepard, 1869.

Smith, Joshua Hett. *An Authentic Narrative of the Causes Which Led to the Death of Major André.* London: Mathews and Leigh, 1808.

[Smith, Joshua Hett, defendant] "Trial of Joshua Hett Smith for Complicity in the Conspiracy of Benedict Arnold and Major

André." *The Historical Magazine,* Vol. X (1866), Suppl., pp. 1–5, 33–38, 65–73, 97–105, 129–138.

Smith, Justin H. *Arnold's March from Cambridge to Quebec.* New York: G. P. Putnam's Sons, 1903.

———. *Our Struggle for the Fourteenth Colony.* 2 vols. New York: The Knickerbocker Press, 1907.

Smith, Richard. *Diary of Hon. Richd. Smith, Delegate from New Jersey to the Continental Congress, 1774–1776.* Library of Congress, MSS. Div.

Smith, William. *Memoirs.* Vol. 6 and 7. William Smith Papers, Manuscripts Division, New York Public Library.

Sparks, Jared, ed. *Correspondence of the American Revolution: Being Letters of Eminent Men to George Washington.* 4 vols. Boston: Little, Brown and Company, 1853.

Sparks, Jared. *The Life and Treason of Benedict Arnold.* New York: Harper & Brothers, Publishers, 1860.

Spears, John R. "Benedict Arnold—Naval Patriot." *Harper's Monthly Magazine,* Vol. CVI, No. DCXXXII (January 1903), pp. 277–81.

Squier, Ephraim. "Diary of Arnold's Expedition to Quebec." In Kenneth Roberts, *March to Quebec* (see), pp. 615–28.

Stanley, George F.G. *Canada Invaded, 1775–1776.* Toronto and Sarasota: Samuel Stevens Hakkert & Company, 1977.

Stansbury, Joseph, and Dr. Jonathan Odell. *The Loyal Verses of . . . relating to the American Revolution.* Albany, N.Y.: Joel Munsell, 1860.

Starke, John, *et al.* "An Open Letter to Captain Pringle." *The Bulletin of the Fort Ticonderoga Museum,* Vol. I, No. 4 (July 1928), pp. 14–20.

Stevens, B. F. *Facsimiles of Manuscripts in European Archives Relating to America, 1773–1783.* 25 vols. London, 1889–1898.

Stevens, John Austin. "Benedict Arnold and His Apologist." *Magazine of American History,* Vol. IV, No. 3 (March 1880), pp. 181–91.

Stewart, George, Jr. *The Story of the Great Fire in St. John, N.B.* Toronto: Belford Brothers, 1877.

Stockbridge, J. C. "The Case of Major André." *Magazine of American History,* Vol. III, No. 12 (Dec 1879), pp. 739–42.

Stocking, Abner. "Journal." In Kenneth Roberts, *March to Quebec* (see), pp. 541–69.

Stone, Frederick D. "Philadelphia Society One Hundred Years Ago, or the Reign of Continental Money." *The Pennsylvania Magazine of History and Biography,* Vol. III (1879), pp. 361–94.

Stone, William L. *The Campaign of Lieut. Gen. John Burgoyne and the Expedition of Lieut. Col. Barry St. Leger.* New York: Da Capo Press, 1970 (originally published in 1877).

————. *Life of Joseph Brandt—Thayendanegea.* New York: George Dearborn and Co., 1838.

Sutherland, Lucy S. *The East India Company in Eighteenth-Century Politics.* London: Oxford University Press, 1952.

Swift, Samuel. *History of the Town of Middlebury.* Middlebury, Vt.: A. H. Copeland, 1859.

Talleyrand, Prince Charles-Maurice de. *Memoirs.* 2 vols. London: The Grolier Society, n.d.

Tallmadge, Benjamin. *Memoir.* New York: The New York Times & Arno Press, 1968 (originally published in 1858).

Taylor, J. G. *Some New Light on the Later Life and Last Resting Place of Benedict Arnold and of his Wife, Margaret Shippen.* London: George White, 1931.

Teed, Eric L. "Footprints of Benedict Arnold Late Major General Congressional Army of the American Colonies, Late Brigadier General British Army." New Brunswick Historical Society *Collections,* No. 20 (1971), pp. 57–97.

Tessier, Yves. *An Historical Guide to Quebec.* Quebec: Société Historique de Quebec, 1985.

Thacher, James. *Military Journal of the American Revolution.* New York: The New York Times & Arno Press, 1969 (originally published in 1862).

————. "Observations Relative to the Execution of Major John André as a Spy in 1780." *The New-England Magazine,* Vol. 6 (May 1834), pp. 353–64.

Thayer, Captain Simeon. "Journal of his March Through the Wilderness to Quebec." In Kenneth Roberts, *March to Quebec* (see), pp. 243–94.

Thompson, Maj. Gen. E. R. "Sleuthing the Trail of Nathan Hale." *Intelligence Quarterly,* Vol. 2, No. 3 (October 1986), pp. 1–4.

Thomson, Jason P. *Digest of the History of the Second Company Governor's Foot Guard of Connecticut.* New Haven, Conn.: Price, Lee & Adkins Co., 1898.

Tower, Charlemagne. *The Marquis de La Fayette in the American Revolution.* 2 vols. Philadelphia: J. B. Lippincott Company, 1901.

Tucker, P. C. *Gen. Arnold and the Congress Galley.* 1860.

United States Continental Congress. *Journals.* Ed. Worthington C. Ford and others. 34 vols. Washington, D.C.: Government Printing Office, 1904–1937.

Van Doren, Carl. *Secret History of the American Revolution.* New York: The Viking Press, 1941.

Van Schaack, Henry C. *The Life of Peter Van Schaack.* New York: D. Appleton & Co., 1842.

[Varick, Richard, subject] *The Varick Court of Inquiry to Investigate the Implication of Colonel Varick (Arnold's Private Secretary) in the Arnold Treason.* Ed. Albert Bushnell Hart. Boston: The Bibliophile Society, 1907.

Vital Records of Norwich. 2 vols. Hartford, Conn.: Society of Colonial Wars in the State of Connecticut, 1913.

Walker, Lewis Burd. "Life of Margaret Shippen, Wife of Benedict Arnold." *The Pennsylvania Magazine of History and Biography,* Vol. XXIV (1900), pp. 257–66, 401–29; Vol. XXV (1901), pp. 20–46, 145–90, 289–302, 452–97; Vol. XXVI (1902), pp. 71–80, 224–44, 322–34, 464–68.

Wallace, Paul A.W. "Historic Hope Lodge." *Pennsylvania Magazine of History and Biography,* Vol. LXXXVI, pp. 115–42.

Wallace, Willard M. *Connecticut's Dark Star of the Revolution: General Benedict Arnold.* Hartford, Conn.: The American Revolution Bicentennial Commission of Connecticut, 1978.

———. *Traitorous Hero.* New York: Harper & Brothers, Publishers, 1954.

Ward, Christopher. *The War of the Revolution.* 2 vols. New York: The MacMillan Company, 1952.

Ware, Joseph. *A Journal of a March from Cambridge, on an Expedition Against Quebeck, in Colo. Benedict Arnold Detatchment.* Peter Force Transcripts, Series 7E. Library of Congress, MSS. Div.

Warren, Captain Benjamin. "Diary on the Battlefield of Saratoga." *Journal of American History,* Vol. 3 (1909), pp. 201–16.

Washington Crossing, Pa. The David Library of the American Revolution. Sol Feinstone Manuscripts.

Washington, D.C. Library of Congress. British Museum Manuscripts Project.

———. MSS. Div. Mrs. Archibald Crossley Autograph Collection.

———. MSS. Div. Nathanael Greene Papers.

———. MSS. Div. John Hancock Papers, 1774–1776. 4 vols.

———. MSS. Div. James McHenry Papers, 1775–1781.

———. MSS. Div. Miscellaneous Manuscripts Collection.

———. MSS. Div. William Arthur Oldridge Collection. Official Writings of General George Washington's Headquarters Staff

———. MSS. Div. Timothy Pickering Papers.

———. MSS. Div. Jonathan Trumbull Papers, 1774–1796. Peter Force Transcripts, Series 7E.

————. MSS. Div. George Washington Papers.

Washington, D.C. National Archives. *The Papers of the Continental Congress, 1774–1789.*

Washington, George. *Diaries, 1748–1799.* Ed. John C. Fitzpatrick. 4 vols. Boston and New York: Houghton Mifflin Company, 1925.

————. *Writings.* Ed. John C. Fitzpatrick. 37 vols. Washington, D.C.: United States Government Printing Office, 1931–1940.

————. *Writings.* Ed. Jared Sparks. 12 vols. Boston: Ferdinand Andrews, Publisher, 1839.

Watson, John F. *Annals of Philadelphia and Pennsylvania.* 4 vols. Philadelphia: Carey and Hart, 1845.

Watson, W. C. "Arnold's Retreat After the Battle of Valcour." *Magazine of American History,* Vol. VI, No. 6 (June 1881), pp. 414–17.

Webster, J. C. *Historical Guide to New Brunswick.* Saint John, N.B.: N.B. Government Bureau, 1944.

Weigley, Russell F. *The American Way of War.* New York: Macmillan Publishing Co., Inc., 1973.

Wells, Bayze. "Journal." *Collections of the Connecticut Historical Society,* Vol. VII (1899), 239–96.

Westcott, Thompson. *The Historic Mansions and Buildings of Philadelphia.* Philadelphia: Porter & Coates, 1877.

————. *The Official Guidebook to Philadelphia.* Philadelphia: Porter and Coates, 1875.

Wetmore, A. H. "Benedict Arnold's Residence." In *Benedict Arnold in New Brunswick,* p. 10.

Weyl, Nathaniel. *Treason.* Washington, D.C.: Public Affairs Press, 1950.

"Who Took Ticonderoga?" *The Bulletin of the Fort Ticonderoga Museum,* Vol. IV, No. 3 (Jan. 1937), pp. 55–87.

Wiener, Col. Frederick Bernays. "The Greed of Benedict Arnold: Siren Call to Treason." *Army,* Vol. 24, No. 5 (May 1974), pp. 43–47.

Wilkinson, James. *Memoirs of My Own Times.* 3 vols. Philadelphia: Abraham Small, 1816.

Willyams, Cooper. *An Account of the Campaign in the West Indies in the Year 1794.* London: T. Bensley, 1796.

Wilson, Lavalette. "André's Landing Place at Haverstraw: A Mooted Question Settled." *Magazine of American History,* Vol. XIII, No. 2 (February 1885), pp. 173–76.

Yeaton, Heidi. *Reminiscences of Phippsburg: A Tale of Three Villages.* Privately printed, n.d.

Index

ABOUT THE AUTHOR

CLARE BRANDT spent six years researching and writing *The Man in the Mirror*. Her first book, *An American Aristocracy: The Livingstons*, was published in 1986. She lives in the Hudson Valley.

ABOUT THE TYPE

This book was set in Caslon, a typeface first designed in 1722 by William Caslon. Its widespread use by most English printers in the early eighteenth century soon supplanted the Dutch typefaces that had formerly prevailed. The roman is considered a "workhorse" typeface due to its pleasant, open appearance, while the italic is exceedingly decorative.

Lake Erie

N

KILOMETERS

0   100   200

0   100   200

MILES

PENNSYLVANI

VIRGINIA

James River

Richmond

Yorktown

Portsmouth

APPALACHIAN MOUNTAINS

NORTH
CAROLINA

SOUTH
CAROLINA

GEORGIA